# Environmental Law and Sustainability after Rio

THE IUCN ACADEMY OF ENVIRONMENTAL LAW SERIES

**Series Editors**: Kurt Deketelaere, *University of Leuven, Leuven, Belgium* and Zen Makuch, *Imperial College, London, UK*

As environmental law increases in importance as an area of legal research, this new series will bring together some of the most current research carried out by the IUCN Academy of Environmental Law, a global network of environmental law scholars. The important issues addressed in the papers in this series were first presented at the Academy's annual colloquia. The series will present original research analysis and assessment, along with a much-needed synthesis of the state of environmental law. Directions as to the positive role that environmental law can play at a global level are also emphasized. This series will prove essential reading for scholars throughout the world with an interest in cutting edge environment-related issues, and will no doubt play an important role in shaping future debate.

Titles in this series include:

Compliance and Enforcement in Environmental Law
Toward More Effective Implementation
*Edited by Lee Paddock, Du Qun, Louis Kotze, David L. Markell, Kenneth J. Markowitz and Durwood Zaelke*

Environmental Law and Sustainability after Rio
*Edited by Jamie Benidickson, Ben Boer, Antonio Herman Benjamin and Karen Morrow*

# Environmental Law and Sustainability after Rio

*Edited by*

Jamie Benidickson
*Faculty of Law, University of Ottawa, Canada*

Ben Boer
*Sydney Law School, University of Sydney, Australia*

Antonio Herman Benjamin
*Justice, High Court of Brazil (STJ),*
*Professor, Catholic University of Brasilia*

Karen Morrow
*School of Law, University of Swansea, Wales, UK*

THE IUCN ACADEMY OF ENVIRONMENTAL LAW
SERIES

**Edward Elgar**
Cheltenham, UK • Northampton, MA, USA

Published by
Edward Elgar Publishing Limited
The Lypiatts
15 Lansdown Road
Cheltenham
Glos GL50 2JA
UK

Edward Elgar Publishing, Inc.
William Pratt House
9 Dewey Court
Northampton
Massachusetts 01060
USA

A catalogue record for this book
is available from the British Library

Library of Congress Control Number: 2011925761

ISBN    978 0 85793 224 2  (cased)

Printed and bound by MPG Books Group, UK

# Contents

# Contributors

**Marcelo Nogueira Camargos**
Marcelo Camargos is a Brazilian environmental lawyer. He holds a Master's degree in International Law and Environmental Law at the Catholic University of Santos, and was the recipient of a scholarship from the Coordination for the Improvement of Higher Level Education (CAPES). He specialises in protected areas, traditional populations and cultural heritage law.

**Fernanda de Salles Cavedon**
Fernanda de Salles Cavedon is Environmental Law Professor and researcher at the Universidade do Vale do Itajaí – UNIVALI, Brazil and a Master and Doctor in Juridical Science at UNIVALI. She is a PhD candidate in Environmental Law in the Environmental Law Doctoral Program of the University of Alicante, Spain. She has published a wide range of books, book chapters and articles on environmental law.

**Miriam Alfie Cohen**
Miriam Alfie Cohen holds a PhD in Social Sciences from the Universidad Iberoamericana, Campus Santa Fe, Mexico City. Her work revolves around governance, environmental risk, environmental movements and democracy. She is a Research Professor of the Department of Social Sciences, Universidad Autónoma Metropolitana-Cuajimalpa, and is at Level II within the National System of Researchers in Mexico.

**José Augusto Fontoura Costa**
José Augusto Fontoura Costa is a Professor in Environmental Law at the University of São Paulo, Santos Catholic University and the State University of Amazonas in Brazil.

**Arlindo Daibert**
Arlindo Daibert holds a JD from the State of Rio de Janeiro University Law School and an LLM in Environmental Law from Pace University School of Law, NY, USA. He is Senior Partner of the Escritório Daibert de Advocacia (law firm), in the City of Rio de Janeiro, Brazil and an Attorney at the City of Rio de Janeiro Attorney General's Office.

### Javier de Cendra de Larragán

Javier de Cendra is an energy and environmental lawyer at the UCL Energy Institute. He completed a first degree in law and economics, after which he gained an LLM in international, European and comparative energy and environmental law. His PhD thesis undertook a fundamental legal analysis of EU climate change law and policy and the way in which benefits and costs of climate mitigation measures have been distributed among countries, among economic sectors and within sectors.

### Adrián de Garay Sánchez

Adrián de Garay Sánchez holds a PhD in Anthopology from the Universidad Autónoma Metropolitana, Mexico City. He is a Research Professor of the Department of Sociology Universidad Autónoma Metropolitana-Azcapotzalco, and is at Level II within the National System of Researchers in Mexico.

### Joseph W. Dellapenna

Joseph Dellapenna is a Professor of Law at Villanova University School of Law where his scholarly interests focus on water management and on international and comparative law. His writings in the water law field include *Waters and Water Rights* (2001) (co-author), a leading reference work on water law in the United States. He has served as Rapporteur for the Water Resources Committee of the International Law Association with the charge of redrafting the Helsinki Rules on transboundary water management in light of subsequent developments in international water law and international environmental law. He has also acted as consultant to numerous private parties and foreign governments.

### Anél du Plessis

Anél du Plessis is an Associate Professor at the Faculty of Law, North-West University (Potchefstroom Campus), South Africa. She holds a BA in Law from Potchefstroom University for Christian Higher Education, and an LLM and LLD from North-West University. She lectures in administrative law, law of delict, law of contract, legal pluralism and property law. Anél's doctoral thesis was on the fulfilment of the constitutional environmental right in the local sphere of government. Her research interests focus on environmental, human rights and local government law. She is the assistant editor of the *Potchefstroom Electronic Law Journal*. Anél is a member of the IUCN Academy's Governance Committee.

### Willemien du Plessis

Willemien du Plessis is a Professor of Law at North-West University (Potchefstroom Campus) South Africa. She holds B Jur, LLB, LLD and MA in Environmental Management degrees from the Potchefstroom University for Christian Higher Education. She teaches in the areas of environmental law, land and land registration law, legal history, foundations of South African law, property law and South African environmental law. Her research interests include environmental rights and governance, comparative environmental law, comparative constitutional law, local government law, development law, human rights law and property law. Willemien is the co-chair for the IUCN Academy's Research Committee.

### José Juan González

José Juan González is a Professor of Environmental Law at the Universidad Autónoma Metropolitana, Mexico. He is a fellow of the Mexican National System of Researchers, and has published a number of treatises in the field of environmental law. From 1992 to 1996 he was the Chief of the Legal Office of the General Attorney's Office for Environmental Protection. He has collaborated as external adviser for the Commission for Environmental Cooperation, the Inter-American Development Bank, the United Nations Environment Programme, the United Nations Development Programme and the World Meteorological Organization. He is a member of the IUCN Academy's Governing Board.

### David Hodas

David Hodas is a Professor of Law of Widener University School of Law, at Widener's Delaware campus. He holds a BA from Williams College, a JD from Boston University School of Law in 1976 and an LLM in Environmental Law from Pace University. He teaches and writes in the areas of environmental law, climate change law, administrative law, constitutional law, international environmental law and sustainable energy law. He was a member of the Governing Board of the IUCN Academy of Environmental Law from 2008 to 2010.

### Emmanuel Kasimbazi

Emmanuel Kasimbazi is a Senior Lecturer at the Faculty of Law, Makerere University as well as a legal consultant and advocate. He holds an LLM from the University of Calgary, Canada and a PhD from the University of Kwazulu-Natal, Durban, South Africa. He teaches Environmental Law and Policy at both undergraduate and postgraduate level. He has consulted for a number of international and national agencies.

### Robert Kibugi

Robert Kibugi is a Tutorial Fellow at the School of Law, University of Nairobi, currently on leave to pursue doctoral studies at the Faculty of Law, University of Ottawa, Canada, where he is also a part-time professor. He is an advocate of the High Court of Kenya and holds LLB and LLM degrees from the University of Nairobi. His scholarship in environmental law focuses on sustainability in land use, integration of sustainability, poverty and food security issues, land management and access to environmental justice.

### Flavia Rocha Loures

Flavia Rocha Loures holds a JD from the University of Paraná in Brazil, and an LLM with a focus on international groundwater law from Vermont Law School, USA. She is currently a Senior Program Officer working on international water law and policy at the World Wide Fund for Nature in Washington DC.

### Nicola Lugaresi

Nicola Lugaresi is an Associate Professor of Law at the University of Trento Law School. His fields of research expertise include administrative law, environmental law and water law. He teaches in these areas at undergraduate and postgraduate levels.

### Karen Morrow

Karen Morrow is a Professor of Environmental Law in the School of Law, Swansea University. She holds an LLB from Queen's University of Belfast and an LLM from King's College London. She is an editorial board member of the *Environmental Law Review* and a co-editor of the *IUCN Academy of Environmental Law e-Journal*. Her research interests cover environmental law and policy and the law and policy of sustainable development, encapsulating domestic, EU and international dimensions and the interplay between them.

### Charles Odidi Okidi

Charles Odidi Okidi is Director of the Centre for Advanced Studies in Environmental Law and Policy (CASELAP) at the University of Nairobi. His areas of specialization include environmental law; legal and policy issues in transboundary resources; marine and coastal resources; institutional and policy arrangements for natural resources management; environmental education; public international law; international and comparative environmental law and policy; international water policy and law; law of the sea; and law and development.

### Alexander Paterson

Alexander Paterson holds BSocSci, LLB and LLM degrees from the University of Cape Town, where he is an Associate Professor. He lectures in environmental law at both undergraduate and postgraduate level. Prior to joining the Institute, he practised as an environmental attorney and worked as an environmental consultant. He has also worked in the NGO sector, monitoring the progression of environmental legislation through Parliament. His areas of legal research include biodiversity, protected areas and incentive-based regulation. He is co-editor of the *IUCN Academy of Environmental Law e-Journal* and assistant editor of the *South African Journal of Environmental Law and Policy*.

## Nicholas A. Robinson

Nicholas Robinson is the Gilbert and Sarah Kerlin Distinguished Professor of Environmental Law at Pace University School of Law, New York, USA. He served as Deputy Chair and then Chair of the IUCN Commission on Environmental Law. He was the founding Chair of the IUCN Academy of Environmental Law. He has worked on the development of environmental law since 1969, when he was named to the Legal Advisory Committee of the President's Council on Environmental Quality. He founded Pace's environmental law programs, and is the author of several books and many articles. He teaches a range of environmental law courses. In 2009, the Pace University Board of Trustees conferred on him the position of University Professor for the Environment for his significant contribution to scholarship in the field of environmental law, both in the USA and abroad.

## Werner Scholtz

Werner Scholtz obtained his doctorate in law at Leiden University, The Netherlands in 2001. He is a Professor of Law at the Potchefstroom Campus of North-West University, South Africa and a Research Associate at the South African Institute for Advanced Constitutional, Public, Human Rights and International Law. His recent research focuses on the issues of global environmental security, sovereignty and global environmental degradation.

## Fernanda Sola

Fernanda holds an LLB from the Law School of Sorocaba and a Master in Environmental Law from the Catholic University of Santos in Brazil. She is a Professor in Environmental Law at the São Carlos Federal University at the Sorocaba Campus. She has been engaged in a research project 'Law, Natural Resources and Environmental Conflicts: The Amazon Cooperation Treaty.' Her interests include environmental law, shared management of water resources, administrative law and international environmental law.

## Ricardo Stanziola Vieira

Ricardo Stanziola Vieira is an Environmental Law Professor and researcher at the Universidade do Vale do Itajaí – UNIVALI, Brazil and holds Master in Law and Doctor in Human Science degrees from the Federal University of Santa Catarina, Brazil. He undertook a postdoctoral programme in the Centre de Recherches Interdisciplinaires en Droit de l'Environnement, de l'Aménagement et de l'Urbanisme (CRIDEAU) at the University of Limoges, France.

**Mekete Bekele Tekle**
Mekete Bekele Tekle is an Assistant Professor of Law, School of Law of Addis Ababa University, Ethiopia. He holds an LLB from Addis Ababa University and an LLM from the University of Nairobi, Kenya. He teaches environmental law, law of taxation, law of succession and property law. His research interests focus on environmental law and in particular biodiversity and biotechnology law. He has published in law journal articles and book chapters in a number of countries.

**Solange Teles da Silva**
Solange is a Brazilian environmental lawyer, who obtained her PhD at the University of Paris 1, Panthéon-Sorbonne. She is a Professor of Law at the State University of Amazonas in Manaus and at Mackenzie University in São Paulo. She is the coordinator of research groups on sustainable development and law, and law, natural resources and environmental conflicts. She is the International Director of Law for a Green Planet, Director of Publications at the Institute of Law and Citizenship Studies Brazil, Associate Editor of *Fundação Getulio Vargas Law Review* and a member of the Research Committee of the IUCN Academy of Environmental Law. Solange has been a visiting professor at Valencia University in Spain, University of Paris-Sud in France and Georgia State University in the United States.

# Acknowledgements

As editors, on behalf of the IUCN Academy of Environmental Law, we take this opportunity to record our thanks and appreciation to our Brazilian hosts, the Brazilian School of Environmental Law and Policy and the Law for a Green Planet Institute, for their excellent support in the Academy's 2007 colloquium locations of Rio de Janeiro and Parati. Particular thanks are due to Kelen Meregali and her team for their diligent attention to the administrative arrangements that underpin any successful international gathering.

Thanks are also due to the United Nations Environment Programme for the contributions it has made on a continuing basis to facilitate the participation of scholars from developing nations at the Academy's colloquia.

The editors are also grateful to the University of Ottawa for its continuing support of the Academy's endeavours. In addition, Ben Boer acknowledges the infrastructure support of the Sydney Law School, together with that of the Law Department of the European University Institute in Italy, where he was the holder of a Fernand Braudel Senior Fellowship in 2010.

For the production of this book, we owe a debt of gratitude to Joanna Howse in Sydney for her copy editing and conversion of the chapters into camera-ready copy. Her patience and forbearance are very much appreciated.

Finally, we would like to express our appreciation for the support of the team at Edward Elgar in the United Kingdom and in particular for the editorial and practical guidance of Ben Booth, Rebecca Hastie and Laura Seward.

*Jamie Benidickson, Antonio Herman Benjamin, Ben Boer and Karen Morrow*

# 1. Introduction: environmental law and sustainability after Rio

## Jamie Benidickson, Ben Boer, Antonio Herman Benjamin and Karen Morrow

The fields of environmental and sustainability law, despite strong historical roots and antecedents, are by no means fully elaborated and mature fields of scholarship and professional practice. It is possible, nonetheless, to identify landmarks or milestones in their development and to reflect upon the significance of what has been put in place. The 1992 United Nations Conference on Environment and Development in Rio de Janeiro, commonly referred to as the Earth Summit, and the adoption of Agenda 21 and the Rio Declaration on Environment and Development clearly represent one such landmark.

It is appropriate, particularly in the field of environmental law, both to commemorate past achievements as well as to take a realistic view of their shortcomings. In recognising achievements, we are able to celebrate and express appreciation for the very significant accomplishments of an earlier generation of researchers, advocates, negotiators and practitioners. The success of their efforts to safeguard the environment gives us hope, an outlook that is not always in good supply. On the other hand, the process of assessment necessarily invites reflection on the shortcomings and limitations of our current situation and encourages a salutary reminder that much remains to be done to secure the foundations of environmental protection and sustainability on a global, national and local basis.

The fifteenth anniversary in 2007 of the Rio conference provided a sufficient temporal perspective to attempt the undertaking of an assessment of progress in environmental law in the realm of sustainability. The Brazilian organisers of the Fifth Annual Colloquium of the IUCN Academy of Environmental Law thus invited participants from the Academy's member institutions as well as the broader global university community to convene in Rio de Janeiro and in the heritage town of Parati for presentations and debates under the general theme 'Rio + 15: A Legal Critique of Ecologically Sustainable Development'. This book contains selected papers from that significant colloquium, and forms part of the continuing series of IUCN Academy of Environmental Law colloquium proceedings. Each of the contributions has been updated by their authors where necessary to take account of subsequent developments. We have chosen to name the book *Environmental Law and Sustainability after Rio*, to urge the more expansive notion of 'sustainability' that has become prevalent after the 2002 Johannesburg World Summit on Sustainable Development, encompassing the three pillars of environmental, economic and social development, as well as Goal 7 of the United Nations Millennium Development Goals, which is directed to ensuring environmental sustainability.

While a great deal has been achieved in the field of environmental law since the 1990s, the extraordinary environmental crises facing humanity in the 21st century indicate a continuing urgent need for the generation of robust policies and frameworks concerning ecological, social/cultural and economic sustainability. This book identifies a variety of ways in which such sustainability can be progressed and implemented at global, national and local levels through appropriately innovative legal mechanisms.

The volume is divided into five sub-themes. In the first part, the history, principles and concepts associated with sustainability are canvassed. Nicholas Robinson of Pace University School of Law, who presented the colloquium's distinguished lectures, is one of the pioneers of environmental law in the United States and globally. He dedicates his colloquium contribution to Professor Oleg Stepanovich Kolbasov of Russia (1927–2000). In doing so, he celebrates their joint contributions to the development of environmental law over many difficult years of the Cold War, and emphasises how international collaboration in passionate and applied scholarship contributes to the vitality of the discipline. Professor Robinson's broad-ranging historical analysis and contemporary diagnosis concludes that 'the realization of environmental norms is found in the context of compliance procedures and decisions, as well as the recognition that a community's environmental rights are as important as an individual's human rights', and that 'environmental law can induce or force design of new technologies, and can save us from our proclivity to excess'. His inspired essay emphasises the important responsibility that environmental lawyers have to build a more robust and resilient environmental law.

Charles Okidi's review of capacity building in environmental law in African universities traces the evolution of the field of environmental law over a 40-year period, emphasising the significant role of universities, particularly in terms of expanding the range of environmental law subjects, the publication of specialised journals and the formation and role of the Association of Environmental Law Lecturers of African Universities.

Anél du Plessis canvasses an important theme of the Rio Conference, analysing developments in relation to Local Agenda 21s. She argues that the use of a rights-based approach by municipalities to local environmental governance may contribute to a more enforceable and hence more effective Local Agenda 21 regime. She concludes that the domestic implementation of international environmental soft law deserves greater attention, and that encouraging local government compliance with these norms will contribute to more sustainable human environments at the local level.

The Brazilian experience with the innovative 'socioambientalismo' concept and its significance for sustainability law is the subject of analysis in the chapter by Fernando de Salles Cavedon and Ricardo Stanziola Vieira. They urge the use of this concept as a paradigm for constructing and consolidating a body of domestic and international environmental law capable of promoting harmonisation between socio-economic issues, environmental protection and ethnic and cultural diversity.

A sociologically oriented chapter by Miriam Alfie Cohen and Adrián de Garay Sánchez promotes the concept of the 'risk society', in which they identify the precautionary principle as the spearhead of political change at the local and global level. They argue that the idea of the risk society, taken together with the precautionary principle, should form the new basis for environmental law. They conclude that with the environmental risks that the world now faces, 'the implementation of this new environmental management paradigm cannot be delayed'.

Nicola Lugaresi's study of environmental economics in the context of public procurement decisions considers practice in this field in the European Union. He argues that '[W]hile economic analysis cannot be neglected, public powers should have the capacity to resist regulation and management derived exclusively from prevailing economic considerations'. His conclusion proposes that Principle 16 of the Rio Declaration, on the internalisation of environmental costs and the use of economic instruments, should be interpreted broadly, or rewritten, to take into account also the 'externalization of environmental advantages, in order to address environmental, economic, ethical and equity expectations'.

Part Two of the volume is devoted to philosophical and practical aspects of environmental rights, access to justice and liability issues in the context of sustainability. Werner Scholtz examines the development of the New International Economic Order first put forward in the 1970s, and argues for a 'southern' perspective on the concept of intergenerational equity. He calls for a 'continuous commitment of all states, rich and poor, to pursue a New International Sustainable Development Order which addresses the needs of the poor without depleting the means of future peoples'.

Karen Morrow focuses on issues of public participation in environmental decision-making within the courts in the United Kingdom, in the light of developments in this field in Europe. One of her main conclusions is that the third pillar of the Aarhus Convention, access to justice, is effectively rationed in the United Kingdom because of the costs of legal representation and the potential liability for unsuccessful defendants, which can lead to profound cynicism of the value of public participation.

Robert Kibugi takes a broader approach in exploring the conceptual nature of access to justice and how it is achieved through judicial institutions and in particular the Kenyan National Environment Tribunal, canvassing the expansion of locus standi through judicial and legislative action, and the use of the *suo moto* jurisdiction.

José Juan González examines recent trends in environmental liability in a number of Latin American jurisdictions and suggests an alternative approach, involving imposition of liability without proof of damage. He identifies a variety of barriers to this new paradigm, and concludes that more legislative development is required to ensure adequate restoration of the environment.

The chapter by Arlindo Daibert looks at another aspect of liability, concerning environmental torts, with Brazilian developments as his main focus. He explores the ideas of diffuse societal environmental rights and material and moral diffuse damages, arguing that these concepts require 'extending standing to sue in order to facilitate stronger societal control of actions interfering with the environment and the maintenance of sustainability'.

Part Three focuses on particular aspects of natural resources law and sustainability. Joseph Dellapenna and Flavia Loures examine treaty-making processes and reform in the context of the final shape, scope and text of the Draft Articles on the Law of Transboundary Aquifers and Aquifer Systems, in the light of the provisions of Agenda 21 and the Rio Declaration on Environment and Development. Their analysis reveals some serious faults with the Draft Articles, for which they recommend some specific practical remedies.

The rights of farmers and plant breeders are the subject of the chapter by Mekete Tekle, specifically looking at the agricultural sector in Ethiopia in the light of sustainability issues. He concludes that Ethiopia can claim to have 'a national law that balances and protects the respective rights of the communities, farmers and breeders in line with most of the international treaties and soft laws of both international and regional nature', the like of which is yet to be seen in other countries.

Part Four contains several chapters concerning energy, climate change and sustainability. David Hodas critically assesses the contribution of international law on sustainable energy in the context of the work of the

Commission on Sustainable Development, arguing that 'we must make the law sustainable-energy friendly; build the right policies in law, and sustainable energy investments will follow'. His postscript notes that '[T]ragically, as UNFCCC meetings avoid concrete discussion about how to shift to a more sustainable, low carbon world economy, international talks increasingly become disconnected from real-world policy, science and law'.

Willemien du Plessis examines the challenges of regulating cross-border gas pipelines in the context of the Rio Declaration, Agenda 21 and the 2002 Johannesburg Plan of Implementation. She questions whether in this context, the goals of the Rio Declaration, the Energy Charter, and other relevant instruments can be effectively achieved.

Javier de Cendra de Larragán incisively examines the legal foundations of climate policy in the European Union, concluding that the concept of burden sharing of liability within the Union has increased its degree of consistency with the relevant legal principles of the Union's climate change regime, and has thus contributed to its legal robustness.

Emmanuel Kasimbazi usefully surveys initiatives to combat climate change from the perspective of the developing world, using Uganda as a case study. He looks in particular at the barriers to implementing, inter alia, Clean Development Mechanism obligations under the Kyoto Protocol, concluding that Uganda's efforts under Kyoto are constrained by a number of factors, most of which are outside the legal framework.

Part Five concludes the volume, focusing on the fundamental area of nature conservation and sustainability. Alexander Paterson analyses the innovations introduced in recent years in South Africa concerning the role of contract in implementing elements of the Convention on Biological Diversity through comprehensive legislative mechanisms. He observes that 'Laws are living instruments subject to constant change' and concludes that 'a little tinkering with the formulation of the current contractual mechanisms should see them achieving the lofty ideal of co-opting the public as the future stewards of biodiversity regulation in South Africa'.

The nature of legal protection afforded to mangrove swamps and their contribution to Brazilian sustainability is the subject of detailed scrutiny by Marcelo Nogueira Camargos and Solange Teles da Silva. They set out the vital role that mangroves play in the Brazilian coastal environment and use this as a springboard for a discussion of the legal issues, as well as the importance of the Brazilian Constitution with respect to mangrove protection. They observe that land use planning and environmental zoning are important instruments for conserving mangroves, but conclude that for these provisions to be effective, the participation of all stakeholders, including traditional populations, must be ensured.

In the last chapter, José Augusto Fontoura Costa, Solange Teles da Silva and Fernanda Sola critically discuss the contribution of the Amazonian Cooperation Treaty to the harmonisation of environmental law on a regional basis. They provide an overview of Amazonian geography, highlighting the relationship between socio-diversity and biodiversity in the region. They canvass the need for a more international treatment of environmental problems in the Amazon using international regime theory. They conclude that since the present regional regime does not include dispute resolution or delegation rules, domestic law is still the main driver of environmental regulation, and that consequently the diffusion or educational role of the Treaty and its function as a political forum are its most important attributes.

In addition to the essays included in this volume, numerous papers from the 2007 colloquium have been published elsewhere, and for that reason do not appear here. As editors, we thank those authors for their contribution to the colloquium and congratulate them for their success in making the results of their scholarship more widely available through legal periodicals, books, and on-line journals.

Insofar as the Academy's Annual Colloquium provides an opportunity for the organisation's various committees to conduct business, this introduction allows us to mention several other significant achievements. An extensive discussion of a draft curriculum on Enforcement and Compliance of Multinational Environmental Agreements was held during the colloquium. This session, effectively a multilateral seminar on the challenges and opportunities of teaching international environmental law, was conducted in connection with a project carried out by the Academy in close collaboration with the United Nations Environment Programme. Special acknowledgement should be given to Carl Bruch of the Environmental Law Institute in Washington who served as lead consultant, and to principal authors Jorge Caillaux of Peru and Loretta Feris from South Africa. The resulting materials are available through UNEP and the IUCN Academy for instructional use around the world.

In addition, during the colloquium, the Academy's Research Committee confirmed the direction of another recently completed programme of legal research on climate change and developing countries. The chief result of that work is *Climate Law and Developing Countries: Legal and Policy Challenges for the World Economy*, published by Edward Elgar in 2009 under the editorship of Ben Richardson, Yves Le Bouthillier, Heather McLeod-Kilmurray and Stepan Wood.

PART ONE

# History, principles and concepts of sustainability

# 2. Reflecting on Rio: environmental law in the coming decades

## Nicholas A. Robinson[*]

## 1. INTRODUCTION

Environmental law has matured greatly since the 1972 Stockholm Conference on the Human Environment. It was given a tremendous boost by the 1992 Rio de Janeiro UN Conference on Environment and Development (UNCED, or the 'Earth Summit'). Nevertheless, the persistence of excessive natural resources exploitation and pollution underscores a sobering fact: environmental law worldwide remains unable to attain its remedial objectives. Environmental law success stories have occasionally demonstrated that the legal norms, rules and procedures can work effectively, but to be globally successful on a continuing basis these legal regimes will need to be scaled up enormously.

All nations at UNCED agreed upon Agenda 21, an action plan to promote sustainable development.[1] The urgent need for universal cooperation to formulate the recommendations of Agenda 21 had been articulated in 1987 in *Our Common Future*, the report of the UN World Commission on Environment and Development (1987). The principles of the 1992 Rio Declaration on Environment and Development[2] were reaffirmed in Johannesburg in 2002 at the UN World Summit on Sustainable Development, adding important recommendations on energy efficiency and on the alleviation of poverty.[3]

In 1987, *Our Common Future* recommended the robust elaboration of environmental law, and proposed relevant legal principles in its Annex 1. Yet even five years later, when Chapter 8 of Agenda 21 called on each nation to build up its national laws for environment and development, and in Chapters 28 and 29 called for all nations to enhance international law and organisation, Agenda 21's drafters were tepid in their support of 'environmental law' as such. In order to find consensus for the adoption of Agenda 21, the term environmental law was dropped from discussion, in deference to 'the law of environment and development', with the occasional alternative reference to 'sustainable development law', the precise meaning of which was not elaborated.[4] The financial commitments needed to build the capacity for providing a legal foundation for sustainable development were stripped from the text of Agenda 21.[5] Even when the nations met in Monterrey, Mexico,[6] to pledge the funding for implementing Agenda 21, the commitments turned out to be mostly symbolic.

In addition to Agenda 21 and the Rio Declaration, the nations that met in Rio de Janeiro in 1992 signed the UN Framework Convention on Climate Change[7] and the UN Convention on Biological Diversity,[8] both landmark multilateral environmental agreements which embraced new global environmental norms, structured the system for their legal implementation and incorporated recommendations from *Our Common Future*. It took another two years to complete negotiations for the UN Convention to Combat Desertification,[9] now referred to as one of the 'Rio Conventions'.

Notwithstanding the aspirations for realising sustainable development, the UN system is still plagued with doubts and even resistance to environmental law. Despite the work of such bodies as the Business Council for Sustainable Development (Schmidheiny, 1992) and the World Environment Center,[10] there remain governmental and business interests who oppose environmental law reforms on the supposition that they will harm or retard economic development. These perspectives have prevented the agreement of any international legally binding agreement on the stewardship of the Earth's remaining forests, or their reforestation and afforestation.[11] The United Nations Forum on Forests, convened annually each northern spring under the auspices of the UN General Assembly, has made scant progress.[12] Separate efforts to address indigenous issues and oceans policy have also fallen short. In due course, treaties will be needed to strengthen world-wide forest policy and to enlist the nations of indigenous peoples as full partners in the General Assembly in stewardship of the Earth's terrestrial and marine environment.

Similarly, although the United Nations General Assembly established the Commission on Sustainable Development (CSD) to continue the deliberations of the Rio Earth Summit and oversee the implementation of Agenda 21, states have not supported use of the CSD as the strategic body to shape concrete measures for sustainable development. Rather, the CSD has remained a place to exchange views, educate diplomats and their governments about issues, and occasionally advance some dimension of international cooperation associated with sustainable development. The CSD has not yet produced significant new agreements to advance each of the chapters of Agenda 21.

Despite the lukewarm embrace of environmental law by some governments, both national and international environmental law have continued to develop. The United Nations Environment Programme (UNEP) has served as the catalyst for a number of important multilateral environmental agreements (Tolba and Rummel-Bulska, 2008), and has supported the national and international elaboration of environmental law systematically through its Montevideo programmes.[13] UNEP has also been engaged in capacity building for environmental lawyers through its global environmental law training programmes, and the preparation of comprehensive training manuals.[14] Despite many past positive efforts, since 2004 UNEP has been reducing its focus on the progressive development of environmental law, and has been criticised for not adequately realising synergies among the MEAs and integrating environmental programmes.[15]

At this point after the Earth Summit, we should have sufficient perspective to critically appraise what UNCED did to advance environmental law. How did it shape legal concepts of sustainability and promote the consolidation of the norms of sustainability within the paradigm of environmental law? What legal doctrines and methods need to be refined and enhanced in the coming decades if environmental law is to help all nations attain sustainability in all its aspects?

In retrospect, and on the positive side, the accomplishments of the Earth Summit itself are truly extraordinary. Agenda 21 represents a global consensus. The Earth Summit's products are concrete evidence that states can coalesce to find policy agreement in the face of serious environmental threats. They also offer lessons about the shortcomings that states encounter on follow-through and implementation.

We take the concept of 'sustainable development' for granted today, but we cannot over-estimate how difficult it was in 1987 to move nations to adopt it. The Brundtland Commission gave the idea worldwide popularity. In the lead-up to the Earth Summit, nations turned to Ambassador Tommy Koh, who had chaired the UN Conference on the Law of the Sea, to chair the preparatory committee for UNCED and the UNCED deliberations in Rio de Janeiro (Koh, 1993). His leadership was exemplary.

Agenda 21 remains a remarkable blueprint for the reforms that governments are called upon to realise through environmental law and policy. The Earth Summit was a crucial station on the way to the development of a global set of norms to inform environmental law. From the 1980s, the IUCN Environmental Law Programme had provided the leadership for adoption of the UN World Charter for Nature, and many of these concepts were embodied in the Rio Declaration, the Climate Change Convention, the Convention on Biological Diversity and other multi-lateral agreements thereafter. From the 'soft law' principles embodied in the 1972 Stockholm Declaration on the Human Environment, reflected in various provisions of the Rio Declaration on Environment and Development, a body of 'hard law' has begun to emerge internationally. The Convention on

Biological Diversity embodies as norms the conservation and sustainable use of nature, and inter-state cooperation 'for the conservation and sustainable use of biological diversity' (Arts 5 and 6). The 1992 UNFCCC embodies the duty to protect the climate system in national actions through international cooperation (Arts 3(5) and 5) and to use the precautionary principle (Art 3). The elements embodied in Rio Declaration Principle 10 on access to information, public participation and access to justice, and Principle 17 on environmental impact assessment were incorporated into the Aarhus Convention.[16] The 1994 Convention to Combat Desertification embodies norms to give priority to securing people from the deleterious impacts of desertification and drought, and to cooperate internationally (Arts 2 and 3). The 2002 Rotterdam Convention on the Prior Informed Consent Procedure for Certain Hazardous Chemicals and Pesticides in International Trade[17] and the 2001 Stockholm Convention on Persistent Organic Pollutants[18] establish the norms that states shall not expose their citizens or those in other states to hazardous chemicals without adequate protective precautions in place. Thus, over these years, the doctrine of binding international environmental law norms has become clearer. Many nations have now amended their national constitutions to establish a right to the environment as a foundation for their national environmental rules and procedures.

In addition to the increasing congruence of domestic legal norms that was encouraged by international environmental law developments, many nations adopted their own national versions of Agenda 21, to guide domestic law reforms to build sustainable development practices. Results include New Zealand's 1991 Resource Management Act, which codified much of its land use and natural resource regime around the paradigm of sustainable development,[19] and Australia's federal legislation, the Environment Protection and Biodiversity Conservation Act 1999, which incorporated the concept of ecologically sustainable development and associated principles as foundations for decision-making. Legal regimes for environmental impact assessment have been enacted throughout the world. Legal frameworks for environmental management systems exist throughout the European Union, North America and other regions. Companies worldwide have promulgated policies and practices for corporate social responsibility towards the environment, and for health and safety compliance. Many nations now have laws to curb pollution and conserve flora and fauna, although some are still in rudimentary form. Dedicated administrative systems have become standard, with environmental protection agencies functioning within the vast majority of nations.

## 2.　ENVIRONMENTAL LAW SINCE 1992

Despite the impressive gains that characterise environmental law around the world, and its measurable benefits for providing environmental protection in many sectors, the implementation of Agenda 21 falls short of what nations promised to do in 1992. This reality is starkly evident when comparing the current body of environmental laws with the reports about environmental degradation problems provided from relevant scientific disciplines. Measured by the continuing reports of the IUCN Species Survival Commission or the UN Intergovernmental Panel on Climate Change, or the conditions documented by the UN Millennium Ecosystem Assessment, the remedial measures of environmental law are not effective in averting or reversing trends in environmental degradation. All recent scientific studies analysing environmental degradation indicate that the scale of global and national problems largely outstrips the capacity and scope of contemporary environmental law. This is true, for instance, in relation to urban air pollution, the depletion and contamination of aquifers and surface water supplies, and the accumulation of chemical and industrial wastes and the loss of biodiversity.

These phenomena will grow as we add several billion more people to our planet in the coming decades. This growth produces such demands that, without structural reforms, the world's economy may grow four times from its present size, to some US$140 trillion in annual global output (Speth, 2004, p. 21). Such projected growth imposes demands on Earth's biological and other natural systems that they cannot sustain

This brief recitation of sectors where environmental law is weak or non-existent shows that one of the core lessons of the 1992 Earth Summit has not been embraced. Decisions concerning the sustainability of the natural environment ought not to still to be the product of 'business as usual' decision-making, or exploitation beyond sustained yields, or simply because of human whim. Scientific study and an understanding of natural systems must inform decisions. Although the UN World Charter for Nature provides that 'Earth's natural systems shall not be impaired',[20] extensive volumes of scientific reports show that we humans have in fact impaired essential natural systems, sometimes to the point of being irretrievable.

While environmental degradation endangers public health and the environment in all nations, it is especially troubling in developing nations, where poverty levels often prevent remedial and protective measures. If these patterns of polluting the biosphere and consuming Earth's natural capital continue, the well-being of many human societies will be severely compromised. Agenda 21 discusses the underlying causes that drive these patterns, especially concerning unsustainable consumption and human demographics. Population issues have rarely been the focus of law. With the exceptions of China, which attempts to limit family size, and states such as Russia that experience negative population growth rates, nations have not adequately addressed their population growth challenges. Moreover, there is virtually no legal focus on human migration, even though sea-level rise will engender millions of environmental refugees and increasingly force a 'retreat' from the coasts, while the attraction of urban centres draws vast numbers from rural areas to produce mega-cities.

As to consumption, there has been little use of economic instruments or regulations to curb the appetite of the affluent. Indeed the world's economy has grown based on patterns of international trade and production of consumer goods. The many political disputes about the social or ecological 'fairness' of the economic 'free trade' agreements expose the problems nations experience with the consumption issues identified in Agenda 21. As the gaps between the world's developed and developing regions grow, population and consumption issues become more divided.

Clearly, these unsustainable patterns of behaviour both in human encounters with nature and among human beings provoke basic questions: What are the fundamental jurisprudential foundations of environmental law? What relationship do the core norms of environmental law bring to these environmental, social and economic questions?

In light of the trends since 1992, it seems clearly too facile simply to link 'environment and development', as Agenda 21 does. Environment and development are not 'equals' and a policy instrument such as Agenda 21 cannot amalgamate the two into one. Development can exist only within the capacity of the environment to sustain it. It is also unrealistic to act as if the 2002 Johannesburg Declaration on Sustainable Development makes any advancement in the integration of development and environment when it states that sustainable development rests on three interdependent and mutually reinforcing pillars of 'economic development, social development and environmental protection'.[21] These pillars are not equal; the volume of law promoting development is huge and has been driving government decision-making for centuries, while much of the law related to social welfare dates only from the late 19th century, and then mainly for developed countries. The law relating to environmental protection, on a global basis, is still weak, and is only one generation old. The economic agenda dominates decision-making and is a tall pillar. The social/cultural sector, for example, meeting the needs of the poor and disadvantaged as articulated in the UN Millennium Development Goals,[22] including women and children – for their housing, human health services, or education – is still dictated to by the economic sector. Thus the social sector remains modest in comparison with the economic development pillar. The third pillar is the shortest; the ecological dimension is simply reduced to the utilitarian goal of 'environmental protection'. The resources for environmental protection are inadequate.

These unequal pillars cannot support a level roof. If they are regarded as the three legs of a stool, they are so lopsided as to be useless. The very symbol of three such pillars at best merely states a policy aspiration, and does not exist in practice anywhere. Reciting the policy mantra of these three pillars reflects the limited and shallow understanding of the policy makers. Development continues largely unabated as an economic driver, blind to the social and environmental externalities it generates; commerce or traditional patterns of economic development overwhelm environmental stewardship and many social priorities as well. Business as usual persists, with social and environmental reforms being effectively realised only in a few regions, such as Scandinavia.

From the perspective of the scientific reports cited above, the dominant economic 'business as usual' model is manifestly inadequate. It is wholly anthropocentric and is not grounded in the reality of what is happening to the Earth. This need not be so. In Costa Rica a different model prevails; there, the government's environmental and ecological agenda is given priority to guide the economic, agricultural and other sectors. In Bhutan, the Buddhist concept of happiness at least theoretically infuses environmental and economic laws, and animates a balance in which environment is maintained above economic growth and markets. In some traditional societies where indigenous people have been able to continue to live in more or less natural settings, customary law recognises a balance and sustains humans and their roles within nature. But these remain rare examples from which we can draw some lessons about what may be wrong with the prevailing conceptualisation and implementation of environmental law in much of the world.

Properly recognised, the normative jurisprudence of environmental law should not be regarded as a handmaiden to economic growth and development. As Professor Kolbasov recognised, human legal systems need to be grounded in ecology (Kolbasov, 1976). Environmental law should be informed by what scientists tell us about how natural systems function, and not the other way around. Environmental law should not be used as a methodology to allow human engineering of nature, but is rather the means by which society can contain human excess. For two centuries, humans have been fashioning laws for nature conservation, to sustain species of wild animals or retain natural habitats in parks and reserves. Unfortunately, the dominant society generally regards such conservation efforts as being tangential to the mainsprings of economic and social life. The 'sustainable yield and use' of wild nature is often seen as the objective of nature protection laws, but this instrumental aim is too narrow. The primary objective must be to respect the integrity of non-human living systems and species and protect them for their intrinsic worth, not their economic use for humans. We have altered the carbon cycle, the hydrologic cycle and the nitrogen cycle; we are tampering with the very essence of the Earth's biosphere, and are posing a threat to human and other life on this planet.


## 3.   A 'SUCCESS' STORY: THE STRATOSPHERIC OZONE REGIME

Humans *have* used environmental law to reverse such destructive behaviour and must learn to replicate their successes. One significant example is the worldwide campaign to protect the stratospheric ozone layer from destruction by ozone-depleting substances, such as chlorofluorocarbons. The world community acted in unison when it progressively negotiated, ratified and implemented the 1985 Vienna Convention to Protect the Stratospheric Ozone Layer[23] and the 1987 Montreal Protocol on Substances that Deplete the Ozone Layer[24] and related agreements. The basic norms in the Vienna Convention are clear: 'to protect human health and the environment against adverse effects resulting or likely to result from human activities which modify or are likely to modify the ozone layer' and cooperate internationally to do so.[25] An international regime, based on science, has induced every nation to adopt implementing legislation and set up national administrative agencies, addressing all phases of the manufacture, use of and trade in ozone-depleting substances. Nations have transformed the market and built an epistemic community of civil servants acting with one shared aim: to protect the thin layer of $O_3$ molecules found at the top of Earth's atmosphere. Governments have listened to what scientists have said, and we have learned to act with solidarity and measurable effectiveness.

Through the Montreal Protocol we are simultaneously protecting the atmosphere from this particular class of greenhouse gas (each CFC molecule is many thousands of times more effective in retaining heat than is a $CO_2$ molecule). As a measure of success of the ozone regime, the Intergovernmental Panel on Climate Change reported on 5 May, 2007, that '[T]he emissions of ozone depleting substances controlled under the Montreal Protocol, which are greenhouse gases, have declined significantly since the 1990s. By 2004, the emissions of these gases were about 20 per cent of their 1990 level'.[26]

How did this success story come about? What can be learned from it to apply to other environmental sectors? The legal regime for protecting the stratospheric ozone layer is holistic, linking local to national to global conduct, and establishing forums for both public and private sectors. The

Vienna Convention required scientific cooperation to study the threat to the ozone layer, with an agreement to act if a threat was found. When the ozone hole was discovered over the Antarctic, studies intensified and states convened in Montreal in 1987 to agree on a 50 per cent phase-out of chlorofluorocarbons (CFCs). In 1990, states convened in London to agree on a nearly 90 per cent phase-out. A fund was established to build capacity in states that required assistance to establish the national systems to secure CFCs and eliminate their use. At a meeting in Copenhagen, a compliance system was established to ensure all states observed the agreement. In 2007, China agreed to eliminate the manufacture and use of a CFC substitute, HCFC, and agreement was obtained to eliminate the last ozone-depleting substances. National reports document the progress in each country as the substances are eliminated. Sustained leadership by diplomats, national civil servants and non-governmental organisations have been key to this success.

While scientists currently do not know whether the stratospheric ozone layer will in fact regenerate new $O_3$ molecules once these ozone-depleting substances are removed from the atmosphere, we can take some comfort that an environmental law regime has remade a technological and trade system, with the purpose of protecting life for people and nature. Perhaps if human health had not been at risk of skin cancer and cataracts, we might not have had the political support just to safeguard a remote, invisible, natural system of the Earth.

But is not the lesson clear? We must now strongly regulate such phenomena as the nitrogen cascade and persistent organic pollutants. We do not need to wait until the illnesses or dead zones wipe out life in either human or natural settings.

The ecological foundations of environmental law are deeper than Agenda 21. It requires diligent study of natural systems, knowledge of accumulated baseline data about what constitutes healthy environments, healthy animals and healthy human bodies. It requires the identification of acts and substances that can harm the environment and its living components, including people. It requires procedures and measures to avert or eliminate the harm or threat of harm, and to allow proposed development activities only when all mitigation mechanisms have been identified and implemented. This is the essence of the precautionary principle of environmental law.[27]

## 4. EXPLORING MORE ROBUST ENVIRONMENTAL LAW NORMS

Has not the jurisprudential foundation for stewardship of nature always been a part of environmental law? How can stewardship principles be strengthened? If we trace its roots, we see that stewardship as a norm has struggled to emerge from the practice of nature conservation and, more recently, environmental protection and management, and now moves towards shaping a new transformative environmental paradigm. The reality is that Earth can provide adequate habitat for all species, including humans, but only if people learn to make room for the flora and fauna. If human civilisation is to continue, people need to invent new patterns of co-existence with both other species and the cycles of life on Earth. They will need to retool all technologies to reserve space for Earth's natural systems to function 'normally', without the degrading influence of the human 'footprint'. To do so, they will need to affirmatively act to enhance resilience and promote restoration of natural systems.

There are five substantive dimensions to how environmental law must be advanced if we are to realise the objectives of Agenda 21. (1) The legal regimes for nature conservation dating from the mid-19th century have their place. Parks and protected areas need to be expanded and protected from impacts from adjacent land uses or distant pollutants or the loss of the habitat elsewhere associated with migratory species. This is a significant task in its own right. (2) The pollution control laws need to be advanced into their next phase. All pollution should be regarded as waste, and the generation of waste needs to be designed out of the manufacturing and agricultural production systems. Laws to induce the invention of new technological processes are needed; 'technology forcing' has been too timid and inadequate in scale. Full life-cycle product analysis is needed for everything we manufacture and must be reflected in pricing. Mass transit should be the default and standard system, and personal motor vehicles retired. As a transition, the internal combustion engine needs to yield to motors based on non-carbon fuels, such as hydrogen and electricity. All pollutants need to be measured in order to incorporate these 'externalities' entirely into the financial sectors of the economy. (3) Environmental Management Systems, whether formalised or informal ones such as the International Standards Organization's ISO-14000 series, are both too timid in scope and inconsequential in scale to have a material impact on stimulating sustainable manufacturing processes. The widely used system of environmental impact assessment is so weakly deployed that it has not generated the reformed practices promised. It needs to be revised to mandate elimination or maximum reduction of all adverse environmental impacts. All proven management systems now should be universally enhanced and used. (4) Similarly, land use laws, whether as 'town and country planning' or 'zoning' have a bias towards 'green field' development, rather than retrofitting and rehabilitating existing urban centres. To sustain natural systems, land use laws need to prioritise rehabilitating what now is built, rather than always seeking new buildings which entail destroying essential areas for agricultural soils, habitat for other species and open space for people. (5) Finally, the laws for the exploitation of nature need to be rescaled. The human cull of renewable resources is so over-extended that major reductions will be needed if reproductive systems are to be maintained so that a harvest can be ensured in the future. For non-renewable sources of energy, all carbon fuels extraction will need to end; oil is best used as a feed stock for the petrochemical industry and we cannot afford to burn it until it is lost; electricity needs to be generated directly from sunlight, wind and hydro. Coal needs to be left in the ground, to avert further releases of carbon dioxide as a greenhouse gas. A revolution is needed in the distribution and storage of electricity. Current alternative energy efforts are at too small a scale to meet current and projected needs. Environmental law needs to accelerate such efforts.

For each of these substantive legal reforms, parallel procedural environmental laws need to be enhanced. To effectively manage the planet's natural systems to serve humans and nature alike, complete transparency is needed. Full disclosure should apply to all environmental impacts, including financial disclosure by companies and individuals who exploit natural resources Freedom of information laws, rules for the public dissemination of environmental information and procedures for environmental reporting to stakeholders must be enhanced and made universal. The Aarhus Convention offers a template for information access, public participation and access to justice to seek redress of any departures from observance of environmental due process of law. Institutional innovations must be expanded into each nation, such as the establishment of agencies like Brazil's Ministério Público and the establishment of environmental courts or 'green' benches. Stakeholders need clear rights to locus standi and judicial review. Public defenders' offices for the environment need to be expanded beyond the few places where they now exist. Environmental education, at all levels, also needs to be promoted.

These challenges are currently perceived as the immediate next steps in the progressive development of environmental law. Even so, this perception is shared largely only by environmental law professors, environmental court judges, scientists, conservation leaders and environmental ministry professionals, but generally not by legislators, diplomats, the media, business corporation officers or the general public. Agenda 21 is of continuing relevance as the foundation for 'sustainable development'.

However, even if Agenda 21 were fully embraced and implemented, a further agenda of reform qualitatively different in scope and content is required, with a more intensive and more highly leveraged role for environmental law. Should the fundamental ground norm in environmental law be that of the physicians: Do No Harm? Where there is injury or illness, heal. End the clear cuts and burning of flora, and cease the wholesale culling of wild species. Restore what has been lost over the past 4,000 years through reforestation and afforestation. As people retreat from the coastlines because of sea level rise, take the opportunity to restore estuaries and once lost wetlands and mangroves, and plant new wetlands and new mangrove forests. Help natural habitats and other species to move inland along with people, and redesign the harbours and coastal resorts and promote kinetic, wind and solar for generating electricity in lieu of the fossil fuel facilities situated along the coasts now. Replace static systems of coastal zone management with a dynamic and integrative new regime of Adaptive Coastal Zone Stewardship to produce resilience in coastal land uses and infrastructure, and be a learning system that reiteratively addresses new coastal conditions as they arise.

The pattern of adaptive stewardship needs to expand to all geographic places and all sectors of human activity. This will require: (1) defining clear, adaptable objectives to address the needs of people and nature together; (2) providing for scientific assessment and data collection and the restating of baselines from which to measure both physical environmental change and progress towards stated objectives; (3) open and regular dissemination of environmental reports; (4) ensuring all environmental decision-making is transparent and guarantees public participation; and (5) review of the decisions every five years or so, to apply the latest environmental scientific information, and then adapting the decisions as appropriate. Under this model, decision-making is not static, bound by time or place, as it is now, but dynamic and cyclical, accommodating environmental change at the core and involving both horizontal and vertical coordination.

In light of constantly changing conditions, every environmental stewardship system also needs to be consciously transformative. Socio-economic society must emerge as socio-ecologic society in order to adjust nimbly to these new conditions. The human economy will do well only when the environment does well. Environmental law needs to require economic entities to measure and adapt to environmental conditions, not ignore them, as is the currently governing neo-classical economic model. Taken to its logical ends, this model is ecologically illiterate and is largely a cardboard ideology, unable to guide the livelihoods of humans or other species through the challenges that life is contemplating. Sensible conventions of macro-economic and micro-economic analysis will continue to be useful, but economic disregard for nature must end; economics must serve ecological decision-making, not the other way around, or the deterioration of environmental conditions will diminish both economic and ecological analysis. The unique calling of environmental law is to integrate these two spheres of knowledge, and provide the decision-making framework for their application.

Environmental law provisions for establishing adaptive stewardship also must cut across time. Just as environmental problems accumulate as a result of past human behaviour, decision-makers must think in terms of future generations today. Environmental policy pays lip service to the principle of inter-generational equity, but does little to implement this norm. In order to temper the excessive appetite of the current generation, environmental laws must establish a bright line, placing the resources needed for future generations off limits for current exploitation. This can be done by extending the legal concept of trusteeship, with courts made capable of adjudicating the needs of current and future generations; otherwise, environmental justice will at best be ephemeral.

To make the transformation from contemporary 'business as usual' models for sustainable development will not be easy. In order to shift socio-economic decision-making from ignoring impacts on human health and nature, the next generation of environmental law will need to enact directives that make protection of the environment the default position. Departure from protection should be discrete and only when the environmental impacts are essential and all concomitant harm is mitigated, off-set and compensated.

## 5.   DEVELOPING MORE ROBUST STEWARDSHIP

Heuristic efforts to frame and legislate basic norms for environmental stewardship have been a major feature of international relations over the past several decades. IUCN's Commission on Environmental Law undertook the initial analysis to support the drafting and adoption of the World Charter for Nature, adopted by the UN General Assembly (Burhenne and Irwin, 1986; Lausche, 2008).[28] The Charter is an important statement of norms necessary for supporting environmental law, and many of its values have been adopted in the UN Convention on Biological Diversity. Nonetheless, the stated norms in the Charter have yet to be integrated into the mainstream of environmental decision-making.

There have, however, been repeated efforts to restate the ethical values for how humans should interact with nature. The Rio Declaration on Environment and Development restated many of the principles of international law for sustainable development, but did not address the deeper challenge of agreeing on an ethical framework for the environment. The proposal that UNCED adopt an 'Earth Charter' to become a common moral code of conduct did not find consensus with the nations assembled in Rio. The campaign for such an instrument was taken up by a dedicated group of leaders[29] who consulted widely over a period of years and prepared the 2004

Earth Charter,[30] a restatement of the values and norms that might guide humans in caring for the Earth.

While it is a well-conceived ethics framework, the Earth Charter is for the most part *de lege ferenda*, a statement of norms that needs still to become a part of binding international law. First steps in this direction include the endorsement of the Earth Charter by UNESCO and IUCN. Like its predecessor, the UN World Charter for Nature, many of the norms for nature are not yet *lex lata*, or established international law. Environmental law specialists need to examine which of the Earth Charter's norms already reflect prevailing international law. It is important to clearly understand which components are *lex lata* and which are *de lege ferenda*; too often the debate has been 'all or nothing'. Of course, the Earth Charter could (and perhaps should) be adopted as a treaty, to provide hard law guidance to nations and their decision-making. The Earth Charter's norms, as statements of basic principles of international law, are embedded in how humans fit into and grow out of nature. They can be characterised as natural rights, not of the type dreamt up by natural philosophers, but rather as fundamental rights arising from what we have learned of nature and the discipline of ecology. This was the view of the Supreme Court of the Republic of the Philippines in the decision of *Oposa v. Factoran*.[31] Many of the Earth Charter's principles underpin the rules of environmental law embodied in the multilateral environmental agreements. Its norms are akin to the provisions in the constitutions of states that confer a right to the environment, and provide the elaboration of how to apply that right in various circumstances.

The ethical framework of the Earth Charter is consistent with many of the teachings of different religions. This has been demonstrated, for example, by IUCN in its work with Islamic states. The publication *Environmental Protection in Islam*[32] makes clear that the Holy Qur'an requires the protection of God's creation. The teachings of Buddhism, as reflected for instance in the laws of Bhutan, require that nature be respected as a precursor to development. When neo-classical economic norms justify greed or aggrandisement of economic gain while ignoring adverse environmental consequences, or when corruption undermines the rule of law, then the protection of nature must depend upon a higher law.

An ethical framework also underpins the science of ecology, distinguishing that science from other disciplines (Leopold, 1949). Before there is a more widespread observance of environmental laws, there will need to be an appeal to the stronger normative foundations that should bolster environmental stewardship. As a secular instrument, the Earth Charter can be used by all states to provide a common legal foundation for a more robust, worldwide environmental law regime.

# 6. TRANSFORMING ENVIRONMENTAL LAW TO PROVIDE RULES FOR RESILIENT ADAPTATION

We should understand that environmental law is at once grounded upon and informed by basic principles of stewardship of life on Earth, such as those reflected in the World Charter for Nature and the Earth Charter. Through legal scholarship, we need to reassess the present body of international and national environmental law in the light of these principles and norms. One such exercise is found in the international restatement of norms for sustainable development in the draft Covenant on Environment and Development and its accompanying commentary.[33] The Draft Covenant is designed to be a hard law instrument that can mirror the consensus of Agenda 21. However, as indicated by the choice of words in its very title 'environment and development', the Draft Covenant itself needs to be revised and strengthened. In order to better reflect an adequate ethical wellspring, it needs to be recast as a 'Covenant on Earth Stewardship'. At present, however, states are not even ready to adopt the Covenant as a faithful legal reflection of Agenda 21 and the Rio Declaration on Environment and Development, and it is admittedly much weaker than the Earth Charter.

Growing international awareness of environmental degradation, of climate change impacts and of natural resource scarcities, is making it more likely that states will come to recognise that they need the stewardship principles of the Earth Charter, in much the same way as they recognised the need for a Universal Declaration of Human Rights in 1948. Environmental law builds the reciprocal relationships of governmental rights and obligations to care for the Earth. Just as states act with solidarity for the protection of human rights, so they must come to act with respect for all aspects of the environment.

In 1992, the Earth Summit laid the basis both for building the multilateral environmental agreements and national environmental legislative systems. It was a milestone, but it should not be seen as an end in itself. The current corpus of international environmental agreements has become the basis for a continuing process. Nations need to rethink and enhance institutions previously established. Reforms such as the constituting of the UN Commission on Sustainable Development after UNCED need to be rethought, as do the institutional reforms arising from the 1972 Stockholm Conference, such as the creation of the modest United Nations Environment Programme. States have not been ready to do so (Robinson, 2002). The coming decades will witness a further phase of elaborating environmental law at all levels of government, wherever pollution, ecosystem degradation, resource depletion or climate change impacts are experienced. Environmental law professors, practising lawyers and judges will need to more explicitly orient their proposals and advice in light of the Earth Charter. We must test the application of the law against these basic jurisprudential concepts. Where the proposed action or advice is at variance with the core values, they must be revisited and re-examined.

It is more likely than not that states will act on specific reforms, step by step, further elaborating the system of MEAs, but will not adopt wholesale the vision of the Earth Charter. Thus, it will probably not be by establishing any new global administrative or political institutions that environmental law will be strengthened. Rather, there will be an elaboration of a much more sophisticated, holistic and integrated system of environmental law at international, national and sub-national levels. One focus for the coming elaboration of environmental laws will be through comparing the effectiveness of different types of national legislation, and the integration of these laws at the regional levels (Adams, 1997; Robinson, 2002).

At the international level, it must be ensured that MEAs are implemented thoroughly at the national level, in the same manner as has been done with the Vienna Convention and its Montreal Protocol, and the Convention on Trade in Endangered Species (CITES).[34] These regimes illustrate the kinds of more complete legal regimes which must become the norm in every area of environmental management and conservation. The elaboration of environmental law will require replicating what we have learned from these international, national and local examples.

Where Agenda 21 includes recommendations that have not yet been implemented, these now need to be considered in light of the Earth Charter principles, and then made the subject of a treaty negotiation or the enactment of national or local legislation. Where an Agenda 21 recommendation is already in effect, its implementation must be compared with the Earth Charter principles and, if necessary, enhanced through new rule-making. Where procedures consistent with Rio Principle 10 have not been adopted, national provisions akin to those of the Aarhus Convention need to be enacted.

It is in the process of formulating and applying environmental law that environmental stewardship arises and is realised. No single enactment or decree can be expected to reshape human conduct into 'sustainable' practices. No Earth Charter, however well elaborated, will induce the reformed behaviour. Rather, it is through a multiplicity of reflective and cautiously deliberative actions that environmental stewardship may emerge.


## 7.  BEHAVIOURAL DOUBTS

Notwithstanding the rational recommendations for a more robust environmental law regime promoted by the Rio Conference, we are still very distant from realising the effectiveness of such a regime, for the following reasons. First, inertia is a powerful force, and stimulating change is thus difficult. Second, most political leaders are preoccupied with immediate problems and many are ignorant of the scientific reports about global environmental degradation. They are not alert to local environmental degradation. Environmental law needs to build additional requirements for self-education, such as personally certifying annual, public environmental reports. Third, our ethics tend to be shallow, and are still grounded in the concepts of balancing 'environment and development', a process which almost always favours development interests. Some argue that formally adopting the Earth Charter is valuable in order to broaden shared ethical horizons and deepen our ethical commitments. Fourth, entrenched patterns of perpetuating 'business as usual' are still seen as valid and self-validating for those who enjoy them. New ethical rules alone will not change this pattern.

Perhaps our inability to act in the face of environmental degradation is a behavioural trait. As Mancur Olson wrote in 1965, 'Rational, self-interested individuals will not act to achieve their common or group interests' (Olson 1965, p. 2). Environmental lawyers need to learn from this. It should induce each government and interest group to perceive what is needed to sustain natural systems beyond the needs of any one government or interest group, and then induce the necessary collective decision-making. The invention by the National Environmental Policy Act 1969 (NEPA) of the EIA process sought to do this. Economic instruments, such as deposits on beverage bottles to promote recycling or environmental taxes and charges similarly are used to induce changes in behaviour. If behavioural studies show that many humans will not act on enlightened self-interest, environmental legal processes for public participation and transparency, despite their growing support, may not be enough to make environmental law more robust. To build the common protection of the environment and to achieve sustainability, much stronger substantive codes and regulations will be needed.

Moreover, given the slow pace of establishing environmental law regimes and the accelerating pace of global environmental degradation, environmental law by itself cannot quickly enough become the needed holistic system, responsive to all environmental threats, and administered consistently across all countries. Even absent the limitations of a deficient observance of the rule of law or of shortcomings in the capacity to enact or implement environmental laws, it will take time to negotiate and enact all the environmental laws needed to achieve a satisfactory system of environmental regulation on a global basis. In the interim, we need to recognise and adhere to a common set of environmental norms. We need to enhance and use scientific knowledge about our environment. We need to ensure that all stakeholders and members of the public have access to a transparent and fair decision-making process about the environment. Out of such a system, and no doubt with a struggle in many jurisdictions, environmental stewardship can emerge.

## 8.   THE UNIVERSITY'S OBLIGATIONS TOWARDS ENVIRONMENTAL LAW

Efforts around the world to build the capacity and scope of environmental law will be fundamental as we cope with the predicted global population increase. Our university systems will have to grow also, to keep pace with the demand for education, but also to provide vision and perspective, with the realisation that in ecological education lies the future of the biosphere.

However intimidating the environmental threats, if we believe in civilisation, then human society can and must rise to the occasion, and the universities must lead the way. Thomas Berry put it succinctly: 'The universities must decide whether they will continue training persons for temporary survival in the declining Cenozoic Era or whether they will begin educating students for the emerging Ecozoic ... it is the time for universities to rethink themselves and what they are doing' (Berry, 1999). The teaching of environmental law is a major contributor to this ongoing rethinking of the role of the university. Within law schools, environmental law departments must be enhanced and should make systemic links to the arts and sciences in both environmental law teaching and research. In the tradition of the sciences, environmental law seeks to integrate knowledge of the biosphere into all decision-making. While clarifying and elaborating a set of values based in nature, environmental law motivates reform by celebrating the beauty of nature and the creativity of human culture, or mourning their loss, in the tradition of the humanities. The world's parks and protected areas echo with the works of poets, naturalist essayists and song writers. The art galleries bring the mind's eye to nature. Environmental law is growing beyond merely being a professional preparation for practising lawyers, into a field that expands, integrates and applies environmental knowledge.

Environmental law is a transformative field. It promotes the clean-up of wastes, the remediation of damaged ecosystems and the phase-out of harmful technologies, while encouraging benign innovations. Universities need to educate students to sustain values that money cannot buy, the essential quality of life's elements: clean air and potable water, open space and tree-lined streets, human health, city parks and vast natural protected areas with myriad flora and fauna beyond human dimensions. Human love of nature is a theme in the literature and art of every nation, and the teaching of this shared heritage should increasingly become a core focus of the university.

Universities must imagine and explore such innovations. We shall need to fashion new and sometimes patently controversial new procedures and rules. Environmental law faculties must undertake this challenging work.

How we teach and what we research in the coming decades will be enormously important. Just as Agenda 21 urged universities to build capacity in this field of law for environment and development, so we must design environmental law to leverage societies to implement the rest of Agenda 21's recommendations.

Universities should consider themselves well suited to this task. We teachers understand 'intergenerational equity' better than most. We know that we owe an enormous debt to our own teachers, and in striving to meet the expectations that our teachers set for us, we repay our indebtedness by our own teaching, mentoring, and research and service to our students. We must operate intergenerationally as we build the capacity in our students for their future of hope. University law faculties can take the lead in advancing major innovations in environmental law. The IUCN Academy of Environmental Law, which engages a wide range of the world's law faculties, has an important role to play in achieving the unrealised parts of Agenda 21. To do so more effectively, the IUCN Academy needs to link to other related institutions which promote environmental studies. Within each university, the law school and its environmental law section needs to interact with other schools and departments concerned with environmental stewardship.

## 9. CONCLUSION

By strengthening environmental compliance procedures, environmental laws can guide the multiple actions required for implementing environmentally sustainable standards. The realisation of environmental norms is found in the context of compliance procedures and decisions, as well as the recognition that a community's environmental rights can be seen as being on the same level as an individual's human rights. As the world struggles to accommodate several billion more people over the next few decades there will be a rush for short-term fixes. We are apt to make the same mistakes we have made in the past. Environmental law can provide the long-term perspective and sustain long-term solutions.

If we have learned anything as we established our field of environmental law, it is that legal tools exist to challenge the governance paradigms that imperil Earth's biosphere (Koh and Robinson 2002). Environmental law can induce or force design of new technologies, and can save us from our proclivity to excess. In order to evolve towards actions based on the principles of an Earth Charter, we need to muster disciplined and thoughtful decision-making, based on clear processes. If governments benignly ignore what scientists are discovering and reporting about natural conditions on the Earth, then we shall compound our environmental problems and weaken environmental law.

The way towards a more robust and resilient environmental law is in our hands.

## NOTES

\*    This chapter is dedicated to the memory of Professor Oleg Stepanovich Kolbasov, the 'Father' of what he chose to call 'ecological law' in the Russian Federation and the former Union of Soviet Socialist Republics (USSR). From his research as a legal scholar in water resources law, beginning in the 1970s, Oleg Kolbasov built the theoretical and scholarly foundations for environmental law as the founding director of the Environmental Law Centre of the Institute of State and Law in the Russian Academy of Science. He was vice chairman of the IUCN Commission on Environmental Law and co-chaired the USA–USSR Bilateral Environmental Law Cooperation Negotiations from 1974 to 1992. When the USSR came to an end in 1989, Professor Kolbasov served as Deputy Minister of the Environment for Russia and helped frame the regional seas agreement for the Caspian Sea. He was also instrumental in Russia's support for the negotiation of the Aarhus Convention. His publications and lectures inspired a generation of environmental law specialists in Russia and abroad. He won the respect and affection of all who came to work with him. His daughter, Professor Irina Olegova Krasnova, a member of the IUCN Academy of Environmental Law's Governing Board, continues his environmental law teaching and scholarship in Moscow. He and I explored the realm of détente for our two nations during the Cold War; we came to have an abiding respect and deep affection for each other, as fellow conservationists. He is deeply missed.

1.   Agenda 21, UN Doc. A/CONF. 151/26 (1992), available at: http://www.un.org/esa/dsd /agenda21/.

2.   Rio Declaration on Environment and Development, UN Doc. A/CONF.151/26 (Vol. I) available    at    http://www.unep.org/Documents.Multilingual/Default.asp?documentid =78&articleid=1163.

3.   Johannesburg Declaration on Sustainable Development and the Plan of Implementation of the World Summit on Sustainable Development (WSSD), UN Doc. A/CONF. 199/L-6 rev. 2 (4 September 2002).

4.   Agenda 21, Chapter 8, paras 8.19 and 8.20.

5.   See the edition of Agenda 21 edited for IUCN as IUCN's Environmental Law & Policy Paper No. 27 in 1993, which retained the estimates of financial commitments needed to implement each of the recommendations in Agenda 21.

6.   Monterrey Consensus of the International Conference on Financing for Development and Follow-up Report, UN Doc. A/CONF. 198/11 (2002), reproduced in N.A. Robinson, *Strategies toward Sustainable Development: Implementing Agenda 21* (2004) at 655, et seq.

7.   UNFCCC, 31 (1992) ILM 849.

8.   (1992) 31 ILM 818; the initial draft of the Convention on Biological Diversity was ·prepared by members of the IUCN Commission on Environmental Law and the IUCN Environmental Law Centre.

9.   Convention to Combat Desertification in those Countries Experiencing Serious Drought and/or Desertification, Particularly in Africa (1994) 33 ILM 1328.

10. The World Environment Center began in 1974, at the behest of the UN Environment Programme's Executive Director, Maurice Strong, to build understanding and cooperation between environment ministries and multinational companies.

11. A Non-legally Binding Authoritative Statement of Principles for a Global Consensus on the Management, Conservation and Sustainable Development of all Types of Forests was negotiated in 1992; at http://www.un-documents.net/for-prin.htm.

12. The United Nations Forum on Forests produced a more substantial instrument in 2007: Non-Legally Binding Instrument on all Types of Forests in April 2007. It was adopted by the UN General Assembly (Resolution 62/98) in December 2007.

13. UNEP Periodic Review of Environmental Law, adopted by the UNEP Governing Council in 2001 (Montevideo Programme) http://www.unep.org/law/About_prog/montevideo_ prog.asp Montevideo Programme IV is being prepared; see http://www.unep.org /Law/About_prog/montevideo_prog.asp.

14. For example, *Judicial Handbook on Environmental Law, 2005*, *Manual on International Environmental Law* (UNEP, 2006); for UNEP publications see http://www.unep.org /law/Publications_multimedia/index.asp.

15. See the report of the United Nations Joint Independent Panel. T. Iomata, 'Management Review of Environmental Governance within the United Nations System', UN Doc. JIU/REP/2008/9 (2008), at http://www.unjiu.org/data/reports /2008/en2008_3.pdf.

16. The 1988 Aarhus Convention on Access to Information, Public Participation in Decision-making and Access to Justice in Environmental Matters implements Principle 10 of the 1992 Rio Declaration on Environment and development.

17. http://www.pic.int/incs/dipcon/c)/English/Conf-2.pdf (entered into force 24 February 2004).

18. http://chm.pops.int/Convention/tabid/54/language/en-US/Default.aspx.

19. Section 5 (1) states: 'The purpose of this Act is to promote the sustainable management of natural and physical resources'.

20. UN World Charter for Nature, UN Doc. UNGA Res. 37/7 (1982).

21. UN Johannesburg Declaration on Sustainable Development, Para. 5 (2002).

22. Millennium Declaration, UN Doc. UNGA Res. 55/2 (8 September 2000).

23. Vienna Convention, (1985) 26 ILM 1529.

24. Montreal Protocol, (1987) 26 ILM 1550.

25. Vienna Convention Arts 2 and 3.

26. See the Ozone Secretariat's reports at www.unep.org/ozone.

27. The precautionary principle's application in the area of conservation of biodiversity and management of natural resources is set out in guidelines endorsed by the IUCN Council in 2007: *Guidelines for Applying the Precautionary Principle to Biodiversity Conservation and Natural Resources Management*, at http://cmsdata.iucn.org/downloads/ ln250507_ppguidelines.pdf

28. UN Doc. UNGA Res. 37/7 (1982).

29. Including Mikhail Gorbachov of Russia, Ruud Lubbers of the Netherlands and Steven Rockefeller of the USA.

30. Available at http://www.earthcharterinaction.org/content/pages/Read-the-Charter.html.

31. Supreme Court of the Philippines, No. 101083 (30 July 1993).

32. Available at http://cmsdata.iucn.org/downloads/eplp20en.pdf.

33. The IUCN Draft Covenant on Environment and Development was launched at the UN General Assembly's 50th anniversary conference on Public International Law at the UN Headquarters in New York in 1995; the fourth edition was completed in 2010, and is available at http://data.iucn.org/dbtw-wpd/edocs/EPLP-031-rev3.pdf.

34. Convention on the International Trade in Endangered Species, developed by IUCN; see http://www.cites.org/eng/disc/text.shtml.

# REFERENCES

Adams, Trevor (1997), 'Environmental Law in the European Communities', in N.A. Robinson (ed.), *Comparative Environmental Law and Regulation*, Dobbs Ferry, New York: Oceana Publications.

Berry, Thomas (1999), *The Great Work: Our Way into the Future*, New York: Bell Tower.

Burhenne, Wolfgang E. and Will A. Irwin (1986), *The World Charter for Nature: Legislative History, Commentary*, 2nd edn, Berlin: Erich Schmidt Verlag.

Koh Kheng Lian and Nicholas A. Robinson (2002), 'Regional Environmental Governance: Examining the Association of Southeast Asian Nations (ASEAN) Model', in Daniel Esty and Maria H. Ivanova (eds), *Global Environmental Governance: Options and Opportunities*, New Haven: Yale School of Forestry and Environmental Studies.

Koh, Tommy T.B. (1993), 'The Earth Summit's Negotiating Process: Some Reflections on the Art and Science of Negotiation', in Nicholas A. Robinson (ed.), *Agenda 21: Earth's Action Plan*, Dobbs Ferry, New York: Oceana Publications.

Kolbasov, O.S. (1976), *Ecological Law*, Moscow: Progress Publishers.

Lausche, Barbara (2008), *Weaving a Web of Environmental Law*, Berlin: Erich Schmidt Verlag.

Leopold, Aldo (1949), *A Sand County Almanac*, New York: Oxford University Press.

Olson, Mancur (1965), *The Logic of Collective Action: Public Goods and the Theory of Groups*, Cambridge, Massachusetts: Harvard University Press.

Robinson, Nicholas A. (2002), 'Befogged Vision: International Environmental Law Governance a Decade after Rio', *William & Mary Environmental Law and Policy Review*, **27**, 299.

Robinson, Nicholas A. (2004), *Strategies toward Sustainable Development: Implementing Agenda 21*, Dobbs Ferry, New York: Oceana Publications.

Schmidheiny, Stephan (1992), *Changing Course: A Global Business Perspective on Development and the Environment*, Business Council for Sustainable Development, Boston, Massachusetts: MIT Press.

Speth, James (2004), *Red Sky at Morning, America and the Crisis of the Global Environment*, Yale, New Haven and London: Note Bene.

Tolba, Mustafa and Iwona Rummel-Bulska (2008), *Global Environmental Diplomacy: Negotiating Environmental Agreements for the World, 1973–1992*, Cambridge, Massachusetts: MIT Press.

United Nations Commission on Environment and Development (1987), *Our Common Future*, Oxford: Oxford University Press.

# 3. Capacity building in environmental law in African universities

## Charles Odidi Okidi

## 1. INTRODUCTION

At dinner in New York only a few years ago, a group of lawyers was surprised by my explanation of environmental law teaching and research in Africa and the role of the United Nations Environment Programme (UNEP) in promoting institutional developments in this field. As environmental lawyers themselves, they shared the once-popular assumption that African countries were hostile to environmental law because it was inconsistent with their ambitions for development; an assumption originating in the atmosphere preceding the 1972 Stockholm Conference on the Human Environment.[1]

This chapter reviews developments in environmental law teaching, research and institutional capacity building in Africa during the formative years from 1978 to the present. In 1978, a Workshop on Environmental Education and Training took place in Nairobi. The event revealed very little evidence of actual teaching and research on environmental law in Africa. Twenty-five years later, in 2004, the first Symposium on Environmental Law by African scholars took place in Nakuru. Between these two landmarks, the range of environmental law activity increased significantly, supported and encouraged by a number of international initiatives under the auspices of the UNEP and other UN agencies. A second symposium at Entebbe in 2006 demonstrated the scope of further developments and adopted a number of instruments to institutionalise an association for environmental law in Africa and spelled out conditions for its sustainability.

## 2. THE CONTEXT

The initial problem faced in assessing concern for environment lies in definition. Initially, environmental concern was understood in terms of public health or urban and industrial pollution. However, as the meaning broadened, the concerns extended to poor physical planning, deforestation, adverse agricultural practices and land use. Within most African countries, the majority of these still narrowly construed concerns were understood to belong to industrialised countries of the west. What was considered as environmental law was construed accordingly.

Gradually, environment came to be linked to sustainable development. Through the Stockholm Declaration and its principles, the scope of environment became more widely understood (Okidi, 1997), setting the stage for a more comprehensive understanding of the relevance of environmental law. The broader meaning extended to the totality of nature and natural resources and included the context within which they exist and interact, as well as the infrastructure constructed to support socio-economic activities. We now take our cue from the Brundtland Commission Report *Our Common Future* (WCED, 1987) and the Rio Principles[2] which are premised on integration of environmental exigencies into development planning and management to meet the interests of the present generation without compromising the interests of future generations. The scope of environmental law in university curricula must be correspondingly broad.

Environmental law encompasses common law doctrines, civil law norms, constitutional provisions, treaty law and general principles of law which seek to promote intra- and inter-generational equity through rational management of the environment and its resources. In other words, the primary function of environmental law is to ensure that the present generation is able to enjoy the environment and its resources without jeopardising the ability of future generations to enjoy the same.

African countries have demonstrated a widespread acceptance of this extended understanding of environmental law. This is evident from the broad range of treaties, soft law and hortatory instruments adopted since the advent of independence of the former colonies. The principal examples of such instruments include: the 1968 African Convention for the Conservation of Nature and Natural Resources, a revised version of which was adopted in 2003 (UNEP, 2005); Lagos Plan of Action and Final Act of Lagos, 1980;[3] African Priority Programme of Economic Recovery, 1985;[4] Bamako Convention on the Ban of the Import into Africa and the Control of the Transboundary Movement and Management of Hazardous Wastes within Africa, 1991 (UNEP, 2005); and the Treaty Establishing the African Economic Community 1991.[5] These developments show that, as a group, African countries have been positively disposed to accept environmental law either as legal obligation or at the hortatory level.

The general acceptance of environmental law by African countries is also demonstrated by the fact that over 40 African countries, out of 53, have enacted framework environmental laws of different levels of sophistication, in addition to the wide array of sectoral and functional laws with environmental implications.[6] It is equally significant that some 35 African countries have entrenched environmental provisions in national constitutions, lifting environment to the highest legal order of the country (Bruch et al., 2001). Accordingly, those universities which may wish to teach environmental law have a wide array of laws to base their work on.

At the global level, environmental education has received authoritative support. The first global forum providing for a declaration of environmental principles was provided by the Stockholm Conference on the Human Environment in 1972.[7] Principle 19 urged that environmental education be given to the younger generation as well as to adults to build enlightened opinion and responsible individuals who will protect the environment. Additionally, Principle 20 called for scientific research and the free flow of environmental information.

Principle 9 of the Rio Declaration on Environment and Development is equally germane. It urges states to cooperate to strengthen endogenous capacity building for sustainable development with an emphasis on scientific and technological advancement. However, one would understand that to extend to legal regimes which regulate, control or otherwise facilitate such scientific capacity building. Principle 10 advocates public participation and enjoins states to facilitate and encourage public awareness. These are possible only with education at all levels.

Agenda 21[8] is much richer on matters of environmental education. Chapter 36 addresses the promotion of environmental education, public awareness and training, while Chapter 37 urges the establishment of national mechanisms and international cooperation for capacity building in developing countries. Further, Chapter 36 acknowledges the contribution of the Intergovernmental Conference on Environmental Education organised by UNESCO and UNEP and held at Tbilisi, Georgia, in 1977. The three programme areas discussed in Chapter 36 are: (a) re-orienting education towards sustainable development; (b) increasing public awareness; and (c) promoting training.

## 3.   THE AFRICAN AGENDA

Nearly six years after Stockholm, UNEP funded a Workshop on Environmental Education and Training in African Universities, convened under the aegis of the Accra-based Association of African Universities (AAU) and organised by the University of Nairobi, in December, 1978.[9]

Invitations were sent to 75 universities, all members of AAU, asking them to nominate scholars teaching any environmental subject to attend. Ultimately, only 40 universities were represented. Twenty five papers were presented but only one was on environmental law. In that paper, 'Teaching and Research in Environmental Law in African Universities', the author sought to set out an agenda for teaching environmental law in Africa (Okidi, 1980). The paper recommended a comparative approach to the teaching of environmental law in Africa and emphasised the inextricable relationship between research and teaching, urging environmental law lecturers to engage in workshops with scholars from diverse backgrounds in order to facilitate peer review and intellectual dialogue. Other specific recommendations emphasised that:

- teaching and research in environmental law should be undertaken in an interdisciplinary context so that the relationship between legal developments and other environmental disciplines are kept under constant review;
- scholars should publish environmental law journals to provide outlets for scholarly research reports; and
- strong libraries are required to provide access to environmental law materials from other continents.

Those participating at the 1978 workshop were also urged to build up links with policy makers so that environmental law would be incorporated within relevant policy domains. Similarly, African environmental law scholars were encouraged to appeal to United Nations agencies, especially UNEP, for support in their work, particularly research and teaching materials as well as workshops and journal publications. Moreover, conference delegates were reminded of the desirability of seeking collaborative links with universities involved in research and teaching in environmental law in industrialised countries. While the foregoing points may appear mundane today, their emphasis in a continent where environmental law was not on obvious offer may have been salutary when universities agreed to discuss environmental education in December 1978.

## 4.   REVIEWING THE DECADE OF ACTIVITY AND DISCOVERY: 1995–2006

While the 1978 workshop resulted in no further or immediate effort to convene teachers or researchers on environmental law in Africa to pursue the agenda set out above, a further environmental law symposium in 2004 revealed that a great deal of activity in research and teaching of environmental law was actually initiated during the ensuing quarter century. Two developments may have been catalytic.

## Impact of the United Nations Conference on Environment and Development

Preparations for the 1992 United Nations Conference on Environment and Development were highly orchestrated in most countries. With the conference itself highlighting the integration of environment and development as well as intra- and inter-generational equity, a new epoch had arisen in environmental thought. There was a growing popular movement and widespread action with which all professionals wanted to identify.

## Inter-Agency Project on Environmental Law and Institutions in Africa

As if in response to the recommendations advanced at the 1978 workshop, an initiative known as the Partnership for the Development of Environmental Law and Institutions in Africa (PADELIA)[10] was launched shortly after UNCED. With a grant of US$5 million from the Dutch Government, the project was housed at UNEP under the supervision of an inter-agency Steering Committee comprising FAO, IUCN, UNDP, the World Bank, the Dutch Government and UNEP itself. Suffice to state that this initiative may well have influenced activities in teaching and practice in environmental law in Africa.

The first phase of the project, 1995–2002, operated in only seven countries: Burkina Faso, Kenya, Malawi, Mozambique, São Tomé and Príncipe, Tanzania and Uganda. The second phase commenced in 2002 and included six additional countries, namely Mali, Niger, Senegal, Botswana, Lesotho and Swaziland. This phase is still continuing.

The project formally encompasses the national policy domains focusing on development of environmental law, both framework and sectoral statutes, as well as on strengthening government institutions to facilitate implementation of such laws. Although the project was not directly connected to teaching and research in African universities there were, however, three ways in which the project, as an African activity, spread environmental law to the universities.

### Utilisation of local legal, policy and technical capacity

The project deployed legal, policy and technical capacity available locally to review the status of environmental policy and law and to develop draft laws for local enactment. Notably, project implementation rejected use of imported or itinerant consultants to work in project countries. Instead, project managers recruited local lawyers, particularly lecturers from the universities, and guided them through the work of evolving the laws. All drafts were placed before national consensus-building workshops with the participation of a diverse range of stakeholders. After revisions, taking into account views from the workshops, the draft bills were sent to the Attorneys-General for formal drafting and the legislative process. This procedure demystified environmental law and popularised it within and outside the universities and could have substantially promoted teaching of the subject even by lawyers who had no formal training in environmental law.

### The range of activities encouraged close collaboration

A number of activities under the project included non-project country participants. For instance, a workshop to discuss implementation of conventions related to biological diversity was held in Maputo, Mozambique in June–July 1997. One result was that it was decided there should be a handbook to guide African states on policy development and teaching related to treaties on biological diversity. This work involved representatives from over 20 African countries and from the Ramsar Secretariat, the Convention on Migratory Species, the Convention on International Trade in Endangered Species and the Organization of African Unity, resulting in a book circulated to all African countries and available globally.[11]

Another example under this category was a workshop targeting industrialists, to discuss environmental law and its enforcement as well as the role of the private sector in promoting compliance at Kisumu, Kenya, in 1997. This was attended by four industry representatives accompanied by a lawyer and a scientist from South Africa, São Tomé and Príncipe, Mozambique, Malawi, Mali, Kenya, Guinea, Gabon and Burkina Faso, resulting in recommendations and a book distributed to all African countries. Such a process further demystified environmental law and promoted efficacy. Such exercises involved individuals from many African countries and again enhanced interest in teaching environmental law.

### Academic publications resulting from the project

The project generated over 30 publications between 1996 and 2002. The first and most striking publication was the Compendium of Judicial Decisions on Matters Related to Environment, one volume on International Decisions and three on National Decisions. These were stimulated by the Workshop on Judicial Intervention in Environmental Cases, which was held for judges at Mombasa, Kenya in September 1996. Decisions from diverse jurisdictions presented for discussions by the judges were used for training lawyers from similarly diverse African countries at a workshop in Kampala, Uganda in August 1997. The same was done for the ten volumes and two supplements of the Compendium of Environmental Laws of African Countries.[12]

Another solid set of publications generated by the project addressed the development and harmonisation of environmental law in East Africa with reference to seven subject areas: environmental standards; environmental impact assessment; wildlife; forestry; hazardous wastes; hazardous and toxic substances; and shared water resources in the Lake Victoria basin. With an additional book on synergies and complementarity in initiatives related to environmental law, the eight books were distributed to African countries to offer guidance to environmental law-making for various jurisdictions.[13]

Importantly, the project generated diverse materials that could offer analogies for teaching and research in environmental law. However, even those who did not directly use the materials were inspired into considering teaching and research in the field. In fact, as the Project Steering Committee deliberated on dissemination of the publications, they urged that documentation or resource centres be established in project countries, preferably at all universities. These would accommodate the publications for purposes of policy, legislation, teaching and research. This had been one of the agenda items at the 1978 African Workshop.

During Phase I of the African Environmental Law Project, the Steering Committee considered the possibility of convening a Symposium of environmental law lecturers to discuss their experience and seek ways of mutual assistance, but for various reasons the majority of Steering Committee members thought the idea could wait.

## Discovering the Scope of Capacity, Teaching and Research at the Nakuru Symposium

During the second half of the 1990s, the range of activities, including the encouragement of teaching and research generated by the UNEP/UNDP/Dutch Joint Project, had the effect of demystifying the subject. An opportunity to convene a meeting of environmental law teachers then arose when it was confirmed that the University of Nairobi, through its Centre for Advanced Studies in Environmental Law and Policy (CASELAP), was to host the Second Colloquium of the IUCN Academy of Environmental Law in October 2004. CASELAP approached UNEP through PADELIA, the successor to the UNEP/UNDP/Dutch Joint Project, to support the participation of scholars teaching environmental law in African universities in the Colloquium.

The two parties agreed to revive an earlier concept paper proposing convening a symposium of such lecturers and to conduct it back-to-back with the Colloquium. Twenty-three participants from as many countries attended and a total of 25 papers, including contributions from two UNEP officers, were presented.

The papers from roughly half of the countries of the continent indicate what had been happening in teaching and research in environmental law in African universities. The information presented below is gleaned from a 580 page report of the Nakuru Symposium.[14] Notable highlights in relation to educational developments in environmental law are summarised below.

At the undergraduate level, environmental law courses have been introduced at the University of Asmara, Eritrea; the University of Zimbabwe;

and the University of Ghana, Legon, where a course was offered as early as 1996. At the University of Nairobi, Kenya, elective courses including environmental and natural resources law, law of the sea, and land use planning are available to students in the final year of the LLB programme. Environmental law and policy courses are taught in Uganda at both Makerere University and Uganda Christian University. In Nigeria, courses on environmental law and policy, introduction to elements of environmental law, biotechnology regulation and control law have been taught at Delta State University in Abraka. Undergraduate environmental law courses and directed research studies are also available in Nigeria at Ahmadu Bello University in Zaria. At the National University of Lesotho, environmental law was first introduced as an elective course in the LLB programme in 1983. Environmental law is an elective at the University of Malawi where the international law course also provides an opportunity for the study of international environmental law. The Institute of Marine and Environmental Law at the University of Cape Town, South Africa, offers an elective environmental law course to upper year students in the LLB programme. Environmental law was first offered as an elective course at the University of Sierra Leone in 2004. The University of Dar es Salaam offers environmental law to upper year undergraduates in Tanzania alongside such related courses as cultural property and antiquities law, natural resources law, regulatory law, and law of the sea.

Graduate studies in environmental law have been introduced at a number of African universities, such as Tanzania's University of Dar es Salaam. At the University of Ghana, environmental law is offered as an elective available to students with no prior background in the subject in a course whose scope extends to historical evolution of environmental law, principles of international environmental law, the Ghanaian environment, and European Communities environmental law. At the University of Nairobi, students pursuing the thematic LLM in Environment and Natural Resources may select from courses including international environmental law, law on transboundary natural resources, the marine environment and the law, natural resources law, law and control of pollution, physical planning and development law, public property and public trust doctrine, legal regulation of power and energy sectors, and international maritime law. Makerere University, Uganda, offers both LLM and LLD degrees in environmental law.

The curriculum proposed for the LLM at Delta State University in Abraka, Nigeria, encompassed courses on international environmental issues in business, environmental and toxic torts law, environmental justice, environmental litigation, comparative environmental law, energy and natural resources law, conservation law, biotechnology regulation and law relating to control of science, animal welfare law, environmental negotiation and skills law, environmental impact assessment law, and advanced international environmental protection law. Thesis-based LLM and PhD programmes at Ahmadu Bello University in Zaria, Nigeria, permit students to pursue environmental law topics at an advanced level. At the Institute of Marine and Environmental Law at the University of Cape Town, LLM candidates may opt to specialise in either of the two fields. Courses taught include international law of the sea and coastal zone law as well as environmental law, international environmental law, marine resources law, and marine pollution law. Other proposals for graduate studies in environmental law have been under consideration at the University of Sierra Leone and at Makerere University in Uganda.

The existence of journals publishing work in the environmental law field is also noteworthy. These include the *University of Nairobi Law Journal*; *East African Law Journal*; *University of Malawi Student Law Journal*; *Journal of Law and Social Justice*; *Eastern Africa Law Review*; *Journal of Law and Development*; *Nyerere Law Journal; East African Journal of Peace and Human Rights*; *Makerere Law Journal* and *Zimbabwe Law Review*.

## Outcome of the Nakuru Symposium

The Nakuru gathering resulted in a set of recommendations:

- Participants should share information obtained, lessons learned and materials received at the symposium with colleagues at home and with other stakeholders;
- Efforts should be made by university lecturers and professors to develop courses in environmental law that are tailored to cultivate the best qualities in students that would allow the application of environmental law to meet sustainable development objectives;
- University lecturers and professors should create and update teaching and research materials;
- University environmental law lecturers and professors should contribute and participate in environmental law making, policy formulation and implementation;
- African university administrators should respond adequately to the dire need for environmental law teaching in African universities;
- University lecturers and professors should identify research areas and develop criteria for determining research priorities based on their circumstances;
- University research should be responsive to the sustainable development needs of African societies and sensitive to opportunities to relieve Africa's debt burden;

- Initiatives should be taken to create journals and other outlets for research findings to make them accessible to stakeholders for use in resolution of environmental issues and problems;
- Research is required on the role that natural resources play in fuelling and maintaining conflicts in Africa and on the potential of ensuring security through sustainable and equitable use of natural resources.

A declaration drafted at the Nakuru Symposium recognised, among other things, that:

- Environmental law is critical in promoting sustainable development;
- University scholars in environmental law have a social responsibility to contribute to the promotion of sustainable development;
- There can be no sustainable development without sound environmental laws, and their enforcement;
- Promoting sustainable development through environmental law requires capacity building of judges, lawyers, policy makers and implementers, legislators, civil society and other stakeholders;
- Environmental governance depends on capable, well-trained and adequately-funded academics in order to ensure that solutions are relevant to African circumstances;
- While African solutions to African problems are desirable, university scholars in environmental law should learn from others and tailor knowledge and experience acquired to suit local circumstances;
- Africa's sustainable development should be enhanced and ensured by an environmental law research agenda primarily driven and conducted by African scholars for the benefit of Africans using traditional, national, regional and international tools and initiatives;
- There is a need to develop, compile and publish textbooks and other teaching materials and create and maintain a data bank of relevant African environmental law materials and profiles of African environmental law scholars; to encourage collaborative and inter-disciplinary research; and to compile an African environmental law reader and a journal of environmental law and policy in Africa;
- Continuing legal education for university scholars in environmental law is essential;
- It is imperative to mainstream environmental education in African university curricula.

The Symposium resolved that the secretariat of the Association of African Environmental Law Scholars established at the Nakuru meeting would be at CASELAP at the University of Nairobi.

## 5.   THE SECOND IUCN ACADEMY COLLOQUIUM

Capacity building is a multi-dimensional phenomenon which gains strength and vitality with application and practice at different levels of rigour. The same is true with the development of scholarly competence: scholarly capacity is enhanced by the frequency and intensity of exposure to scholarly discourse and debate. That is why the participation of African environmental law scholars in regional and global conferences is viewed partly as mutual peer engagement in scholarly discourse and partly as an element of the process of enhancing the stock of knowledge and capacity. The range of African environmental law scholarship presented at the Nairobi IUCN Academy Colloquium in 2004 was very wide (Chalifour et al., 2007). Topics addressed included: Climate Change Adaptation and Mitigation; Transboundary Environmental Assessment; Community Rights to Genetic Resources in Africa; Wildlife Conservation Easements; Property Rights in Wildlife Management; Sustainable Use of Wetlands; Environmental Assessment; Urban Planning and Management; Integrated Environmental Governance and Land Use; Sustainable Land Use; Kenya's National Environment Tribunal and Public Complaints Committee; the Environmental Impact of Refugees; Environmental Assessment of the Oil and Gas Industry; and Land Use Conflicts.

It can be remarked that 15 of some 30 papers contributed from the entire sub-Saharan Africa were by African researchers; clear evidence that African scholars are ready to participate in scholarly discourse in environmental law, just in case some people were still in doubt. Further, the conference organisers requested papers related to land use law. The response indicated that a significant number of environmental law scholars are already doing research, or at least that they have sufficient theoretical grounding to prepare high quality papers.

It is pertinent to conclude that considering the situation in December 1978 which was discussed earlier, there is a vastly increased capacity for teaching and research in environmental law in Africa. It will be interesting to see the extent to which such experts can now respond to the challenges of environment and development and the role of law in finding solutions to environmental problems.

## 6.   THE SECOND SYMPOSIUM ON ENVIRONMENTAL LAW IN AFRICA – ENTEBBE

The first symposium of African environmental law scholars at Nakuru in 2004 had assigned CASELAP, in collaboration with a Steering Committee and UNEP, to make arrangements for a Second Symposium to be held after two years. It was convened at Entebbe, Uganda, with the financial assistance of UNEP in September 2006.

The Entebbe symposium had two principal components: delegates initially addressed business matters relating to the future of the Association of Environmental Law Lecturers of African Universities (ASSELLAU), while the second part of the gathering was devoted to academic exchange. Forty participants drawn from 20 African countries represented 35 university law schools.

On the business side, the symposium adopted a Constitutive Instrument for ASSELLAU designating CASELAP as the Secretariat of the Association. Accordingly, symposium participants requested the Chair, as a member of CASELAP, to effect registration of ASSELLAU as an international learned and non-profit organisation in Kenya. CASELAP was accordingly requested to designate an internal focal point and to appoint an interim Executive Secretary. The symposium also agreed to establish an African Journal of Environmental Law and Policy. The Symposium adopted the Entebbe Declaration in the same spirit as the one at Nakuru.

In deciding the format and content of the scientific conference the Steering Committee recalled that the Nakuru Symposium and the IUCN Academy Colloquium had demonstrated that there was already considerable competence in environmental law in African universities. Therefore, they proposed that the Entebbe Symposium should explore the application of theories and practice of environmental law to the resolution of some pressing problems of Africa. The general theme selected was 'New Horizons in Environmental Law, Natural Resources and Poverty Eradication'.

Again, the individual record demonstrates the extensive scope of contemporary activity in African environmental law. Nearly 40 papers addressed a very wide range of topics, including: community-based natural resources management; nature conservation and customary law; the right to water and poverty alleviation; environmental enforcement; forest and wildlife management for sustainable development in marine and aquatic resources management; legal issues relating to problem animals and local communities; traditional communities and wildlife conservation legislation; poverty, biodiversity and decentralisation; good governance of World Heritage sites; effective and equitable protected areas; forest resources; biodiversity conservation; food security and the environment; conserving and utilising indigenous biological resources; biodiversity; biotechnology and wealth creation; contractual arrangements for sustainable natural resources management; transboundary natural resources; poverty alleviation and wealth creation; constitutions and sustainable development; juridical pluralism and natural resources management; and the conservation of nature and natural resources in Africa.

A few conclusions may be drawn on these presentations. The Entebbe Symposium represented the highpoint in the new initiatives to promote scholarship in environmental law in Africa. The participating scholars not only engaged in extended discussion examining the application of environmental law to development; they also institutionalised ongoing arrangements by adopting a constitutive instrument and creating a permanent administrative office.

The grand aspirations of the scholars are captured in what they called the 'Entebbe Declaration on a Strategy for Teaching of and Research in Environmental Law and Policy'.[15] The scholars urged UNEP, within its current mandate, to foster inter-regional partnerships to further advance teaching and research in environmental law.

## 7.   GENERAL OBSERVATIONS

In noting the evolution of capacity building in environmental law in Africa, one has to say that, in comparison with the baseline year, there is now a good deal of teaching and research in environmental law in Africa, but that there is still a rather narrow range of courses compared to the subjects covered by the papers cited above. The topics taught could certainly expand if there was a regular exchange of syllabi in environmental law among, for example, members of the IUCN Academy of Environmental Law.

The agenda set out in 1978 urged that teaching of environmental law be linked to research to take advantage of the contribution of active researchers to classroom instruction, a point raised forcefully in the Entebbe Declaration. As environmental law lecturers press university managers to support teaching of the subject, they must raise the problem of scarce research funding. It is vital that African scholars begin creative solicitation of research funding, and in particular to pursue opportunities for collaborative research and joint funding with foreign scholars. It may be useful to look at the possibility of a major role for the IUCN Academy and its member universities in this regard.

The 1978 recommendations included active engagement in conferences and workshops, the result of which is evident from the three conferences surveyed. A further proposal was made in 1978 for development of interdisciplinary curricula in environmental law, which one can only continue to urge for further consideration.

A number of universities now publish journals contributing to the dissemination of African environmental law research, possibly in response to encouragement offered during the 1978 meetings. These include *The South African Journal of Environmental Law and Policy* (from 1994) and the *East African Law Review* (published for over 30 years), although the *East African Law Journal* and the *Journal of Environmental Policy and Law in Africa*, both from Nairobi, ceased publication. If the participation of African environmental law scholars at Nakuru, at the IUCN Academy's second

Colloquium, and at the Entebbe symposium is anything to go by, there will be no shortage of solid scholarly papers in the future.

One of the other items raised in the 1978 agenda was the need facing African environmental law scholars to create an information pool. It was thus decided to establish such a database to support research, teaching and collaboration; UNEP/PADELIA agreed to support this initiative.

In 1978, it was further emphasised that environmental law scholars should establish rapport with officials in relevant policy domains. Considerable progress may be seen. In all 13 African countries, under PADELIA, local experts make direct inputs as national advisors and consultants. The survey of national-level activities showed where impacts have been made. For instance, university lecturers in Kenya, Tanzania and Uganda contributed to the development of framework environmental laws. They have also participated in training the judiciary in environmental law.

In 1978, African environmental law scholars were also encouraged to solicit resources through the UN system to support the range of their activities. Very clearly, as demonstrated above, UNEP/PADELIA, which involves the participation of other UN agencies, has facilitated these activities. As more African universities become members of the IUCN Academy they may, as a collective regional association, discuss the question of organisational sustainability in order that ASSELLAU can continue to develop into a vibrant learned society.

Despite this progress, important additional measures remain to be taken. The need for links with learned societies elsewhere was highlighted in the Entebbe Declaration. As ASSELLAU matures, this should be a priority. Further deliberate measures must be pursued to attract environmental law scholars from North Africa.

It is clear that there is now enhanced competence in environmental law in Africa. Capacity is evolving and will gain rapid and increasing competence so long as the resolutions at Nakuru and Entebbe are pursued. However, even if the structures proposed at Entebbe in 2006 do not become fully vibrant, momentum has been established and the participants who have been identified and recruited can be expected to find their place in the global orbit of environmental law experts.

## NOTES

1.   Stockholm 1972 Report of the United Nations Conference on the Human Environment, United Nations Environment Programme, http://www.unep.org/ Documents.Multilingual/Default.asp?documentid=97.
2.   *Rio Declaration on Environment and Development* (1992) UN Doc. A/CONF.151/26 (Vol. I) available at http://www.unep.org/Documents.Multilingual/Default.asp?documentid =78&articleid=1163.

3. See generally, Organization of African Unity, *Lagos Plan of Action for the Economic Development of Africa, 1980–2000* (International Institute for Labour Studies, 1982), http://www.uneca.org/itca/ariportal/docs/lagos_plan.PDF.

4. Organization of African Unity, *Africa's Priority Programme for Economic Recovery 1986-1990* (adopted by the African Heads of State and Government in July 1985). This programme was later renamed and adopted by the UN General Assembly as the United Nations *Programme of Action for African Economic Recovery and Development 1986–1990* (Eighth Plenary Meeting, 1 June 1986 A/RES/S-13/2).

5. East African Community, *Treaty Establishing the East African Community – 1999*, available at http://www.eac.int/.

6. Compiled from UNEP, *Compendium of Environmental Laws of African Countries: Framework Environmental Laws and Environmental Impact Assessment Regulations*, Vols 1 to 8; see http://www.unep.org/padelia /publications/laws.html.

7. *UN Declaration on the Human Environment*, (1972) 11 ILM 1416.

8. Agenda 21, available at http://www.un.org/esa/dsd/agenda21/.

9. The author was Secretary to the Planning Committee and Associate Secretary for the Workshop. It is important to observe that the first decade of UNEP saw very strong staffing of the Environmental Education and Training Unit (EETU) at UNEP. The chief of the Unit was Dr. Victor Johnson, a scholar from Fourah Bay College, Sierra Leone with Dr. Peter Mwanza, former Principal of Chancellor College University of Malawi, and Dr. S. Bhoojedhur, a former senior lecturer at University of Mauritius.

10. This project is otherwise known as the UNEP/UNDP/Dutch Joint Project on Environmental Law and Institutions in Africa. For more information see http://www.unep.org/padelia/index.htm; for a summary of the project see Elizabeth Mrema (2003).

11. UNEP/UNDP/Dutch Joint Project, *Handbook on the Implementation of Conventions Related to Biological Diversity in Africa* (UNEP) (December 1999), available at http://www.unep.org/padelia/publications/handbook11.htm.

12. See note 6.

13. UNEP, PADELIA, http://www.unep.org/padelia/publications/ publication.htm.

14. The manuscript is entitled *Reflections of African Scholars on Environmental Law*, Proceedings of the Symposium of Environmental Law Lecturers held at Merica Hotel, Nakuru 29 September to 2 October 2004 under the aegis of UNEP (PADELIA) and University of Nairobi (CASELAP) (UNEP, Nairobi, March 2005).

15. For full text of the Entebbe Declaration, see UNEP (2006).

# REFERENCES

Agenda 21, UN Doc. A/CONF. 151/26 (1992), available at: http://www.un. org/esa/dsd /agenda21/.

Bruch, Carl, Coker Wole and Chris Van Arsdale (2001), 'Constitutional environmental law: giving force to fundamental principles in Africa', *Columbia Journal of Environmental Law*, **26**, 131–211.

Chalifour, Nathalie, Patricia Kameri-Mbote, Lye Lin Heng and John R. Nolon (eds) (2007), *Land Use Law for Sustainable Development*, Cambridge: Cambridge University Press.

Mrema, Elizabeth (2003), 'PADELIA – A Review', *Environmental Policy and Law*, **33** (5), 204–218.

Okidi, Charles (1980), 'Environmental law in African universities', *Environmental Policy and Law*, **6**, 18–22.

Okidi, Charles (1997), 'Incorporation of general principles of environmental law into national law with examples from Malawi', *Environmental Policy and Law*, **27** (4), 327–335.

United Nations Environment Programme (UNEP) (2005), *Register of International Treaties and Other Agreements in the Field of the Environment*, Nairobi: United Nations Environment Programme.

United Nations Environment Programme (2006), *Biannual Bulletin of Environmental Law*, 22, UNEP, Division of Environmental Law and Conventions, available at: http://www.unep.org/law/PDF/ Environmental-law-Bull-2006.pdf.

World Commission on Environmental and Development (WCED) (1987), *Our Common Future*, Oxford: Oxford University Press.

# 4.  Local Agenda 21: a rights-based approach to local environmental governance

## Anél du Plessis[*]

## 1.  INTRODUCTION

Chapter 28 of Agenda 21 is entitled 'Local Authorities' Initiatives in support of Agenda 21',[1] known as LA 21. It envisages that local authorities should play a crucial role in fulfilling Agenda 21's objectives.[2] Unfortunately however, LA 21 merely serves as an unenforceable international blueprint; its successful implementation depends on strategies, plans, policies and processes adopted by state parties and their municipalities. The fact that LA 21 is not legally enforceable means that, like many other international policies and instruments, it may have very limited real-life impact at the level of local communities all over the world. This is problematic at a time when the achievement of sustainable environments for communities has become increasingly important.[3]

The Earth Summit in 1992 spawned the development of a good deal of new environmental law. Various contemporary national constitutions and international human rights instruments, for example, compel positive environmental action on the part of national bodies because of the introduction of *enforceable* environmental rights in legislation. Noticeably, clear parallels exist between the obligations of states, as well as national bodies, as expressed in Agenda 21, and the realisation and protection of domestic environmental rights. Jurisprudence furthermore shows that the type of positive action required of local authorities in terms of environmental rights generally corresponds with the action envisaged by LA 21.[4]

This chapter proposes that the use of a rights-based approach by municipalities to local environmental governance (LEG) may contribute to a more enforceable and hence more effective LA 21 regime. It focuses on the correlation between the environmental obligations of municipalities as expressed in LA 21 and the obligations under national constitutions, and on how this correlation may feed into local environmental governance. The chapter employs the overlap in obligations in terms of environmental rights and LA 21 to show that a municipality's response to an environmental right can simultaneously facilitate fulfilment of its LA 21 obligations. The primary aim is to illustrate how a rights-based approach to LEG may beneficially reflect state obligations as found in international soft law and domestic constitutional law. Towards that end, the theoretical observations are substantiated by a critical review of positive experiences and learning curves in South Africa.

## 2.   AGENDA 21, LA 21 AND LOCAL ACTION 21 REVISITED

### Agenda 21

Agenda 21 is a blueprint for governmental action in all areas in which people of the 21st century impact on the environment (Picolotti and Taillant, 2003).[5] It is directed at, among other things, a balanced and integrated approach to environmental and developmental questions, the improvement and restructuring of decision-making processes through public participation and the achievement of various goals related to the conservation and management of natural resources. A key objective of Agenda 21 is to improve the social, economic and environmental quality of human settlements (see para 7.4), which certainly imposes positive obligations on, *inter alia*, local authorities. Implementation of Agenda 21 is the voluntary responsibility of national governments (see Preamble and para 1.3) and its successful implementation depends on the initiatives of individual countries, with significant emphasis on public participation. Paragraph 3.7 states that sustainable development must be achieved at every level of society and that a community-driven approach to sustainability should be followed. The integration of environmental and developmental decision-making processes is crucial. Agenda 21 proclaims that governments in partnership with, amongst other entities, their local authorities, are key role-players in this regard (paras 8.2 and 8.4). The extended objective of Agenda 21 is to promote, in the light of country-specific conditions, integration of environment and development objectives through appropriate laws and regulatory programmes, instruments and enforcement mechanisms at all levels of government (paras 8.5, 8.16 and 8.17–8.22).

## Local Agenda 21

LA 21 translates Agenda 21 into a framework for local authorities/municipalities. It is often described as an instrument that seeks local solutions to global challenges. This intention is particularly evident in paragraph 28.1. It relies on voluntary commitment and action on the part of the municipalities of signatory countries. As a local-government-led, community-wide participatory effort to establish a comprehensive action strategy for environmental protection, economic prosperity, and the well-being of local communities at local level, it facilitates implementation of Agenda 21's key objectives through local authorities and their constituent communities. It highlights community participation, assessment of current conditions, target setting for achieving specific goals, monitoring and reporting.[6] A large number of local authorities around the world have instigated LA 21s over the years – although these may not necessarily be named as such.[7]

The primary objective of LA 21 is, by its nature, for local authorities to adopt a 'Local Agenda 21'. A Local Agenda 21 refers to a concerted and implementable long term programme that bears Agenda 21's goals in mind. A Local Agenda 21 needs to develop from a local process of consultation, consensus-building and community participation towards the preparation of sustainable development strategies. It also envisages cooperation between local authorities (including between local authorities in different parts of the world), exchange of information and experience and the involvement of women and youth in decision-making, planning and implementation processes (see paragraph 28.2 (b)–(d)). The objectives of LA 21 were initially accompanied by deadlines, many of which to date have proved to be unattainable. This does not, however, render the objectives void.

LA 21 raises a range of practical questions. What should be the format of a municipality's Local Agenda 21? What type of considerations must be included in the programme and what are the key steps, features and delineations that a municipality should bear in mind? LA 21 itself provides no answers. Lafferty and Eckerberg argue that this should be interpreted as an omission by design. This absence of particulars arguably reflects 'the considerable variation in central-local authority domains across the member states as well as the wide diversity in specific types of local and regional authority within countries' (Lafferty and Eckerberg, 1998, p. 2). Instead of outlining in detail the content areas/activities of a pre-ordained plan or programme, LA 21 calls for innovation, creativity and individualism. The message conveyed is that it is up to the municipalities of signatory countries to initiate and coordinate dialogue among citizens, local organisations and private enterprises in order to design a Local Agenda 21 programme that fits the needs of local people (Lafferty and Eckerberg, 1998, p. 3). LA 21 merely serves as the initiator – no specifics are provided.

Clearly the design and implementation of a Local Agenda 21 require the interpretation and 'adaptation' of LA 21 to suit the unique conditions and challenges of a country, as well as various local communities within its borders (Lafferty and Eckerberg, 1998 p. 3). Dynamic development of domestic environmental law frameworks may compel the Local Agenda 21 of a municipality to be aligned both with Agenda 21 and LA 21 as well as with the relevant legislation of the country. The extraction of positive obligations from local authorities in terms of environmental provisions in a country's constitution could potentially complement the design and subsequent implementation of a municipality's Local Agenda 21 insofar as a constitution may reveal the pressing developmental and environmental needs of the people. Apart from substantive environmental provisions, rights such as access to information and just administrative action have also received increased attention in environmental contexts globally and should therefore also be employed to inform and augment a municipality's Local Agenda 21. In addition, international law has also recognised the key role of procedural rights in environmental contexts.[8] These ideas are considered further below.

## Local Action 21

The term 'Local Action 21' was coined at the 2002 UN World Summit on Sustainable Development Local Government Session as a motto for the second decade of the Local Agenda 21 movement.[9] It established a mandate for local authorities worldwide (albeit still voluntary) to move from a mere agenda for action to actual and concrete action. The aim is to ensure the accelerated implementation of sustainable development strategies by local authorities. Municipalities are expected to pay particular attention to factors that could prevent them from becoming sustainable in different ways. These factors may include, for example, poverty, injustice and exclusion, insecurity and conflict, unhealthy environments and the vulnerability of human and natural resources. Local Action 21 requires municipal sustainability management in terms of a well-designed and inclusive Local Agenda 21 programme and calls for both specificity and detail. An effective programme for action requires an integrated focus on the priority concerns of individual communities – which reinforces the key role of participatory decision-making and inclusiveness in the Local Agenda 21 context.[10]

## 3. THE NEED FOR ENFORCEABILITY OF LA 21

### Introduction

The issue of how these internationally-developed soft-law frameworks relate to rights in domestic contexts is now considered. Various rights have a bearing on the environment of people generally; for example, the rights to life, dignity, information, just administrative action and health. The focus here is on how domestic substantive constitutional rights to a quality environment often require positive state action – especially where they are of a socio-economic nature.[11] With reference to existing jurisprudence, it also focuses on how the required positive state action resembles the positive action required in terms of Agenda 21, LA 21 and Local Action 21. One should, however, consider how all of these obligatory actions may feed into local environmental governance.

### Local Environmental Governance

The aim here is to show how a rights-based approach to local environmental governance (LEG) may be beneficial to further developing state obligations in terms of both international soft law and domestic constitutional law. The definition developed by Nel and Du Plessis (2004) and adapted by Kotzé (2006)[12] states that environmental governance is:

> The collection of legislative, executive, judicial, administrative and private functions, processes and instruments used by the public and private sectors to ensure sustainable behaviour by all as far as governance of activities, products, services, processes, tools and livelihoods are concerned, both in a substantive and procedural sense.

This generic definition applies to all government levels and all organs of state, including municipalities, as well as to private sector governance. As far as this chapter appraises environmental governance in the local government context, it uses the term LEG.[13]

### A Rights-based Approach to Local Environmental Governance

A review of the literature shows that many national constitutions contain substantive provisions on peoples' claims to a quality environment – whether in the form of a fundamental environmental right or an environmental directive principle (Lavrysen and Theunis, 2007).[14] The constitutions of many democratic countries also provide for and regulate local authorities/municipalities. In the most elementary sense, a rights-based approach to LEG implies that constitutional environmental rights should stimulate and serve as a foundation for the development of domestic environmental and local government law in a particular country. It also means that the governance endeavour of municipalities at all times should be aligned with the subjective environmental right of people where such a right exists.[15] A rights-based approach to LEG presumably requires national legislatures and municipalities to divine from the constitution what the fundamental environmental entitlements of people are. The questions that authorities should pose with regard to constitutional environmental provisions include:

- Does the provision imply environmental threshold levels?
- Are future generations included as beneficiaries of the provision?
- Has a court of law to date suggested any tools or mechanisms for fulfilment or realisation of the provision?
- What can the people of a country rightfully expect in terms of their constitutional environmental right (or environmental norm, direction or principle)?
- How does the environmental provision link with other constitutionally entrenched rights such as the procedural right of access to information or just administrative action?

The answers to these questions should assist municipalities to plan and govern in a way that is conducive to furthering the constitutional environmental entitlements of community members. In a nutshell: If a particular country's constitution contains an environmental provision, it should be interpreted purposively for and at local government level. It subsequently should inform LEG as a means to facilitate fulfilment of the environmental claims of individuals or communities.


## 4.  LINKING A RIGHTS-BASED APPROACH TO LEG WITH LA 21 AND SUSTAINABLE COMMUNITY ENVIRONMENTS

A rights-based approach to LEG means that the spirit and purposes of a country's provisions regarding environmental rights should inform and direct the way in which its municipalities govern natural resources, environmental media and the relationship between people and their environment. Environmental rights unfortunately are often ambiguously phrased, requiring 'concerted efforts' and 'reasonable and other measures' to further their substantive content. So while environmental rights generally necessitate positive action on the part of authorities, the exact meaning and parameters of such action remain tacit. The position with the obligations of authorities in terms of LA 21 is, however, slightly less problematic than with environmental rights generally. Although LA 21 also is not very specific on the positive action to be taken by municipalities to further the objectives of Agenda 21, at least it provides a framework for the inclusion of specifics in a municipality's own Local Agenda 21.[16]

The thorough development and implementation of a realistic Local Agenda 21, directed at effective local environmental management by a municipality, could also play a significant role in meeting its constitutional environmental obligations, where they are provided for. It is submitted that the inclusive and participatory development and conscientious implementation of a Local Agenda 21 programme by a municipality that progressively addresses the primary environmental needs and concerns of its community (and future generations), may go a long way in persuading a court of law of such a municipality's attempt to fulfil the environmental rights claims of its people. The manner in which a rights-based approach to LEG and LA 21 could contribute to the establishment of a sustainable environment for communities is illustrated below with reference to the constitutional environmental claims and LA 21 endeavours in South Africa.

## 5.  LA 21: THE SOUTH AFRICAN EXPERIENCE

### Introduction

This chapter has introduced the idea that overlaps between the obligations of authorities in terms of a country's provisions on environmental rights and the objectives of Agenda 21 could be mutually reinforcing. The focus falls on local authorities, reviewing developments concerning the environmental right and LA 21 in South Africa, with some concluding critique and observations on the practices of the city of Cape Town.

### The Environmental Right

South Africa is extraordinarily rich in natural resources and biodiversity and the environment (especially in a narrow 'natural resource conservation' sense) always has been a priority of the Republic. However, an extended legal definition of the 'environment' and of environmental rights protection came into being only after the adoption of the Constitution of the Republic of South Africa, 1996 (the Constitution). Today the Constitution contains an enforceable fundamental environmental right. Section 24 states:

Everyone has the right:

(a) to an environment that is not harmful to their health or well-being; and

(b) to have the environment protected, for the benefit of present and future generations, through reasonable legislative and other measures that:

(i) prevent pollution and ecological degradation;

(ii) promote conservation; and

(iii) secure ecologically sustainable development and use of natural resources while promoting justifiable economic and social development.

Should one wish to go by a traditional classification, section 24(a) shows features of a civil and political right and section 24(b) that of a socio-economic right (Glazewski, 2005).[17] The contemporary (post-1996) environmental framework law serves to promote the section 24 environmental right and the South African legislature has made deliberate efforts to acknowledge this right in various laws, such as the National Environmental Management Act 1998, the National Water Act 1998, the National Heritage Resources Act 1999, the National Environmental Management: Protected Areas Act 2003, the National Environmental Management: Biodiversity Act 2004, the National Environmental Management: Air Quality Act 2004, and the National Environmental Management: Waste Management Act 2008.

In the absence of a flagship Constitutional Court case on section 24, *dicta* from available decided cases must be relied on for jurisprudential interpretation of the environmental right. The South African Supreme Court of Appeal in *Director: Mineral Development, Gauteng Region and Sasol Mining (Pty) Ltd v Save the Vaal Environment and Others*[18] stated that:

Our Constitution, by including environmental rights as fundamental justiciable rights, by necessary implication requires that environmental considerations be accorded appropriate recognition and respect in the administrative process in our country.[19]

Five years later in BP Southern Africa (Pty) Ltd v MEC for Agriculture, Conservation and Land Affairs, the Court held that:

By elevating the environment to a fundamental justiciable human right, South Africa has irreversibly embarked on a road, which will lead to the goal of attaining a protected environment by an integrated approach, which takes into consideration, *inter alia*, social-economic concerns and principles.[20]

In Fuel Retailers Association of Southern Africa v Director-General Environmental Management, Department of Agriculture, Conservation and Environment, Mpumalanga Province and Others,[21] the Constitutional Court made it clear that:

> Our Constitution does not sanction a state of normative anarchy which may arise where potentially conflicting principles are juxtaposed. It requires those who enforce and implement the Constitution to find a balance between potentially conflicting principles. ... The principle that enables the environmental authorities to balance developmental needs and environmental concerns is the principle of sustainable development.[22]

and that:

> The need to protect the environment cannot be gainsaid. So, too, is the need for social and economic development. How these two compelling needs interact, their impact on decisions affecting the environment and the obligations of environmental authorities in this regard, are important constitutional questions.[23]

These statements reiterate the socio-economic nature of the environmental right. They also show that the realisation of this right requires affirmative action. It requires, amongst other things, explicit recognition in and alignment with authorities' administrative processes and implies the need for a concerted and integrated approach towards the environment, environmental media and the relationship between people and their environment (Feris and Tladi, 2005; Horsten, 2007).[24] Section 24 of the Constitution requires that a balance be struck between the potentially conflicting ideologies of economic growth, social prosperity and protection of the environment. The state will breach its duty to fulfil the environmental right when there is an absence of ample action or when its actions are insufficient or inappropriate.[25] The decision in the widely celebrated international environmental rights case of *Social and Economic Rights Action Centre for Economic and Social Rights (SERAC) v Nigeria*,[26] also feeds into this line of interpretation.

Any legal duty implies the existence of a responsible person or entity. It can be argued that the legislative and executive branches of government at all levels (inclusive of local government), should be accountable for the fulfilment or realisation of section 24. To enforce the duty to achieve the environmental right, it is submitted that the judiciary should evaluate the policies and practices (environmental governance endeavours) of government. Such evaluation should question whether or not existing measures (policies and practices) are reasonably adequate to fulfil the right (Brand, 2005). On the basis of the internal limitation clause attached to all socio-economic rights in the Constitution, a standard of 'reasonableness' exists in South Africa (Du Plessis, 2009).[27] Municipalities together with other state bodies hence must take reasonably adequate action in response to the environmental right. Therefore, when the duty to fulfil the environmental right is breached, authorities will only be able to justify such contravention before a court of justice when the contravention proves to have been reasonable under the circumstances.

This chapter shows how local government could employ environmental rights as pathways to also further LA 21 activities and to establish a sustainable human environment. Therefore it is important to note that the Constitution, apart from the widely applicable environmental right, makes it clear that municipalities have environmental obligations. Bekink argues that one of the 'most critical functions' of local government in South Africa is to 'rebuild local communities and environments and, further, to establish a foundation for a democratic, integrated, prosperous and non-racial society' (Bekink, 2006). The Constitution identifies five core objects of local government generally, namely to: provide for a democratic and accountable government for local communities; ensure sustainable provision of services; promote social and economic development; promote a safe and healthy environment; and encourage public involvement in local government affairs.[28] These objectives largely echo the objectives of Agenda 21 and LA 21 but still give little concrete direction to municipalities as to the means for their achievement.

## LA 21 Developments

With 283 municipalities, South Africa has a system of 'wall-to-wall' local government. This means that the entire land area (including rural areas) falls within the jurisdiction of at least one municipality. In response to the voluntary obligations of Agenda 21 and LA 21 and some mandatory constitutional obligations, the South African legislature included a chapter in the Local Government: Municipal Systems Act 2000 (Systems Act) on the compulsory development of Integrated Development Plans (IDPs) by each municipality.[29] The rights-based approach to LEG in South Africa culminated in the notion of integrated development planning. The IDPs themselves translate into Local Agenda 21 programmes. The Systems Act requires municipalities to adopt these single and inclusive five-year strategic plans for development. An IDP integrates and coordinates municipal planning and takes into account proposals for the development of the municipality; aligns the resources and capacity with the implementation of the plan; forms the policy framework and general basis on which annual municipal budgets must be based and which must be compatible with provincial and national development. IDPs should ensure: integration of social, economic and environmental concerns by incorporating the latter into municipal level planning; poverty, gender and socio-economic analysis; formulation of strategic development guidelines; development of alternative assessment and prioritised criteria; the setting of indicators; impact assessment and assessment of strategic and policy compliance. Provision is furthermore made in the Systems Act and environmental laws for the inclusion of environmental sector plans such as disaster management plans and waste management plans in all IDPs. Municipalities are further required to review their IDPs annually in consultation with communities and stakeholders.[30]

The IDP of a municipality is the principal planning instrument which guides and informs municipal budgetary processes. The IDP system has been designed, *inter alia,* to facilitate municipalities' simultaneous compliance with section 24 of the Constitution and to incorporate and give effect to the characteristics of LA 21. Hypothetically, it is possible for the IDPs to facilitate commitment to significant affirmative local government environmental action, as required by article 24 of the Constitution and LA 21. Nevertheless, some LA 21 focus areas such as the need for partnerships and the exchange of environmental information have been neglected in the IDP legal framework. Whether or not the IDPs, as legally constructed products of national local government law, are in fact beneficial to municipalities' fulfilment of the constitutional environmental right and the LA 21 objectives, cannot be concluded based on a review of law alone. As a practical example, the IDP of the City of Cape Town is considered below.

**The City of Cape Town**

The City of Cape Town has almost doubled in size over the past 20 years and its area has grown by 40 per cent since 1985.[31] It hosts some 3.2 million people, including large squatter settlements on the city's fringes and unemployment has grown from 13 per cent to almost 28 per cent over the past 10 years. This obviously poses numerous challenges to the city's local authorities. Nevertheless, South Africa takes pride in Cape Town. It has become known for progressive environmental action. In compliance with the legal obligation to draft and implement an IDP, Cape Town established its first IDP (Local Agenda 21) in 2002. The 2006/2007 IDP (hereafter the IDP) explicitly referred to both the constitutional environmental mandate(s) of the municipality and the section 24 environmental right of its community members.[32] Thus the environmental right clearly fed into at least the design of Cape Town's IDP at that point. The IDP was an extensive document – reminiscent of a historic *status quo* report and planning instrument. At the time, it reflected the needs and challenges of Cape Town that related to the environmental, economic and social sustainability of its communities.[33] Yet the IDP failed to concretise and break down the environmental obligations of the municipality in terms of both the Constitution and internationally recognised instruments such as LA 21.

The IDP acknowledged the Systems Act's requirement that each municipality in South Africa should monitor the levels of development, identify development priorities (as targets) and identify indicators for the monitoring of performance. However, in the environmental context, the IDP only included indistinctively formulated aims such as 'to ensure that high levels of services are maintained and extended' and 'the Roads and Stormwater Department will start or continue implementing the following strategic interventions: eradication of backlogs and increasing accessibility of marginalised communities to basic services through extending the road network in required areas, including informal settlements'. The IDP lacked time-frames or clear strategies showing when or how these aims should be accomplished. This deficiency implies that although the IDP contained vaguely formulated targets (aims), no performance indicators existed to accompany the former and to facilitate measurement of performance over time.[34]

In the environmental context, the IDP contained a number of strategic themes comprising strategic objectives, high level outputs and council inputs and resources that will be allocated to achieve outputs. One of the strategic themes was, for example, economic development and job creation. One of the strategic objectives of this theme was to increase the number of economic opportunities available in order to achieve an economic growth rate of 6 per cent per annum. One of the high-level outcomes in order to reach the former objective was to position Cape Town as a leading African city in meeting its energy needs in a sustainable way. One of the envisaged outputs listed that must be achieved in the short term was to purchase renewable energy, and the related council inputs included to facilitate the development of the biofuels industry and mandate strategic partnerships with, *inter alia*, the then Department of Environmental Affairs and Tourism and independent power producers. With reference to this specific theme and some other environmental strategic themes and objectives contained in the IDP, it seems as if its development had been inspired largely by economics. There has been little emphasis on the socio-environmental needs of community members such as the provision of electricity, potable water and sanitation.

Although some objectives and correlating performance indicators were included in the IDP, it lacked realistic and quantifiable targets and performance indicators as well as concrete strategies that could be employed by the municipality and local community to measure the achievements of the municipality. Targets and indicators can be of great assistance in measuring achievements, not only in terms of the IDP, but also in terms of the section 24 environmental right and LA 21. The initial absence of clear targets and performance indicators hence could defeat the purpose of an IDP, namely to serve as a clear policy direction for a municipality. It similarly could have detrimental effects on the sharing of environmental information with community members and on environmental reporting.

Cape Town's 2006/2007 IDP lacked some of the inherent features of a long-term cyclical programme. It merely referred to the notions of organisational performance management cycles, targets and key performance indicators, without going into much detail. Although the budget system of Cape Town was aligned with the then strategic themes and broad strategic objectives of the IDP, a clear performance management cycle has not been provided for.[35] The reasons for this may be a fear or inability to commit to clearly formulated targets or mere capacity needs in establishing clear targets – many of which should be based on, *inter alia*, scientifically valid and reliable environmental data. Conversely, one truly positive feature of the IDP has been the significant weight afforded to the establishment of partnerships (as called for by Agenda 21 and LA 21) at local, national and international level.

It is encouraging to note some progressive changes in the City of Cape Town's most recent (revised) 2007–2012 IDP.[36] From the outset it is made clear that the 2007–2012 IDP aims to balance development with the conservation of natural areas, thereby ensuring a high-quality natural environment to complement and stimulate social and economic development. The 2007–2012 IDP is seen as the foundation of the city's development of a 'long term city development strategy' for the next 30 years; it makes ample provision for objectives, measurable targets and performance measures. Targets are set for, *inter alia*, the reduction of the city's carbon footprint, electricity consumption, climate change adaptation, the improvement of air quality and upgrading of informal settlements. The 2007-2012 IDP is further aligned with various targets for development that have been set at the national level. Progress has also been made in relation to the setting of targets and the design of measures to estimate performance and the IDP deals much more explicitly with the socio-economic and environmental dimensions of development. However, the IDP still lacks clear strategies and action steps to show exactly how the municipality intends to reach its objectives and targets. For example, some projects and plans are loosely referred to but these are not clearly tied to the objectives and target dates. It is also not clear whether performance will be measured in-house only and whether or not the community and/or a third party auditor will, over time, be involved in the process to measure and report on, for example, the municipality's performance in relation to the objectives set in the 2007–2012 IDP. One still does not get the idea that the city has adopted a truly cyclical approach in the design, implementation and review of its IDP.

Generally, Cape Town's 2006/2007 and 2007–2012 IDPs illuminate a number of (potential) generic challenges concerning the IDP/LA 21s generated in South African municipalities, especially when taking into account that the City of Cape Town harbours considerably more resources than, for example, medium-sized or small municipalities in South Africa. These include, in brief:

- Gaining a practical understanding of the meaning of sustainability in individual municipalities in all sectors;
- Ensuring strong political support for the strengthening of sustainability in both the planning and implementation of municipalities' IDPs;
- Developing the skills required to ensure the sustainability of strategies and projects within the IDP process;
- Ensuring that there is adequate human and financial capacity within the municipality's plan to effectively implement and manage interventions for the strengthening of sustainability;
- Developing the institutional structures required for an inter-sectoral approach to addressing sustainability issues;
- Obtaining the baseline information concerning the current state of the environment and defining the limits of acceptable change of social, economic and biophysical resources;
- Identification of appropriate targets and indicators and the development of an effective monitoring system;
- Too little accountability on the part of local councils – attention should be paid to time frames and deliverables and the process of assessing progress;
- Making trade-offs between the various elements of sustainability (i.e., social, economic and biophysical concerns) that will lead the municipality towards its vision of a desirable future; and
- Development and implementation of clear strategies and projects that may not show short-term gains, but which could assist the municipality in moving towards sustainability.

Bearing in mind some LA 21/urban sustainability developments in Europe, for example,[37] it is argued that a cyclical approach towards IDP development may go a long way to addressing some of the listed challenges. A cyclical approach implies processes aimed at: a baseline review, target setting, political commitment, implementation, monitoring and evaluation and reporting with national and provincial support, and capacity investment.

This chapter shows that South Africa has formally absorbed LA 21 into its local government law, and that by means of IDPs it is theoretically possible for municipalities to draft Local Agenda 21s that facilitate simultaneous fulfilment of the obligations in the section 24 environmental right in the Constitution and LA 21. However, the Cape Town example indicates that a rights-based approach to local environmental governance requires a good deal more development and analysis by municipalities. Even where an environmental right, combined with framework laws, compel LA 21 developments in municipalities, only clear targets and performance indicators can prevent mere linear planning as opposed to cyclical action. Whereas local environmental governance in South African municipalities is informed and directed by the enforceable constitutional environmental right, actual programme development by municipalities still requires refinement. Thus the need for a legally obligatory and hence specifically enforceable LA 21 programme development in South Africa should be acknowledged as a valuable and important step in transforming unenforceable international soft law into domestically enforceable provisions.

## 6. CONCLUDING OBSERVATIONS

Forever imprinted in the history of development of environmental law, the Rio accomplishments cannot be allowed to languish. Contemporary environmental challenges (such as pressures on cities and towns to create more sustainable environments for people) and developments (such as increased focus on peoples' basic rights and the accompanying entrenchment of rights in domestic constitutions) impact on the Agenda 21 objectives. It also impacts on the achievement of this soft-law instrument's voluntary objectives. LA 21 has been the Agenda 21 for local authorities since LA 21 was established in 2002. It ought not to be viewed as a mere agenda but as a requisite for actual and concrete action on the part of municipalities. There is a need for specificity and detail in the Local Agenda 21s of municipalities that should culminate in concrete environmental targets and performance indicators. Nevertheless, no matter how ambitious and laudable the goals of Agenda 21, LA 21 and Local Action 21 may be, these instruments remain legally unenforceable, unless they are rendered so by constitutional provisions combined with enactment and implementation of domestic legislation.

Changes in political climate in many countries have resulted in the establishment of and/or alteration to their domestic constitutions in recent years. An increasing number of constitutions contain a set of enforceable fundamental rights with accompanying obligations on the part of, *inter alia*, local authorities. Provision is often also made for an environmental right for people. Unlike the content of the international soft law instruments referred to above, environmental rights in general are legally enforceable. These rights often require that all levels of government (inclusive of local authorities) take positive action as part of their obligation to fulfil such rights towards the establishment of a sustainable human environment.

This chapter introduced the possibility for national governments to apply a rights-based approach to LEG in order to create a more enforceable LA 21 regime in domestic contexts. The correlation between the environmental obligations of municipalities in terms of LA 21 and national constitutions and how this correlation may feed into LEG served as primary point of departure. To give some life to the otherwise abstract analysis in this chapter, some South African developments were critically examined. The obligatory and hence legally enforceable LA 21 programme development in this country revealed a valuable and important step in arming unenforceable international soft law with domestic bite, by introducing, through local government law, the notion of integrated development planning. Inspired by the environmental right in the Constitution and LA 21, these developments have since compelled all municipalities in the country to generate and implement IDPs. Nevertheless, the Cape Town example, based on the status quo in 2007 and 2010 respectively, shows that although LEG in South African municipalities is informed and directed by the enforceable constitutional environmental right and local government law, actual IDP development by municipalities remains in need of further refinement. Clear targets and performance indicators as well as strategies to achieve objectives should, *inter alia*, be included in IDPs to prevent mere linear planning as opposed to cyclical action. It must furthermore be made clear who is or will be involved in the process of monitoring performance – this is important in order for the IDP to retain its legitimacy. Bearing in mind Local Action 21, cyclical action is key in the move towards the achievement of sustainable environments.

The domestic legal implementation of international environmental soft-law, in the light of increased international environmental pressures, deserves much more attention. This chapter has indicated that it is possible to take an enforceable approach to LEG to encourage local government compliance and thus to contribute to more sustainable human environments at the local level.

## NOTES

\*     The author wishes to thank her faculty and the National Research Foundation of South Africa for the financial support for the preparation of the paper on which this chapter is based. She is also grateful to Professor Erika de Wet for her insightful comments.
1.     http://www.un.org/esa/sustdev/documents/agenda21/english/agenda21chapter28.htm.

2. Fulfillment of the objectives requires, amongst other types of action, local consultative processes, cooperation between local authorities, exchange of information and representation of women and youth in decision-making, planning and implementation processes.

3. See for example the report on the *State of the World's Cities 2006/2007*, United Nations-Habitat, available at http://www.unhabitat.org/pmss/listItemDetails.aspx?publication ID=2101.

4. See for example *Social and Economic Rights Action Centre for Economic and Social Rights (SERAC) v Nigeria, African Commission on Human and Peoples' Rights*, Comm. No. 155/96 (2001) of the African Commission on Human and Peoples' Rights, the South African case of *Residents of Bon Vista Mansions v Southern Metropolitan Local Council* 2002 (6) BCLR 625 (W), *Guerra and Others v Italy* (1998) and *López Ostra v Spain* (1994), decided by the European Court of Human Rights, Strasbourg.

5. Picolotti maintains that Agenda 21 is also 'significantly involved with elements that rightly belong to the conceptual universe of human rights'.

6. Summarised from United Kingdom initiative on Local Agenda 21s at http://www.gdrc.org/uem/la21/la21.html.

7. ICLEI–Local Governments for Sustainability brochure at http://www.iclei.org/fileadmin/user_upload/documents/Global/About_ICLEI/brochures/ICLEI-intro-2009.pdf.

8. See Convention on Access to Information, Public Participation in Decision-making and Access to Justice in Environmental Matters of 1998 (Aarhus Convention) (1999) 38 ILM 515.

9. At the 2002 World Summit on Sustainable Development Local Government Session in Johannesburg, South Africa, local government leaders from around the world as well as representatives from the United Nations Development Programme, United Nations Environment Programme, UN-HABITAT and the World Health Organization, joined the International Council for Local Environmental Initiatives (ICLEI) in launching Local Action 21 as the next phase of LA 21. See *Local Action 21: From Agenda to Action* at http://www.localaction21.org/.

10. See further ICLEI – Local Governments for Sustainability at http://www.iclei.org/index.php?id=iclei-home.

11. Today various contemporary national constitutions compel positive action on the part of organs of state in terms of enforceable environmental rights or principles. For example, the South African Constitution provides that everyone has the right to an environment that is not harmful to their health or well-being; and to have the environment protected, for the benefit of present and future generations, through reasonable legislative and other measures (Constitution of South Africa Ch. 2 Article 24).

12. Environmental governance arguably also requires consideration of juridical principles such as the principle of legality, the *trias politica* and the principle of checks and balances.

13. LEG is not an activity or notion separate from local governance generally, being dependent on exactly the same infrastructure and mechanisms as local governance in the ordinary sense of the word, although it establishes an inter-related and focused variant of local governance. For a definition of LEG see Du Plessis (2009 p. 156).

14. While section 24 of the Constitution of the Republic of South Africa, 1996 provides for the right to 'an environment that is not detrimental to health or well-being', the Constitution of Namibia, 1990, for example, refers in chapter 95(1) to the right of people to have policies implemented aimed at the maintenance of ecosystems, essential ecological processes and biological diversity and the utilisation of living resources on a sustainable basis; for other examples see Lavrysen and Theunis (2007).

15. Alignment requires, amongst other activities, deliberate state and local government action in the form of such things as an integrated environmental management programme.

16. LA 21 has been designed to facilitate interactive and integrated long-term sustainable development planning at local government level; the obligations that it introduces mirror those of environmental rights generally.

17. Glazewski remarks that the inclusion of an environmental clause in the Constitution 'lays the foundation for the development of an environmental law jurisprudence in South Africa' which serves as the vehicle for legal recognition of the notion of sustainable development.
18. *Director, Mineral Development, Gauteng Region and Sasol Mining (Pty) Ltd v Save the Vaal Environment and Others* 1999 (2) SA 709 (SCA).
19. 1999 (2) SA 709 (SCA) [719]; see also Jan Glazewski (2005, pp. 16, 67).
20. *BP Southern Africa (Pty) Ltd v MEC for Agriculture, Conservation and Land Affairs* 2004 (5) SA 124 (W) [32].
21. *Fuel Retailers Association of Southern Africa v Director-General Environmental Management, Department of Agriculture, Conservation and Environment, Mpumalanga Province and Others* 2007 CCT 69/06.
22. Ibid. at [93].
23. Ibid. at [41].
24. See section 7(2) of the Constitution. Note that whereas international and regional environmental rights often impose merely implicit obligations on states to take positive action to fulfil environmental rights, section 24(b) of the Constitution places a specific duty on the state to regulate in favour of environmental protection by means of reasonable legislative and other measures.
25. See also 1987 Limburg Principles on the Implementation of the International Convention on Social, Economic and Cultural Rights UN Doc. E/CN.4/1987/17 at http://www.acpp.org/RBAVer1_0/archives/Limburg%20Principles.pdf, principles 17, 18, 27, 28, 32, 35–41, 45, 52 and 72.
26. In the SERAC case, African Commission on Human and Peoples' Rights, Comm. No. 155/96 (2001) the observations of the Commission show what a rights-based approach may mean for and demand of environmental governance generally, but also of local environmental governance in particular.
27. The standard of reasonableness in relation to section 24 is discussed in greater detail in Du Plessis (2009).
28. Section 152 of the Constitution.
29. See chapter 5 of the Systems Act. For the explicit links drawn between the IDP system in South Africa and LA 21, see Department of Provincial and Local Government Local Pathway to Sustainable Development in South Africa Summary Document on the IDP–LA 21 Relationship: http://www.buildnet.co.za/akani/2002/nov/02.html. Note that the IDP system in South Africa is part of the country's proof of commitment towards the vision of the New Partnership for Africa's Development (NEPAD).
30. It has been argued that an IDP must be renewed annually to ensure that municipal planning takes changing circumstances into account.
31. The reasons for this growth are mainly economic in nature and include the fact that Cape Town is home to an array of industries varying from tourism, manufacturing, mining and the drilling for oil to the import and export of goods. Furthermore, many major companies have headquarters in the city and the real estate market in the Western Cape Province is generally booming.
32. The IDP acknowledges that the Constitution is the primary determinant of local government functions – especially those pertaining to the environmental right, the right of access to information and the more general local government functions contained in chapter 7 of the Constitution. The City of Cape Town's latest IDP of 2007–2012 is available at http://www.capetown.gov.za/en/IDP/Pages/default.aspx. The 2006/2007 IDP is on file with the author.
33. The IDP states that all stakeholders' expectations and input on pressing issues within the local communities for the identification of priority issues and needs were considered to the extent possible. The priority issues identified by the community as part of the processes of public participation were housing, jobs and crime, and not environmental concerns. This has been the case despite the fact that Cape Town is located in a highly sensitive and vulnerable ecosystem; that the environment is one of the strongest assets driving tourism in the city and that rising levels of pollution threaten the river system.

There are also high levels of air pollution. Furthermore, Cape Town is situated in the heart of the Cape Floral Kingdom and many species that occur in the Cape Floral hotspot of biodiversity are found nowhere else in the world. The Cape Floral Kingdom hosts almost 9000 different plant species and many animal species; the region was inscribed on the World Heritage List in 2004. Cape Town also has the dubious distinction of being one of the earth's mega-disaster areas – areas that have already seen the loss, or are on the verge of losing, a significant part of their biodiversity. The biodiversity extinction rate in Cape Town is reported to be the highest for any metropolis in the world.

34. It is noted, however, that some quantifiable targets are contained in the IDP; these relate to the management of HIV/AIDS and tuberculosis among community members.

35. Apart from the IDP functioning as a separate local government policy, the City of Cape Town has an Integrated Metropolitan Environmental Policy (IMEP) which contains a number of issue-specific environmental strategies aimed at, amongst others: environmental education and training, biodiversity, coastal zone management, air pollution, heritage and catchment- and storm-water river management.

36. City of Cape Town *Five-Year Plan for Cape Town, Integrated Development Plan 2007–2012,* available at http://www.capetown.gov.za/en/IDP/Documents/IDP%202010%20-%202011/IDP201011ReviewMay2010.pdf

37. See *inter alia* http//:www.localsustainability.eu and http://www.localtargets21.org/.

# REFERENCES

Bekink, Bernard (2006), *Local Government Law,* Durban: LexisNexis Butterworths.

Brand, Danie (2005), 'The Right to Food', in Danie Brand and Christof Heyns (eds), *Socio-Economic Rights,* Pretoria: Pretoria University Law Press.

Du Plessis, A. (2009), *Fulfilment of South Africa's Constitutional Environmental Right in the Local Government Sphere,* LLD thesis, North West University, Potchefstroom Campus, pp. 379–397.

Feris, Loretta and Dire Tladi (2005), 'Environmental Rights', in Daniel Brand and Christof Heyns (eds), *Socio-Economic Rights,* Pretoria: Pretoria University Law Press.

Glazewski, Jan (2005) (2nd edn), *Environmental Law,* Durban: LexisNexis, Butterworths.

Horsten, Debra (2007), 'Adjudicating Issues involving Socio-Economic Rights', in Francois Venter and Anél du Plessis (eds), *Politics, Socio-Economic Issues and Culture,* Faculty of Law, Northwest University: Potchefstroom, available at http://ajol.info/index.php/pelj/article/viewFile/43478/27013.

Kotzé, Louis J. (2006), *A Legal Framework for Integrated Environmental Governance in South Africa and the North West Province,* Wolf Legal Publishers.

Lafferty, William A. and Katarina Eckerberg (eds) (1998), *From the Earth Summit to Local Agenda 21,* London: Earthscan.

Lavrysen, Luc and Jan Theunis (2007), 'The Right to Protection of a Healthy Environment: A Glance over the Borders and a Glance Back', in *Liber Amicorum Paul Martens,* Brussels: Larcier.

Nel, Johan and Willemien du Plessis (2004), 'Unpacking integrated environmental management: a step closer to effective co-operative governance', *SA Public Law,* **1,** 181–190.

Picolotti, Romina and Daniel Taillant (eds) (2003), *Linking Human Rights,* Tucson: University of Arizona Press.

# 5. Brazilian 'socioambientalismo' and environmental justice

## Fernanda de Salles Cavedon and Ricardo Stanziola Vieira

## 1. INTRODUCTION

This chapter examines the concept of Brazilian 'socioambientalismo' and environmental justice as a paradigm for constructing and consolidating a body of domestic and international environmental law capable of promoting harmonisation between socio-economic issues, environmental protection, and ethnic and cultural diversity. Given the complexity of contemporary environmental problems, it is argued that the evolving paradigm of 'sustainability' requires the integration of these factors in environmental decision-making.

We adopt the hypothesis that environmental law as it is presently manifested, with its strong technical-regulatory characteristics, may be poorly suited to address environmental conflicts involving social complexity and diversity. We argue that it needs to accommodate social, economic, political, cultural and ethnic issues that influence the treatment of contemporary conflicts.

Effective management of environmental conflicts must consider variables such as social and environmental exclusion, differences of power distribution in decision-making processes and the vulnerability of those who are disproportionately exposed to environmental costs and risks. Adoption of the concept of 'socioambientalismo' and environmental justice may contribute to re-conceptualising environmental law in order to deal with social complexity and the challenges of sustainability beyond their technical, scientific and juridical dimensions.

It is not our intention to formulate a definitive conception of the 'Law of Sustainability' incorporating 'socioambientalismo' and environmental justice, but rather to present some new social and juridical considerations, that may lead to more comprehensive understanding. The 'Law of Sustainability' is a juridical paradigm under construction that requires much more research and reflection to be consolidated, or even possibly to be refuted. As François Ost says, 'La tâche de dire le droit est donc bien une oeuvre herméneutique, un travail toujours recommencé' ('Declaring the law is a continuing hermeneutic task') (Ost, 1991, p. 272).

## 2. THE DEMAND FOR SUSTAINABILITY AND THE LIMITS OF ENVIRONMENTAL LAW

The established technical and regulatory character of environmental law is well known. Scholars such as Martin Mateo (1991) emphasise the relationship between environmental law norms and the state of scientific and technical knowledge, referring in particular to the influence of the natural sciences. These linkages, in conjunction with the traditional logic of legal conflict resolution, underpin and reinforce limitations and weaknesses in environmental law in the face of contemporary environmental complexity, especially within the broader context of social, economic, cultural, political and ethnic factors.

Contemporary environmental conflicts involve widely diffuse claims, including the rights of future generations, alongside factors beyond the scope of traditional scientific and legal considerations. Indeed, social stakeholders defend divergent understandings of approaches to managing environmental goods. This calls for revision and adjustment of existing juridical instruments and procedures.

Alonso and Costa outline a sociology of environmental conflicts that identifies key characteristics of these disputes. Environmental conflicts are structurally conditioned by the interaction of groups which encapsulate various interests and values. Motivation for conflict is grounded in a dispute over control of environmental goods by these groups as well as a struggle for power to affirm a conception of reality that corresponds to their own interests and values (Alonso and Costa, 2002, pp. 125–126).

Hannigan contributes an important observation to the theory that environmental conflicts are socially constructed from contextual factors, arguing that the power relationships involved in this process must also be considered (Hannigan, 1995, p. 246).

The manner in which a given conflict is socially constructed (Fuks, 2001) as well as the way in which it is transformed through the process of public presentation and communication ultimately influence the manner in which the dispute is decided. The conflicting visions, interests, stakeholders and other elements that were not publicised during its development and, accordingly, did not reach the judicial arena, will not form part of the conflict's juridical universe.

This analysis supports the observation that environmental conflict has two phases, each involving different levels and strategies of dispute. The first phase encompasses social construction, the definition of the contours, elements, stakeholders, visions and interests that characterise the dispute at its point of entry into the judicial system. The second phase occurs within the juridical process. In this way, Fuks says that 'a conflict only reaches judicial expression when it has acquired a sufficient degree of maturity to be well defined' (Fuks, 2001, p. 28). At this stage, the social construction of the conflict is supplemented or transformed by its juridical construction. The dispute is now governed by environmental rules and legal arguments, with the judge holding decision-making power. In this phase the conflict becomes more visible to the public and is legitimated by its entry into the judicial system.

Acselrad describes environmental conflicts as having four constitutive dimensions: symbolic appropriation, physical appropriation, duration and spatial extent (Acselrad, 2004, p. 27). The first two are related to the contexts in which power relationships are defined and the manner in which physical capital (in this case, the environment) may be appropriated. Differential power over physical resources may derive from the capacity of stakeholders for influence within political and legal institutions, from economic competition, or from the exercise of force (Acselrad, 2004, p. 23). The second dimension of conflict, symbolic appropriation of resources, refers to the permanent tension in environmental conflicts between different interests and conceptions about forms of appropriating environmental resources.

These considerations represent a challenge to traditional legal approaches to environmental law because the interests involved are diffuse in nature and extend beyond the typical sphere of interpersonal conflicts. The object of the conflict – the environment – is not only economic in nature, but also represents non-physical value. Furthermore, environmental conflicts are related to the interests of future generations. The environment is a common good with all the challenges that this classification brings. Thus, consideration about the type of interests involved and the underlying objectives of the parties in conflict must be at the centre of environmental conflict analysis. In this vein, Rubens and de Araújo emphasise the distinctive configuration of diffuse environmental interests and the tension between them and liberal juridical models (Rubens and de Araújo, 2002, pp. 243–244; Maciel, 2001, p. 18).

Limitations in the judicial treatment of environmental conflicts may be the result of traditional legal conceptions. Ferraz Jr (2001, p. 87) and Melo (1998, p. 68) observe that juridical principles have conflict resolution as their essential function. With its focus on norms, concepts and institutions, the legal system (centred on the formal aspects of the decision) leaves out the real or actual experience of environmental conflict, as well as its axiological aspects – the fundamental values at stake. It constructs a parallel 'juridical reality' that defines what is juridical or not, the conflicts that must and can be decided, and how they are decided. Instead of being structured by the nature of things, it forces new configurations of reality, in order to fit them within its abstract concepts. It promotes a kind of 'de-problematisation' of conflict, creating a sense of security. But by eliminating the polemical and controversial aspects of environmental conflicts, the legal process makes their complete resolution difficult. It creates an appearance of conflict resolution, imposing a decision within the limits of the dogmatic system, characterised as the only possible way to re-establish social peace (De Andrade, 1996, p. 8). In this context, it is important to mention that Ferrari, instead of referring to conflict resolution, opts for the expression 'treatment of the declared conflicts' (Ferrari, 1989, p. 114). He understands that the juridical models do not present definitive solutions for situations of conflict. Indeed it is possible that judicial procedures contribute to the reproduction of conflict.

Based on all these factors, we consider that environmental conflict acquires the condition of juridical conflict when stakeholders appeal to legal arguments and norms to fix its contours, adopting the judicial way as a strategy. The insertion of the conflict into the judicial arena serves to publicise and institutionalise it. This contributes to the definition of the legitimate scope of conflict, to the construction of valid arguments and to legitimisation of the conflict. Introduction to the legal process also generates at least the symbolic expectation of a definitive decision whose enforcement may be guaranteed.

As environmental conflicts have a high level of complexity, demanding analysis of social, economic, political and cultural factors, it is necessary to extend the scope of environmental law. This 'extended' environmental law, capable of considering these factors in the treatment of conflicts, may be understood as a 'Law of Sustainability'. Its scope extends beyond the protection and management of environmental goods to encompass the social, economic, political, cultural and ethnic factors involved in the management process. The 'Law of Sustainability' is accordingly directed to achieving sustainability in a complex, multicultural and globalised society, marked by social and economic inequalities and reflecting divergent interests and visions about the use and management of the environment. In the specific context of this chapter, we analyse the Brazilian 'socioambientalismo' and the environmental justice conceptions for their contribution to the construction of the 'Law of Sustainability'.

## 3.  'SOCIOAMBIENTALISMO' AND THE LAW OF SUSTAINABILITY

In recent decades, environmental law has assumed a more open and multidisciplinary character, but this has resulted in a dilemma without precedent: on one side the advance of science and technology, on the other, the traditional, rational and positive values of law. Both science and law, in their modern formulation, have experienced a process of 'secularisation' distancing them from their origins (Pierucci, 2003, p. 153) and seeking to eliminate value-oriented dimensions, either positive or negative (Marramao, 1999, pp. 49–50). Environmental law is located in the centre of these complex challenges and represents a new 'hope' (Petrella, 2004) of possible legal regulation in both state and non-state public spheres (Habermas, 2003). In order to fulfil this function, a new perspective has become necessary for environmental law.

Brazilian 'socioambientalismo' is similar to the environmental justice movement and certain European and international trends and experiences (Acselrad, 2004; Acselrad et al., 2004; Alonso and Costa, 2002). The adoption of the 'socioambientalismo' approach as a paradigm for environmental law entails the claim that its technical and scientific aspects should be supplemented by the influence of social, economic, political, ethnic and cultural concepts such as exclusion, empowerment, socio-economic vulnerability and access to information. All these elements can play a significant role in the treatment of environmental issues and in the possibilities available to communities to advance their interests and to protect their conception of the environment.

The 'socioambientalismo' approach recognises traditional knowledge and cultural perceptions of the environment as determining factors in the treatment of conflicts, as well as sources for the renewal of environmental law in its evolution towards a 'Law of Sustainability'. As argued by Santilli, 'the new paradigm of development based on "socioambientalismo" must promote and enhance the cultural diversity and the consolidation of democratic process in the country, with ample social participation in environmental management' (Santilli, 2004, p. 34).

The 'socioambientalismo' approach thus has a close relationship with the improvement of structural conditions for the exercise of citizenship and environmental democracy. It encourages the formation of participatory decision-making procedures and promotes understanding that environmental issues must be resolved on a collective basis.

The 'socioambientalismo' approach can ultimately be understood as a new juridical paradigm, since this extended vision of the challenges and pathways to sustainability calls for effective implementation through the legal system.

This new juridical paradigm has been under construction in Brazil since the Federal Constitution of 1988 (Marés, 2002, p. 93; Santilli, 2004), which recognises and protects a set of rights and interests of collective character. Such collective rights include the environment, culture, sustainable socio-economic development and respect for all ethnic groups and their ways of life. The 'socioambientalismo' approach calls for these rights to be analysed and interpreted on an integrated basis, since they cannot be effectively implemented in isolation. Marés presents 'socioambientalismo' as a new juridical paradigm, recognising the existence of a 'Socio-environmental Law' that 'transforms public policies into collective rights'. In this context, it is essential to define the object of this new law, that is, 'socio-environmental' goods as legal goods (Marés, 2002, ch. 38). It is in this context that the Instituto Socioambiental, a Brazilian non-governmental organisation dedicated to the promotion of 'socioambientalismo', proposed the adoption of the term 'Socio-environmental Law', as follows:

> the Constitution established the basis of a modern Law – the Socio-environmental Law that is defined as a new paradigm of citizenship law, encompassing and extending beyond individual rights. It is not a linear extension of the social and environmental rights foreseen in the national legal system, but another set resulting of the integrated understanding of these rights, characterized by tolerance between peoples and the search for shared and sustainable development (Instituto Socioambiental, 2004, p. 190).

By this means, the close interconnection between the juridical paradigm of 'socioambientalismo' and its contribution to sustainability is established. This relationship results from acknowledgement in the 'socioambientalismo' approach of the intrinsic linkages between the natural and built environment and the diverse forms of material and symbolic appropriation of the environment by communities based on their knowledge, their culture, their forms of life and their connections with their surroundings. The object of legal protection is no longer the environment as such, but the various relationships between human communities and the environment.

It must be emphasised that the 'socioambientalismo' approach is a product of dialogue between the environmental, social and civil rights movements, seeking to promote a fusion of their agendas on the understanding that their ability to achieve common aspirations could be strengthened through collaboration. The 'socioambientalismo' initiative emerged during the second half of the 1980s and was recognised in the 1990s, with this new paradigm being accepted in both legal and political spheres.

It is possible to identify parallels between 'socioambientalismo' and the environmental justice movement. The latter, born in the United States, offers a sense of cohesion amongst groups and movements that have in common the fight against various forms of injustice, inequality and environmental exclusion. Dobson underlines the movement's composition and its contribution to political awareness (Dobson, 1998, p. 22) as the two main characteristics. It is configured from the fusion of two agendas: the civil and human rights agenda and the environmentalist agenda.

The conception of environmental justice developed by the movement has as its central focus the equitable distribution of environmental risks, costs and benefits, independent of discrimination based on such factors as ethnic group, income and social status. The environmental justice movement also promotes equal access to environmental resources and to the decision-making processes on environmental issues. These objectives call for the creation of structural conditions favourable to the organisation and empowerment of society as an active stakeholder in the environmental management process. It is based on the argument that certain groups – vulnerable on the basis of their social, economic, or ethnic character and lacking access to information – are disproportionately exposed to environmental costs and face greater difficulties with participating in environmental decision making (Acselrad, 2004).

The challenges of environmental justice are underscored by the tendency for interests with more economic power and political capacity to prevail in disputes over access to environmental resources. Accordingly, the operational structure of the capitalist economy produces a distribution of environmental costs and benefits that are based on social conditions with environmental risks falling disproportionately on those of inferior social and economic status (Gould, 2004).

The environmental justice agenda, therefore, is based on a new conception, that of environmental exclusion, which is more specific than social exclusion. From the perspective of inequality and environmental exclusion, it can be also said that environmental law is not equally accessible to all. There can be 'flexibility' in its application as a consequence of the weakness of groups and communities in respect of political articulation and power, or even of the economic status or ethnic composition of affected communities.

In this sense, the juridical paradigm of the 'socioambientalismo' and the conception of environmental justice offer greater opportunities for consideration of variables such as social and environmental exclusion and disproportionate vulnerability that are part of the inherent complexity of environmental conflicts.

One of the most innovative aspects of this debate is the renewal of all environmental law, understood in its international, regional (for example, European) and national dimensions. That also represents a renewal of the law itself. This 'innovative trend' of international law and of environmental law more specifically, finds support among a number of authors (for example, Ost, 1991; Morand, 1999; Monediaire, 2005; Delmas-Marty, 2006).

The principle of sustainable development also represents one of the icons of this renewal effort. This principle has usually been presented in the form of three pillars: economic effectiveness, environmental protection and social equity, with respect for culture being a later addition to the concept of social equity.

Monediaire stresses the importance and the challenges of recognising sustainable development as a legal principle and argues for a new perception of law to bring this about. Monediaire (2005) has named this 'droit post-moderne mondialisé' (globalised postmodern law), and in the environmental context as a new 'Droit du development durable' (Sustainable Development Law), which is more versatile and flexible, and adjusted to address the complexity and great transformations that characterise the contemporary world.

Various expressions have been employed to convey similar ideas and concepts: 'Sustainable Development Law' (Monediaire, 2005), 'Law of Sustainability',[1] 'Socioenvironmental Law' and 'Environmental Justice'. These can cause misunderstandings and conceptual problems. However, we point out the general and common aspects of the concepts that have been formulated. We submit that the contributions brought by 'socioambientalismo' and environmental justice can assist in defining the 'Law of Sustainability'.

Sustainability extends beyond the mere preservation and conservation of environmental resources and the legal and technical analysis of the environmental dilemmas faced by humanity. It requires the promotion of quality of life in all its dimensions, including: job and income creation; equitable human and economic development; access to education and information; the possibility of exercising citizenship and democratisation of decision-making processes, as well as the promotion of multiculturalism, alongside measures to address social inequality and environmental exclusion. These objectives of the 'Law of Sustainability' are therefore broader than the traditional objectives of environmental law.

Accordingly, 'socioambientalismo', together with environmental justice, in calling for a more extensive interface between social and environmental concepts as well as for consideration of a wider range of variables in approaching environmental issues, can be understood as theoretical and practical supports for the 'Law of Sustainability'.

# 4.   JUDICIAL CREATIVITY AND THE LAW OF SUSTAINABILITY

A juridical paradigm more suited to addressing the complex social and environmental interactions demanded by sustainability needs to be formulated and concretely implemented. Implementation of the 'Law of Sustainability' requires that it be adopted not only in the context of elaborating public policies and producing legislation at the international level, but also in the treatment of environmental conflicts at the local level.

It is important to consider the deep modifications introduced in the treatment of the environmental conflicts in the judicial sphere. The transformative effect of new concepts is most apparent in relation to the judicial function and judicial decision-making in the treatment of environmental conflicts. The multiple interests and perspectives relevant to environmental conflicts, the various elements that exert influence over their social and juridical form, and the scope of judicial decisions are factors that, instead of being excluded through the elimination of fundamental values, offer opportunities for judicial treatment to more appropriately align the juridical system with social and environmental necessities.

The judicial context represents an important mechanism for incorporating elements of the 'socioambientalismo' approach and environmental justice into environmental law. Moreover, it offers a pathway to social empowerment in the sense that the judicial adoption of elements of the 'socioambientalismo' approach has the potential to alter or influence the core of environmental law. By taking advantage of opportunities for public participation in the judicial context, environmentally excluded communities can enhance their ability to influence environmental decisions and may influence these decisions in directions that promote a more equitable distribution of environmental benefits.

## Normative Production in the Judicial Context: Creative Judicial Decision-making

Judicial decision-making is not only an exercise in formal logic. It is also influenced by value-based, interpretative and argumentative attitudes (Siches, 1973; Dworkin, 1986; Capelletti, 1993; Perelman, 1996; Alexy, 2001; Atienza, 2005). Siches notes that judicial application of law, especially in times of intense social transformation, requires judges to undertake more complex exercises of thinking, reasoning and creativity involving value choices. However, this understanding of the judicial role may conflict with the ideals of juridical security and certainty that do not readily deal with complexity. The authors assert that this criticism does not undermine the idea of law as presenting a solution to all conflicts. Rather, it reinforces the creative role of the judge who must find the appropriate norm for each case, even if the norm is not clearly formulated or must be derived from general principles (Siches, 1973, pp. 16–17).

Accordingly, judicial decision-making must extend beyond an exercise of deductive formal logic, and demands the development of approaches to argumentation that are capable of justifying the manner in which the judge's decision has been crafted, as well as the incorporation of social, political and perhaps moral variables (Atienza, 2005, p. 18). Thus, it is possible to consider that judicial decisions acquire a creative and transformative potential when faced with the complexity of environmental conflicts and the growing necessity of recognising new rights, such as those related to sustainability.

The exercise of creative activity is not confined to situations in which gaps exist in the legal order. Principles, given their flexibility and generality, are more capable of being adapted to concrete cases. Thus judicial creativity must be understood to encompass new interpretations of existing norms, adaptation of general juridical principles to concrete cases and the articulation of new concepts and norms applicable to new configurations of reality or social demands.

Through the judicial resolution of environmental conflicts it is possible to incorporate new elements into the juridical system, as well as to promote the transformation of existing elements. Aguiló Regla considers that 'the judicial creation of norms refers to the fact that the objective application of legal process contributes to its own configuration' (Regla, 2000, p. 103). In seeking to resolve specific cases, judges frequently need to transform the norms that are to be applied. However, it is necessary to justify the decision, setting out its reasons. To do so, the judge must use a universal criterion, so that the decision can also be universal. When judges select the normative premise that will support their decision, they draw upon numerous criteria. However, the decision, now based on some universal criterion, creates future consequences, since the system of precedent calls for the same decision to be taken under similar circumstances.

Thus, when an environmental law decision incorporates 'socioambientalismo' or environmental justice by means of re-interpretation or reference to some general principle, it promotes the transformation of environmental law in ways that may contribute to its renewal and expansion in the direction of the 'Law of Sustainability'. In this way, creative judicial decisions can contribute to the transformation of technical environmental law to a more open and dynamic state that is better suited to addressing complex interactions between environment, society, economy, politics and culture, that comprise the quality of life in all of its aspects.

However, the 'Law of Sustainability' also requires the creation of structural conditions more favourable to the exercise of citizenship, making society an active participant in its overall construction. So, groups that are able to pursue environmental conflicts in the judicial context can – with reference to 'socioambientalismo' and environmental justice arguments used to delineate the broader outline of those conflicts – influence the law's configuration, thereby producing judicial decisions that incorporate the sustainability dimension.

## Judicial Powers and Decisions in Environmental Conflicts

The judges' powers and the nature and scope of judicial decision-making in environmental matters have been revised in a manner that reflects the possibilities of creative transformation. Judicial protection of the environment not only represents the utilisation of procedural instruments in the treatment of environmental conflicts, it also represents a way of exercising citizenship and of distributing power and environmental benefits consistent with a strategy of guaranteeing and recognising environmental rights through the adoption of 'socioambientalismo' and environmental justice principles.

Ferrajoli, understanding law as a system of guarantees structured around fundamental rights, emphasises the reinforcing role of judges as protectors of rights established by the constitution (Ferrajoli, 2001). This model promotes changes in classical positivism relating to the redefinition of the judge's role and the revision of the forms and conditions concerning the application of norms. Through interpretative work, the judge must consider the consistency of legal norms with the constitutional text. The authors thus would attribute a more critical role and a certain liberty to judges to find the limit of fundamental rights under the constitution. The judge must become the critic of invalid norms, motivated by their contents, and must re-interpret them within the meaning of the constitutional framework (Ferrajoli, 2001).

Cappelletti (1993) emphasises that in protecting an array of diffuse rights, judges exercise a high degree of interpretative discretion (p. 129). Mass social conflicts and the need to protect diffuse interests were some of the causes of the transformation of the judicial role. The new judicial responsibilities and powers are justified because the rights involved are fluid and programmatic, and accordingly require the judge to interpret them with a higher degree of activism and creativity (pp. 59–60). This greater attention by the judges to guarantee the protection of environmental rights and interests is further justified by the difficulties of representing these interests when they are confronted with private claims. It is also important to consider the intergenerational character of environmental protection and the role of judges as 'guardians' of the rights of future generations in environmental conflicts. The judges also have more liberty in the production and analysis of evidence. Mirra defends more liberty for judges to analyse the technical information and proof in a more critical and rational way, including the power to refute conclusions based on procedural elements (Mirra, 2002, p. 244).

The judge must consider all facts and arguments that could contribute to the construction of the judicial decision, not only the technical and scientific ones. Thus the social, political, cultural, ethnic and economic factors cannot be disregarded. This liberty in the consideration of evidence and in the construction of arguments helps to make judges important stakeholders in the transition to a 'Law of Sustainability'. From this perspective, it is possible to conclude that judicial power has an environmental function that, in the context of Brazilian law, derives from a Constitution which attributes to the public the duty to defend and preserve the environment for the benefit of present and future generations.

The exercise of judicial power in connection with environmental decision-making is a responsibility shared by public authorities and by society. The effectiveness of environmental rights must be guaranteed through the exercise of creative judicial interpretation, guided by constitutional direction to realise environmental juridical values. Effective representation of environmental interests must also be guaranteed by means of judicial activism that will safeguard the integrity of the environment. In this way, the application of environmental law principles through the exercise of judicial power also helps to advance social empowerment.

The scope of judicial activism and the enlargement of judges' powers to produce norms are not unlimited. As proposed by Ost, the judge who endeavours to incorporate sustainability dimensions into environmental decisions may resemble Hermes rather than Jupiter or Hercules (Ost, 1991). In Ost's interpretation, Jupiter, constrained by a pyramidical and codified conception of law, is unable to undertake a mission calling for creativity to extend the limits of existing norms. Marked by juridical and political monism, and confined by a deductive and linear rationality, Jupiter's conception of law is unable to respond to the complexity of environmental conflicts. This conception of law is antithetical to the 'Law of Sustainability'.

The judicial Hercules contrasts sharply with Jupiter's approach. Hercules represents the super-judge who carries the weight of the whole world in his arms, and is capable of solving all conflicts, however complex or controversial they may be. Hercules' law is a law of concrete cases, in contrast to the abstraction of Jupiter's code. It is important to recognise the efforts of Hercules, but the challenges posed by sustainability do not arise only in the arena of conflicts of interests; that is only one of the possible strategies. The model of Hercules is also limited in practice. Hercules, an ideal figure to inspire judicial activity aimed at applying law in accordance with justice, stands in sharp contrast with the human condition of judges who will never be able to replicate his divinity.

So, the judge most capable of promoting the 'Law of Sustainability' is Hermes (Ost, 1991, pp. 244–245), for whom law is considered as a net, with multiple points of inter-relationship. Within the net model, Hermes, the messenger, the great mediator and communicator, is able to gather together all the factors, stakeholders, variables, interests and values characteristic of environmental conflicts. This concept of a net allows Hermes to contribute to the construction of a more dynamic and flexible law, and a more dialectical judicial procedure that facilitates participative decision-making. In this way, the 'Law of Sustainability' can be characterised as 'Net Law'.

### Judicial Activism and Social Empowerment: Participation in the 'Law of Sustainability'

The next step in this analysis is to consider if judicial intervention based on the 'socioambiental' approach and environmental justice can contribute to a more equitable distribution of power in environmental decision-making, an important element in the 'Law of Sustainability'. Alternatively, one might inquire whether such judicial decision-making is inconsistent with democracy. The theoretical basis for this discussion comes from Dworkin (2000), who examines the search for 'the right answer' in 'hard cases', where judges decide with reference to political morality. In so doing, he examines the role of political convictions in decisions respecting the interpretation of law, considering the circumstances in which this is consistent with legitimate democratic decision-making. Dworkin discusses how judges decide, and in particular how they should decide controversial cases, asking if these decisions can and/or must be political decisions. He elucidates the proposition that 'judges must and do serve their own political convictions in deciding what the law is' (Dworkin, 1985, p. 3). Deciding in a political way does not mean deciding in accordance with the specific interests of political groups, but instead involves 'their own convictions about matters of principle' (ibid.). Dworkin (1985) first considers the 'argument from democracy' (p. 18)[2] against judges making political decisions. Here he identifies flaws in the claim that controversial cases can be resolved with reference to the rule book applied according to the will of responsible legislators. He then turns to consider the 'argument for democracy' in support of principled political decision-making by the judiciary by inquiring: 'Do judicial decisions on matters of principle (as distinct from policy) offend any plausible theory of democracy?' (p. 24).

There are two aspects to the analysis. The first is related to the question: 'Are there institutional reasons why a legislative decision about rights is likely to be more accurate than a judicial decision?' (Dworkin, 1985, p. 24). Dworkin emphasises the difficulty of establishing that legislative decisions inherently enjoy a greater likelihood of being correct than judicial ones. Although decisions about rights will be better if based on more information, there is no evidence that legislators have more information than judges. Moreover, Dworkin observes that legislators are exposed to more external influence and pressure than judges (pp. 24–25).

The second aspect of the 'argument for democracy' is related to the question: 'are there other reasons of fairness, apart from reasons of accuracy, why legislation should be the exclusive strategy for deciding what rights people have?' (Dworkin, 1985, p. 25). Here, Dworkin addresses considerations relating to public respect for law and concerns about political stability if decisions about rights were to be made outside the legislative forum. He does not consider either of these arguments determinative against a role for the courts in respect of political principle, in part because public attitudes about the comparative legitimacy of courts and legislatures are certainly subject to evolution. (pp. 25–26).

In addition to considerations of accuracy and political stability, people prefer decisions about rights to be made by legislative bodies on grounds of fairness. 'Democracy supposes equality of political power, and if genuine political decisions are taken from the legislature and given to courts, then the political power of individual citizens, who elect legislators and not judges, is weakened, which is unfair' (Dworkin, 1985, p. 27). It is difficult to measure this loss of power by citizens and Dworkin understands that some citizens win more than lose in a transfer of political power from the legislature to the judiciary: 'For individuals have powers under the rights conception of the rule of law that they do not have under the rule-book conception. If their rights are recognized by a court, these rights will be enforced in spite of the fact that no Parliament had the time or the will to enforce them' (ibid.). Citizens and groups whose interests did not reach the legislative sphere and who are without representation in the legislative process, can see their interests and rights recognised by the judiciary: 'If courts take the protection of individual rights as their special responsibility, then minorities will gain in political power to the extent that access to the courts is in fact available to them, and to the extent to which the courts' decisions about their rights are in fact sound' (p. 28).

Dworkin concludes that there is no reason to believe that transferring decision-making powers about rights from the legislators to the judges could damage the democratic ideal of political power equality; it can even promote it.

Cappelletti (1993) reaches similar conclusions concerning the democratic legitimacy of judge-made law. He presents five arguments to refute the suggestion that judicial creativity is anti-democratic.

First, given that political representatives do not necessarily reflect majority opinion or a consensus of the governed, and are frequently linked to interest groups, judges are 'more free' as decision makers (pp. 94–95). Secondly, the judiciary itself can claim a measure of representativeness. Even amongst countries in the civil law system, judges in the superior courts are politically nominated, and have, accordingly, a certain legitimacy derived from the nomination process. The court's activities and decisions are subject to a certain degree of public control, making them more responsible to society than other administrative decision-makers (pp. 97–98).

The third and fourth arguments are related to the potential of courts to contribute to the democratisation of decision-making. On the one hand, through access to justice, groups otherwise excluded from decision-making institutions for socioeconomic, informational as well as ethnic reasons, can find an empowerment space in the courts, where they have an opportunity to influence decisions that affect their interests. As Cappelletti explains, decision-making processes involving legislative and executive authority tend to be remote from the daily life of the citizenry, and are frequently highly bureaucratised, whereas judicial procedure permits community groups to initiate claims, to contribute to the definition of those claims and to be heard (p. 100). In addition, judges have more proximity to the reality of daily life and social conflicts, since they are called upon to resolve specific disputes that emerge from the social dialectic.

The fifth argument asserts that the protection of fundamental rights and liberties is essential to the maintenance of democracy. The judiciary can certainly contribute to the maintenance of democracy when acting in a dynamic and creative way, and by preserving checks and balances to counterbalance the weight of political power and that of other powerful groups (p. 107).

## 5.　CONCLUSIONS

Environmental law, despite certain innovative considerations such as concern for intergenerational interests and intangible values, nevertheless reflects traditional characteristics of the modern era. These elements, notably an emphasis on the production of norms and comprehensive codification, together with a strong connection to technical–scientific rationality, limits the capacity of environmental law to address the complex, dynamic and multi-party features of environmental matters in the postmodern era. This chapter has argued that social, economic, political, cultural and ethnic factors that have a significant weight in contemporary environmental conflicts are not appropriately considered in conventional environmental law. The search for a new juridical paradigm that is capable of accommodating all this complexity is encapsulated in the 'Law of Sustainability'.

The Brazilian 'socioambientalismo' approach and environmental justice contribute significantly to the challenge of incorporating more factors than the environment *stricto sensu* when constructing a 'Law of Sustainability'. The 'socioambientalismo' approach represents an enlarged conception of environmental matters, capable of integrating all the multiple elements in the relationship between environment and society. It promotes the connection of technical–environmental factors with the social, economic, political, cultural and ethnic context. It is capable of recognising traditional knowledge and custom as well as their cultural connection with the environmental context, as determining factors in environmental conflicts. Environmental justice promotes awareness that the treatment of environmental conflicts requires the consideration of such variables as social and environmental exclusion, environmental racism, differences in the distribution of decision-making power and the vulnerable position of those who bear environmental costs disproportionately.

The 'Law of Sustainability', which this chapter has not endeavoured to conceptualise in any definitive way, may be understood as a form of postmodern law. Marked by its incompleteness, dynamic nature and interdisciplinary character, the 'Law of Sustainability' takes the form of a 'net law' as proposed by François Ost. Without disregarding technical and scientific considerations, the 'Law of Sustainability' is a social construct capable of considering cultural, political, economic and ethnic issues with the same level of seriousness.

By adopting a creative posture through judicial activism and incorporating considerations of 'socioambientalismo' and environmental justice into its decisions, the judiciary can play a fundamental role in the construction of the 'Law of Sustainability'. This creative activity can promote the incorporation of new elements into the juridical system, as well as the reformulation of existing norms, concepts and institutions. Judicial initiatives can strengthen and empower civil society, thereby promoting a better distribution of power in environmental matters.

We reiterate, finally, that the processes are dialectic and that the juridical, social, political, economic, cultural and ethnic complexities of sustainability do not allow a unique, simple or 'true' answer. It is necessary to dream in order to construct possible emancipation scenarios capable of meeting the complex demands of sustainability. Without imagined 'utopias' we may be confined by paralysis, conformity and resignation, which are inconsistent with increasingly frequent claims for transformation emerging from the dynamic interaction between environment and society.

## NOTES

1. At the Universidad de Alicante (Spain) this conception has been developed further, especially through the creation of a Master's Program on the Law of Sustainability.
2. Dworkin states: 'Political decisions, according to this argument, should be made by officials elected by the community as a whole, who can be replaced from time to time in the same way. That principle applies to all political decisions, including the decision what rights individuals have, and which of these should be enforceable in court. Judges are not elected or re-elected, and that is wise because the decisions they make applying the rule book as it stands to particular cases are decisions that should be immune from popular control. But it follows that they should not make independent decisions about changing or expanding the rule book, because these decisions should be made in no way other than under popular control'.

## REFERENCES

Acselrad, Henri (ed.) (2004), *Conflitos Ambientais no Brasil*, Rio de Janeiro: Relume Dumará, Fundação Heinrich Böll Pub.

Acselrad, Henri et al. (ed.) (2004), *Justiça Ambiental e Cidadania*, Rio de Janeiro: Relume Dumará, Fundação Ford Pub.

Alexy, Robert (2001), *Teoria da Argumentação Jurídica*, Landy: São Paulo.

Alonso, Ângela and Valeriano Costa (2002), 'Por uma sociologia dos conflitos ambientais no Brasil', in Héctor Alimonda (ed.), *Ecología Política. Naturaleza, Sociedad y Utopia*, Buenos Aires: CLACSO.

Atienza, Manuel (2005), *Las Razones del Derecho: Teorias de la Argumentación Jurídica*, Mexico: Universidad Nacional Autónoma de México.

Cappelletti, Mauro (1993), *Juízes Legisladores?* Porto Alegre: Sergio Antonio Fabris Pub, pp. 92–107.

De Andrade, Vera Regina Pereira (1996), *Dogmática Jurídica: Escorço de sua Configuração e Identidade*, Porto Alegre: Livraria do Advogado.

Delmas-Marty, Mireille (2006), *Le Pluralisme Ordonné – Les Forces Imaginantes du Droit (II)*, Seuil: Paris.

Dobson, Andrew (1998), *Justice and the Environment – Conceptions of Environmental Sustainability and Dimensions of Social Justice*, Oxford: Oxford University Press.

Dworkin, Ronald (1985), *A Matter of Principle*, Cambridge, Massachusetts: Harvard University Press.

Dworkin, Ronald (1986), *Law's Empire*, Cambridge, Massachusetts: Harvard University Press.

Dworkin, Ronald (2000), *Uma Questão de Princípio*, São Paulo: Martins Fontes.

Ferrajoli, Luigi (2001), *Derechos y Garantias – La Ley del más Débil*, Trotta: Madrid.

Ferrari, Vicenzo (1989), *Funciones del Derecho*, Madrid: Editorial Debate.

Ferraz Jr, Tércio Sampaio (2001), *Introdução ao Estudo do Direito – Técnica, Decisão, Dominação*, São Paulo: Atlas.

Fuks, Mario (2001), *Conflitos Ambientais no Rio de Janeiro: Ação e Debate nas Arenas Públicas*, Rio de Janeiro: Editora UFRJ.

Gould, Kenneth (2004), 'Classe social, justiça ambiental e conflito politico', in Henri Acselrad et al., *Justiça Ambiental e Cidadania*, *Relume Dumará*, Rio de Janeiro: Relume Dumará, pp. 67–80.

Habermas, Jürgen (2003), *Direito e Democracia – entre Facticidade e Validade*, Rio de Janeiro: Tempo Brasiliero.

Hannigan, John A. (1995), *Sociologia Ambiental – a Formação de una Perspectiva Social*, Lisbon: Instituto Piaget.

Instituto Socioambiental (2004), *Almanaque Brasil Socioambiental*.

Maciel, Débora Alves (2001), 'Conflito social, meio ambiente e sistema de Justiça: notas sobre o novo papel do Ministério Público brasileiro na defesa de interesses difusos', *Plural: Sociologia* USP, 18.

Marés, Carlos Frederico (2002), 'Introdução ao direito socioambiental', in André Lima (ed.), *O Direito para o Brasil Socioambiental*, Porto Alegre: Sérgio Antônio Fabris Editor.

Marramao, Giacomo (1999), *Céu e Terra: Genealogia da Secularizaçao*, São Paulo: UNESP.

Mateo, Ramón Martin (1991), *Tratado de Derecho Ambiental – Volumen I*, Madrid: Trivium.

Melo, Osvaldo Ferreira (1998), *Temas atuais de Política do Direito*, CMCJ–UNIVALI Sérgio Antonio Fabris Editor: Porto Alegre.

Mirra, Álvaro Luiz Valery (2002), *Ação Civil Pública e a Reparação do Dano ao Meio Ambiente*, São Paulo: Juarez de Oliveira Pub.

Monediaire, Gérard (2005), *L'Hypothèse d'un Droit du Développement Durable in Patrick Matagne, Les Enjeux du Développement Durable*, Paris: L'Harmattan.

Morand, Charles-Albert (1999), *Le Droit Néo-moderne des Politiques Publiques*, Paris: Librairie Générale de Droit et de Jurisprudence.

Ost, François (1991), 'Júpiter, Hercule, Hermès: trois modèles du juge', in Pierre Bouretz (ed.), *La Force du Droit – Panorama des Débats Contemporains*, Paris: Éditions Esprit, pp. 242–245.

Perelman, Chaïm (1996), *Ética e Direito*, São Paulo: Martins Fontes.

Petrella, Ricardo (2004), *Désir D'Humanité – Le Droit de Rêver*, Brussels: Editions Labour.

Pierucci, Antônio Flávio (2003), *O Desencantamento do Mundo. Todos os Passos do Conceito em Max Weber*, São Paulo: Editora.

Regla, Josep Águiló (2000), *Teoría General de las Fuentes del Derecho (y del Orden Jurídico)*, Barcelona: Editorial Ariel.

Rubens, José Morato Leite and Patryck de Araújo Ayala (2002), *Direito Ambiental na Sociedade de Risco*, Rio de Janeiro: Forense Universitária.

Santilli, Juliana (2004), *Socioambientalismo e Novos Direitos – Proteção Jurídica à Diversidade Biológica e Cultural*, São Paulo: Peirópolis.

Siches, Recasens (1973), *Nueva Filosofia de la Interpretacion del Derecho*, Mexico: Porrúa.

# 6. Risk society and the precautionary principle

## Miriam Alfie Cohen and Adrián de Garay Sánchez

## 1. INTRODUCTION

Environmental risk evaluation has become a key category of analysis that is capable of assisting in the examination of the vulnerability of economies in the face of ecological deterioration. It also reveals the way in which decisions taken in the industrial era have resulted in serious collateral damage. Against this backdrop, this chapter seeks to demonstrate the need for a new form of environmental management that adopts the recognition of environmental risk as its point of departure, and subsequently, the precautionary principle. Both of these concepts have become elements of change in decisions taken within the sphere of environmental policy and the present context of sustainability.

The industrial era was preceded by several profound transformations: the shift from closed to open economies, the broadening of political channels and structures and the processes of secularisation, among others. All these contributed to an increasingly more modern world (Giddens, 1990; Ritzer, 1993; Berian, 2004).[1] Despite scientific and technical advances, the growing gap between the model of economic development adopted and the natural environment within which it operated was unforeseen. Instead, we witnessed an unbridled and indiscriminate process of industrialisation which, until the end of the 1970s, seemed to be without limitation in its growth and expansion. Nonetheless, exponential population growth, combined with the depredation of non-renewable resources, the profligate use of non-renewable energy resources and the deterioration of renewable resources marked the beginning of a new era in which human existence itself came under threat (Dobson, 1989; Dryzek, 1997).

The industrial revolution was the pivot that unleashed an economic, scientific and technological boom. For many years, the image of hundreds of chimneys emitting smoke into the environment represented progress and economic power. The smokestack economy symbolised a new era of civilisation which severed all ties with the limitations and shortcomings of the past. But the industrial revolution generated other evils, including the ecological crisis confronting the planet today.

The process of industrialisation entailed not only expansion; in most countries, growth was poorly planned and resulted in the deterioration of environmental conditions (Eckersley, 1992; Gibbs, 1995; Manes, 1997). The widespread growth of industrial production, together with the inappropriate, intensive and systematic exploitation of natural resources, expanded in an uncontrolled fashion without any appreciation of future impacts.

Unanticipated environmental harm subsequently placed limitations on human activity, with the result that the relationship between society and nature has come under increasing scrutiny. While it was formerly true that as a species humans had been characterised by our domination and possession of nature, today the tables have been turned, as it would seem that nature has become a destructive force that we are no longer in a position to control. The occurrence of an environmental crisis on the planet is no longer a remote possibility. On the contrary, if the present trends are not reversed, a high risk situation will develop within two or three decades (Shabecoff, 2000; Shettler, 2000).

Even where the powerful forces of economic globalisation are most tangibly apparent, the other side of the coin is exposed; environmental problems cannot be isolated and viewed exclusively in their regional or national dimension. Environmental questions have become global issues in which we are all immersed.

One characteristic of this global era is threats of serious or irreversible damage to the environment and human health. We live in an age of uncertainty. Nowhere is this truer than in the reality of international environmental issues. Will continued emissions of carbon dioxide and other greenhouse gases lead to global warming? Is acid rain responsible for the decline in North American temperate forests? Do ocean driftnets threaten the sustainable management of fisheries? What are the effects of shipboard waste incineration on the marine environment? These are some of the many questions for which existing science has provided no definitive answers in a timely manner, even though we have a reasonably good grasp of some of the consequences. Precaution is a necessary process where ecological interdependence is recognised and translated into policy actions. We have to initiate deliberations on the appropriate response to environmental threats about which there is scientific uncertainty (Tristram and Jotterand, 2004; Martuzzi and Bertollini, 2005).

The precautionary principle translates scientific uncertainty borne by exposed populations into policy uncertainty borne by state and non-state actors, which then prompts these actors to take a much more coordinated approach to policy making to manage possible ecological crises.

Accepting that contemporary society is characterised by environmental risk, this chapter focuses on two lines of enquiry. First, we seek to unravel the way in which environmental risk becomes an integral category of analysis, by exploring the vulnerability of economies vis-à-vis ecological deterioration and, in this manner, demonstrate how the decisions made in the industrial era have led to serious collateral damage. Second, we attempt to inquire, analyse and understand the need for a new form of environmental management which adopts, as its point of departure, the situation of environmental risk and, subsequently, the precautionary principle, both being instruments of change in the decision-making process pertaining to environmental issues.

## 2.  ENVIRONMENTAL RISK: INTEGRAL CATEGORY OF ANALYSIS

The shaping of a new world 'order' pursuant to the globalisation process takes on particular characteristics in specifically defined areas. Global developments interact with local circumstances and conditions to result in increasingly more complex, differentiated and specialised realities. These are the direct result of this new process and represent different sides of the same coin. The process of globalisation is understood here in broader terms, which implies not only transformation in the economic order, but also and more importantly, changes at the political, geostrategic and even cultural levels. In this sense, globalisation and 'world-wideness' (the boom in media, cultural and assessment integration) are two parallel processes (Bauman, 2000, 2004; Beck, 2002; Lash and Lury, 2007).

This new reality can no longer be studied, analysed and understood according to theoretical categories formulated in the eighteenth and nineteenth centuries. The use of these concepts and categories, as Ulrich Beck (1992) points out, can lead us to an 'iron cage', enclosing social sciences in a cul-de-sac and bringing to a close the explanation of new phenomena and events. For this reason, the theory of Reflexive Modernity and the categories with which it works allow us to understand the characteristics of an unedited world panorama which is different, complex and contradictory and which emanates from that second era of modernity, characterised by risk, contingency and ambivalence (Alfie, 2005).[2]

To the extent to which Reflexive Modernity is a new theory and centres its analysis on a radically changing reality, in the socio-political as well as the economic or techno-scientific spheres, many of its proposals will be severely questioned by older schools of thought. What cannot be denied is the fact that, come what may, to take risks in theoretical construction opens the way to enormous possibilities in the field of the social imagination. To envisage a world which, thanks to new concepts and categories, is entirely different from that which prevailed until the end of the Cold War, serves as a stepping stone to the possibility of questioning and advancing the analysis of processes of global and local interaction that result in *glocal* realities, meant here to depict the hybridisation of the global and the local.

Reflexive Modernity is the result of the pernicious consequences of industrial society, which have led us to a situation of risk in which it is increasingly difficult to confirm a series of events with any security and certainty. Risk becomes pivotal in these societies and we are all immersed in the phenomenon: institutions, actors and politics. In a broader sense, however, risk can lead to the discovery of original intellectual horizons which redefine the modernity script (Luhman, 1998; Giddens, 2001).[3]

According to Ulrich Beck, we need a new sociological imagination aware of the paradoxes and specific challenges of Reflexive Modernity and which, at the same time, is sufficiently strong to drill holes in the walls of abstraction in which routine academic analyses are trapped. The order which emanated from Industrial Modernity guaranteed the security and certainty of the world. These two characteristics are severely questioned with the emergence of global risk, an integral category which allows us to rethink today's world and its diverse problems.

If it is agreed that risk is the key element of this Reflexive Modernity, it is important to clarify that this not only refers to the resulting damage. Risk begins where our confidence in security terminates, and ceases to be relevant on the occurrence of catastrophe. The concept of risk, therefore, characterises a peculiar intermediary between security and destruction. The sociology of risk is not a science of potentialities and judgments concerned with probabilities. The concept of risk (risk = accident severity x probability), while on the one hand adopting the form of calculation of probabilities in Industrial Modernity, is defined in this current societal era by cultural standards of tolerable living, which means that the risks allude to an interdisciplinary relationship: knowledge and technical capacity are combined with cultural perceptions and norms.

Risks and the perception of risks are 'non-desired consequences' of Industrial Modernity: we do not look for risks; it is they that find us.

The political, ideological and economic decisions made in the industrial era that have resulted in climatic change, holes in the ozone layer and nuclear disasters and so on, point to the failure of the capacity of individual nation-states to manage environments on their own. However, this is not due only to the global dimension of risks but also to indeterminacies and uncertainty inherent in the diagnoses of the risks themselves.

While it is true that risk refers to a calculation of probabilities immersed in a cultural and evaluative context, it cannot be denied that, today, it is impossible to determine with absolute certainty the magnitude and dimensions of the risks. The unintended consequences of decision-making play a key role in the effects of risks. It is clear that from the moment of decision, the security and control of social thought and political action are lost.

For the social sciences, risk is something more than merely novel and cannot be understood from the rationalist point of view. The traditional distinction between the layperson and the expert is no longer applicable; risk must be understood as a socio-cultural phenomenon. It is a vision where living conditions involve constant uncertainty; where we do not have a secure scientific perspective on our ambiguous future.

In this sense, risk takes on different aspects in different types of modernity. In the context of Industrial Modernity, it signifies a form of calculating unforeseeable consequences. The calculation of risk is based upon forms and methods to make foreseeable what is unforeseeable (calculation of probabilities, scenarios, statistical representations, standards and preventive organisations) but, to the extent to which the industrialisation process advances and the process of de-traditionalisation is activated (time–space separation), new types of uncertainty emerge. They range from the ontological sphere to the political. These new risks become apparent as a result of the intervention of three categories of participants: through the participation of scientific experts, in the role played by the producers and via the action of analysts and beneficiaries. Efforts to limit and control risks can actually extend the range of uncertainties and introduce new dangers (Giddens, 2001).

The contemporary concept of risk encompasses a particular synthesis of knowledge and ignorance that results from fusing the evaluation of risks based on empirical knowledge, decision-making and performance with risks immersed in uncertainty and indeterminacy. What emerges as a consequence is the category of 'manufactured uncertainty'. This introduces a double referent: on the one hand, greater and better knowledge, but at the same time, a state of ignorance or lack of knowledge. That is, new risks stem from those things that are still not known or are no longer known. The inability to perceive 100 per cent all the consequences of risk characterises this second phase of modernity and opens the panorama to a series of contingencies and unforeseeable events.

Reflexive Modernity generates a society based on knowledge, information and risk; a threatening sphere of possibilities, impotence and alarm is thus established. The responses to this scenario are rooted in cultural answers which span the range from indifference and ignorance to unrest and radicalism. One example of radicalism in the environmental arena can be characterised as the Theological Environmental Movement, where Gaia is the new religious paradigm, or the Deep Ecology Movement, adherents of which want to return to the lost green paradise and deny all the technological progress of modern society.

To highlight the distinction between those who adopt the decisions on risks and those who are obliged to face the consequences of the decisions of others (in other words, the danger) becomes the key issue of analysis.

The risk society opens a new panorama where scientific uncertainty contributes to policy uncertainty, the inability to take decisions with no risk. If we agree that this risk society is a characteristic of our world, globalisation can be understood as a process where the nation-state ceases to be a universal actor, while the decisions of others, the conformation of differentiated values and the multiplicity of agencies become pivotal elements of this new reality.

Against this backdrop it is important to know how vulnerable a particular society is to new global risk. And if the nation-state is no longer the exclusive political actor, how important is the role of non-state actors in the decision-making when dealing with risk?

The relevant themes and challenges pertaining to global risk include: to attempt to find alternative solutions to a changing reality; to formulate functions for new institutions and forums; to inquire into unknown forms of social relations; to set up action networks; and to analyse practices imbued with freedom and responsibility (Beck et al., 1994).

The risk is of such magnitude that the experts no longer have the last word: events can harm us all and permanent alertness would seem to be the order of the day; there are no last-minute sanctuaries. It will be the task of researchers to gear inquiry towards the aspects of the impact; that is to say, towards the form in which these risks can affect us. The problem of vulnerability holds centre stage in the awareness that, while it is true that risks have an impact on all and sundry, the effects can vary. There will be countries, actors, organisations and institutions which will be more sensitive and vulnerable to the adverse effects experienced in the second era of modernity.

In order to understand the cultural and political dynamic of the Society of Risk, it is necessary to establish that risks are in evidence in the global as well as the local sphere. Contemporary risks are of a hybrid nature. They are created by humankind, and combine politics, ethics, mathematics, media, technologies and cultural perceptions. This unfamiliar situation leads to the impossibility of characterising, with exclusive and restrictive categories, the world that surrounds us. Ambivalence is promoted as a mode of resisting fixed-category thought processes, while providing a plethora of expectations and cultural dynamics. The conjunction 'and' hinders the creation of dead-end and absolute concepts, which explains why it is so complicated to understand the global Society of Risk (Bauman, 1998, 2000).

The Society of Risk becomes, in Reflexive Modernity, a society observing itself as in a mirror. Its activity and its objectives are transformed into the centre of controversies, both scientific and political, in that it provides room for ambivalent concepts which destroy distinctions and reconnect antitheses. For example, in the industrial era social movements tended to be very specific, like the struggle for land. Nowadays one can point to a variety of movements that endorse not only a struggle for land but also advocate women's rights or environmental justice. Thus, the theory of the Society of Risk develops an image that converts the circumstances of modernity into contingencies and ambivalence. These circumstances are subject to continuous discussion and political reorganisation.

The new situation in which risk, contingency and ambivalence are the axes that allow us to understand *glocal* reality is epitomised in one of the most intractable and widespread problems facing us in different contexts and latitudes – the environmental crisis. The environment represents the best example of the society of global risk, given that the impacts on water, air and soil are of such a magnitude and capacity that they reach beyond frontiers, motivate global mobilisations and lay the bases for new discussions on risk and vulnerability. The environmental problem shapes trans-frontier actions and creates international institutions beyond state power (Rodriguez, 2003).

The deterioration of the environment places us in a situation of risk. In measuring the environmental vulnerability of different societies, we witness a break with familiar categories, while the panorama of expectations, perceptions and ignorance expands. A series of unforeseeable contingencies begins to flourish. The environmental problem generates controversy among agencies, industrialists, non-governmental organisations (NGOs), experts and insurance companies, among others. There are neither agreements nor controls, there is no order, and politics is once again at the centre of discussion.

What is certain is that environmental impacts are viewed as the result of the processes of industrialisation and urbanisation. Ecological damage often becomes visible only years after its impact has actually begun. The gap between the origins of environmental harm and the eventual consequences is a central problem with implications for conflict and debate in the realms of social construction and scientific explanation. The less risk divulged publicly, the greater the risk produced in the vulnerability of actors, institutions and countries.

Environmental problems cannot continue to be studied using categories originally applicable to industrial society. In the same vein, the design of political actions ought not to pursue that same logic. Environmental deterioration is not an external affair. It should be analysed within the context of all social institutions and therefore it should be the responsibility of these institutions to recognise the reality of the risks. Rather than negate the existence of environmental risks, social institutions must seek out their origins and come up with possible solutions to counteract them.

Intensifying environmental catastrophes and downturns in living standards caused by interlocking crises of energy, water, food and violent conflicts leave us with the idea of seeking global solutions to change this environmental risk. We have adopted a global treaty for climate change; we have pledged to protect biodiversity; we are committed globally to fighting the encroachment of deserts. The big challenge now is to turn those fragile and unfulfilled global commitments into real solutions. The greatest successes in global cooperation should combine: a clear objective, an effective technology, a clear implementation strategy and a source of financing.

Risk societies are characterised by the paradox of growing environmental degradation combined with an expansion in environmental rights and regulation. They are tacitly incongruous because they guarantee neither greater knowledge of the deterioration nor prevention of the damage already done.

## 3. ENVIRONMENTAL MANAGEMENT: RISK AND PRECAUTIONARY PRINCIPLE

We have argued that environmental questions can be analysed today from another perspective, where risk is an integral (or inherent) element of decision-making. Accordingly, it would seem worthwhile to look into the need for a new policy design which would immediately address the deterioration which decisions made in the industrial era have led us to.

The main characteristic of Reflexive Modernity lies in the fact that it inaugurates a stage in which risks will be accompanied by multiple options. Political, economic and cultural decisions will not refer to one sole alternative. The options make it possible to unfold a horizon of different possibilities and, subsequently, of multiple risks. The contingencies present themselves to us as an integral part of the decision made, in that it is impossible to calculate 100 per cent the results of our chosen option. Accordingly, the unexpected, and that which cannot be calculated, will be present on a permanent basis.

That is why citizens and policymakers alike are aware that science may be incapable of identifying safe levels of resource exploitation or pollution. This may be a result of (a) uncertainty as data unavailability; (b) uncertainty as indeterminacy, when an ecosystem's complexity does not permit reliable predictions; or (c) uncertainty as ignorance, when scientists are unsure of the right questions to ask, let alone how to find the right answers. In the face of such uncertainties, scientific experts often cannot identify with confidence the level of risk borne by ecosystems and or communities (Carter, 2000; Hughes, 2001; Maguire and Ellis, 2005; Saltelli and Funtowicz, 2005; Gérard, 2006).

The evaluation of risk becomes a necessary mechanism which allows us to identify the negative consequences of an activity and the risk calculation involved in such consequences. The result is two-fold: on the one hand, a quantitative and qualitative report of the anticipated effects and, on the other, an approximation of the uncertainties discovered. In the new context, risk evaluation is an instrument for decision-making and for the definition of risk management policies.

Risk and its impacts can be visualised in differing spheres of social life: in relations between genders, in labour transformations, in the disenchantment produced by institutions, in the impotence of science or in the changes presented to family structures. However, it is in the environmental sphere where the significance of risk can be more clearly appreciated. The scientific and technological upsurge that accompanied Industrial Modernity led to an accelerated process of horizontal and vertical industrialisation which, today, threatens to exhaust natural resources and energy sources. Industrialisation also increased contamination with imminent environmental risks.

The most important distinguishing factor of Industrial Modernity was the accelerated scientific and technological development implemented in the processes of industrialisation. Technology spearheaded economic growth, facilitating a new rationality in which science and economic growth went hand in hand.

The result of technical–industrial rationality did not lead to the situations hoped for: technological progress failed to create absolute control over the results. While various economies grew exponentially, it was not possible to calculate (because this was no longer perceived to matter) the damage caused to the environment and the collateral effects involved. It was thought, mistakenly, that technology represented a medium of rational control where gain was guaranteed. It took several decades to realise the consequences of those decisions and the environmental risks that the unbridled use of technology has brought about.[4] It is in the phase of the risk society, according to Beck, that the recognition of the incalculability of the dangers unleashed by technical–industrial deployment obliges one to self-reflect on the fundamentals of the social context and a review of the existing conventions and basic structures of rationality (Beck, 1996).

This scientific and technological development was brought about by scientists and engineers who had categorically failed to calculate the social and environmental costs of their decisions. They set in motion a series of transformations, at that time beyond question, under the meta-social halo of science, which guaranteed the one and only truth. It should be mentioned that today irrefutable truths do not exist: science is no longer regarded as the sole guarantor of rationality; risk also has an impact on scientific advancement, while consideration is given to the presence of methodological doubt as a guide to all types of research: there are no guarantees, there is no more order without disorder. As science contains methodological doubt, it does not guarantee the success anticipated. Now, everything is brought into question.

Faced with this situation, environmental management suggests that decisions in matters of technology can no longer be taken in isolation. It is now considered necessary to rethink the effects of risk in three spheres:

(a) A new temporal horizon that considers the medium- and long-term consequences and establishes the research steps to be taken, together with the evaluation, design and management stages involved;

(b) The non-intentional collateral effects, as well as the negative or perverse effects; and

(c) The irreversible nature of the effects, intentional or not.

This vision no longer encompasses the possibility of calculation of all the risks. In the face of a world out of control, where new decisions provoke new risks which, in turn, require the formulation of new alternatives, it is clear that the use of statistical probabilities for the prevention of risk is a method limited by the inability to put to the test an infinite number of variables in one space and at the same time. Accustomed to obtaining the maximum benefit at the maximum risk, statistical analysis was the ad hoc tool to calculate the utility in security frameworks. For example, if we look at Latin America in the 1950s, the use of pest control and fertilisers in a vast land to produce more crops was a policy of growth to detriment of the environment. Governments called it 'The Green Revolution'.

Nevertheless, the uncertainty which today promotes scientific and technological development can no longer guarantee pertinent decisions which statistics were capable of enhancing some 15 to 20 years earlier. While statisticians base their decisions on subjective calculations and seek to guarantee the maximisation of gain and greater satisfaction, the uncertainties that we experience limit the success that was formerly promised and anticipated.

The new dilemma today is to act or not to act. The contingencies guarantee no security whatsoever; knowledge is to be found in uncertainty. Probability, which is subjective, facilitates a distancing from rationality (costs-goals) and so-called scientific objectivity. Today, our choices and actions move in a new context of minimum rationality. Risk and uncertainty are not, and are not lived as, externalities, and technology is neither good nor bad; this gives rise to unforeseeable consequences.

The original wager on technology proposed to put into practice everything that was technologically possible; scientific innovation was assumed to be implementable without limitations. This approach led, however, to unanticipated environmental results, including impacts at the global level. Such a panorama included varying alternatives and risks, and it was for this reason that the precautionary principle acquired a key role in environmental management (Raffensperger and Tickner, 1999; Riechmann and Tickner, 2002).

The approach to the analysis of risk comprises three elements: risk assessment, risk management and risk communication. The precautionary principle is, above all, a risk management tool.

The precautionary principle was heralded as the most important new policy approach in international environmental cooperation. Enshrined in the 1992 Rio Declaration on Environment and Development, the principle has also been incorporated into a number of international environmental instruments. It has become a fully-fledged and general principle of international law and has crystallised into a norm of customary international law.

In essence, the precautionary principle says that some types of risk are worse than others, so actions should be biased accordingly. It thus represents a rejection of 'risk neutrality', which measures risk purely as the product of the magnitude and probability of harm. Generally, the law uses two techniques to resolve uncertainties: the burden of proof to determine the risk of uncertainty and evidentiary presumptions to bridge gaps in knowledge. The burden of proof is an appropriate means of resolving uncertainty when one's knowledge, though incomplete, defines a probability distribution of possible environmental effects.

The precautionary principle has been more clearly defined by the establishment of evidentiary presumptions. Such presumptions are often used when knowledge is so limited that uncertainties cannot be quantified. Under such circumstances, presumptions based on other, similar situations whose uncertainties can be quantified serve to bridge gaps in knowledge and help make qualitative judgments possible.

Some argue that the principle imposes a positive obligation to act as soon as a plausible threat is identified; others maintain that it is not a legal principle at all but only a policy guideline to be taken into account along with many other policy factors. In any case, the principle is employed in a wide range of international instruments including within the European Union and even in institutions that do not explicitly recognise the precautionary principle, such as the World Trade Organization (Cranor, 2004; Ricci et al., 2004; Lafranchi, 2005; Gardiner, 2006).

The precautionary principle thus challenges policymakers and stakeholders to deliberate explicitly and to act in their role as arbiters and actors of risk to the benefit of society. On the one hand, politics is present in at least two ways. First, acceptable levels of risk cannot be assessed scientifically, even in conditions of perfect information, since acceptable risk will vary from one society to another. Secondly, one does not make decisions about risks in a vacuum. A choice to cease an activity when a certain level of risk is reached must be made in light of the full range of impacts that cessation will have. If an environmental protection measure will impose costs and consequences in the form of decreased economic rents, increased threats of disease, decreased food production, or excessive policing costs, for example, decision makers must consider values and societal priorities to determine whether the environmental measure should be adopted. Judging what is an 'acceptable' level of risk for society is pre-eminently a political responsibility. Indeed, if something goes wrong, those in charge of risk management are accountable.

On the other hand, one important element of the precautionary principle is democracy. If faced with scientific uncertainty, we need to set goals, and choose the safest alternative to achieve these goals. These processes involve values and ethics; it is not something that scientists or government bureaucrats can decide alone. We need to bring affected parties to the table: stakeholders, NGOs, citizens and enterprises. This gives us a chance as a public to set the goals that we want to drive toward; it helps get on the table a much wider array of options to resolving problems and looking for alternatives (Dickson and Cooney, 2005; Peel, 2005; Saltelli and Funtowicz, 2005; Fisher et al., 2006).

That is why the precautionary principle is put forward as a guide in the elaboration of public policies, particularly in the regulation of technological risks in situations of uncertainty. The majority of existing formulations on the precautionary principle coincide when defined as a 'protection action demand' concerning our surroundings or public health, even when there is no firm scientific evidence to establish a relationship between cause and effect.[5]

As Raffensperger and Tickner (1999) argue: 'When an activity is presented as a threat to human health or the environment, precautionary measures must be taken, even when certain cause-and-effect relations have not been established scientifically in their entirety.' The main issue is that the precautionary principle seeks to manage scientific uncertainty; it is a tool that can give us standards and flexible norms for a specific time and place, it can teach us about precaution as a practice where monitoring, identification and anticipatory actions have to be taken in the light of a risk society.

From a legal point of view, the precautionary principle generates a new legal culture that implies different levels of deliberation and decision. The principle must be flexible and cannot be expected to eliminate all risks entirely. Reducing the chances of irreversible environmental damage caused by inappropriate laws or public decisions, and enforcing environmental matters from a multi-level governance perspective is part of the new environmental agenda.

In the context of risk and taking the precautionary principle as a guide, two essential tools are required to reform environmental management: the theory of scenarios and the prisoner's dilemma (Shettler, 2000; Rodriguez, 2003).

(a) The theory of scenarios: *by acting as if the worst were to occur*, which implies the need for precaution, is the most rational scenario vis-à-vis constant uncertainty and risk. The precautionary principle functions within this new framework of decision-making as the best form of caution. The intention, therefore, is to ensure that the principle acquires social value and is adopted as a law, as a right and a factor in the decisions of public life. If we take the precautionary principle into account, it is possible to estimate decisions taken in risk and assess harmful effects. It is a question of assessing negative consequences, as well as quantitative, qualitative and irreversible effects. The decision-making then implies a constant evaluation of the risk that generates management policies. The management of separation of variables, which supposedly leads to objectivity, can no longer exist. Instead, what is required is constant management evaluation, an interpretation evaluation in which there are political and social values, and which leads to several decisions: protection, revision of instruments and technical–industrial uses (Parga y Maseda, 2001; de Sadeleer, 2002; Sands, 2003; de Climent, 2006).

(b) The prisoner's dilemma: *by establishing concrete and specific agreements* that are suitable to all, the precautionary principle can be privileged in a new risk culture and the limitations of the ominous 'free rider' scenario and the prisoner's dilemma may be alleviated. ('Prisoner's dilemma' refers to an aspect of game theory which endeavours to show why two people who might be expected to cooperate do not do so; 'free riders' are known as social actors who take all the benefits without any commitments.) Attitudes favouring optimal individual benefits may be modified toward a preference for optimal collective outcomes through negotiation about risk and agreements such as the Kyoto or Cartagena protocols. Cooperation, in other words, becomes a calculated preference that stems from risk. Thus, the mission of outside authorities, national governments and international agencies is to draw up and promote agreements between the different social actors at the local and global level in the face of environmental deterioration.

## 4. CONCLUSIONS

Risk imposes upon us new forms of exercising and executing policies. What emerges is the need for a new environmental management system, in which the combined elements of risk and the precautionary principle promote the need for concrete and specific agreements between different social actors. The so-called stakeholders (actors who have a stake in the decision) today have a fundamental importance in environmental management, where governments are the focal point of agreements between the industrial sector, NGOs and the overall community, as expressions of multi-level governance.

Industry should undertake to reduce contamination rates, to introduce more transparent ways of operating and to take specific action on commitments with the other three actors. The NGOs take part as allies and overseers of these new forms of cooperation and, accompanying them, the community's role will be to point out the social, health and environmental consequences that such agreements produce. It will be possible then to talk about a new co-responsibility in the decision-making process, in which transparency, the increase of rights and visibility become key factors in new environmental management.

To think of the worst possible scenario becomes the weapon to confront risk. The precautionary principle is the spearhead of political change at the local and global level. Responsibility and information now go hand in hand. It is a question, subsequently, of restructuring agencies and agents, which will lead not only to credible institutions but also to actors exploring new forms of participation.

Reform of what already exists, the criss-crossing of integration policies in the decision-making process, decentralisation, concrete and specific agreements instigated by local governments and international agencies designed to strengthen cooperation, mutual benefit and the reduction of the optimum individual advantage in favour of the common good: these are the main tasks to be pursued. Bearing in mind the global environmental risks facing us today, implementation of this new environmental management paradigm cannot be delayed.

# NOTES

1.      All sociological theory has an interpretation of the construction of the Modernity process.
2.      Reflexive Modernity is understood here as the move from the industrial era to that of risk, which is carried out in an anonymous and imperceptible manner in the course of autonomous modernisation in accordance with the model of latent collateral effects. For a better understanding of the term, see Alfie (2005).
3.      The concept of risk is not new in today's society. Nevertheless, the debate on risk has been mainly situated within the technical-scientific or rationalist perspective, that is to say, the risk prevailing in fields such as engineering, medicine or business administration.
4.      Technical–industrial effects are experienced in a more chaotic and perverse manner by the so-called 'emerging' societies in that, while certain Southern countries have availed themselves of particular technologies, in general terms this is not cutting-edge technology nor does it represent the most important scientific advances, which has resulted in serious deterioration of our environment.
5.      The precautionary principle has been implemented in many jurisdictions, including Germany, the Netherlands and Australia, resulting in concrete agreements between different actors as well as legislation.

# REFERENCES

Alfie, Miriam (2005), *Democracia y Desafío Medioambiental en México: Retos, Riesgos y Opciones en la Nueva Era de la Globalización*, Universidad Autónoma Metropolitana-Azcapotzalco, Mexico: Ediciones Pomares.

Bauman, Zygmunt (1998), *Globalization: The Human Consequences*, New York: Columbia University Press.

Bauman, Zygmunt (2000), *Liquid Modernity*, Cambridge: Polity Press.

Bauman, Zygmunt (2004), *La Sociedad Sitiada*, Mexico: FCE.

Beck, Ulrich (1992), *Risk Society: Towards a New Modernity*, London: Sage.

Beck, Ulrich (2002), *La Sociedad del Riesgo Global*, Madrid: Siglo XXI de España Editores.

Beck, Ulrich, Anthony Giddens and Scott Lash (1994), *Reflexive Modernization: Politics, Tradition and Aesthetics in the Modern Social Order*, Cambridge: Polity Press.

Berian, Josexto (2004), *Modernidades en Disputa*, Madrid: Anthropos.

Carter, Bob (2000), 'When science fails, just use the precautionary principle', *Institute of Public Affairs Review*, **58** (4) 33–35.

Cranor, Carl F. (2004), 'Some legal implications of the precautionary principle: improving information-generation and legal protections', *International Journal of Occupational Medicine and Environmental Health*, **17** (1), 17–34.

de Climent, Zlata Drnas (2006), *Aspectos Conceptuales del Principio de Precaución Ambiental*, Córdoba, España, Academia Nacional de Derecho y Ciencias Sociales de Córdoba, available at http://www.acaderc.org.ar/doctrina/articulos/artprincipioprecaucion.

de Sadeleer, Nicolas (2002), *Environmental Principles: From Political Slogans to Legal Rules*, Oxford: Oxford University Press.

Dickson, Barney and Rosie Cooney (eds) (2005), *Biodiversity and the Precautionary Principle*, London: Earthscan.

Dobson, A. (1989), *Green Political Thought*, London: Routledge.

Dryzek, J. (1997), *The Politics of the Earth: Environmental Discourses*, New York: Oxford University Press.

Eckersley, R. (1992), *Environmentalism and Political Theory: Toward an Ecocentric Approach*, Albany: State University of New York Press.

Fisher, Elizabeth, Judith Jones and René von Schomberg (eds) (2006), *Implementing the Precautionary Principle: Perspectives and Prospects*, Cheltenham, UK and Northampton, MA, USA: Edward Elgar.

Gardiner, Stephen M. (2006), 'A core precautionary principle', *The Journal of Political Philosophy*, **14** (1), 33–60.

Gérard, Mégie (2006), 'From stratospheric ozone to climate change: historical perspective on precaution and scientific responsibility', *Science and Engineering Ethics*, **12**, 590–606.

Gibbs, L. (1995), *Dying from Dioxin: A Citizen's Guide to Reclaim Our Health and Rebuilding Democracy*, Boston: South End Press.

Giddens, Anthony (1990), *The Consequences of Modernity*, New York: Macmillan.

Giddens, Anthony (2001), *Runaway World*, London: Routledge.

Hughes, Johnathan (2001), 'How not to criticize the precautionary principle', *Journal of Medicine and Philosophy*, **1**, 441–464.

Lafranchi, Scott (2005), 'Surveying the precautionary principle's ongoing global development: the evolution of an emergent environmental management tool', *Boston College Environmental Affairs Law Review*, **32**, 679–720.

Lash, S. and C. Lury (2007), *Global Culture Industry: The Mediation of Things*, Cambridge, Massachusetts: Polity Press.

Luhman, Nicholas (1998), *Sociología del Riesgo*, Universidad Iberoamericana Mexico: Triana

Maguire, Steve and Jaye Ellis (2005), 'Redistributing the burden of scientific uncertainty: implications of the precautionary principle for states and non-state actors', *Global Governance*, **11**, 505–526.

Manes, Christopher (1997), *Green Rage: Radical Environmentalism and the Unmaking of Civilization*, London: Little Brown and Company.

Martuzzi, Marco and Roberto Bertollini (2005), 'The precautionary principle, science and human health protection', *Human Ecology Risk Assessment*, **11** (1), 63–68.

Parga y Maseda, Patricia Jiménez (2001), *El Principio de Prevención en el Derecho Internacional del Medio Ambiente*, Madrid: ECOIURIS.

Peel, Jacqueline (2005), *The Precautionary Principle in Practice: Environmental Decision-making and Scientific Uncertainty*, Annandale, Australia: Federation Press.

Raffensperger, Carl and John Tickner (1999), *Protecting Public Health and Environment: Implementing the Precautionary Principle*, Washington, DC: Island Press.

Ricci, Paolo F., Louis A. Cox Jr. and Thomas R. MacDonald (2004), 'Precautionary principles: a jurisdiction-free framework for decision-making under risk', *Human & Experimental Toxicology*, **23**, 579–600.

Riechmann, Joan and John Tickner (2002), *El Principio de Precaución*, Barcelona: Icaria.

Ritzer, George (1993), *Teoría Sociológica Clásica*, Mexico: MacGraw Hill.

Rodríguez, Alejandro Gómez (2003), 'El principio de precaución en la gestión internacional del riesgo medioambiental', *Política y Sociedad*, **40** (3), 35–43.

Saltelli, Andrea and Silvio Funtowicz (2005), 'The precautionary principle: implications of risk management strategies', *Human and Ecological Risk Assessment*, **11**, 69–83.

Sands, Philippe (2003), *Principles of International Environmental Law*, Cambridge: Cambridge University Press.

Shabecoff, Phillip (2000), *Earth Rising, American Environmentalism in the 21st Century*, Washington, DC: Island Press.

Shettler, Thomas (2000), *Generations at Risk*, Boston, MA: MIT Press.

Tristram Engelhardt, Jr., H. and Fabrice Jotterand (2004), 'The precautionary principle: a dialectical reconsideration', *Journal of Medicine and Philosophy*, **29** (3), 301–312.

# 7. Measuring the environment through public procurement

## Nicola Lugaresi

### 1. THE ENVIRONMENT, ECONOMIC ANALYSIS AND MARKETS

From a legal point of view, the environment resembles Rubik's cube. The different sides symbolise different components of environment, economics and the social, cultural and political context which law must consider separately, but must bring back to unified alignment. Facing environmental issues without considering the relationships among the different components that must ultimately be integrated means ignoring the combination and the array of colours on the other sides of the cube. You can get a side of a single colour, but you are very likely to mix up the other sides in the process. Economic analysis is one aspect of administrative discretion in environmental decision-making; it must not to be neglected, and should not be considered in isolation.

Economic analysis may contribute, alongside political and legal evaluations, to further understanding and knowledge, operating from an ostensibly neutral perspective. Through assessments supported by numerical criteria, alternative solutions to a specific issue are organically weighted, pointing out the most economically advantageous one. At first glance, economic analysis may seem a very rational and verifiable way to deal with environmental issues, but it may seem, on the other hand, a 'colder' one. If uncritically adopted, without appropriate consideration of the environmental peculiarities (and of the legal specificities), economic analysis may constitute a weakness of decision-making systems. It risks subordinating protection of public environmental (and therefore social) interests to predominantly economic interests. The Rubik's cube would not be carefully handled: if forcefully adjusted, it will eventually be broken.

Economic analysis must consider the peculiarity of environmental issues. Under a stricter legal point of view, environment is simultaneously a set of public commodities and resources, a cross-sectional value, and the expression of composite public interests. These must be introduced, assessed and protected in a multitude of decision-making processes, both on the political and administrative levels. As a commodity, and as a resource, environment is naturally and intrinsically subject to economic evaluations. As a value, and as an interest, it is traditionally and desirably subject to more complicated assessments. While economic analysis cannot be neglected, public powers should have the capacity to resist regulation and management derived exclusively from prevailing economic considerations. Indeed, environmental considerations should have a role in decision-making processes where economic concerns traditionally predominate.

Environment, as a commodity and a resource, is subject to the law of the market, but as a value and an interest, it is subject to the intervention by public authorities, through which market failures and distortions must be corrected. Endorsing the primacy of economic analysis means uncritically relying on markets, even though the market is just one among many regulators and must be integrated with others. Economic analysis contributes to the adoption of political choice first, and administrative discretion afterwards, but it cannot replace traditional assessments and evaluations of public interest. The public interest must first be identified, delimited and then protected.

The discretion of policy-makers should be limited by the measurability of impacts on the public interest, considering environmental, economic and social consequences. Economic analysis is an element of that discretion, but when it comes to sustainable development there are aspects that cannot easily be weighed. The role of law is to find a satisfactory balance.

## 2.  THE POLLUTER PAYS PRINCIPLE AND THE INTERNALISATION OF COSTS

Principle 16 of the Rio Declaration on Environment and Development,[1] states:

> National authorities should endeavour to promote the internalisation of environmental costs and the use of economic instruments, taking into account the approach that the polluter should, in principle, bear the cost of pollution, with due regard to the public interest and without distorting international trade and investment.

Principle 16 concerns the relationship between environment and economics, and as such we should expect to find analogous provisions in other fundamental soft law documents adopted in the international arena. However, this is not the case. Neither the 1972 Declaration of the United Nations Conference on the Human Environment,[2] nor the 2002 Johannesburg Declaration on Sustainable Development,[3] though addressing economic issues, deal with the internalisation of environmental costs – the polluter pays principle – or the use of economic instruments in the way the Rio Declaration does. The approaches of the Stockholm Declaration (see Principle 8, Principle 10 and Principle 11), and of the Johannesburg Declaration (see Principle 5 and Principle 14) are more general in nature. They are directed toward a vague concept of sustainable development and to international relationships, mainly between developed and developing countries.

The Rio Declaration, instead, tries to influence national legal systems by calling for the adoption of an environmental liability scheme. Principle 16 expressly refers to the polluter pays principle and to the connected criterion of internalisation of costs, to be obtained not only by rules, regulations and penalties, but also by means of economic and consensual instruments. The polluter pays principle is affirmed somewhat cautiously. According to Principle 16, the polluter 'should' bear the cost of pollution, and in doing so it must take into account not only the 'public interest', but also the need to not distort 'international trade and investment'. When broadly interpreted (considering other environmental negative impacts, beyond pollution) Principle 16 of the Rio Declaration can underpin (and has supported) environmental liability, environmental damage, environmental taxes and environmental insurance (that is, the internalisation of costs of authorised, allowed, or illegal activities). However, it cannot appropriately promote the externalisation of advantages.

A simple case illustrates the situation. San Giorgio a Cremano is a little town close to Naples, in the Campania Region of Italy. Campania has experienced a serious waste management crisis, due to several factors, primarily the insufficient resort to waste separation in the collection process. San Giorgio a Cremano was no exception. Then the local authorities introduced incentives for the waste brought to the separate collection sites (the incentives start at 0.203 Euro/kilo for paper to 0.445 Euro/kilo for aluminium, and concern cardboard, glass and plastic as well). As a result, in 2006, the quantity of separate collection amounted to one ton a day.[4]

While it can be argued that citizens, out of a sense of civic responsibility, should have practiced separate collection of waste without needing incentives, it must be noted that such incentives represent both an ethical principle and a practical goal. As long as some citizens adopt environmentally appropriate behaviour, which contributes to both environmental improvements and public financial savings, they should be rewarded. Moreover, these incentives are promoting a change in citizens' approach to environmental behaviour. Unfortunately, while the incentive offered was insufficient to spare San Giorgio a Cremano from the waste crisis, it was a first step.

Environmental law and policy have increasingly resorted to economic and consensual instruments, shifting their attention to the promotion of environmental improvements rather than the prosecution of environmental harms. Obviously, it is not a substitutive process, but an integrative one. Still, the goal is to rely more on market-based instruments and less on the traditional 'command and control' system. What is missing or at least still underrated, is the alternative process of rewarding virtuous behaviours which can provoke environmental progress. On this line of reasoning, eco-labels[5] and eco-management schemes such as the Eco-Management and Audit Scheme in the European Community,[6] and ISO 14000 are market-based instruments, but their (marketing) benefits are available mainly to companies, not to individual citizens. Moreover, they are not directly linked to the environmental advantage acquired, but more to the increase of profits due to the altered perception by sensitive consumers (or professional buyers). Similarly, companies, and not citizens, are the intended beneficiaries of environmental agreement initiatives.[7]

Is there a different way to achieve higher levels of environmental protection through economic instruments directed not only to companies and public administrations, but also to citizens? Is there an opportunity to identify a principle complementary to 'polluter pays', which allows a measurable externalisation of environmental advantages and promotes change in personal behaviour and patterns of economic activity? Is there such a principle that could be named the 'non-polluter gains'?

This chapter seeks to analyse recent European Union market-based approaches to environmental issues and sustainable development, with specific reference to 'green procurement', and its possible theoretical significance for a broader and deeper interpretation of Principle 16. While Principle 16, as mentioned, seems limited to the 'polluter pays' principle and, in general, to the internalisation of environmental costs, this chapter explores whether it has been implicitly perceived as a principle connecting behaviours, both vicious and virtuous, to economic consequences. In other words, can Principle 16 live a 'second life', integrating environment and economics, public interest and markets, economic analysis and administrative discretionary choices?

## 3.  THE EUROPEAN UNION APPROACH TO MARKET-BASED INSTRUMENTS

The European Community, which adopted its Fifth Environment Action Programme in 1993, not surprisingly just after the Rio Conference of 1992 and while the Maastricht Treaty was independently introducing an autonomous Community environmental policy, has acknowledged the role of markets in the pursuit of environmental protection targets. Accordingly, the Community has promoted new instruments, such as economic and fiscal incentives, which go beyond traditional 'command and control' measures and which are directed to 'internalizing all external environmental costs'. The Fifth Programme, '*Towards Sustainability*', adopts an economic approach, based on pricing mechanisms and economic valuations that should consider the environmental costs of production, taking into account that some environmental assets cannot and should not be priced.[8] In other words, economic measurement of the environment is one important tool in the decision-making process, but it is not exclusive and may be displaced when higher interests, even though not measurable, are at stake.

The Sixth Community Environment Action Programme, adopted by Decision no. 1600/2002/EC of 22 July 2002, accordingly, promotes a strategic approach that involves the market and all stakeholders.[9] The Programme, based on fundamental Community environmental principles,[10] emphasises the relevance of cost–benefit analysis,[11] in order to integrate the three components of sustainable development (environmental, economic and social/cultural) when environmental measures must be adopted (Art. 2, §4). The Sixth Programme consequently encourages the reform of subsidies that have considerable negative effects on the environment and are incompatible with sustainable development (Art. 3, §4), the consideration of tradable environmental permits (Art. 3, §4) and the use of fiscal instruments, among other measures (Art. 3, §4).

One of the main goals of the European Union, once it acknowledged and absorbed the principle of sustainable development, has been the integration of environmental considerations into other policies. Economic analysis has become one of the criteria to help national and EU institutions' decision-making processes. The problem is that environmental and economic choices often seem to collide. Analysis of the provisions seeking to implement sustainable development through economic instruments, specifically in the context of public procurement, provide insights about theoretical issues and practical matters faced in the decision-making processes.

In 2007 the Commission of the European Communities adopted a Green Paper on market-based instruments for environment- and energy-related policy purposes (28 March 2007, COM2007, 140 final). The document advocates the advancement of market-based instruments in the Community, valued for their flexibility and effectiveness (point 1). Market-based instruments can intervene in the market in a cost-effective way, with some advantages over regulatory instruments, such as 'giving a value to the external costs and benefits of economic activities', allowing industry flexibility ('and thus lower overall compliance costs'), and giving companies incentives to pursue 'dynamic efficiency' through technological innovation (point 2.1). While the Green Paper focuses on taxes, charges and tradable permit systems, it is open to other market-based instruments.

Consensual, cross-sectional instruments (like eco-management and audit schemes, eco-labels, environmental agreements and environmental accounting) allow a different approach to environmental issues. This flexibility is attractive to the most sensitive and efficient companies, which can act in a proactive way, founding their activities not only on legitimate economic expectations, but also on more appropriate courses of action. A different approach is also available to public authorities now forced to think and act in more dynamic ways, no longer exclusively connected to the traditional permit–control–penalty pattern. Consensual instruments, by considering the economic consequences of policy choices and based on economic analyses, try to use markets and competition to gradually raise the level of environmental protection. But again, something is missing. The role that consensual and economic instruments leave to the citizens is relevant in principle, but they are not individually rewarded. Whether for economic reasons, or for lack of consideration, the result is an ethical asymmetry between the way in which companies and individuals are treated.

Measurability is a further consideration. It might be easier and cheaper to weigh the costs to be internalised with reference to companies than the advantages to be externalised with reference to companies and citizens. But it is a contradiction that consensual and economic instruments ignore the role that the externalisation of advantages by companies, public administrations and citizens can have in improving environmental protection; advantages that can be measured. The one ton a day of separated waste collected in San Giorgio a Cremano is a clear example.

As long as market and economic analysis are involved, measurability is needed. The integration between environmental and economic considerations has to be weighted at some point, which means that apples and oranges must be compared.

## 4.   THE INTEGRATION OF ENVIRONMENTAL CONSIDERATIONS INTO TRADITIONAL DECISION-MAKING PROCESSES: GREEN PROCUREMENT

There are different ways to consider the economic analysis of environment-related issues, and to integrate economic instruments into the political and legal processes devoted to pursuing the range of public interests associated with sustainable development. The most interesting issues arise when environmental considerations are to be integrated into a very 'procedural' sector. Public procurement provides an example. Decision makers must address principles like fair competition, transparency and non-discrimination, and undertake a phase of 'weighting' different criteria. The greening of public procurement demonstrates the intertwined relationship among economic analysis and legal analysis, markets and law, economic interests and public interests, and, ultimately, price criteria and environmental criteria.

The Sixth Environment Action Programme expressly promoted green public procurement, taking into account the environmental characteristics of products while respecting Community principles and rules on competition and the internal market (Art. 3, §6).

In 2001 the European Commission adopted an Interpretative Communication on public procurement.[12] The Communication analytically faced delicate issues dealing with the interaction between two very different sectors and associated EC policies. On one side is the public procurement sector, characterised by strict procedures, where the direction of the prevailing regulatory trend has been (not without opposition) towards a gradual reduction of administrative and technical discretion, in order to promote competition, guarantee transparency, and limit distortions (often pathological) of the market. On the other side is the environmental sector, characterised by a progressive extension of its scope, and by its recognised cross-sectional nature and strategic relevance, all of which is bound to heighten the problems connected to the delimitation of its boundaries.

The meeting between the two sectors led the Commission to try to define principles, objectives, procedures and limits for the introduction of environmental considerations into public contracts – postulating that environmental goals may be pursued through a partial adjustment of market rules. The Communication acknowledges the relationship between sustainable development and public procurement, in order to favour environmentally-friendly products and services. The 'greening' of the public procurement policy, which is one of the many components of Single Market policy, may help in 'greening' the market through the environmental performance of contracts awarded by public authorities, but also through changes induced in industry and consumers' purchasing behaviours.

The Court of Justice of the European Communities has further clarified the new integrating approach, and confirmed its reasons and rationality in the European Community perspective. All the while, the Court has addressed the public procurement sector concerns, connected to the market adjustment mentioned above.

In 2002[13] the Court of Justice stated that the integration of environmental considerations into the public contracts procedure is compatible with the Treaty, but specified limits and precautions to be respected.[14] In particular, the Court dealt with the criteria to be used in the most economically advantageous tender, stating that the Directives do not limit the use of criteria to those of a purely economic nature, citing aesthetic characteristics.[15] Quoting article 6 of the EC Treaty,[16] the Court therefore admits 'the possibility for the contracting authority of using criteria relating to the preservation of the environment when assessing the economically most advantageous tender'.[17]

Not surprisingly, in two later cases,[18] the Court had to intervene to correct inappropriate measures of implementation. These clearly showed the main danger of the new approach, that is, a distorted application that would ultimately broaden the discretion of the contracting authority to an absolute freedom of choice, while curbing competition and altering or suppressing the public tender procedures. Requirements of 'equal treatment and transparency of procedures for awarding public contracts' must be met by the award criteria.[19]

The new approach has been codified by new public contracts directives.[20] These, taking case law into account, transposed the contents of the Interpretative Communication of 2001 into rules, defining how environmental considerations could be integrated in the different stages of the public contracts process, including: the definition of the subject matter of the contract; candidate selection; award of the contract; and contract execution. Actually, the first opportunity for considering environmental performance related to a contract is in a phase preceding the application of the public contracts directives, that is, the definition of the subject matter of the contract (for example, building design, methods of cleaning). How this is done depends more on the sensitivity of the public authority than on regulatory criteria.

What is interesting in the green procurement discipline is twofold: on one side, the legal system has to assess apples and oranges, compare their values, and make and justify choices based on these grounds; on the other side, the greening of public procurement acts not only through the internalisation of costs, but also through the externalisation of advantages. Or, at least, it should.

# 5. ECONOMIC INTERESTS AND ENVIRONMENTAL INTERESTS

The discipline of 'green procurement' involves many general environmental issues, and requires political, legal, economic and social evaluations. What are the effects of this new 'environmentally sustainable' public contract policy, with reference to the higher costs for the contracting authorities and to the modification of the competitive balance? What are the environmental advantages that can be reasonably obtained in the medium and long terms? What is the impact on the market, on public administration, on companies, and on economic policy choices? To what extent can environmental policy influence public contracts policy without distorting it? To what extent can traditional administrative procedures accommodate environmental expectations? Beyond such general questions, the most interesting point is related to specific economic evaluations occurring in the final, and most delicate, stage of the procedure. This raises a more practical question: to what extent can environmental considerations modify the economic framework for awarding the contract?

There are several hypotheses, some of which cause neither interpretative nor application problems. The 'environmental choice' may be directly the cheaper one. This occurs where the more 'environmental' product is less expensive than the traditional one; or, the 'environmental choice' may indirectly be less costly. This occurs where the buying price is higher, but considering the whole life-cycle (including use, maintenance and disposal) the contracting authority ultimately saves. With reference to such cases, environmental considerations are redundant, as economic choices and environmental choices substantially overlap. The different 'environmental surplus value' of the different tenders is not neutral though, as it may determine a different ranking and, in the end, a different winner. When the Communication on public procurement of 2001 states that the 'environmental soundness' of a product (which does not necessarily determine an economic advantage for the contracting authority) could be 'translated' into economically measurable criteria (environmental running costs, energy efficiency costs, recycling and waste treatment costs),[21] it stays on the safe side, but, somehow, states the obvious.

Other cases are more complicated. A more expensive 'environmental choice', with reference to a specific contract, may become more convenient if derived advantages, often in the long run, are acknowledged. By way of example, one service might cost more than others, but would make it possible to save money as a result of lower health expenses. In such a situation, the public advantages, connected to general public interests, external to the contract but linked to its objectives, are assessed, transformed into economic evaluations and internalised. Once the limit of the connection with the objective of the contract is respected, a further limit, still with reference to the contracting authority, seems to operate, according to the Court of Justice (and to the Commission). The Court, in the *Concordia Bus* case, states that non-economic factors 'may influence the value of a tender', but states that it does so 'from the point of view of the contracting authority'.[22] In the same terms, the Communication of 2001 acknowledges that in the award phase of the contract, through the most economically advantageous tender, the criteria applied 'shall generate an economic advantage for the contracting authority'.[23] The directives of 2004 on public contracts refer to the most economically advantageous tender 'from the point of view of the contracting authority',[24] or 'entity'.[25]

On a first, stricter, reading, it appears that the advantages, economic or environmental, should be associated with the specific mandate or operations of the contracting authority. Such a reading would address legitimate concerns, trying to avoid an abuse of environmental reasons in order to adopt preconceived and unaccountable choices, and to favour, or disadvantage, some candidates. On the other hand, the same reading would prevent contracting authorities from adopting choices where environmental advantages for the public administration as a whole (and for the community) might be reached.

A second, intermediate, reading, would not preclude the contracting authority from seeking environmental advantages, taking into account that, in order to avoid distorted interpretations, the other limit, namely connection to the object of the Treaty, pointed out by the Court would be sufficient. In this case the economic advantages would be enjoyed by the public as a whole (reserving the option to identify trade-off mechanisms among public administrations, as long as measuring economic advantages, direct or indirect, immediate or deferred, are viable). The practical challenges, in relation to this interpretation, would be associated with environmental improvements, externalising advantages, and rewarding behaviours.

In other circumstances, environmental advantages can be produced, but there are no detected economic advantages to be internalised, or there are economic losses to be considered. In these cases, the contracting authority must assess conflicting, or at least not completely convergent, public interests. Environmental protection is often a luxury, as the development curve of countries shows: environmental expenses grow when a certain level of development is met, and from then on environmental protection becomes a necessity and therefore a mainstream public interest. Also, as with other non-material luxuries, the value is not always measurable, as it is often associated with a feeling (for example, of well-being).

A third, expansive reading, could then overcome not just the 'contracting authority' limit, but also the 'measurable' limit, allowing consideration of environmental non-economic or anti-economic factors when the contracting authority, or other public authorities, could enjoy a public interest advantage. That would lead to a broad opening, particularly for contracts concerning local authorities, considering that environmental interests are naturally regarded as interests enjoyed by the inhabitants of a particular territory.

With reference to public contracts, resolutely ruling out the chance of an environmental anti-economic choice would betray the very reason for the Interpretative Communication of the Commission, of the rulings of the Court of Justice and of the reform of the Directives concerning public contracts. Moreover, it would render the abovementioned solution according to which the advantages, economic or environmental, must be referred exclusively to the contracting authority, even more irrational and short-sighted. Potentially anti-economic choices determined by different public interests are not new, both at a general[26] and at a more specific level.[27]

The Court of Justice confirmed the interpretation according to which environmental considerations may determine anti-economic choices, and environmental advantages may refer to the community as a whole, not only to the community living on the territory of the contracting authority (local or otherwise). In the EVN AG case of 2003, several points of a most economically advantageous tender were allotted to the utilisation of renewable energy sources, which were more expensive than traditional sources. The Court held that there was a no misapplication of the law because of the negative economic consequences, or because of the 'extraterritoriality' of the environmental advantage. Rather, the misapplication arose because the criteria adopted in order to award the points to the tenders were illogical, not very transparent and largely based on non-verifiable previews. This resulted in 'unjustified discrimination'.[28]

In this respect, national regulations which utilise quotas can also be mentioned. It is the law itself that predetermines the contents of an array of contracts, imposing a percentage of environmentally friendly products (paper, plastic, tires ...). Quotas reduce (or suppress) discretion both at the time of the choice of products to be bought and, *de facto*, at the time of the award of the contract, as environmental considerations are moved back with reference to the most economically advantageous tender (which can be consequently replaced only by the lowest price). It is a different way to externalise environmental advantages.

## 6.  'MEASURABILITY' OF ENVIRONMENTAL ADVANTAGES AND DISCRETION

Environmental protection is something that can be paid for, and usually is. Environmentally sustainable choices may cause additional costs in public contracts. The point is how this can happen and to what extent it can be allowed, comparing interests of a different nature, through both administrative and technical discretion, when economic and environmental interests can be equally served, or when the legislator does not predetermine the pattern (as in the 'quotas' system).

'Measurability' of environmental aspects is not a prerogative of 'green procurement'. Measurability can be the numeric expression of the internalisation of more defined environmental costs. Article 9 §1 ('Recovery of costs for water services') of the Directive 2000/60/EC,[29] commonly known as the *Water Framework Directive*, states the principle of recovery of the costs recovery of water services, including environmental and resource costs. Measurability can be the quantification of environmental liability and environmental damage. Article 2 of the Directive 2004/35/EC[30] defines costs with reference to many factors: assessing costs; administrative, legal and enforcement costs; data collection costs; monitoring and supervision costs; and other general costs (Art. 2, §16).

Measurability is also the tool, especially with reference to economic sectors, to limit the administrative discretion which environmental considerations, due to their relevance and extent, might otherwise allow. There is a twofold meaning to the measurement of environmental advantages. The first refers to the economic advantage derived, directly or indirectly, from choices due to environmental considerations. The second refers to the environmental 'value' of the choices, to be compared and weighed together with other public and private interests. The former refers to technical discretion, the latter to administrative discretion.

With reference to green procurement, the most interesting and delicate profile is given by the numerical comparison that, in a procedure ruled by the most economically advantageous tender, concerns different aspects of the tender and, therefore, affects different interests. The general and political choices pointed out at European Community level (through Directives) and at a national level (through domestic laws), are transposed in evaluations connected to administrative discretion first (what kind of contract, its contents, its clauses), and then finalised in technical discretion.

Environmental aspects, like economic ones, are relevant at all levels: political choices (environmental considerations can, and must, be integrated in other policies); administrative choices (in a specific public contract, environmental characteristics can obtain high grades, to be added to other grades given for other characteristics); technical choices (in the range of the maximum grade obtainable for environmental characteristics, the final grade is awarded, through a comparison of the different tenders).

In the last stage, that is, determining the most economically advantageous tender, the comparison between the economic value and the environmental value is obtained through the measuring of both, each of which must be awarded points. The process is easier for the economic aspects, as the points stem from a mathematical calculation. It is harder for environmental aspects, which, as previously noted, can include economic implications. The points must be given through both an internalisation of economic costs and the externalisation of environmental advantages.

In the awarding stage, which represents the decisive and most sensitive moment of the process, especially when environmental considerations imply negative economic considerations, it is a matter of apples and oranges. It is not a choice between environment and economics, which would be an impossible choice. It is not a matter of fundamental principles anymore; it is not Cézanne's *Pommes et Oranges*, where apples and oranges coexist to create a masterpiece. It is a critical bookkeeping matter, which, nonetheless, would remain arid and inadequate if it did not take into account the very same principles. A choice between apples and oranges for a diet would not be based exclusively on economic aspects (price) or other measurable aspects (calories, vitamins), but also on taste, variety, season and, why not, colour. These are all relevant, if non-measurable, criteria. In order to pursue the well-being of our society, our legal system should be as flexible, as strong and as considerate to choose, to some extent, colours instead of money.

Public procurement can be 'greened' at different stages of the decision-making process: definition of the subject matter of the contract, selection of the candidates, award of the contract and execution of the contract. The profile linked to measurability represents, if not the final act, certainly the decisive point where principles should be implemented, as they express the environmental value of the choices, potentially set against the economic value. It is therefore the time when bookkeeping and philosophy meet, when principles and mathematics interact, when the scales convey the relevance of values. Administrative discretion logically precedes technical discretion, but when the process of measuring cannot be based on definite criteria, signs of the evaluation of interests often remain in the weighting process as well. Environmental considerations are present throughout the entire process of public decision-making.

# 7.  CONCLUSIONS: MEASURABILITY, ECONOMIC ANALYSIS, EXTERNALISATION OF ADVANTAGES AND A NEW RIO PRINCIPLE 16?

Economic analysis requires measurability, as it weighs the economic impact of political and administrative choices. Administrative discretion can use measurability, as it simplifies choices and provides criteria to evaluate interests, based on numbers. Technical discretion can use measurability as well, since scientific and technical criteria are used to weigh different profiles. Measuring environmental advantages facilitates their externalisation, as they can be integrated in the economic, administrative and technical evaluations.

But decisions respecting public interests, like environmental protection, cannot be confined exclusively to economic and measurable criteria. Measuring environmental aspects does not always make them comparable to economic aspects. Sometimes one orange is more appropriate and cherished than one, two or more apples. Measuring the economic impact of environmental protection may add some data, but cannot represent the solution to be adopted in every case. This can be a step forward in environmental protection. Consider, assess, measure, compare, but, in the end, choose according to fundamental interests, people's expectations, and ethics. Measurement is a precious tool: the externalisation of advantages can use it, but does not 'need' it.

Principle 16 of the Rio Declaration deals with the internalisation of environmental costs, the polluter pays principle, and the use of economic instruments. Effective environmental protection requires us to go further, so we need to interpret the wording of Principle 16 broadly, or be prepared to rewrite it. The following amendments to the principle point in the direction that a future international agreement might take:

> National authorities should endeavour to promote the internalization of environmental costs and the externalization of environmental advantages, in order to address environmental, economic, ethical and equity expectations; economic and consensual instruments must be used, in order to integrate the traditional instruments devoted to the protection of the environment; the polluter pays principle and the non-polluter gains principle must be taken into account with reference to governments, companies, and citizens, with due regard to public and community interests, without distorting international trade and investment, in order to acquire a high level of protection and improvement of the quality of the environment.

# NOTES

1.  Rio Declaration on Environment and Development UN Doc. A/CONF.151/26 (Vol. I), at http://www.unep.org/Documents.Multilingual/Default.asp?documentid =78&articleid=1163.
2.  Stockholm Declaration, United Nations Conference on the Human Environment at http://www.unep.org/Documents.Multilingual/Default.asp?documentid=97&articleid=150 3.
3.  Johannesburg Declaration on Sustainable Development at http://www.un.org/esa/sustdev/documents/WSSD_POI_PD/English/POI_PD.htm.
4.  *Ideambiente*, 3/2007, at www.apat.gov.it/site/_contentfiles/00144100/144158 _Ideambiente _03_2007.pdf p. 8.
5.  See http://europa.eu/legislation_summaries/consumers/product_labelling_and_ packaging/l28020_en.htm.
6.  See http://europa.eu/legislation_summaries/enterprise/business_environment/l28022 _en. htm.
7.  See http://europa.eu/legislation_summaries/enterprise/interaction_with_other_policies/ l281 26_en.htm.
8.  *European Community Fifth Environment Action Programme*, point 7; see http://ec.europa. eu/environment/archives/env-act5/pdf/5eap.pdf.
9.  Note 7, Recital 14: see http://ec.europa.eu/environment/natres/pdf/final_report_wg1.pdf.
10. Note 7, Art. 2, §1: see http://ec.europa.eu/environment/natres/pdf/final_report_wg1.pdf the Programme 'shall be based particularly on the polluter pays principle, the precautionary principle and preventive action, and the principle of rectification of pollution at source'.
11. *European Community Sixth Environment Action Programme*, Art. 2, §3: 'analysis of benefits and costs, taking into account the need to internalise environmental costs'.
12. Interpretative Communication on the Community law applicable to public procurement and the possibilities for integrating environmental considerations into public procurement (4 July 2001 COM2001 274 final).
13. CJEC 17 September 2002, case C-513-99, *Concordia Bus*.
14. CJEC 17 September 2002, case C-513-99, §64: 'the contracting authority may take criteria relating to the preservation of the environment into consideration, provided that they are linked to the subject-matter of the contract, do not confer an unrestricted freedom of choice on the authority, are expressly mentioned in the contract documents or the tender notice, and comply with all the fundamental principles of Community law, in particular the principle of non-discrimination'.
15. CJEC 17 September 2002, case C-513-99, §55: 'It cannot be excluded that factors which are not purely economic may influence the value of a tender from the point of view of the contracting authority. That conclusion is also supported by the wording of the provision, which expressly refers to the criterion of the aesthetic characteristics of a tender'.
16. European Community Treaty, Art. 6: 'Environmental protection requirements must be integrated into the definition and implementation of the Community policies and activities'.
17. CJEC 17 September 2002, case C-513-99, §57: the Directive 'does not exclude the possibility for the contracting authority of using criteria relating to the preservation of the environment when assessing the economically most advantageous tender'.
18. CJEC 10 April 2003, joined cases C-20/01 and C-28/01, Federal Republic of Germany; CJEC 4 December 2003, case C-448/01, EVN AG.
19. CJEC 4 December 2003, case C-448/01, §59: 'it is for the national court to determine, taking account of all the circumstances of the case, whether ... the award criterion at issue in the main proceedings was sufficiently clearly formulated to satisfy the requirements of equal treatment and transparency of procedures for awarding public contracts'.
20. Directive 2004/17/EC of 31 March 2004 coordinating the procurement procedures of entities operating in the water, energy, transport and postal services sectors; Directive

      2004/18/EC of 31 March 2004 on the coordination of procedures for the award of public
      works contracts, public supply contracts and public services contracts.
21.   Interpretative Communication on the Community law applicable to public procurement
      and the possibilities for integrating environmental considerations into public procurement,
      §3.1.
22.   CJEC 17 September 2002, case C-513-99, §55.
23.   See note 21.
24.   Directive 2004/18/EC, Art. 53 §1.
25.   Directive 2004/17/EC, Art. 55, §1.
26.   See the Court of Justice case law concerning the award of contracts and the condition of
      employment of long-term unemployed persons: CJEC 20 September 1988, case 31/87,
      *Beentjes*, where the Court stated the compatibility with the Directive of such a condition,
      to be mentioned in the contract notice, 'if it has no direct or indirect discriminatory effect
      on tenderers from other Member States'.
27.   Not surprisingly the CJEC quotes the aesthetic criterion, traditionally accepted as one of
      the non-economic criteria of the most economically advantageous tender.
28.   CJEC 4 December 2003, case C-448/01, EVN AG, §69.
29.   Directive 2000/60/EC of 23 October 2000 establishing a framework for the Community
      action in the field of water policy.
30.   Directive 2004/35/EC of 21 April 2004 on environmental liability with regard to the
      prevention and remedying of environmental damage.

PART TWO


# Environmental rights, access to justice and liability issues

# 8.   A sustainable and equitable legal order

## Werner Scholtz[*]

## 1.   INTRODUCTION

The world is characterised by enormous disparities between developing and developed states (Anand, 2004, p. 103; Johnston, 1998–1999, p. 36; Kingsbury, 1998, p. 599). The existing inequality in the distribution of desired goods between states has resulted in demands by the developing states that the formal sovereign equality[1] of states must be extended to incorporate material equality through recourse to equitable measures (Simpson, 2004, p. 39). Thus, the developing states demanded the establishment of a New International Economic Order (NIEO). The NIEO, requiring the pursuit of distributive justice, could result in the birth of a more just world (Franck, 1995, p. 47).[2] International law, however, has never been transformed pursuant to equity as desired by developing states (Mickelson, 2000, p. 64).[3] Lately, the grievances of the economically disadvantaged have been supplemented by a rising concern regarding the circumstances of future generations. This concern is referred to in international environmental law as 'intergenerational equity'. Intergenerational equity also has links with the notion of distributive justice. Some of the primary principles of the NIEO have experienced a revival in the field of international environmental law. Thus, it is of interest to determine whether and how the concerns pertaining to future generations may present opportunities to diminish inequality and increase equity between developed and developing states.

Section 2 of this chapter briefly introduces the notion of equity in international law. Equity and the primary principles of the NIEO receive attention in Section 3. Section 4 investigates intergenerational equity, and Section 5 contains a critical analysis of intergenerational equity. Then the way intergenerational equity may promote a more equitable international order is canvassed.

## 2.   EQUITY IN INTERNATIONAL LAW

According to the traditional Western view of equity, it is important to understand the distinction between 'equitable principles' and recourse '*ex aequo et bono*' (Janis, 1983, p. 9; Falk, 1999, p. 411; Kaur, 2002, p. 328). Under Art. 38(2) of the Statute of the International Court of Justice (ICJ), the ICJ may decide cases *ex aequo et bono* with the consent of the parties. The power to decide a case *ex aequo et bono* has sometimes been described as a grant of discretion to a judge to act as a legislator (Janis, 1983, p. 10). Western doctrine further distinguishes (Janis, 1983, p. 12) between equity *intra legem*,[4] *praeter legem*[5] and *contra legem*.[6]

Continental shelf allocation has invited the application of equitable principles in international law as illustrated in the North Sea Continental Shelf[7] cases and subsequent decisions of the ICJ.[8] The ICJ explained that it applied an equitable principle *intra legem* in order to reach a decision in the North Sea Continental Shelf cases, but various scholars, such as Kaur, are of the opinion that the court actually applied distributive justice (Kaur, 2002, p. 317). Franck, for instance, opines that the Court has introduced a notion of distributive justice without departing from Article 6(2) of the Geneva Convention on the Continental Shelf of 1958 (Friedmann, 1970, p. 236; Blecher, 1979, p. 87; Franck, 1995, p. 63).

Equity further has become very important in relation to the development of equitable standards for the allocation and sharing of resource benefits (McIntyre, 2007, p. 121).[9] Another development of interest is 'common heritage equity' pertaining to resource allocation (Baslar, 1998, p. 227).


## 3.   DEPARTURE FROM TRADITION: EQUITY AND THE NIEO

The Third World equity doctrine differs from the traditional Western concept (Nawaz, 1980, pp. 113–122 and Khurshid, 1980, pp. 108–112). It needs to be viewed in the context of the call for a New International Economic Order. In the 1970s the achievement of political independence of former African and Asian colonies strengthened the position of developing countries and led the latter to reconsider the whole international economic system. Far-reaching demands were put forward concerning the reshaping of international relations and the equitable distribution of wealth between developed and developing countries (Cassese, 1986, p. 364).[10] It appeared to the developing countries that the economic order served the interests of the developed world (Hossain, 1980, p. 2). It was through the process of decolonisation that developing countries acceded to the international system and acquired formal sovereignty, but the former colonies soon realised that mere political independence was not enough and they also needed to struggle for economic independence (Bedjaoui, 1979, p. 87).

The introduction of a new international and economic order was seen a prerequisite to decolonisation (Bedjaoui, 1979, p. 86). Developing countries demanded measures to remedy the colonial past and promote economic independence. In 1974, the United Nations General Assembly accordingly adopted a Declaration on the New International Economic Order,[11] with a Programme of Action[12] and a Charter of Economic Rights and Duties of States.[13]

## The Primary Principles of the NIEO

The Declaration contains various references to the notion of equity. The preamble, for instance, proclaims that the establishment of a new international economic order must be:

> based on equity, sovereign equality, interdependence, common interest and co-operation among all States, irrespective of their economic and social systems which shall correct inequalities and redress existing injustices, make it possible to eliminate the widening gap between the developed and developing countries and ensure steadily accelerating economic and social development and peace and justice for present and future generations.[14]

The Charter is of great importance for the pursuit of an NIEO as it is an instrument which seeks to provide for change and a redistribution of wealth and power (Tiewul, 1975, p. 686).[15] The developing world required affirmative action similar to the initiatives in municipal constitutional law (Hossain, 1980, p. 5). This is also evident from the structure of the Charter, as it sets out provisions which resemble directives in constitutional law. The Charter therefore is a code that contains basic principles in various spheres of international economic relations. The Charter merely refers to the 'Economic Rights and Duties' of States, but it is suggested that it has a broader application, and in this sense it is an economic Charter in the non-exclusive sense (Tiewul, 1975, p. 658).[16]

In this discussion, it is important to reflect on the references in the Charter to solidarity, cooperation and preferential treatment. Article 18 refers to the importance of solidarity, as it reads that: 'In the conduct of international economic relations the developed countries should endeavour to avoid measures having a negative effect on the development of the national economies of the developing countries'. Various articles deal with the issue of cooperation.[17] Article 8, for instance, asserts that: 'States should co-operate in facilitating more rational and equitable international economic relations and in encouraging structural changes in the context of a balanced world economy in harmony with the needs and interests of all countries, especially developing countries, and should take appropriate measures to this end'. Note that 'should' instead of 'shall' is used. These are recommendations and are not couched in obligatory language.

The principle of preferential treatment is perhaps one of the most important elements of the NIEO, which is reflected in nineteen articles in the Charter (see Arts 5, 6, 8, 9, 11, 12, 13, 14, 15, 17, 18, 19, 22, 24, 25, 26, 27, 29 and 30). For example, Art. 19 states: 'With a view to accelerating the economic growth of developing countries and bridging the economic gap between developed and developing countries, developed countries should grant generalized preferential, non-reciprocal and non-discriminatory treatment to developing countries in those fields of international economic co-operation where it may be feasible'.

The Charter introduced norms that were perceived by developed countries as a radical departure from international law and accordingly as non-binding (Bulajić, 1980, p. 60). The view of the developing world was that the Charter was a legally binding document. Although various General Assembly Resolutions were adopted in relation to the NIEO, these never were really implemented in full (Bollecker-Stern, 1980, p. 69). The resolutions did, however, have a political impact. Perhaps one of the reasons for the demise of the NIEO was the fact that it was characterised by the imposition of new unilateral obligations on the developed world (Cullet, 1999, p. 566). The developing world furthermore did not have much to bargain with in order to induce the developed world to agree to the new order.

In a subsequent development, the International Law Association (ILA) commenced work on the notion of the NIEO in 1980 (Makarczyk, 1988, p. 160). The 'Declaration on the Progressive Development of the Principles of Public International Law Relating to a New International Economic Order' (Seoul declaration) was adopted in 1986 (Makarczyk, 1988, p. 174).[18] The Preamble incorporates the list of principles. It makes it clear that the incorporated principles are generally recognised legal principles, but that other principles can become binding through their acceptance in treaty law or as customary international law. Accordingly, it seems that each principle needs to be examined in order to clarify the binding character of the principle. The ILA presented 12 principles, which are deemed to be most important. Several of these principles are examined here.

The substantive legal principles are introduced by the 'The Principles of Equity and Solidarity and the Entitlement to Development Assistance' (para. 3). The Declaration notes that: 'Without ensuring the principle of equity there is no true equality of nations and states in the world community consisting of countries of different levels of development' (Para. 3, subpara. 1). It further states that: 'The principle is also an integral element of the interpretation of the law by international courts or arbitration panels and may be applied by them to supplement the law'.

In relation to solidarity, the Declaration notes that the principle 'reflects the growing interdependence of economic development, [...] states have to be made responsible for the external effects of their economic policies [...] states, should conduct their economic policies in a manner which takes into account the interests of other countries [...] they should seek to avoid any measure which causes substantial injury [...] in particular to the interests of developing states and their peoples' (para. 3, subpara. 2).

Para. 4 includes the duty to cooperate. The list also includes 'the international protection of the natural environment', but it is not clear whether 'natural environment' refers only to flora and fauna, or whether it has an extended meaning. Furthermore, it states that 'the protection, preservation, and enhancement of the natural environment for the present and future generations are the responsibility of all states' (para. 7, subpara. 5). The principles in paragraphs 8, 9 and 10 pertain to equality. Paragraph 10 deals with substantive equality, including the preferential and non-reciprocal treatment of developing countries in the areas of international economic, financial and monetary relations.

The notion of equity forms the source for principles, such as solidarity and cooperation in the Charter (Makarczyk, 1988, p. 115).[19] The duty of cooperation furthermore is a result of the principle of solidarity, to which it gives effect (Makarczyk, 1988, p. 116). The notion of equity derived from the economic inequality between the developed and developing world differs from the notion of equity as a form of corrective justice, which may be applied by a judge in certain cases. The 'equity' that is required by the developing world is a norm which would rectify the unequal distribution of wealth in the world. This implies a preference for some sort of distributive justice (Harris, 2000, p. 55).

## 4.  EQUITY AND INTERNATIONAL ENVIRONMENTAL LAW

A form of equity which also has strong ties with distributive justice is that of intergenerational equity. It primarily entails a two-fold concept: the present residents of the earth hold the earth in trust for future generations and at the same time the present generation is entitled to reap benefits from it. The most comprehensive and important scholarly contribution on the legal discourse pertaining to intergenerational equity has been made by Edith Brown Weiss (Brown Weiss, 1989).[20] According to Brown Weiss, 'the use of equity to provide equitable standards for allocating and sharing resources and benefits, lays the foundation for developing principles of intergenerational equity'. This means that the principles of intergenerational equity can be built on the use by the ICJ of equitable principles in its decisions.

The basic proposition of Brown Weiss's proposal is that each generation is both a custodian and a trustee of the planet for future generations as well as a beneficiary of its fruits (Brown Weiss, 1989, p. 17). This imposes not only obligations on the current generation, but also provides the latter with rights. Brown Weiss uses this premise to develop rights and duties as well as strategies for the implementation of her proposal. However, she realises that not all countries are wealthy enough to promote sustainable development and it is for this reason that she makes provision for intragenerational equity which requires that 'wealthier countries and communities, which will benefit from protecting the general planetary environment for future generations, to contribute to the costs incurred by poor countries and communities in protecting these resources' (Brown Weiss, 1989, p. 28). In general, every generation has the duty to pass the planet on in no worse a condition than it had been received in as well as to provide access to its resources and benefits and a duty to repair the damage done by previous generations where these generations failed to adhere to the first duty (1989, p. 24).[21]

Three basic principles of intergenerational equity may be distinguished (Brown Weiss, 1989, p. 38). The first principle is referred to as the principle of the 'conservation of options'. According to this principle, each generation should conserve the diversity of the natural and cultural resource base so that it does not unduly restrict the options for future generations. The principle of the 'conservation of quality' entails that each generation must maintain the quality of the planet so that it is passed on in the same condition as it was received, to enable future generations to enjoy a quality of life comparable to that of the previous generation. In terms of the principle of 'conservation of access' each generation should provide its members with equitable rights of access to the legacy of past generations and in addition should conserve this access for the future.

The notion of intergenerational equity has been affirmed in international environmental law and jurisprudence. Judge Weeramantry referred to intergenerational equity, *inter alia*, in the *Nuclear Test Case* of 1995 in which New Zealand challenged France's underground nuclear tests in the Pacific. Judge Weeramantry opined that 'The case before the Court raises [...] the principle of intergenerational equity – an important and rapidly developing principle of contemporary environmental law'.[22] Judge Weeramantry also reaffirmed that the use of nuclear weapons could pose a serious danger to future generations.[23] The notion of intergenerational equity has received recognition in various international legal documents that represent both hard and soft law. The Stockholm Declaration is but one example. Principle 1 reads: 'Man [...] bears a solemn responsibility to protect and improve the environment for present and future generations'. Intergenerational equity also is prominent in the 1992 Rio Declaration: 'The right to development must be fulfilled so as to equitably meet developmental and environmental needs of present and future generations' (Principle 3). Intergenerational equity has also received recognition in various other treaties, including the 1946 International Convention for the Regulation of Whaling, the 1973 Convention on International Trade in Endangered Species of Wild Fauna and Flora, the 1979 Convention on the Conservation of Migratory Species of Wild Animals, the 1974 UN Charter on the Economic Rights and Duties of States, the 1992 Convention on Biological Diversity and the 1992 Framework Convention on Climate Change.

The World Commission for Environment and Development (WCED) defined the concept of sustainable development to mean that the present generation must meet its own needs without compromising the needs of future generations.[24] This has, in general, become the most accepted international description of sustainable development.[25] The notion of intergenerational equity accordingly is an element of sustainable development (Sands, 2003, p. 253).[26] Intergenerational equity has however been extensive critiqued.

## 5. INTERGENERATIONAL EQUITY: A SOUTHERN PERSPECTIVE

The South frequently is referred to as a 'grudging partner' in international environmental law negotiations (Mickelson, 2000, p. 53; Beyerlin, 2006). The unwillingness of developing states, however, needs to be viewed in the context of the fact that the North and South have differential interests. Whereas the South has 'environmental problems of poverty', the North faces environmental problems deriving from the 'excess of affluence' (Ntambirweki, 1990–1991, p. 907). The Stockholm Declaration recognises the aforementioned differential interests. The developing countries asserted their influence during the Stockholm conference and their interests were acknowledged in the Declaration (see Principles 8, 9, 10 and 11). However, the victory that the developing countries achieved at the Stockholm conference did not last long. In general, the environmental problems deriving from the 'excess of affluence' mostly have been the main concern of international environmental law (Ntambirweki, 1990–1991, p. 924). It is, therefore, not always unjustified that the developing countries view the environmental initiatives of the developed world with scepticism. Developing countries fear that the global environmental agenda, which they perceive as an agenda of the North, may hamper their economic growth (Speth, 2004, p. 789). The different interests of the North and South also may be evident in the distinction between intergenerational and intragenerational equity. The North mostly focuses on the pursuit of intergenerational equity, whereas the South is sceptical of intergenerational equity, while the major part of the current generation does not have the means to address their most basic needs. How can one expect poor people to shoulder the burden of future generations? Furthermore, these future generations as a consequence also will include generations of the North, which implies that these people will need to ensure the affluence of future (Northern) generations. The connection with future generations is vague and it is difficult to see why current generations should make sacrifices for future generations (Gillespie, 1997, p. 117), especially the poor. Intergenerational equity focuses too much on future justice and does not really address the injustices of the past (Mayeda, 2004, p. 48).[27]

Another point of critique is that intergenerational equity does not reflect the fact that equity is not merely an abstract concept (Mayeda, 2004, p. 42). Equity must be applicable between separate individuals or groups. For example, redistributive equity might be imposed on the relationship between developed and developing countries in order to pursue equality. However, this is not possible in the instance of future generations as they constitute a mere abstract group. Intergenerational equity further requires us to make assumptions about what future generations will value (D'Amato, 1990; Gündling, 1990; Mayeda, 2004, p. 48).[28] In order to make these assumptions we will use our own present values to establish the future values. These present values do not always aspire to equity as is reflected by the growing inequality of the current world order. This may mean that current inequity will be passed on to future generations.

However, the main problem with intergenerational equity is the assumption that intragenerational equity is an extension of intergenerational equity (Brown Weiss, 1989, p. 21), a viewpoint which entrenches the primary importance of intergenerational equity and demotes intragenerational equity to an incidental matter. While intergenerational equity acknowledges intragenerational equity, too much weight is accorded to intergenerational equity.

Thus, equity first needs to be achieved in our present generation in order to bestow an equitable world upon future generations. This does not mean, of course, that we should not pay heed to the interests of future peoples, but that one should disregard the dualism implicit in the distinction between the two forms of equity Too much focus on future generations makes the issue of equity abstract and does not address the dire needs of billions of people living in the world today. However, doing away with the notion of intergenerational equity and introducing a new concept is not a very plausible solution, as already it has been embedded in international environmental law. Rather, a re-interpretation of intergenerational equity is suggested.

The Brundtland Report defines sustainable development as development 'that meets the needs of the present without compromising the ability of future generations to meet their own needs'. The first part refers to present needs and the promotion of equity for the current generation. Thus, equity in the present should not result in a situation where future generations are unable to meet their needs. It is not the other way around: the needs of faceless future generations should not be pursued as a primary goal, with the needs of the current poor perhaps receiving attention thereafter as an incidental matter. Accordingly, in order to pursue future equity, the world needs first to address current inequity (Chowdhury, 1992, p. 256).[29] This amounts to a call for some sort of distributive justice (Chowdhury, 1992, p. 240). The process of distributive justice is, however, qualified by the needs of future generations. This implies a check on current generations. There is no need to make a rigid distinction between the different forms of equity. The equity that is needed must be unlimited in relation to time and space. The acceptance of the importance of intragenerational equity also serves the self-interest of the North, as assistance to the South may prevent environmental destruction that can be seen as a prerequisite for development. In this sense, development which is more sustainable may be pursued.

## 6. TOWARDS A SUSTAINABLE AND EQUITABLE INTERNATIONAL LEGAL ORDER

It is clear that intergenerational equity is something quite different from the traditional view of equity in international law (Falk, 1999, p. 426; Yokota, 1999, p. 584). Intergenerational equity as discussed above is not a rule or source of law. It may be categorised as an ideal or goal, which may challenge the inequity of the current system and guide change in the pursuit of present and future equity. The pursuit of this form of equity may introduce a more equitable international environmental order. Thus, intergenerational equity guides international standard setting and law making pursuant to a new sustainable development world order (Ginther, 1995, p. 30). This process of change has to be seen in the context of the calls for a NIEO. The developing world demanded change to ensure the progressive continuance of the process of decolonisation and the achievement of *de facto* sovereign equality. The NIEO movement has not delivered the necessary results, as the developing world did not have sufficient bargaining power to induce change. The proposals also implied the imposition of unilateral obligations on the developed world, which were not accepted. In general, there was no reason for the developed world to effect radical changes pursuant to equality. Self-interest dictated no necessity for a new order. However, global environmental threats demand change. Developing countries now have more bargaining power as developed countries need them to address global environmental problems in a cooperative manner, as illustrated, for example, by the implementation of the Montreal Protocol.[30] The current environmental crisis therefore presents the South with opportunities to pursue a new order.

While the NIEO has become obsolete, several of its underlying principles have experienced a revival in the environmental field. The most important principles, namely solidarity, cooperation and preferential treatment (now known as differential treatment) will be discussed briefly to examine whether their revival may support the promotion of equity in international environmental law.

## Solidarity

Solidarity implies that states would, through joint or separate action, pursue an outcome that benefits all states or at least does not gravely interfere with the interests of other states (MacDonald, 1995, p. 259). Thus, states should not take into consideration only their own interests in shaping their international interests but also those of other states or the interests of the community of states, or both (Wolfrum, 1995b). Furthermore, the principle of solidarity may aim to ameliorate inequalities of particular states in comparison with others. This implies that in aiming to realise a common goal, some states may have to contribute more than others (ibid.).

Solidarity accordingly implies some form of reciprocity (MacDonald, 1995, p. 280). 'Reciprocity' in this context does not imply equal obligations and therefore does not preclude preferential treatment. Developed countries may, for instance, provide developing countries with assistance, whereas developing countries have the duty to use the assistance efficiently. Solidarity 'should be conceived as the impetus behind genuine cooperative effort on the part of all states. Differences in resources and capacities mean that there will be differences as to how states meet their obligations, but the fact remains that all states share these obligations' (ibid.). Translated into the field of international environmental law, this means that the contributions to funds[31] are not to be seen as charity, but as a realisation of the principle of solidarity. The obligations of the developing countries entail their cooperation in international measures to promote sustainable development. For this purpose, the developing countries need to use the provided funds efficiently.

The principle of solidarity therefore implies that states might need to choose actions that do not interfere with the general well-being and interests of the international community, in particular the interests of developing states. This implies that narrow self-interest must yield to communal interests. Solidarity is of extreme importance in the global pursuit of international environmental equity.

## Cooperation

It is the principle of cooperation that actually gives effect to solidarity. International environmental matters necessitate the imperative of cooperation (Stoll, 1996, p. 39). Although no universal definition exists,[32] it is clear that a characteristic of cooperation is that states aim to achieve common ends (Stoll, 1996, p. 42).[33] The interdependence of actors necessitates coordination. Constructive international relations may be referred to as cooperation (Schreuer, 2001, p. 164).

The United Nations Charter affirms the importance of cooperation. As one example, Art. 1 states that it is one of the purposes of the United Nations Charter 'to achieve international cooperation in solving international problems of an economic, social, cultural, or humanitarian character'.

Principles 5, 7, 9, 12, 13, 14 and 27 of the Rio Declaration elaborate on the concept of cooperation. Verschuuren states: 'Co-operation is no longer simply aimed at the prevention of damage in neighbouring states, but at sustainable (economic and social) development for the whole community, especially developing countries' (Verschuuren, 2003, p. 59). Various environmental treaties also refer to the principle of cooperation. Article 5 of the Convention on Biological Diversity, for instance, reads: 'Each Contracting Party shall, as far as possible and as appropriate, cooperate with other Contracting Parties'. The cooperation principle also has been a central issue in various international disputes, such as the Gabčíkovo-Nagymaros case,[34] although the ICJ has never really has defined the cooperation principle.

## Differential Treatment

The use of preferential treatment of the NIEO has been revived in the form of 'differential treatment' (Rajamani, 2006) in international environmental law. The reason for differential treatment has shifted, Cullet has argued, as it now focuses on 'global environmental needs' whereas previously it was more concerned with the development needs of countries (Cullet, 1999, p. 570). He defines differential treatment 'as the instances where the principle of sovereign equality is sidelined to accommodate extraneous factors, such as divergences in levels of economic development or unequal capacities to tackle a given problem' (Cullet, 1999, p. 563).[35] The conceptual basis of differential treatment is, in particular, solidarity. It is the aim of differential treatment to seek equitable and effective results in the current system. This means that the establishment of a new legal order is not necessarily the goal of differential treatment. Differentiation does not entail every deviation from sovereign equality and rather refers to non-reciprocal arrangements that aim to promote substantive equality in the international arena. The deviations mostly relate to a differentiation between developed and developing countries, though no uniform definition exists.

Differential treatment has three main objectives: it aims to achieve substantive equality, to facilitate cooperation among states and to provide incentives to some states for the implementation of their obligations. Two types of international norms can achieve differentiation (Magraw, 1990, p. 73). The first type is referred to as 'differential' norms. Magraw defines this as a 'norm that on its face provides different, presumably more advantageous, standards for one set of states than for another set'. The differential norms that distinguish between developed and developing countries are of interest in this regard.[36] The second type is a 'contextual' norm which implies a norm that 'on its face provides identical treatment to all states affected by the norm but the application of which requires (or at least permits) consideration of characteristics that might vary from country to country'. Contextual norms may be general or limited. General contextual norms refer to norms where the terms of the norm do not limit the characteristics that may be considered.[37] In terms of limited contextual norms, the indeterminacy of the norm is restricted through the terms of the norm.[38] The relevant characteristics that need to be considered are defined. Contextual and differential terms both allow for differentiation. The difference is that contextual terms require further explanation. Further, it is of interest to note that differential and contextual norms *prima facie* may seem beneficial to developing countries, but this may depend on the perspective from which this is viewed.[39]

## Solidarity, Cooperation, Differential Treatment and Equity

What does the aforementioned mean for this discussion of equity? The aspirations of developing countries in their pursuit for a more equitable world order are reflected in the notion of equity in international environmental law. Solidarity constitutes the bedrock of an aspiration towards a new world order. It replaces the mere pursuit of self-interest of states. This implies that in pursuing the common goal of sustainable development, developed states may have to contribute more than others in meeting common obligations. In this regard, cooperation between states gives effect to solidarity. Furthermore, differential treatment may be seen as a practical application of solidarity. The principle which most clearly reflects the essence of differential treatment in international environmental law is the principle of common but differentiated responsibility (Cullet, 1999, p. 577). This implies that the principle of common but differentiated responsibility included in treaties gives concrete effect to the notion of solidarity.

Thus, the basis for the inclusion of differential treatment provisions in treaties is not charity. Differential treatment provisions aim to pursue equity in international environmental law on the grounds of 'need', 'capability' and 'culpability'.[40] 'Need' refers not only to the need of the developing countries to receive assistance from developing countries in order to promote sustainable development, but also to the need of developed countries to attract cooperation of developing countries in order to combat global environmental degradation. 'Capability' alludes to the ability of richer countries to contribute more to solve the common problem of the degradation of the environment. 'Culpability' refers to the exploitation of the developed world of natural resources for their development. The proposed form of equity therefore entails that developed countries are encumbered with more obligations concerning the finding of solutions for global environmental problems. They need to assist developing countries in their pursuit of sustainable development. In this way, the needs of present generations can be reconciled with those of future generations.

## 7. CONCLUSION

This chapter has attempted to dissect the notion of equity in international law, with specific reference to international environmental law. Traditionally, equity is awarded a very restrictive role in international law, and in general, it is used in a corrective fashion to adjust the harshness of law. The inequality that exists between developed and developing countries has accordingly resulted in the demands for the equitable distribution of wealth between rich and poor. The calls for an NIEO have, however, not led to a just world order. The main reason for the failure of the NIEO might have been the lack of sufficient bargaining power of developing countries.

A very important development is the increasing acceptance of intergenerational equity, which needs to be reinterpreted to focus primarily on the position of present generations. The pursuit of equity in this regard may be conducive to development in developing countries and therefore the eradication of global poverty. The implication of this statement is that intragenerational equity should be the primary focus of sustainable development.

The global environmental crisis, however, presents developing countries with the opportunity to pursue a more equitable international environmental legal order. Developed countries cannot address environmental problems on their own. This scenario strengthens the bargaining power of developing countries in the international arena. The most prominent principles of the NIEO discussed above, namely solidarity, the duty to cooperate and preferential treatment, may assist in the pursuit of equity.

Cooperation between rich and poor states is vital to promote substantive equality. It needs to give concrete expression to solidarity. States should not take into consideration only their own interests in shaping their international interests but also those of other states, in particular those of the developing countries. Cooperation based on solidarity also implies that in realising a common goal, some states need to contribute more than others do. Solidarity also forms the basis for differential treatment as it predetermines a different form of reciprocity that does not imply equal obligations, but differentiated obligations in order to achieve the common goal of sustainable development. This means that concerted efforts to combat environmental degradation must be carried out on the basis of differential treatment. Technical and financial assistance as well as technology transfer between developed and developing countries should therefore take place on the basis of solidarity rather than charity.

In this manner, equity may introduce a new environmental order, which reverts to the calls for a NIEO. The difference is that the ecological crisis already has resulted in the acceptance of intergenerational (and intragenerational) equity and the need to address the environmental problem in a cooperative fashion as well as making provision for the preferential treatment of developing countries. The idea of equity in international environmental law therefore does not imply the imposition of radical unilateral obligations on the developed world as portrayed by the demands of the developing countries during the advocacy for a NIEO. The acceptance of equity in this fashion necessitates the required mechanisms to give effect to differential treatment. Therefore, the time is ripe to call for the continuous commitment of all states, rich and poor, to pursue a New International Sustainable Development Order, which addresses the needs of the poor without depleting the means of future peoples.

# NOTES

* I am grateful for the comments of Professor Ulrich Beyerlin and the editors. The usual caveat applies. This publication was made possible through the generous funding of the Alexander von Humboldt-Stiftung.

1.  Article 2(1) of the United Nations Charter.
2.  Article 1(1) of the United Nations Charter refers to justice, without defining the concept. One approach to evaluate justice is to investigate equity in international law. The ICJ observed that: 'Equity as a legal concept is a direct emanation from the idea of justice'. Equity therefore forms the constituent part of justice. See *Case concerning the Continental Shelf* (Tunisia v. Libyan Arab Jamahiriya ICJ), 24 February 1982, ILM 21:225, page 60, para. 71.
3.  This is, for instance, evident from the failure to create a New International Economic Order.
4.  This means that a judge or an arbiter has a certain amount of discretion in interpreting the law, in clarifying obscurities and in filling minor gaps in the law. The judge or arbiter moves within the bounds of international law and does not need to call on legal authority to apply equity.
5.  This is the case where equity is applied in addition to law, where a tribunal is authorised to decide in accordance with international law and equity.
6.  In this case, the arbitrator might act on the basis of absolute equity to the extent of disregarding technicalities of law, such as the rule requiring exhaustion of local remedies.
7.  *North Sea Continental Shelf Cases* ICJ, 20 February 1969, ILM 8:340.
8.  The scope of the present chapter does not warrant an extensive discussion concerning the issue of delimitation.
9.  See the Helsinki Rules on the Uses of Waters of International Rivers 1966, available at http://www.unece.org/env/water/meetings/legal_board/2010/annexes_groundwater_paper/Annex_II_Helsinki_Rules_ILA.pdf.
10. The collective action of OPEC members in achieving an adjustment of oil prices in 1973 provided an impetus for the demands of developing countries.
11. The Declaration was adopted at the sixth session of the UN General Assembly. Resolution 3201-S.VI of 1 May 1974.
12. Resolution 3202-S.VI of 1 May 1974.
13. Resolution 3281-XXIX of 12 December 1974.
14. Para. 1, for instance, states that technological progress is not shared equitably. The Programme of Action for the Establishment of a New International Economic Order (G.A. Res. 3202 (S-VI) of 1 May 1974) also includes references to equity, at para. 1(d).
15. Developed countries raised serious doubts regarding the legal character of the Charter.
16. The Preamble of the Charter also refers to equity.
17. See, for instance, the Preamble, Chapter 1, Arts 4, 8, 9, 11, 12, 13, 17, 19 and 23.
18. ILA, Report of the Sixty-Second Conference, held at Seoul, 30 August 1986. It is interesting to note that the preamble of the New Delhi Declaration of Principles of International Law Relating to Sustainable Development of 2002 (UN Doc. A/57/329) affirms the Declaration; see http://www.ilahq.org.
19. It is, however, interesting to note that the ILA Declaration does not regard equity as a source of law, but rather as something that may be applied to supplement the law.
20. See also Edith Brown Weiss (1990); for a critical analysis of the work of Brown Weiss, see P.A. Baressi (1997) and the reply of Brown Weiss (1997) at 89; see also Gregory F. Maggio (1996–97); Oscar Schachter already referred to the importance of this concept in the 1970s (Schachter, 1977).
21. A generation owes these duties to future generations as a class, irrespective of nationality. Brown Weiss (1989a), p. 27.
22. Request for an Examination of the Situation in Accordance with Paragraph 63 of the Court's 1974 Judgment in the Case concerning Nuclear Tests (New Zealand v. France

case) (Dissenting opinion of Judge Weeramantry), ICJ Report, 22 September 1995, 341. See also Maritime Delimitation in the Area between Greenland and Jan Mayen (Separate Opinion of Judge Weeramantry), ICJ Report, 14 June 1993, 277 (Para. 242).

23. *Advisory Opinion on the Legality of the Threat or Use of Nuclear Weapons* ICJ, (1996) ILM 809 at 888. He furthermore states that: 'Juristic opinion is now abundant, with several major treatises appearing upon the subject and with such concepts as intergenerational equity [...] well established'. See para. 29, page 821. This statement was reaffirmed in the case concerning the *Gabcíkovo-Nagymaros Project* (Hungary v. Slovakia) of 25 September 1997, (1998) 37 ILM 162, para. 53. See also the decision of the Supreme Court of the Philippines in *Minors Oposa v. Secretary of the Department of Environment and Natural Resource*, Supreme Court of the Philippines, No. 101083 (30 July 1993).

24. WCED (1987), *Our Common Future* (Brundtland Report), Oxford University Press: Oxford.

25. The term 'sustainable development' was coined in the Brundtland Report.

26. See also New Delhi Principles: 'the principle of equity is central to the attainment of sustainable development'. It is interesting to note that this principle is referred to as the 'principle of equity and the eradication of poverty'. The paragraph makes it clear that states that have already achieved national intragenerational equity must assist other states in the eradication of poverty where they are capable of this.

27. Mayeda notes that: 'it makes little sense to speak of "equity" between the past and the present, or between past and future, when our past is littered with examples of environmental harmful policies and approaches, and with maltreatment of both humans and the environment'.

28. The focus on future generations generates the most critique; see D'Amato (1990), and critique against the viewpoint of D'Amato by Lothar Gündling (1990).

29. The Environmental Kuznets Curve supports this line of reasoning; see Levinson (2002).

30. Montreal Protocol on Substances that Deplete the Ozone Layer, (1987) 28 ILM 649.

31. See for example Art. 10 of the Montreal Protocol, and the call for a World Solidarity Fund' to eradicate poverty and to promote social and human development in the developing countries. Para. II,7, subpara. (b) Plan of Implementation of the World Summit on Sustainable Development.

32. See Rüdiger Wolfrum (1995a).

33. Stoll distinguishes the 'law on cooperation' from the 'law of cooperation'.

34. (1998) 37 ILM 162.

35. Differential treatment has strong affinities with preferential treatment as conceived in international development law. Differential treatment in this chapter does not refer to the arrangements that increase inequality.

36. See Art. 2 of the Montreal Protocol.

37. See Art. X.2 of the 1972 Convention on International Liability for Damage Caused by Space Objects 18 ILM 899 (1979).

38. An example is Art. 4 of the 1972 World Heritage Convention, which requires that a party 'do all it can to this end, to the utmost of its own resources'.

39. For example, the differential treatment in Art. 5 of the Montreal Protocol that allows developing countries to delay compliance also may be detrimental to the interests of developing countries.

40. 'Need' in terms of current international environmental law may be defined also to include the needs of the developed world as they are dependent on the developing world to combat environmental degradation. This may cancel out the idea of 'charity' which once again superimposes inequality between the 'haves' and 'have-nots'.

# REFERENCES

Anand, Ruchi (2004), *International Environmental Justice: A North–South Dimension*, Aldershot: Ashgate Publishing Ltd.

Baressi, P.A. (1997), 'Beyond fairness to future generations: an intragenerational alternative to intergenerational equity in the international environmental arena', *Tulane Environmental Law Journal*, **11**, 59–88.

Baslar, Kemal (1998), *The Concept of the Common Heritage of Mankind in International Law*, Dordrecht: Martinus Nijhoff Publishers.

Bedjaoui, Mohammed (1979), *Towards a New International Economic Order*, New York: Holmes & Meier Publications.

Beyerlin, Ulrich (2006), 'Bridging the north–south divide in international environmental law', *Zeitschrift für ausländisches öffentliches Recht und Völkerrecht*, **66**, 259–296.

Blecher, M.D. (1979), 'Equitable delimitation of Continental Shelf', *American Journal of International Law*, **73**, 60–87.

Bollecker-Stern, Brigitte (1980), 'The Legal Character of Emerging Norms Relating to the New International Economic Order: Some Comments', in Kamal Hossain (ed.), *Legal Aspects of the New International Economic Order*, London: Frances Pinter Publishers.

Brown Weiss, Edith (1989), *In Fairness to Future Generations: International Law, Common Patrimony, and Intergenerational Equity*, New York: Transnational Publishers Inc.

Brown Weiss, Edith (1990), 'Our rights and obligations to future generations for the environment', *American Journal of International Law*, **94**, 198–207.

Brown Weiss, Edith (1997) 'A reply to Barresi's "Beyond fairness to future generations"', *Tulane Environmental Law Journal*, **11**, 89.

Bulajić, Milan (1980), 'Legal Aspects of the NIEO', in Kamal Hossain (ed.), *Legal Aspects of the New International Economic Order*, London: Frances Pinter Publishers Ltd.

Cassese, Antonio (1986), *International Law in a Divided World*, New York: Clarendon Press.

Chowdhury, Subrata Roy (1992), 'Intergenerational Equity: Substratum of the Right to Sustainable Development', in Subrata Roy Chowdhury (ed.), *The Right to Development in International Law*, Dordrecht: Kluwer Academic Publishers.

Cullet, Philippe (1999), 'Differential treatment in international law: towards a new paradigm of inter-state relations', *European Journal of International Law*, **10**, 549–566.

D'Amato, Anthony (1990), 'Do we owe a duty to future generations to preserve the global environment?', *American Journal of International Law*, **84**, 190–198.

Falk, Richard (1999), 'The pursuit of international justice: present dilemmas and an imagined future', *Journal of International Affairs*, **52**, 409–411.

Franck Thomas M. (1995), *Fairness in International Law and Institutions*, New York: Oxford University Press.

Friedmann, Wolfgang (1970), 'The North Sea Continental Shelf Cases – a critique', *American Journal of International Law*, **64**, 229–236.

Gillespie, Alexander (1997), *International Environmental Law, Policy and Ethics*, Oxford: Clarendon Press.

Ginther, Konrad (1995), 'Comment on the Paper by Edith Brown Weiss', in Winfried Lang (ed.), *Sustainable Development in International Law*, London: Graham & Trotman/Martinus Nijhoff.

Gündling, Lothar (1990), 'Our responsibility to future generations', *American Journal of International Law*, **84**, 207–212.

Harris, P.G. (2000), 'Defining international distributive justice: environmental considerations', *International Relations*, **15**, 51–56.

Hossain, Kamal (1980), 'General Principles, the Charter of Economic Rights and Duties of States, and the NIEO', in Kamal Hossain (ed.), *Legal Aspects of the New International Economic Order*, London: Frances Pinter Publishers Ltd.

Janis, Mark Weston (1983), 'The ambiguity of equity in international law', *Brooklyn Journal of International Law*, **9**, 7–9.

Johnston, Todd (1998–1999), 'The role of intergenerational equity in a sustainable future: the continuing problem of third world debt and development', *Buffalo Environmental Law Journal*, **6**, 36–83.

Kaur, Gurpreet (2002), 'Beyond law or within law? Equitable considerations in international law: an analysis', *Indian Journal of International Law*, **42**, 312–328.

Khurshid, Salman (1980), 'Justice and the New International Economic Order', in Kamal Hossain (ed.), *Legal Aspects of the New International Economic Order*, London: Frances Pinter Publishers Ltd., pp. 108–112.

Kingsbury, Benedict (1998), 'Sovereignty and inequality', *European Journal of International Law*, **9**, 599–625.

Levinson, A. (2002), 'The Ups and Downs of the Environmental Kuznet's Curve', in John List and Aart de Zeeuw (eds), *Recent Advances in Environmental Economics*, Cheltenham, UK and Northampton, MA, USA: Edward Elgar.

Macdonald, Ronald St. J. (1995), 'Solidarity in the practice and discourse of public international law', *Pace International Law Review*, **8**, 259.

Maggio, Gregory F. (1996–1997), 'Inter/intra-generational equity: current applications under international law for promoting the sustainable development of natural resources', *Buffalo Environmental Law Journal*, **4**, 161–223.

Magraw, Daniel (1990), 'Legal treatment of developing countries: differential, contextual and absolute norms', *Colorado Journal of International Environmental Law and Policy*, **1**, 69–99.

Makarczyk, Jerzy (1988), *Principles of a New International Economic Order*, Dordrecht: Martinus Nijhoff Publishers.

Mayeda, Graham (2004), 'Where should Johannesburg take us? Ethical and legal approaches to sustainable development in the context of international environmental law', *Colorado Journal of International Environmental Law and Policy*, **15**, 29–48.

McIntyre, Owen (2007), *Environmental Protection of International Watercourses under International Law*, Aldershot: Ashgate Publishing Ltd.

Mickelson, Karin (2000), 'South, north, international environmental law and international environmental lawyers', *Yearbook of International Environmental Law*, **11**, 52–64.

Nawaz, Tawfique (1980), *Equity and the New International Economic Order: A Note*, Westport, Connecticut: Greenwood Press.

Ntambirweki, John (1990–1991), 'The developing countries in the evolution of an international environmental law', *Hastings International & Comparative Law Review*, **14**, 905–907.

Rajamani, Lavanya (2006), *Differential Treatment in International Environmental Law*, Oxford: Oxford University Press.

Sands, P. (2003), *Principles of International Environmental Law*, Oxford: Oxford University Press.

Schachter, Oscar (1977), *Sharing the World's Resources*, New York: Columbia University Press.

Schreuer, Christopher (2001), 'State Sovereignty and the Duty of States to Cooperate – Two Incompatible Notions (Summary and Comments)', in Jost von Delbrück (ed.), *International Law of Cooperation and State Sovereignty Proceedings of an International Symposium of the Kiel Walther-Schücking Institute of International Law, May 23–26 2001*, Berlin: Duncker & Humboldt.

Simpson, Gerry (2004), *Great Powers and Outlaw States: Unequal Sovereigns in the International Legal Order*, Cambridge: Cambridge University Press.

Speth, James Gustav (2004), 'International environmental law: can it deal with the big issues?' *Vermont Law Review*, **28**, 779–789.

Stoll, Peter-Tobias (1996), 'The International Environmental Law of Cooperation', in Rüdiger Wolfrum (ed.), *Enforcing Environmental Standards: Economic Mechanisms as Viable Means*? Berlin: Springer.

Tiewul, Azadon (1975), 'The United Nations Charter of Economic Rights and Duties of States', *The Journal of International Law and Economics*, **10**, 645–686.

Verschuuren, Jonathan (2003), *Principles of Environmental Law*, Baden-Baden: Nomos Verlagsges, MBH.

Wolfrum, Rüdiger (1995a), 'International Law of Cooperation' in Rudolf Bernhardt (ed.), *Encyclopedia of Public International Law*, North-Holland: Elsevier, pp. 1242–1247.

Wolfrum, Rüdiger (1995b), 'Solidarity Amongst States: An Emerging Structural Principle of International Law', in Pierre-Marie Dupuy, Barbo Fassbender, Malcolm N. Shaw and Karl-Peter Sommermann (eds), *Völkerrecht als Wertordnung: Festschrift für Christian Tomuschat*, Kehl: N.P. Engel Verlag, pp. 1087–1101.

Yokota, Yozo (1999), 'International justice and the global environment', *Journal of International Affairs*, **52**, 583–598.

# 9. The courts and public participation in environmental decision-making

## Karen Morrow[*]

---

## 1. INTRODUCTION

In recent years, enhanced rights for the public to access information and participate in environmental regulation prompted by pursuing the sustainable development agenda have ostensibly wrought considerable change in the operation of environmental decision-making in the UK. This chapter considers the effectiveness of such initiatives and in particular the role of case law and the judiciary in this regard.

Historically, regulatory processes in the United Kingdom have been characterised by an institutional culture that combines elements that are generally hostile to meaningful public participation, notably professionalism and secrecy. In the environmental sphere, problems securing effective engagement are further aggravated by the often highly technical and complex issues involved, especially the difficulties posed by 'asymmetric information' in participation contexts (Lewis, 1999).[1] This is arguably a problem that permeates the whole participation process, founded on differentials in the availability and understanding of information itself. The role of the public in environmental decision-making processes has been fraught with particular difficulty. New systems of legal entitlement to information attempt to address the former, though the fact that much information in the environmental field is intractably technical and confusing to the layman is generally not touched upon.[2]

A number of initiatives, spurred in particular by the UN/ECE Convention on Access to Information, Public Participation in Decision-making and Access to Justice in Environmental Matters 1998 (the Aarhus Convention)[3] have sought to remedy some of the problems encountered in this regard. This chapter will consider recent developments in this area in order to evaluate to what extent, if any, the law has been effective in bringing about changes in the way that environmental decisions are taken.

The promotion of public participation in environmental decision-making is widely regarded as a social good, if not (as yet) a universal norm, and a great deal has been written about its supposed benefits. The confines of this chapter do not, however, allow more than a brief discussion of the rationale for this development. A considerable variety of reasons are commonly given for pursuing the participation agenda, and these are inextricably linked to some of the most fundamental elements of modern governance. They commonly include: democratic values (participation is thought to promote public 'ownership' of decisions that often affect not only the immediate parties to the process in question, but also the broader public interest); accountability (participation can be viewed as endorsing transparent and open decision-making processes and requiring that decisions be adequately justified); improved decision-making (given the complexity of the issues involved in environmental decision-making, methodologies which gather information from a broad range of sources are viewed as likely to be more robust) and education (awareness of salient issues generated on the part of the decision-maker, the applicant, statutory consultees and the public).

As things stand, the democratic credentials of participation have been very much to the fore, but the fact that a great deal of the impetus for legal development in this area has come from the international law of sustainable development requires that the participation agenda be subjected to renewed scrutiny.

## 2.   ROOTS AND GROWTH OF PUBLIC PARTICIPATION IN ENVIRONMENTAL DECISION-MAKING

**International**

At the UNCED in 1992, in particular under the auspices of the Rio Declaration (notably Principle 10) and Agenda 21, and subsequently through the ongoing work of the Commission for Sustainable Development (CSD) and regional groups such as the United Nations Economic Commission for Europe (UNECE), the international community sought to put in place the necessary machinery to progress sustainable development. It would be fair to say that the potential ramifications that such a cultural shift in governance would generate were not fully appreciated at the time. The rhetoric of sustainable development has proved instrumental in shaping the participation agenda in a number of ways, notably requiring engagement not only by states but also by major groups (including business, NGOs, women and indigenous peoples) and even individuals. In this regard participation serves to emphasise the 'bottom-up' decision-making that is integral to the articulation and practice of sustainable development.

In this context public participation in environmental decision-making can be viewed as a key component of sustainable development, contributing to all three interwoven facets of that concept. It is obvious that public participation adds to the social dimension of sustainability by broadening the base of decision-making to bring the community into play, hopefully increasing the range of factors considered and the efficacy and acceptability of the eventual outcome. However, public participation also expands the environmental facet of sustainability, by providing for consideration of alternative and additional perspectives: since environmental decisions rarely affect only the applicant and the regulator but also impose impacts upon other individuals and the host community, it is imperative that these impacts are considered in decision-making processes. This factor shades over into the economic element of sustainable development, as it provides a clear opportunity to underline externalities in decision-making processes, something markedly absent from preceding regulatory regimes.

The UN has continued to actively engage with the participation agenda, not least through the WSSD and the adoption of the Johannesburg Principles on the Role of Law and Sustainable Development[4] and its related work programme.

Actualising public participation as an exercise in improving the democratic credentials of environmental decision-making is, however, a far-reaching and immensely complex task, and one that is perhaps proving to be even more so than may have been envisaged at the time. The Aarhus Convention attempts to import the Rio values relating to public participation to the UNECE area. The Aarhus regime is certainly ambitious, and its implementation has proved problematic (Carnwath, 2004). The Aarhus regime comprises three pillars: access to environmental information; public participation in environmental decision-making; and access to law, in order to challenge decisions that infringe the first two pillars.

**European Union**

The EU is a signatory to the Aarhus Convention, and has therefore adopted a suite of measures to address the Aarhus requirements both in respect of Member States and the Community institutions. These are Directives 2003/4 on public access to environmental information and 2003/35 providing for public participation in respect of certain plans and programmes relating to the environment (the SEA Directive) which apply to Member States. Regulation

(EC) No 1367/2006 and the application of the provisions of the Aarhus Convention relates to Community institutions and bodies.

# 3. UNITED KINGDOM LAW

The UK ratified the Aarhus Convention on 24 February 2005 and has also put legislation in place to address the EU Directives referred to above. This section outlines key aspects of domestic law by reference to the 'three pillars' of the Aarhus Convention.

## Information

The Aarhus Convention and relevant EU laws are primarily implemented in the UK by the Environmental Information Regulations 2004 (SI 2004/3391) (Coppel, 2005).[5] Access to information is foundational in the context of participation, constituting the threshold for other access rights. While this is straightforward in principle, it is considerably less so in practice. The specific Aarhus-based information regime provided by the 2004 Regulations is, on the whole, more generous than that which applies more generally in the UK under the Freedom of Information Act 2000.

## Defining Participation

Participation is a multi-layered activity that can be broken into two main stages: participation in decision-making processes (including policy making) and participation proceedings to challenge the outcomes of said processes. Several regimes that pre-date Aarhus and accord a central role to public participation, notably the EIA and pollution permitting processes, have been amended to give effect to the enhanced public participation requirements. While such provisions do doubtless boost compliance with the Aarhus Convention, the fact remains that the participation arrangements currently in place comprise a complex patchwork of provisions that is arguably more difficult for lay users to access and interpret than it needs to be. A broader provision, laying out clear and simple participation arrangements applicable to environmental regulation more generally, would be desirable in principle and useful in practice. In any event, as the case law discussed below demonstrates, current regulations at best offer comparatively limited opportunities for public participation, which in this context tend to be pragmatic and piecemeal.

## Participation in Decision-making Processes

While this aspect of public participation can be problematic, it is not particularly novel, in particular through its now supposedly well-established role in the Environmental Impact Assessment (EIA) regime. Even in this area however, participation can prove problematic, as demonstrated in *R (on the application of Hereford Waste Watchers Ltd) v Herefordshire County Council* [2005] EWHC 191 (admin), a judicial review of a grant of planning permission for a waste treatment and recycling facility. When the permission was granted, the Council, instead of carrying out an EIA, attached conditions requiring further information with respect to emissions from the site. Hereford Waste Watchers (HWW) argued that lack of information as to the significance of certain environmental effects of the novel waste treatment process that was proposed invalidated the permission, by breaching EIA requirements. HWW argued that it had been deprived of its opportunity to be fully consulted on the potential environmental impacts of the site. Indeed, while Herefordshire County Council may perhaps have had limited experience in dealing with EIA (vastly variable numbers of applications arise across the UK) at this juncture, where the process is well established in principle and practice, failure to adequately address the issue is little short of mystifying.

Elias J upheld HWW's claim on the basis of the EIA argument. He stated (at para 25) that, while the Council's approach may have been adequate to address the practical issues raised, to uphold it would 'frustrate the democratic purpose' of the enhanced consultation requirements of EIA. In this he took a purposive approach, following from Lord Hoffman's speech in *Berkeley v Secretary of State for the Environment Transport and the Regions* [2001] 2 AC 603, 615,[6] which emphasised both the procedural and information requirements of EIA:

> The directly enforceable right of the citizen which is accorded by the Directive is not merely a right to a fully informed decision on the substantive issue. It must have been adopted on an appropriate basis and that requires the inclusive and democratic procedure prescribed by the Directive in which the public ... is given an opportunity to express its opinion on the environmental issues.

> This gets to the heart of public participation in environmental decision-making; while the rights involved are, for the most part, procedural, those rights exist to protect the notion of valid public input into such processes.

Commenting on the *Herefordshire* case, Edwards alludes to the fact that this area of public consultation enjoys enhanced status in consequence of the broader developments in the field, prompted by flourishing sustainability praxis, notably under the Aarhus Convention (Edwards, 2005), which appear to facilitate judicial intervention in cases such as that under consideration.

In *Edwards v Environment Agency* [2006] EWCA Civ 877, Edwards was the nominal claimant in an appeal against a refusal to grant relief in a judicial claim in respect of a Pollution Prevention and Control (PPC) permit issued to Rugby Ltd for continued/altered operation of their cement plant. As part of the process Rugby sought permission to partially substitute the fuel for its kiln with waste tyres; as a result, public health concerns became prominent in the lengthy consultation process. The Environment Agency (EA) sought additional information from Rugby and asked its Air Quality Monitoring and Assessment Unit (AQMAU) to review it. The AQMAU determined that, while the tyre burning was unlikely to cause problems, dust emissions did raise concerns. The EA did not make public all of the information that it received and generated in this process and furthermore refused a request by a member of the public to do so, on the basis that the information was 'integral' to a decision yet to be taken which would be prejudiced if it were released.

The PPC permit was granted with conditions attached requiring a trial of the tyre burning and limiting dust emissions. A claim for judicial review was then instituted. The claim initially focused on the tyre burning issue, as full information was not disclosed until a day or two before the hearing. In response, the claimants changed tack to emphasise the dust issue, and Lindsay J allowed them to reformulate their grounds on the basis that even if the EA had not breached either the EIA or IPPC Directives, the non-disclosure infringed the 'common law duty of fairness to provide fully informed consultation before making its decision' (para 22 CA).

Lindsay J, however, went on to decide that the failure to disclose had not been significant and as such refused to exercise his discretion to grant relief. The claimants appealed. The Court of Appeal upheld the initial decision though it did refer (at para 88) to the 'generally applicable domestic jurisprudence requiring public authorities to act fairly in consultation processes'. The court added that this did not generally require decision-makers to reveal their internal decision-making processes. In this case, however, the court ruled (at para 106) that the information was material and failure to include it in the consultation breached the common law duty of fairness. Nonetheless, the court agreed that the judge had the discretion to refuse relief.

Serious questions arise in *Edwards*. In the first place, it is almost inexplicable how the EA, as a competent regulator with vast experience of public participation requirements in pollution control contexts, could have shown such a cavalier disregard for what fairness required of it in this case.

The institutional culture demonstrated in *Edwards* seems to owe more to a traditional and rather secretive model that excludes the public from what is seen as an *inter partes* process between the applicant and the regulator, than to a modern more democratic style of decision-making.

Secondly the lack of a remedy in *Edwards* makes it is highly questionable that the Aarhus requirements would be satisfied. While the environment may not have been damaged as a result of the flaws in the decision-making process in Edwards itself, this was purely fortuitous. At the very least, more could be done in cases of this type to discourage future repetition of such poor practice: the public interest in good administration has been harmed by failing to penalise such high-handed behaviour and it is arguable that a sanction of some sort would be in order to provide a secure legal underpinning for public participation. One possibility is that decision makers who find themselves in this position should be required to pay a small sum in damages into a fund to facilitate future environmental litigation. This would have the dual advantage of sending the right signals to decision makers and to the public, and it would offer a creative solution to the problem of financing environmental litigation discussed below while creatively interpreting Article 9(5) of the Aarhus Convention, on the establishment of mechanisms to tackle barriers on access to justice.

**Participation in Policy Making**

Participation in the making of policy is arguably more controversial than participation in decision-making processes, invoking direct public input in the strategic political process, rather than premising such involvement on specific concern with particular projects; it is certainly more novel. This is demonstrated in two recent cases. The first is *R (on the application of London Borough of Wandsworth) et al v Secretary of State for Transport et al* [2005] EWHC 314 (admin) which involved complex interlinked challenges to the Government's aviation White Paper, with particular reference to airport provision in the South East of England. The White Paper was adopted after a broad and lengthy consultation process which, given its controversial subject matter, Sullivan J described (at para 311) as an 'impressive attempt' to engage with fraught issues and arrive at a coherent policy response.

The claims in *Wandsworth* expressed various concerns about the consultation exercise. Sullivan J dealt with the claims under a number of headings including: The 'Heathrow challenge', which concerned alleged unfairness in adopting policies that were not 'foreshadowed' in the consultation procedures, was rejected as unfounded. The 'Stansted claim', based on the argument that the policy was unduly prescriptive, succeeded as the court determined that there was inadequate environmental information to justify favouring the preferred option at this stage. The 'Luton claim' succeeded on the basis of fairness, as the proposal had not in fact been consulted on.

What was actually at issue in *Wandsworth* was discontent with the outcome of a consultation and policy making process. In adopting policy in such a complex and controversial area, it is perhaps inevitable that consultation will be flawed in some respects: the question then becomes one of determining which defects will justify judicial intervention. Inclusive consultation, while it may serve to dissipate some disagreement amongst stakeholders, will necessarily result (at best) in a compromise between often wildly divergent perspectives, and it will never satisfy all concerned. The role of the courts in this area is not to tackle disagreements on the merits of policies adopted, nor to 'wield a blue pencil' and simply remove objectionable elements from the policy. The decision adopted to grant declaratory relief in a broad form seems to address the need to vindicate the claims, without straying into the merits. It takes into account that any policy will have adverse effects on some stakeholders and their interests may ultimately conflict not only with the view of the policy maker, but also with those of other stakeholders. The purpose of consultation is not to deliver guaranteed outcomes for participants, but rather to give them an opportunity to air their views and have them considered before a particular course is adopted.

There is a danger that discontented participants may attempt to use the procedural protections offered by Aarhus-based provisions in order to re-open debate, though the broadly purposive approach adopted by the court in *Wandsworth*, and notions of proportionality, will serve to minimise the attractiveness of such a strategy.

If the *Wandsworth* case, taken as a whole, represented a good approach to realising public participation in policy making, then the case of *R (on the application of Greenpeace Ltd) v Secretary of State for Trade and Industry* [2007] EWHC 311 (admin) tells a very different story. Greenpeace sought a quashing order in respect of the Government's decision in 'The Energy Challenge Review Report' 2006 to support building new nuclear power stations in the UK (referred to as 'nuclear new build') as part of the UK's future energy mix. In a 2003 White Paper, the Government had decided against supporting nuclear new build, opting instead to concentrate on renewables. The paper stated (at para 4.86) that:

> Before any decision to proceed with the building of nuclear power stations, there would need to be the fullest public consultation

In 2005 the Secretary of State announced a review of the 2003 paper, promising 'extensive public and stakeholder consultation'.[7] The consultation paper 'Our Energy Challenge' explicitly stated that, because of changed circumstances relating to energy supply, nuclear new build would be reconsidered, but added that at this stage, no policy proposals on the issue were being put forward. In the body of the paper, discussion of nuclear power was extremely limited. An additional summary document 'Our Energy Challenge – Have Your Say' was also issued and a series of consultation events and 'stakeholder seminars' was held.

*The Energy Challenge: Energy Review Report* was published in 2006,[8] stating that the government proposed to facilitate nuclear new build by the private sector. A consultation exercise on nuclear new build was instituted, and a White Paper was promised by the end of 2006. Waste issues were to be resolved on the basis of the forthcoming Committee on Radioactive Waste Management Report.

Greenpeace's challenge to the Energy Review was based on an alleged breach of legitimate expectation that the express promise that a change of policy on nuclear new build would only be adopted following 'the fullest public consultation'. In this regard, it was argued that the 2006 'Consultation Paper' was in fact only an 'Issues Paper', as it was inadequate to attain the status of the former on the basis that: first, it was vague/unclear as to what consultees were being asked to respond to; second, it lacked adequate information for consultees to respond intelligently; and third, it was incomplete, as much of the information on which the Government's decision was based post-dated the consultation exercise. Sullivan J deemed the issue justiciable despite its challenge to a 'high level strategic policy document',[9] as the promise that had allegedly been broken had also been made at the highest level. He added (at para 49):

> Whatever the position may be in other policy areas, in the development of policy in the environmental field consultation is no longer a privilege to be granted or withheld by the executive. The United Kingdom Government is a signatory to … the Aarhus Convention.

It should, however, be noted that the Aarhus Convention leaves challenges to failures in consultation on policy development to the discretion of signatory states and there is considerable room for governments to manoeuvre on this issue. Having referred to Aarhus, Sullivan J went on to pursue the consultation issues through domestic administrative law. He took the view (at para 63) that, while consultation did not have to be perfect in order to escape review (referring to the decision maker's broad discretion in this regard) the court could and would intervene where it found: 'not merely that something went wrong, but that something went "clearly and radically" wrong'.

In this case, Sullivan J found that, reading the 2006 'consultation paper' as a whole, and in context, it did in fact amount to an 'issues paper'. He gave a number of reasons for this including: the minimal time period allowed for consultation;[10] the (limited) express purpose of the document; the very broad nature of the 'key question' posed; allusions to the paper in question forming 'part of a process'; the fact that no 'in principle' question was asked; the content of the summary document; and the lack of substantive coverage. Thus the consultation that had been carried out was deemed to be unfair to the extent that it was seriously flawed, and the outcome unforeseeable to participants. Sullivan J granted a declaration to this effect – though not the quashing order that the claimants sought.

One final issue worthy of comment arising from the *Greenpeace* case is the fact that Sullivan J took the view that, in this case, consultation at common law should be geared to the general public, stating (at para 115) that:

> The public, and not simply those who happened to be 'in the know', were entitled to be given sufficient information … and without [it] they could not be expected to make any, let alone an informed, response.

This approach is both interesting and welcome. The Aarhus Convention itself, partly because of the influence exercised by NGOs in its development, tends to view participation by organised interest groups as a form of proxy for participation by the general public (Morrow, 2005). While this recognises the reality that NGOs play a prominent role in this area, it is not desirable that a prescriptive approach should be adopted and that, in the light of the broader participatory ethos of sustainability, there should always be room for individuals to participate in their own right.

The fact that the purpose of the consultation in both the *Wandsworth* and *Greenpeace* cases was to remove or curtail discussion of controversial issues at subsequent public inquiries greatly concerned the courts and they made full use of the common law concept of fairness in order to ensure that appropriate consultation was undertaken.

## Participation in Litigation (Access to Justice)

Insofar as access to justice, another key aspect of sustainable decision-making is concerned, participation in litigation, while not the only indicator of compliance with the Aarhus requirements (in particular those contained in Article 9) is arguably one of the most significant indices available. In the UK, given the dearth of third party rights to challenge regulatory decisions by appeal, judicial review provides the prime means of challenge. Despite a Department of Environment, Food and Rural Affairs' (DEFRA) statement that judicial review is Aarhus-compliant,[11] this remains open to question, in particular with regard to substantive review. Judicial review does, however, on the face of things, satisfy the procedural review requirement as, while there may be some debate as to the breadth of the grounds of judicial review in UK law in comparison with administrative law in other jurisdictions, differences in this sphere are more often of degree than of type. Key access to justice issues in the Aarhus Convention include standing, remedies and costs.

**Standing**

Article 9(2) of the Aarhus Convention broadly requires that members of the public (including NGOs) with a sufficient interest in the matter/whose rights have been impaired should have access to the courts or other independent review procedures dealing with both substantive and procedural issues raised by the decision in question.

Procedural fetters on standing have long been addressed fairly effectively in the environmental sphere by the willingness of the UK courts to use their discretion[12] on what constitutes a 'sufficient interest' for the purposes of standing/permission generously in judicial review. This is demonstrated in *R v Her Majesty's Inspectorate of Pollution (HMIP) and the Minister of Agriculture, Fisheries and Food, ex parte Greenpeace* [1994] 2 CMLR 548. This case concerned a judicial review of the permitting process applied to the Thermal Oxide Reprocessing Plant (THORP) at the Sellafield nuclear facility. Although the claim ultimately failed on its merits, Greenpeace was granted standing for the purposes of judicial review for a number of reasons: it had members in the local area; it had recognised expertise in the field; and in order to ensure that the matters in hand received the attention of the courts. The approach was more generous still in *R v Secretary of State for Foreign and Commonwealth Affairs, ex parte World Development Movement* [1995] 1 WLR 386, in which standing was accorded to an NGO in a context where, although its members would not be affected by the impugned decision, had it not been allowed to proceed, a serious allegation of potential illegality would not have been subject to legal scrutiny.

Thus it can be seen that courts ultimately enjoy considerable discretion and power when determining access to judicial review, though this discretion is not always exercised in the claimant's favour as, for example, in *Ewing v Office of the Deputy Prime Minister* [2005] EWCA Civ 1583. In this case the courts were called upon the deal with a claim involving that rare but much feared creature, the vexatious litigant. Ewing, who wished to prevent the demolition of a hotel in Weston-Super-Mare had a reputation as one such and, as a result, he faced procedural barriers on standing which he attempted to circumvent by joining with others as 'heritage campaigners', in this case the Euston Trust. His strategy was ultimately unsuccessful. In conclusion, insofar as far as standing is concerned, judicial practice in adopting a broadly generous (though not uncritical) exercise of discretion on standing ensures that judicial review is in compliance with Article 9(2) of the Aarhus Convention.

## Remedies

One issue that arises repeatedly when looking at information/participation cases is the question of what amounts to an appropriate remedy. Article 9(4) of the Aarhus Convention requires that signatory states make available 'adequate and effective remedies, including injunctive relief as appropriate'.

In the UK, while a range of judicial review remedies is available in principle against all public authorities, cases involving the Crown are more complex. In such cases, while injunctions may be awarded against individual ministers, as determined in *M v Home Office* [1993] 3 All ER 537, the courts may not award them against the Crown as such. This would seem to fail to satisfy the Aarhus Convention requirements and is likely to prove a particularly vexed issue in cases involving policy. Having said this, in practice, awarding declaratory relief will normally suffice to 'encourage' the Crown to act, as in the *Greenpeace* case, above.

Another major issue with remedies in the UK case law appears to lie in a general view that when development has been undertaken or permits issued, then the case against the decision is deemed, almost as a matter of course, to become 'abstract', and thus not to warrant a remedy as, for example, *Edwards*. It is, however, at least arguable that, once what should have been protected is lost or the public interest in participation has been thwarted, the best return on public investment in litigation is to use it to send a message about what is and is not acceptable behaviour for decision makers who later find themselves in like circumstances.

## Cost

Article 9(4) of the Aarhus Convention specifically requires that remedies be 'equitable, timely and not prohibitively expensive' and it is in this area, perhaps more than in any other, that the UK is having problems in convincingly pursuing the Aarhus agenda. One of the most significant fetters on public access to the courts is the cost of bringing proceedings. Litigation is, at best, a costly business and the prospect of costs order, should the claimant fail, can have significant potential to dissuade potential claimants from having recourse to the courts. Whilst the public funding system (previously known as legal aid) is available in principle to fund environmental litigation (including public interest litigation, which is doubly problematic) in practice, even where claimants qualify, the civil legal aid system in general is under such intense pressure that the Legal Services Commission can only fund a tiny number of claims of this type. Legal aid in general, and civil legal aid in particular (following the Access to Justice Act 1999), is under immense pressure and is unable to keep pace with increased rights of access to the courts, not least those under the Aarhus Convention, as the Court of Appeal observed in *R. (on the application of Burkett) v Hammersmith (No.2)* [2004] EWCA Civ 1342, discussed below.

The courts have developed their own discretion to costs to facilitate public interest litigation through the adoption of Protective Costs Orders (PCOs) which serve to limit the sums that losing claimants will have to pay in respect of the defendant's costs.[13] The leading case on PCOs is *R (on the application of Corner House Research) v Secretary of State for Trade and Industry* [2005] EWCA Civ 192.[14] Environmental litigation would seem to fall squarely within the requirements identified by Brooke LJ, giving judgement in *Cornerhouse* as justifying the imposition of a PCO. These include the court being satisfied that: the issues raised are of general public importance and require resolution; the claimant has no private interest in the outcome; having regard to the financial resources of the parties, it is fair and just to make an order; and if the order were not made, the claimant would probably discontinue the litigation, and would be acting reasonably in doing so. In addition, the court stated that a claim for a PCO would be strengthened if the claimant's representatives were acting *pro bono*. This is, however, comparatively rare.

While the *Cornerhouse* requirements are less restrictive than those that they replaced, they ensure, as the court intended, that PCOs will still be imposed only in exceptional cases. Thus, although cases have been brought at an increased rate in the wake of *Cornerhouse* (Clayton, 2006) success rates have been low.[15] It would seem therefore that PCOs, at least in their current restricted form, do not appear to be well suited to meeting the Aarhus requirements.

## Costs and Remedies in an Environmental Context

In *R. (on the application of Burkett) v Hammersmith and Fulham LBC (costs)* [2004] EWCA Civ 1342 the Court of Appeal was called upon to deal specifically with costs and participation in the context of the Aarhus Convention. The case concerned a judicial review in respect of a grant of planning permission. 'Outline planning permission', giving consent in principle, had been granted in September 1999 and the claimant, an individual funded by the Legal Services Commission, made a claim for judicial review in April 2000. She failed to obtain leave at first instance and in the Court of Appeal due to delay, but succeeded in the House of Lords and the defendants were ordered to pay her costs.

When the substantive case was finally heard in the High Court the claimant lost and the judge ordered that the defendant's costs at this stage be offset against those that it had previously been ordered to pay. The claimant sought a further judicial review of the judge's decision on costs. The basic argument was that the costs awarded by the Lords 'belonged' to the Legal Services Commission and not the claimant and could not be used to set-off costs ordered against her by the court. The appeal was rejected.

The costs involved in *Burkett* were substantial, amounting to some £135,000, and strongly criticised by the Law Lords on this basis, but they do not in fact appear to be untoward or excessive for such complex proceedings involving multiple hearings and going to the highest judicial level. Their Lordships went so far as to criticise aspects of the claimant's legal team's preparation of the case, although it had satisfied the exacting requirements of the public funding regime. Given the funding and other resource disparities that exist between publicly financed claimants and typically much better resourced defendants, the inequalities that exist between parties and their impacts will necessarily become an issue in cases of this type, as demonstrated for example in the *HWW* case, discussed above, and in *R (on the application of Condron) v National Assembly for Wales* [2005] EWHC 3007 (Stookes, 2007).

Thus access to the courts on paper, and even in practice, does not necessarily ensure that the public interest litigant will be able to present its case to full advantage. The observation that it is difficult to see that judicial review, and the arrangements to fund it, if subjected to close scrutiny, would fully satisfy the Aarhus requirements on costs, does seem to be borne out. The court itself in *Burkett* showed considerable awareness of this problem and its broader implications. In response it took the highly unusual step of adding an addendum to the judgment specifically considering the potential impacts of the current costs regime on environmental law. This referred to a study funded by the Department of Environment, Food and Rural Affairs and led by the Environmental Law Foundation entitled: *Environmental Justice: a report by the Environmental Justice Project*,[16] which examined the central role of costs as a barrier to litigation and thus to compliance with Aarhus.

The *Burkett* case then shows a number of concerns that arise in respect of the costs of public interest litigation on the environment in the UK and their implications. Very real problems arise in public interest litigation where the Legal Services Commission uses scarce funds to support claimants in actions against public bodies which must themselves use scarce funds to defend the action. In each case, the costs are ultimately borne by the wider public, and yet contested issues must be aired as conflicting views of what represents the public interest are inevitable.

Some of the potentially worrying implications of the *Burkett* case appear to have been made manifest in the case of *R (on the application of England) v London Borough of Tower Hamlets & Ors* [2006] EWCA Civ 1742. The Court of Appeal decision here determined a complex claim for judicial review concerning planning permission granted for a housing development project which would require the demolition of the only remaining example of a canal-side loading canopy remaining in London. The claimant here too had the benefit of legal aid. He was successful in obtaining permission to apply for judicial review, but the substantive application was dismissed and the court refused permission to appeal. The developers acted immediately and demolished the canopy. Mr England's counsel refused to act, believing that no further legal aid would be forthcoming, and as a result, his solicitor had to write to the Court of Appeal to seek leave to appeal. The court allowed the solicitor to appear though they dismissed the application as the matters raised – concerning site contamination, at this point – had not been part of the original case. In addition, the court took the view that it was difficult to see that the claimant had a continued interest in the outstanding issues (which concerned EU law) raised by the case, as the structure that he had sought to protect was no more. On a more encouraging note, the court took the view that England's interest in the case, as someone interested in preserving the environment, raised different considerations from private law interests and that the provision of the Aarhus Convention could be relevant in this regard.

## 4.  CONCLUSION

### Culture of Secrecy

The UK exhibits a historic culture of secrecy (Weir, 1999) across the breadth of law and policy-making activity. This has tended to conceal the fact that the resulting legal landscape has been strongly shaped by the lobbying of strong and influential vested interests. Contrary to the ongoing process of Government-heralded 'culture change throughout the public sector'[17] by the implementation of new legislation on access to information (both general and specifically environmental), it is difficult, thus far, to see the Aarhus agenda resulting in any substantial change in this. Having said that, Aarhus has put the issues on the agenda in a much more prominent way than was previously the case and some (rather uneven) progress has been made, though considerable problems remain. It is, however, still comparatively early days in pursuing what will, if it is fully embraced, amount to a profound change in the way in which environmental decisions are made. The cultural shift that will be required to achieve this will be considerable. There are numerous reasons for this, not least the lack of an established expectation of meaningful public participation in governance more generally in the UK. This is the product of numerous complex factors, including a failure to value such input in a system firmly rooted in representative democracy. In the environmental sphere this is aggravated by a professionalised and technocratic approach to decision-making that tends to value scientific input almost to the exclusion of other material (Coyle and Morrow, 2004). Matters are further complicated by attempting to graft ambitious sustainability thinking, which recognises the social and environmental as well as economic implications of regulation, onto a system that has evolved to focus primarily (and only with partial success) on the economic implications. A sustainability-based approach does at least endeavour to address the true import and impact of environmental problems, but it remains the case that it is currently more of an aspiration than a reflection of reality. Forging effective legislation and testing it in the courts is one means of effecting the necessary change, delivering what will ultimately, if successful, cumulatively comprise little short of revolutionary change.

**The Role of the Judiciary in Creating/Advancing Development**

The balance of power in regulation is arguably already beginning to change because of enhanced participation requirements:

> In any highly-regulated field, of which planning and environmental law are paradigm examples, a general right of access to what is held by those doing the regulating is bound to shift the balance of power (Coppel, 2005).

The UK judiciary has taken its time to get to grips with the enhanced public participation agenda (initially in an EIA context and now in the more expansive post-Aarhus context) but has arguably, at best, developed an approach that combines purposive interpretation with pragmatic application. The courts will now look to both the practical and the democratic purposes of participation and to the fact that these would not necessarily be satisfied by 'substantial compliance', necessitating an elaborate paper chase to root out the relevant materials, but could require a single accessible document produced in timely fashion. However, this type of approach does bring to the fore the question of what exactly the 'purpose' in question is. This is demonstrated particularly graphically in the majority decision of the Privy Council in an EIA case concerning construction of a hydro dam, *Belize Alliance of Conservation Non-Governmental Organisations v (1) Department of the Environment and (2) Belize Electricity Co Ltd* [2003] UKPC 63. The Privy Council held that even quite substantial defects in the environmental assessment process were not necessarily to be regarded as fatal. In this case, the project was already irrevocably under way and the environmental 'damage' had been done by the time the case reached court. The view of the majority was that there was little evidence to suggest that anything would be gained by judicial intervention. However, the credibility of the EIA process (in particular in relation to public participation) was also damaged. The latter aspect of the case was not adequately addressed by the Privy Council's approach. Failure to grant remedies in such cases leaves the law looking like an expensive irrelevance. There is potentially a great deal to be said for awarding remedies for the breach of participation requirements in their own right, though these should be proportionately limited in comparison to remedies in respect of actual environmental damage resultant on such a breach.

**Issues of Principle**

As far as participation is concerned, the UK is in the relatively early stages of what will necessarily be a long and profound change process and one in which the judiciary, while it is increasingly coming to grips with the concepts involved, finds itself in a particularly awkward position. While the legal context is beginning to change, it still represents more of a veneer on long-established social mores and political values than a thoroughgoing change of approach. The purposes of participation in the environmental context in the light of its origins must be viewed as having intrinsic value as well as instrumental significance in protecting the environment, and need to be more thoroughly examined and articulated if they are to realise their full potential.

At the most profound level, enhanced public participation represents the grafting of a supplementary role for participative democracy onto the dominant representative democracy model. It is in fact best represented not as an evolution from previous practice but as a revolution in how we take environmental decisions in the modern world. Such a radical change will naturally suffer considerable teething troubles, and questions must remain as to its viability in the long term. If participation is viewed as part of the sustainability agenda, then the implications of how society handles the transition could prove to be of even greater importance than it would at first appear and the problems in realising it more intractable.

While the UK is arguably substantially compliant with the first and second pillars of the Aarhus Convention, in the sense that information is broadly available and participation, in principle at least, is rarely problematic, there are some quite considerable problems in respect of its application. At the present time, however, the most substantial problem in the UK with respect to environmental justice lies with the third pillar; not least in the form of high costs, both for the claimant's own legal representation and in respect of potential liability for those of the defendant if the claim fails. This fact, coupled with the paucity of public funding, ensure that access to justice is effectively rationed:

> Litigation ... is prohibitively expensive for most people unless they are either poor enough to qualify for legal aid or rich enough to be able to undertake an open-ended commitment to expenditure running into tens or hundreds of thousands of pounds (Carnwath, 2004).

Even if the cost barrier is overcome and litigation is undertaken, the question of remedies remains a real and vexed issue. If the current approach prevails and participation is regarded as having primarily instrumental value in the environmental context, it will continue to be sold short. While participation does clearly fulfil such a role, it surely also has intrinsic value in saying something about how environmental decisions are to be taken, recognising that the public interest, in a particularly complex and contested form, is at stake. Until this is clearly recognised, and a strong signal is sent to decision makers that it cannot be ignored without attracting the attention of the courts, it seems that participation will be unlikely to deliver its maximum potential.

These factors may well serve to cause the public to wonder if it is worth the very considerable amount of effort that it requires on their part to engage in environmental decision-making. The public may be granted opportunities to participate in environmental decision-making, but if that contribution is not valued by decision makers, then it is not likely to exert a great deal of influence. This can only breed profound cynicism about the value of public participation both in principle and in practice.

## NOTES

\*     The author would like to thank Carnwath LJ for his helpful comments on an earlier draft, acknowledging that responsibility for the piece as a whole remains her own. For further discussion of a number of the issues raised here, see Morrow (2010).

1.     That is, unequal access to information across the range of participants in decision-making processes.

2.   The requirement of a non-technical summary as part of the Environmental Impact Assessment under EU law is exceptional.
3.   38 ILM (1999), 517 and at http://www.unece.org/env/pp/documents/cep43e.pdf.
4.   Adopted at the Global Judges Symposium, Johannesburg, 18–20 August 2002, at www.unep.org/dpdl/symposium.
5.   Under s. 39 of the Freedom of Information Act 2000 the Regulations govern most environmental cases, though the Act itself may be occasionally be applicable.
6.   Drawing on Lord Hoffman's approach in *R v North Yorkshire County Council, Ex p Brown* [2000] 1 A.C. 397.
7.   Answer to Parliamentary Question, 2 December 2005, United Kingdom Parliament, at http://www.publications.parliament.uk/pa/cm200506/cmhansrd/vo051202/text/51202w26.htm#51202w26.html_wqn4.
8.   United Kingdom Department of Trade and Industry, The Energy Challenge: Review Report, available at http://webarchive.nationalarchives.gov.uk/+/http://www.berr.gov.uk/files/file31890.pdf.
9.   Applying *R (Nadarajah and Abdi) v Secretary of State for the Home Department* [2005] EWCA Civ 1363.
10.  Twelve weeks, the minimum prescribed by the Cabinet Office 'Code of Practice on Consultation', January 2004.
11.  At http://www.defra.gov.uk/environment/internat/Aarhus/pdf/compliance-summary.pdf.
12.  Under s. 42(1),1A Supreme Court Act 1981 (as amended) and Civil Procedure Rule r3.4.
13.  Rule 43(3)(2)(a) of the Civil Procedure Rules.
14.  PCOs were also considered in the Report of the Working Group on Facilitating Public Interest Litigation 'Litigating the Public Interest', July 2006.
15.  Clayton (2006) notes that, of the first five contested cases, only one was successful.
16.  At http://www.ukela.org/content /doclib/116.pdf.
17.  Jack Straw, Hansard, vol. 340, Dec. 7 1999, second reading speech for the Bill that would become the Freedom of Information Act 2000.

# REFERENCES

Carnwath, LJ (2004), 'Judicial protection of the environment: at home and abroad', *Journal Environmental Law*, **16**, 315, 318.
Clayton, R. (2006), 'Public interest litigation, costs and the role of legal aid', *Public Law*, 430–431.
Coppel, Philip (2005), 'Environmental information: the new regime', *Journal of Planning and Environmental Law*, 12.
Coyle, S. and K. Morrow (2004), *The Philosophical Foundations of Environmental Law: Property, Rights and Nature*, Oxford: Hart Publishing.
Edwards, M. (2005), 'Application for planning permission for recycling facility – environmental statement', *Journal of Planning Law*, 1469, 1486.
Lewis, N. Douglas (1999), 'The constitutional implications of participation', in Campbell, David and N. Douglas Lewis (eds), *Promoting Participation: Law or Politics*, London: Cavendish, pp. 1–30.
Morrow, K. (2005), 'Public Participation in the assessment of the Effects of Certain Plans and Programmes on the Environment – Directive 2001/42/EC, the UN/ECE Espoo Convention, and the Kiev Protocol', *Yearbook of European Environmental Law*, **4**, 49–84.

Morrow, K. (2010), 'Worth the paper that they are written on? human rights and the environment in the law of England and Wales', *Journal of Human Rights and the Environment*, **1** (1), 66–88.

Stookes, P. (2007), 'Current concerns in environmental decision making', *Journal of Planning Law*, 536, 545.

Weir, Stuart (1999), 'Participation and passivity: no room at the top', in Campbell, David and N. Douglas Lewis (eds), *Promoting Participation: Law or Politics*, London: Cavendish, pp. 113–116.

# 10. Enhanced access to environmental justice in Kenya

## Robert Kibugi

## 1. INTRODUCTION

This chapter seeks to assess the role of judicial institutions in enhancing access to environmental justice in Kenya. It discusses the conceptual nature of access to justice, and environmental justice in particular, as well as the role of judicial institutions. It then analyses legal mechanisms for access to environmental justice in Kenya, traversing the court system as well as tribunals. It also examines aspects of judicial institutions that enhance access to environment as well as the challenges that they face – and proposes solutions. The final section argues for a framework to enhance access to environmental justice in Kenya by putting forward a case for the courts to exercise *suo moto* jurisdiction in environmental matters of public interest.

## 2. CONCEPTUAL NATURE OF ACCESS TO JUSTICE

### Access to Justice

Effective judicial mechanisms should be accessible to the public, including organisations, so that their legitimate interests are protected and the law is enforced.[1] It is widely recognised that access to justice is one of the most basic human rights, without which the realisation of many other human rights becomes difficult (Bhagwati, 2002).

Access to justice entails much more than improving an individual's access to courts, or guaranteeing legal representation. Access must be defined in terms of ensuring just and equitable outcomes.[2] In addition, easy and unhindered access to judicial redress, particularly to enforce fundamental rights, has emerged as one of the standards of judicial independence.[3]

## Access to Environmental Justice

Environmental justice, often used interchangeably with the term environmental equity, has been defined as the fair treatment of all people without discrimination with respect to the development, implementation and enforcement of environmental laws, regulations and policies.[4] It seeks to ensure that authorities allocate and regulate scarce resources fairly to ensure that the benefits of environmental resources, the costs associated with protecting them and any degradation that occurs are equitably shared by members of society (Shelton and Kiss, 2005).

Access to environmental justice thus refers to effective judicial and administrative remedies and procedures available to a person who is aggrieved or likely to be aggrieved by environmental harm (Shelton and Kiss, 2005, p. 79). In addition, access to environmental justice extends beyond administrative and legal remedies to include public participation in environmental decision making (Eckersley, 2004, p. 4).

Creating a sustainable environment with access to environmental justice requires working with different types of institutions and with various actors such as the police, judicial institutions, social workers, prison officials, community leaders, paralegals, traditional councils and other local arbitrators, and taking into account the linkages between them (Eckersley, 2004, p. 4). This chapter, however, focuses particularly on the role of judicial institutions in enhancing access to environmental justice in Kenya.

## Judicial Institutions and Access to Environmental Justice: A Conceptual Framework

Judicial institutions encompass all entities established by law to adjudicate disputes of an environmental nature or otherwise. Traditionally, the term judicial institutions has always referred to courts of law (the judiciary), as the principal purveyors of justice. In the recent past, however, in addition to specialised divisions within the courts to address specific concerns, there has been a drive for the establishment of quasi-judicial tribunals and Ombudsman-style public environmental committees. As used here, reference to judicial institutions or the judiciary includes the courts and any tribunals established by law to adjudicate over environmental disputes.

Principle 10 of the Rio Declaration requires states to provide effective access to judicial and administrative proceedings, including remedy and redress. States should ensure that their judicial institutions are effective to enhance access to environmental justice for the public. Judicial proceedings should be expeditious, established by law and inexpensive as well as binding on public authorities. Further, the rules on locus standi should be based on national law, but consistent with the objective of giving the public concerned wide access to justice.[5]

Judicial institutions have an important role to play in economic and social issues such as the advancement of the rule of law concerning the environment and sustainable development (Akiwumi, 2007). Judicial institutions have a singular function as arbiters in the balancing act between the interests that present generations value and cherish and the interests to be sustained for the benefit of many unable to speak for themselves because of many constraints placed on them by both procedural and substantive laws, or in view of inhibiting poverty or other socio-economic factors. In this regard, these institutions play a critical role in the enhancement and interpretation of environmental law, and the vindication of the public interest in a healthy and secure environment (Akiwumi, 2007).

Judicial institutions in British Commonwealth countries, such as Kenya, have an additional guide, the *Latimer House Principles and Guidelines*. These recognise and emphasise the fundamental fact that independent, impartial and competent judicial institutions are integral to upholding the rule of law, engendering public confidence and dispensing justice (Commonwealth Secretariat, 2004, p. 10).

The critical place, nature and role of judicial institutions in enhancing access to environmental justice were highlighted by the outcome of the 2002 Global Judges Symposium. The Symposium adopted the 'Johannesburg Principles' which affirmed that an independent judiciary and judicial process is vital for the implementation, development and enforcement of environmental law. The principles emphasise that the fragile state of the environment requires the judiciary, as the custodian of the Rule of Law, to boldly and fearlessly implement and enforce applicable international and national laws to alleviate poverty and ensure that the present generation will enjoy and improve the quality of life for all, while ensuring that the inherent rights and interests of future generations are not compromised.[6] Further, the principles recognise that the poor are the most affected by environmental degradation, hence the urgent need to strengthen their capacity to defend their rights.[7]

Among the principles adopted to guide the judiciary in promoting sustainable development was a full commitment to utilise the judicial mandate to implement, develop and enforce the law, and to uphold the Rule of Law and the democratic process.[8] It was recognised that improvements in public participation, the settlement of environmental disputes and the defence and enforcement of environmental rights were of cardinal importance.[9]

In common law jurisdictions such as Kenya, judicial institutions defined *stricto sensu* (i.e. the courts) often have a law-making function, traditionally through the doctrine of *stare decisis*.[10] Although this doctrine does not prevent re-examination and, if need be, overruling prior decisions, it is a fundamental jurisprudential policy that prior applicable precedent usually must be followed even though the case, if considered anew, might be decided differently by a different judicial tribunal. The policy of judicial precedent is thus based on the assumption that certainty, predictability and stability in the law are the major objectives of the legal system.[11]

In the context of Kenya, the High Court sets precedent for the subordinate courts, while the Court of Appeal sets precedent for both the High Court and the subordinate courts. As institutions involved in access to environmental justice, the courts should use this function to develop environmental jurisprudence and settle the law on diverse aspects in a manner that promotes sustainable development. Judicial institutions are expected to balance the scales between the competing imperatives of socio-economic development and environmental protection (Waki, 2007).

## 3. LEGAL MECHANISMS FOR ACCESS TO ENVIRONMENTAL JUSTICE

With reference to selected judicial institutions – courts, the National Environment Tribunal, the Public Complaints Committee and the Water Appeals Board, this section assesses aspects of the handling of environmental disputes in Kenya.

### The Court System

The High Court is a superior court of record with unlimited original jurisdiction in civil and criminal matters, as well any other jurisdiction that may be conferred on it by the Kenyan Constitution and any other law (s 60). It also doubles as the constitutional court, with the dual mandate to interpret the Constitution (s 67) and enforce the fundamental human rights and freedoms enshrined in the Bill of Rights (s 84). The 1956 Law Reform Act empowers the High Court to exercise supervisory jurisdiction over and adjudicate appeals from decisions of subordinate courts, in addition to judicial review of administrative action (s 8).

The Court of Appeal is a superior court of record with jurisdiction and powers in relation to appeals from the High Court as may be conferred on it by law (s 64). This court sits at the apex of the Kenyan legal system and, when it passes judgment, only a bench of the same court can overturn, distinguish or reverse a previous decision. Its decisions are also binding on the High Court and all subordinate courts.[12] These two superior courts not only have occasion to make law through *stare decisis*, but also enjoy extended jurisdiction in enforcement of environmental and other constitutional rights, as well as appellate functions.

In order to effectively assess access to environmental justice through the court system in Kenya, it is imperative to review the position of the courts in dealing with several key indicators that can act as barometers of the effectiveness of the judicial system. Two such indicators are analysed below: locus standi and the linked aspects of costs and court fees with specific reference to superior courts of record.

### Status of the rule on locus standi

Limitations on the right or standing to sue have historically been among the main hindrances to access to environmental justice. Typically, common law jurisdictions such as Kenya have interpreted locus standi restrictively. It has been held that any litigant must have a sufficient interest over and above that of a mere public-spirited person seeking to bring a matter for judicial determination.[13] The courts have stressed that a person who approaches them for relief is required to have an interest in the subject matter of the litigation, in the sense of being personally adversely affected by the alleged wrong.[14]

In post-colonial Kenya, standing to sue remained a perennial problem facing individuals wishing to use the courts as a forum to ensure environmental protection. The position of the High Court in the renowned case of *Wangari Maathai v Kenya Time Media Trust* in 1989,[15] where the plaintiff sought a temporary injunction restraining the defendant from constructing a proposed 60-story Kenya Times Media Trust complex inside a recreational centre in Nairobi, illustrates the situation. The plaintiff was the co-ordinator of the Greenbelt movement but brought the suit on her own behalf. In dismissing the suit, Dugdale J ruled that 'only the Attorney General can sue on behalf of the public'.[16] The judge also stated that 'the personal views of the plaintiff are immaterial the plaintiff having no right of action against the defendant company and hence no locus standi'.[17]

The traditional and restrictive interpretation of standing to sue subsequently underwent liberalisation through both judicial action and statutory enactment. In 1999, in a radical departure from common law, s 3 of Environmental Management and Co-ordination Act (EMCA)[18] provided that every person in Kenya is entitled to a clean and healthy environment and has a duty to safeguard and enhance the environment. Further, provision was made allowing any person alleging contravention of this right to apply to the High Court for redress (s 3(3)).

At least in the recent past, decisions made by the High Court have been consistent in upholding the literal interpretation of the law. In *Rodgers Muema Nzioka & Others v Tiomin Kenya Limited*,[19] the plaintiff sought a temporary injunction arguing that the titanium mining actions of the defendant would lead to serious environmental and health problems. In granting the injunction, the judge stated categorically that 'the EMCA says that the plaintiff does not need to show that he has a right or interest in the property, environment or land alleged to be invaded'.[20]

In 2006, the High Court arrived at a number of landmark decisions interpreting locus standi liberally. In *Sylvia Endere v Karen Roses Ltd*,[21] the plaintiff sought an injunction to prevent the defendant from excavating, constructing or channeling storm water into the plaintiff's dam. In granting the injunction, the judge stated that 'it is clear that the plaintiff is not a busybody but within her rights under s 3 EMCA to enforce the provisions of that statute if she is of the view that the defendant was likely to contravene the law and cause harm to the environment'.[22]

In Kenya, therefore, statutory provisions have liberalised locus standi in environmental matters as provided by EMCA. This right would, however, be buttressed more firmly if it were entrenched in the Constitution, especially since constitutions generally require two thirds of Parliament to amend them.[23]

## Costs and court fees

The issue of costs and court fees continues to pose a serious challenge in access to environmental justice in Kenya. The courts usually levy fees for the filing of pleadings and other documents. The amounts are fixed administratively and vary depending on the document being filed, the value of the subject matter, the jurisdiction of the court etc.[24] These fees can be prohibitive since not every person seeking access to justice, for instance through enforcement of fundamental rights by a constitutional reference at the High Court, may be able to afford the 10,000 Kenya shillings (approx US$120) filing fee.

Costs pose an even more serious challenge than filing fees. The position under the law is that costs follow the event. Indeed, the Civil Procedure Act 2009 reinforces this position by placing this power to award costs at the discretion of the judge, while reiterating that costs should normally follow the event unless the judge directs otherwise for good reason (s 27(1)). In such a case, the judge will be departing from the established rule. This departure can include rulings that no costs are borne or that each party bears their own costs.[25]

There seem to be positive developments by the High Court in dealing with costs, especially in environmental matters of a public interest nature, but this lacks consistency, with courts of concurrent jurisdiction giving varying orders in similar (environmental) matters. In *Peter K. Waweru v Republic*,[26] the High Court ruled that 'as this is a matter of public interest, each party shall bear their own costs'. Similarly, in the case of *Samson Lereya and 800 others v The Attorney General* the court ordered each party to bear their own costs.[27] However, in similar environmental matters decided by the High Court around the same time, costs were awarded to the plaintiffs as the winners, in *Sylvia Endere v Karen Roses*,[28] and *Peter K. Mwaniki v Peter Njuguna Gicheha and others*.[29]

There are, however, indications that this matter could be resolved. The Chief Justice has stated that a solution is in the offing to address the issue of costs and prohibitive court fees. He has, for example, stated that 'the court shall consider establishing a rule of procedure allowing the waiver of court filing fees for environmental law actions, which the litigants pursue for the common benefit of society. The indigent litigant in public interest matters may also seek the leave of the court to sue as a pauper without paying the costs of instituting the suit.'[30] Recently, the Chief Justice stated that 'the Court may consider waiving the filing fees as well as the party and party costs by an order that each party bears its own costs as happened in the 2006 decision of the High Court of Kenya in *Waweru v Republic*'.[31]

There is indeed provision for an indigent litigant to institute proceedings. Under Order 32 of the Civil Procedure Rules, such a litigant may seek leave to sue as a pauper without paying the costs of instituting the suit, or any party and party costs should they be unsuccessful. There would, however, need to be a statutory amendment to exempt environmental matters of a public interest nature from both party and party costs and court filing fees.

The courts have made progress in easing this challenge of fees and costs, but the level of inconsistency in judgments remains cause for concern. It would be helpful to have statutory provisions exempting public interest environmental matters from costs, and possibly filing fees. In any event, constitutional entrenchment is important, since it equates the fundamental nature of the right to a clean and healthy environment to the fundamental nature of the need for access to environmental justice.

The judiciary has given further prominence to environmental matters with the recent establishment of the Land and Environment Division of the High Court of Kenya.[32] Established to deal with land and environment matters, the division has its own registry and may determine the categorisation of the matters that it may hear. Being a dedicated and specialised section of the superior court, it is expected to go a long way in enforcing environmental rights and ensuring quick settlement of environmental disputes. It has, however, been criticised for being based solely in Nairobi. According to directions issued by the Chief Justice, all land and environmental matters outside Nairobi should be lodged in the appropriate High Court stations upcountry. The division is unlikely to develop complex environmental jurisprudence while restricted to Nairobi only, since environmental disputes are more likely to occur in rural areas.

## The National Environment Tribunal

The National Environment Tribunal (NET) was established by EMCA principally to hear appeals from persons aggrieved by decisions from the National Environmental Management Authority (NEMA).[33] The appeal could be on a number of issues ranging from refusal to grant an EIA licence; imposition of any condition or restriction on a licence; revocation or suspension of a licence; or the imposition of an environmental restoration order or an environmental improvement order (s 129). The Tribunal also has power to give directions to NEMA where the latter refers a matter to it that appears to involve a point of law, or is of unusual importance or complexity (s 132(1)).

The Tribunal comprises five persons including a Chairperson, qualified for appointment as a Judge of the High Court; an advocate nominated by the Law Society of Kenya; a lawyer with qualifications in environmental law and two persons who have demonstrated exemplary academic competence in the field of environmental management (s 125(1)).

Initially restricted to hearing appeals from the decisions of NEMA, its committee or officers, the jurisdiction of the Tribunal was expanded in two respects by the Forests Act in 2005.[34] It now has competence with regard to the grant, suspension, refusal or revocation of an EIA licence under EMCA with regard to planned projects in forests (s 63(1)). The Forests Act also provides that EMCA provisions regarding reference to the Tribunal shall apply to the settlement of disputes arising under the Forests Act (s 53(2)).

The critical issue here is to review how the Tribunal has enhanced access to environmental justice in Kenya. This Tribunal has rendered judgment in a number of appeals brought before it over the last two or three years, demonstrating certain characteristics that aid it in enhancing access to environmental justice.

### Flexibility

The Tribunal has characteristics that make its procedures very flexible and attractive. For instance, any person who is a party to proceedings before the Tribunal has the option to appear in person or be represented by legal counsel (s 132(3)). In order to ensure that persons who elect to represent themselves are not disadvantaged, or intimidated by formality and technicalities by legal counsel representing their opponents, the Tribunal is given the power to regulate its own procedure (s 126(5)). This position is firmly reinforced by the Procedure Rules[35] which provide that, at the beginning of a hearing, the Chairman must explain the order of proceeding which the Tribunal proposes to adopt. Further, the Tribunal is required to 'conduct hearings in such a manner as it considers most suitable to the clarification of the issues before it and generally to the just handling of the proceedings and, so far as appropriate, seek to avoid legal technicality and formality in its proceedings' (Rule 26(2)).

The law also provides that the Tribunal shall not be bound by the rules of evidence as set out by the Evidence Act 1963. In addition to ensuring that the Tribunal receives evidence of any fact which appears to it to be relevant (Rule 26(5) of the Procedural Rules), this exemption also safeguards those appellants appearing in person from having evidence declared inadmissible, since they may not have an appreciation of the rules of evidence. Clearly, in this context provisions allowing persons to represent themselves, relaxation of formality and technicality as well as exemption from the rules of evidence are mechanisms put in place by the law allowing Tribunals, as judicial institutions, to enhance access to environmental justice.

### Interveners in appeals

The position under EMCA with regard to access is very clear; the rule on locus standi has been broadened to allow access to the courts by any person aggrieved over contravention of their entitlement to a clean and healthy environment (EMCA, s 3). In a bid to expand this right to persons not directly linked to the action by NEMA that is being appealed against, but who could be affected by it, the Procedure Rules provide for third party inclusion in hearings. Thus in any proceedings before the Tribunal, it may after an oral or written request, and in its sole discretion, grant intervener status. This status may be granted to any person, corporation or group of persons associated with the pursuit of any of the objectives of EMCA, and in particular those who seek to enforce rights to a clean and healthy environment, where their inclusion would assist the Tribunal in making a decision which will be in accordance with the objectives of EMCA (Rule 26(5) of the Procedural Rules).

It is significant that the Procedure Rules specifically provide for the grant of intervener status to those bodies which seek to enforce rights to a clean and healthy environment. This must, however, be provided for in the constitutions of such organisations, which must be produced to the Tribunal at the time of application (Rule 17(2)).[36] The decision of the Tribunal is binding on any intervener in so far as it relates to matters pertaining to the intervention (Rule 17(4)).

The Tribunal has granted intervener status to third parties on a number of occasions. However, one appeal stands out, that of *Jamii Bora Charitable Trust & Anor v Director General, NEMA & Anor*[37] where the appellant sought to reverse the decision of the respondents, NEMA, in refusing to issue the appellants with an Environmental Impact Assessment (EIA) licence. During the hearing of the appeal, an application was made verbally for leave to be given to a number of organisations to intervene in the proceedings as 'interested parties'. Both the appellants and the respondents had no objection to the application, and the Tribunal took the view that the parties were entitled to participate in the appeal. On the basis of these considerations, the application was granted. In its ruling, the Tribunal reversed the decision of NEMA and issued an EIA licence to the appellants.

The respondents and the interveners jointly appealed to the High Court. During the hearing of this appeal, now known as *Kiserian Pipeline Road Resident Association (KIPRRA), Kenya Wildlife Services (KWS) & Others v. Jamii Bora Charitable Trust & Another*,[38] the respondents raised the issue that all of the appellants, not having been 'parties' in the matter before the Lower Tribunal, were non-suited to bring the appeal. Justice Visram was of the view that admission of a third party intervener does not give such a complainant or an interested party the locus standi to file an appeal against the decision of the Tribunal, that right belonging only to the 'parties' to the proceedings. The judge was of the view that NEMA and the Tribunal are guided by different considerations and procedures from those guiding the High Court in determining issues before them. NEMA and the Tribunal may hear any party who has a complaint or an interest in the matter before them as 'interveners' or 'interested parties' in order to arrive at a just resolution of environmental issues.

Therein lies the problem: whereas granting intervener status enhances access to environmental justice in line with s 3 of the EMCA, the decisions of the Tribunal are not final, being subject to appeal in the High Court. It is entirely possible that the Tribunal will always admit interveners but that the High Court will continue to dismiss any appeals filed by these interveners. There is a need to synchronise the legal position, so that any persons admitted as parties before the Tribunal are also deemed proper parties with full rights of audience before the High Court. This will correct a position which is currently inequitable since, even though the current jurisprudence is that they cannot appeal to the High Court, they are bound by the decision of the Tribunal to the extent of their intervention.

## Costs and filing fees

Generally speaking, Tribunals, and NET in particular, are affordable. In fact, presently, there are no costs levied for filing appeals before NET (Kaniaru, 2007). In addition, rules of procedure provide that the Tribunal shall not normally make an order awarding costs and expenses. The exception is where the Tribunal is of the opinion that a party has acted frivolously, vexatiously or unreasonably in conducting or resisting an appeal. Further, an order for costs may be made in respect of any costs or expenses incurred or allowances paid as a result of an adjournment of proceedings at the behest of a party.[39] Indeed, the Tribunal appears to have set its own precedent in applying this provision literally, and generally making no orders as to costs.[40]

There are, however, certain challenges that currently face the Tribunal which need to be resolved since they may incapacitate it at some point. Here, the discussion is directed to briefly addressing only two issues: the independence of the Tribunal and the linkage of the Tribunal to the High Court.

## Independence of the Tribunal

Ideally, the independence of the Tribunal should be indispensable, both in fact and appearance, thereby making it effective in its roles. There are many facets to be considered when looking at the independence of a judicial institution. The financial independence and operational independence are concentrated on here.

With regard to financial independence, the EMCA does not determine how the Tribunal is to be funded. Provision is only made for remuneration and allowances payable to the Chairman and members. However, it is left to the Minister to determine this remuneration (s 134) and no such determination has been made. The independence of the Tribunal must be jealously protected in order for its decisions to be viewed by the public as truly impartial (Angwenyi 2007). It is important that express provision be made in the law for funding for the Tribunal to be allocated out of the Consolidated Fund directly by the treasury through a vote in the annual budget. Lack of financial independence may compromise the objectivity of the Tribunal in fact or appearance.

Operational independence poses an even greater problem. A reading of s 124 (4) (c) reveals that a member of the Tribunal, including the Chair, may be removed from office by the Minister for failure to discharge the functions of his office or for misbehaviour. No criteria are set out to judge when and how these two conditions are met; the Minister, it seems, will determine the criteria. Thus a member is vulnerable to removal for bogus reasons, including where the government or Minister (officially or to pay homage to political patronage) feels that the presence of any member is an inhibition.

## Linkage to the High Court

Section 3(3) of EMCA provides that any party aggrieved with contravention of their entitlement to a clean and healthy environment can move the High Court for redress. Indeed, a party aggrieved by a decision taken by NEMA or its organs may move the High Court under this provision, and eventually to the Court of Appeal under s 66 of the Civil Procedure Act. On the other hand, if a party similarly aggrieved appealed to the Tribunal, the decision of the latter would be final (s 130(5)). Logically thus, this divergence may generally apply against lodging appeals to the Tribunal since applying to the High Court provided an extra forum to be heard on appeal.

Of course questions arise as to whether s 130 of EMCA, by referring appeals to the Tribunal, ousts the jurisdiction of the High Court. The logical answer is no, since the EMCA confers jurisdiction on environmental matters to the High Court. In addition, the High Court has ruled to this effect in *Republic v NEMA and 2 Others Ex Parte Greenhills Investments Ltd & 2 Others*,[41] where Ibrahim J argued that the High Court retains concurrent jurisdiction with the Tribunal. This conflict is untenable; it is necessary for the courts to affirm the procedure set out in EMCA and require litigants to adhere to the same before moving to the High Court.

In addition, since the decisions of the High Court are final, where it is hearing an appeal from the Tribunal, this creates a rather inequitable position for litigants. One who moves the High Court aggrieved by a decision by NEMA directly has the right to pursue the matter to the Court of Appeal; but one who follows the EMCA procedure is restricted to the High Court. Of course in such a case parties will, if possible, opt for the former. It is time to amend s 130(5) to allow for litigants to appeal to the Court of Appeal from a decision of the High Court.

## The Public Complaints Committee

The Public Complaints Committee (PCC) was established by s 31 of EMCA with powers to investigate any allegations or complaints against any person in relation to the condition of the environment in Kenya. It may also act *suo moto* (see next section) to investigate any suspected case of environmental degradation and report its findings, together with recommendations to the National Environment Council (NEC). While the PCC is not, strictly speaking, a judicial institution, it is considered as such here because it is one of the avenues for access to justice provided by the framework environmental law.

In a bid to ease access to justice by the public, the PCC determines its own procedure. To this end, the draft rules of procedure require that Committee to conduct its business in such manner as to ensure just execution of business and to avoid legal technicality and formality in its proceedings.[42] Further, no fee is to be levied on the lodging or determination of a complaint.[43]

As an enforcement mechanism, any person who fails to comply with an applicable decision of the PCC is guilty of an offence.[44] The other enforcement mechanism available to the PCC is through the National Environment Council (NEC).[45] The PCC reports to and is subject to the direction of the NEC alone. If the NEC were to take prompt steps to act on the recommendations of the PCC, the latter could easily turn out to be one of the most important dispute resolution institutions in environmental management in Kenya (Mumma, 2007).

In *Community Museums of Kenya v Kenya Forestry Research Institute, Forest Department and the Food and Agriculture Organization*,[46] the PCC heard a complaint about the destructive nature of a weed called prosopis juliflora. Among the recommendations made was the eradication of the weed by the concerned Ministries and lead agencies. When this recommendation was not acted upon, a civil suit was initiated before the High Court in *Samson Lereya and 800 Others v The Attorney General, Ministry of Environment and Natural Resources and NEMA*.[47] The initial suit was dismissed for failure to comply with the 1956 Government Proceedings Act, but was filed again as a constitutional reference petition for enforcement of fundamental rights.[48]

Other investigations have concerned issues of deforestation, changes in land use without environmental impact assessment or mitigation measures, quarrying activities, industrial pollution and poor solid waste management practices. In several cases, the respondents have taken remedial action without the need for any enforcement action.

Even though it lacks the power to determine disputes, being restricted to hearing complaints and making recommendations, the PCC serves a valuable role in providing an avenue for dispute resolution that avoids costs and expenses.

## The Water Appeals Board

Established under s 84 of the Water Act,[49] though not yet operational, the Water Appeals Board (the Board) has power to hear appeals at the suit of any person having a right or proprietary interest which is directly affected by a decision or order of the Water Resource Management Authority, the Minister or the Regulatory Board concerning a permit or licence. Further, the Board has jurisdiction to hear and determine disputes arising out of the Water Act (s 85). Membership of the Board comprises a Chairman, qualified to be a judge of the High Court, appointed by the President on the recommendation of the Chief Justice, and two other persons, to be appointed by the Minister (s 84). The members can be removed from office at any time by the person appointing them.[50] This fact potentially vitiates the very independence of judicial institutions that is essential to enhance access to environmental justice.

Draft rules of procedure allow appellants to appear in person, or be represented by an agent such as a lawyer or arbitrator.[51] However, the rules of procedure do not endeavour to reduce legal technicalities and formality. This is obvious from some of the provisions such as the requirement that appeal pleadings are filed in quadruplicate; levying of filing fees; service of appeal with summons; filing of return of service; procedure for amendment of pleadings; requirement to file written submissions etc.[52]

Other provisions make the Appeals Board more user-friendly; for instance the Board may proceed as a Commission of Inquiry,[53] whereby it will not be bound by the rules of evidence.

Provision is made for an order of the Board to be filed in the High Court for enforcement and execution.[54] This position may eventually be the undoing of the Board since, if one has to file an award before the High Court, there is no reason to refrain from moving the Court in judicial review of the administrative decision in question in the first place. The Board should have its own enforcement mechanism, inbuilt in the statute, requiring the Authority or agencies to comply.

In any event, the establishment of this Board is a replication of efforts. Since there is already a National Environmental Tribunal established by the framework law, it would seem logical, in order to build environmental law jurisprudence, promote consistency in decision making, consistency in compliance and basically enhance access to environmental justice, that there should be one order for resolving environmental disputes arising from administrative decisions. Ideally, then, where disputed decisions are made under the EMCA, the Water Act and the Forests Act as well as other sectoral environmental statutes, the appeal should be lodged before the Tribunal. In such a case, once the challenges facing the Tribunal are resolved, the enabling mechanisms under EMCA fall into place, fully enhancing the role of this critical judicial institution.

## 4. TOWARDS ENHANCED ACCESS TO ENVIRONMENTAL JUSTICE – A CASE FOR *SUO MOTO* JURISDICTION

From the court system to the National Environment Tribunal, the Public Complaints Committee and the Water Appeals Board, judicial institutions provide fora for access to justice. They are legal mechanisms granting people audience before these institutions, and act as systems to ensure that the remedies available are consistent with sustainable development. All of these institutions are, however, operating within an adversarial legal system, whereby the presiding judicial officers can only determine disputes brought by aggrieved parties and on the basis of evidence adduced by the parties. The exception is the PCC which has power to investigate environmental degradation on its own motion.

The right to a clean and healthy environment is universal. Environmental degradation, too, affects all, but mostly the poor who may not afford the costs of seeking justice in the courts. Further, it is not possible for the entire society to file a suit to enforce their right to a clean environment. But in extraordinary circumstances, exceptional measures may be required. This could happen where environmentally-harmful activities threaten land held under public trust.

In some jurisdictions, such as Pakistan, the Supreme Court can, in these kinds of cases, assume jurisdiction over a matter of its own accord without being moved by a party, known as *suo moto* jurisdiction. This is done by directly taking judicial notice or cognizance of a matter where the conscience of the court has been so struck by a particular issue that justice demands that the matter be brought for adjudication before it. Such was the situation in *Re Human Rights Case (Environmental Pollution in Balochistan)*[55] where the Supreme Court of Pakistan responded to a daily newspaper report that nuclear or industrial waste was to be dumped in Balochistan in violation of article 9 of the Pakistan Constitution. Following an inquiry by the registrar's office, the Supreme Court ordered that no one could apply for or be allotted a plot for dumping nuclear or industrial waste. This was truly an extraordinary matter, where public authorities had abdicated their duty to safeguard coastal lands, which they held in trust for the public. It therefore called for extraordinary measures such as those taken by the Supreme Court.

Kenya is not immune from situations of such a nature, of similar if not larger magnitude. The critical question to ask is whether the courts in Kenya can invoke *suo moto* jurisdiction to address such critical environmental matters. Although the Court of Appeal has jurisdiction to hear and determine appeals only in cases where there is provision by law (s 84), the High Court of Kenya has unlimited original jurisdiction in civil and criminal matters.

Section 3A of the Civil Procedure Act confers inherent jurisdiction on the High Court to make such orders as may be necessary for the ends of justice or to prevent abuse of the process of the court. Further, under s 84 of the Constitution, the High Court, in enforcement of fundamental rights and freedoms, has the power to make such orders, issue such writs or give such orders as are necessary to protect these rights. With such wide powers, it would be more appropriate for the High Court to take action of its own motion in matters of public interest.

Further, this court has demonstrated a predisposition to issue orders *suo moto* in matters of public interest as demonstrated in the decision of the High Court, as a Constitutional Court, in *Peter K. Waweru v Republic*[56] where the applicants had brought a constitutional reference seeking to quash criminal proceedings brought against them in a subordinate court. The origin of the matter was as follows: the applicants were residents in Kiserian, a township just outside Nairobi, and were prosecuted by a Public Health Officer for discharging raw sewage into a public watercourse. The officer did not, however, comply with the requirement under the Public Health Act to first issue summons to the applicant, prosecuting them directly instead, thus provoking the constitutional challenge.

The judges found that the health officer had failed to comply with the requisite procedure for prosecution, hence denying the applicants due process, and issued *certiorari* to quash the proceedings and an order of prohibition to stop future charges on similar facts. The court further observed that the outcome of the application by the parties would concern the country's treatment of environmental issues raised by the application. They expressed concern that Kiserian Township is located on a water table, with people disposing of effluent and solid waste into the Kiserian River. They stated that the matter raised very serious environmental issues and challenges. The judges stated that:

> the situation described to us could be the position in many other towns in Kenya especially as regards uncoordinated approval of development and the absence of sewerage treatment works. *As a court, we cannot therefore escape from touching on the law of sustainable development although counsel from both sides chose not to touch on it although it goes to the heart of the matter before us.* This larger issue should be of great concern to us as a court ... [Emphasis added].[57]

The court invoked the principle of intergenerational equity, pointing out that water tables and clean rivers are for the present and future generations. They found that under the public trust doctrine, Olkejuado County Council, the competent local authority, as manager of trust lands, was under a duty to make land available for construction of sewerage works. The court ordered *mandamus* to compel the Ministry of Water, the Nairobi Water Services Board and the Olkejuado County Council to construct sewerage treatment works.

This order was made despite the fact that none of these institutions was party to the suit, and the absence of a prayer to that effect. The applicants were also granted the liberty to apply for enforcement if the orders were not complied with within a reasonable time. The court applied the powers granted it under s 84 of the Constitution and issued the writs, orders and directions that were necessary to enforce protection of the fundamental rights. But instead of restricting itself to the rights of the applicants, the court invoked its powers to address the rights of Kiserian residents and Kenyans generally. The matter was not even an environmental one initially, but the court equated the right to a clean and healthy environment to the right to life, which is a fundamental right under the Kenyan Constitution (s 71).

Liberal thinking and interpretation concerning the Constitution and Statutes presents another avenue such as in *Charles Lekuyen Nabori, Samson Lereya & 8 Others v Attorney General & Three Others*,[58] where two of the three-judge bench fully adopted the *Waweru* rationale.[59] Acting *suo moto*, the court also directed the Ministry of Environment to produce a policy working paper on the management and eradication of the plan and present this to Parliament within 60 days for debate and interpretation.[60]

In contrast to the scope of judicial authority in Pakistan, the Kenyan provisions under s 84 expressly require an application to be made before the court. On the other hand, s 3A of the Civil Procedure Act is open ended, allowing the High Court to make such orders as may be necessary for the ends of justice or to prevent abuse of the process of the court. The civil procedure statute is not, however, applied during constitutional reference proceedings; special rules of procedure made under s 84 are applied instead.

Even though there is only one decision so far, there is arguably an established predisposition by the High Court, as a superior court of record, to act *suo moto* in the public interest or to protect group rights. This has entailed issuing orders to entities that were not parties to the suit in order to pre-empt environmental degradation. The provisions conferring inherent jurisdiction on the High Court should be entrenched in the constitution to allow the court to make any orders necessary for the ends of justice. Alternatively, the express requirement for an application to be made in order for powers conferred under s 84 for enforcement of fundamental rights to be exercised by the High Court should be repealed. This would retain the power of the court to make such orders, issue such writs, and give such directions as are necessary to enforce fundamental rights where there is a question of public importance in enforcement.

## 5.  CONCLUSION

Access to justice is critical, but access to environmental justice is an imperative to the realisation of sustainable development. It entails access to effective procedures and remedies for resolutions of environmental disputes, as well as outcomes that are consonant with the dictates of sustainable development. In their work, judicial institutions are always faced with challenges, but these can be remedied through judicial initiative as illustrated in *Waweru*, or through legislative action. The functional aspects that promote the role of these institutions in enhancing access to environmental justice should be guarded jealously. However, judicial institutions, especially the courts, need to venture beyond the adversarial system to take extraordinary steps in extraordinary circumstances, to issue orders to enforce fundamental rights that raise public interest concerns, including the issuing of orders *suo moto*. Prior to legislative and/or constitutional amendments to buttress this power, the courts, especially the High Court, should proceed on the same path as the learned judges in the now-celebrated *Waweru* case. The overall goal, after all, is to enhance access to environmental justice in order ensure sustainable development.

## NOTES

1.  Convention on Access to Information, Public Participation in Decision-Making and Access to Justice in Environmental Matters, adopted at Aarhus, Denmark on 25 June 1998; available at http://www.unece.org/env/pp/. Although this Convention is not applicable to Kenya, it provides a conceptual basis for a national framework to facilitate access to environmental justice.
2.  United Nations Development Programme, *Access to Justice: Practical Note* (2004), 6.
3.  International Commission of Jurists, *Kenya: Judicial Independence, Corruption and Reform* (International Commission of Jurists – Kenya Chapter) (April 2005), 42.
4.  Environmental Justice Research and Resources, *About Environmental Justice*, www.geography.lancs.ac.uk/envjustice/envjusticeboutlancs.htm.
5.  Rio Declaration on Environment and Development, UN Doc. A/CONF.151/26 (Vol. I) at http://www.unep.org/Documents.Multilingual/Default.asp?documentid=78&articleid=116 3 Art. 9.
6.  *Johannesburg Principles on the Role of Law and Sustainable Development*, adopted at the Global Judges Symposium held in Johannesburg, South Africa, 18–20 August 2002, reprinted in UNEP, Global Judges Programme (UNEP) (2005), pp. 14–15.
7.  See note 6, p. 16.
8.  Principle 1.
9.  See note 6, p. 17.
10. *Legal Definition of Stare Decisis*, Lectic Law Library, www.lectlaw.com/def2 /s065.htm.
11. *Moradi-Shalal v Fireman's Fund Ins. Companies* (1988) 46 Cal.3d, pp. 287, 296.
12. Section 65 of the Constitution empowers Parliament to establish subordinate courts with jurisdiction defined in the establishing statute.
13. See Ghanaian Case of *New Patriotic Party v Attorney General* (1999) 2 LRC 283, p. 305.
14. Malawi Human Rights Commission, 'The effect of judicial decisions in Malawi on locus standi and public interest litigation on human rights' (A commentary on the effect of Judicial Decisions No. 1 Draft of November 2006), p. 3.
15. HCCC No. 5403 of 1989, UNEP, *Compendium of Judicial Decisions on Matters Related to Environment, National Decisions* Vol. 1, (1998), pp. 15–18.
16. See note 15, p. 17.
17. See note 15.
18. Act No. 8 of 1999.
19. High Court Civil Case No. 97 of 2001, eKLR [2006], at www.kenyalaw.org.
20. See note 19, p. 3.
21. High Court Civil Case No. 298 of 2005, eKLR [2006], at www.kenyalaw.org.
22. See note 23, p. 3. See also rationale in *Peter K. Mwaniki and 2 Others v Peter Njuguna Gicheha, Limuru Butchers Union and 2 Others* High Court Civil Case No. 313 of 2000, eKLR [2006], at www.kenyalaw.org.
23. See Article 243 Draft Constitution Kenya, on amendment procedure for Bill of Rights at http://kenyastockholm.files.wordpress.com/2010/02/psc_draft_to_coe_-_29-01-0101.pdf.
24. For instance to file a Plaint the fees amount to 1,500 Kenya Shillings (US$24) per player – in addition to a fee levied on the value of the subject matter of the suit; a to file a Constitutional Reference by Originating Motion, the fees are Kenya Shillings 10,000 (US$154) per applicant; affidavits, Kenya shillings 175 (US$3), etc.

25.  ILEG, Public Interest Environmental Litigation in Kenya: Prospects and Challenges (Institute for Law and Environmental Governance, Ecogovernance Series No. 4, 2007), p. 41.
26.  High Court Miscellaneous Civil Application No, 118 of 2000, eKLR [2006], www.kenyalaw.org.
27.  High Court Civil Suit No. 115 of 2006, eKLR [2006], p. 7 at www.kenyalaw.org.
28.  High Court Civil Case No. 298 of 2005, eKLR [2006], at www.kenyalaw.org.
29.  High Court Civil Case No. 313 of 2000, eKLR [2006], at www.kenyalaw.org.
30.  Honourable Chief Justice, J.E. Gicheru, speech on Admission of Advocates to the Roll 7 December 2006, p. 2. (On file with author.)
31.  Honourable Chief Justice, J.E. Gicheru speech to opening of the East Africa Regional Judicial Colloquium on Environmental Law and Access to Justice, Sarova Whitesands Beach Resort, Mombasa, 10–15 April 2007, http://www.ilegkenya.org/ui/images/EA_JUDICIAL_COLLOQUIUM_INTERIM_REPORT-revised%2025%20July.pdf, p. 98.
32.  Gazette Notice No. 301 Dated 10 January 2007 (Kenya Gazette Vol. CIX – No. 7).
33.  Part XII, ss 125.
34.  Act No. 7 of 2005.
35.  The National Environmental Tribunal Procedure Rules, 2003 (Legislative Supplement No. 57, Kenya Gazette Supplement No. 92, 21 November 2003), Rule 26 (1)).
36.  See note 35, Rule 17(2).
37.  Tribunal Appeal No. Net/02/03/2005.
38.  High Court Civil Appeal No. 307 of 2006 (unreported).
39.  Rule 39.
40.  See generally *Narok County Council & Anor v NEMA*, Tribunal Appeal No. NET/0 7 OF 2006; *Nakumatt Holdings v NEMA*, Tribunal Appeal No. NET 01/02/2005; *Jamii Bora Charitable Trust & Anor v Director General*, *NEMA & Anor*, Tribunal Appeal No. NET/02/03/2005 etc., where the Tribunal declined to make any order as to costs despite the parties applying for orders that costs do follow the event against the losing party.
41.  High Court Miscellaneous Application No. 169 of 2004, eKLR [2006], www.kenyalaw.org.
42.  The Environmental Management and Co-ordination (Public Complaints) Regulations, 2007 (Draft of March 2007), Rule 25.
43.  Note 50, p. Rule 5(1).
44.  Rule 26.
45.  Established under ss 4 EMCA.
46.  PCC Complaint No. 67/2005.
47.  See note 27.
48.  High Court of Kenya Petition No. 466 of 2006, *Charles Lekuyen Nabori, Samson Lereya & 8 Others vs. Attorney General, National Environmental Management Authority & 2 Others* (unreported).
49.  No. 8 of 2002.
50.  Fourth Schedule to the Act.
51.  The Water Appeal Board Rules, 2007 – draft of May 2007, Rule 5.
52.  See generally Rules 2–19.
53.  Provision is made under the Commissions of Inquiry Act, Cap 102 Laws of Kenya.
54.  Rule 23.
55.  PLD 1994 Supreme Court 102 reprinted in UNEP, Compendium of Judicial Decisions on Matters Related to Environment, Vol. 1 (UNEP/UNDP, Nairobi, 1998), p. 280.
56.  See note 26.
57.  See note 26, p. 12–13.
58.  See note 48.
59.  See note 48, Judgment by Rawal J, p. 51; and Judgment by Ang'awa J, p. 61.

60. See Ang'awa J, note 48, p. 61. They also granted a prayer by the petitioners for the formation of a Commission to assess and quantify the loss visited upon the environment and the residents by the noxious weed, proposes juliflora. See, Rawal J, note 48, p. 53.

# REFERENCES

Akiwumi, A.M. (2007), 'Role of the judiciary in environmental sustainability in East Africa', paper prepared for the East Africa Regional Judicial Colloquium on Environmental Law and Access to Justice, Mombasa, Kenya, 10–15 April (on file with author).

Angwenyi, A. (2007) 'A Review of the Environmental Management and Co-ordination Act, 1999', in C.O. Okidi, P. Kameri-Mbote & J. Migai Akech (eds), *Environmental Governance in Kenya as a Consequence of the Framework Law*, Nairobi, CASELAP, University of Nairobi.

Bhagwati, P.N. (2002), 'Democratisation of remedies and Access to Justice', speech to First South Asian Regional Judicial Symposium on Access to Justice, 1–3 November, New Delhi (on file with author).

Commonwealth Secretariat (2004), *Commonwealth (Latimer House) Principles on the Three Branches of Government*, Buckinghamshire, Commonwealth Secretariat, Commonwealth Lawyers Association et al., at http://www.thecommonwealth. org/shared_asp_files/uploadedfiles/%7DACC9270A-E929-4AE0 AEF9 4AAFEC 68479C%7D_Latimer%20House%20Booklet%20130504.pdf.

Eckersley, R. (2004), 'The state and access to environmental justice: from liberal democracy to ecological democracy', paper presented at the Access to Environmental Justice, EDO WA Conference, February (on file with author).

Kaniaru, D. (2007), 'Environmental tribunals as a mechanism for settling environmental disputes', paper presented to the East Africa Regional Judicial Colloquium on Environmental and Access to Justice, Mombasa, Kenya, 10–15 April (on file with author).

Mumma, A. (2007), 'Role of administrative dispute resolution institutions and process in sustainable land use management: the case of the National Environment Tribunal and the Public Complaints Committee of Kenya', in J. Nathalie, J. Chalifour, P. Kameri-Mbote, Lin H. Lye and John R. Nolon (eds), *Land Use for Sustainable Development*, New York: Cambridge University Press.

Shelton, D. and A. Kiss (2005), *Judicial Handbook on Environmental Law*, Nairobi: UNEP.

Waki, P.N. (2007), 'Enhancing the role of courts in promoting enforcement and compliance with environmental law', paper presented at the East African Judicial Colloquium on Environmental Law and Access to Justice, Mombasa, Kenya, 10–15 April (on file with author).

# 11. Towards a new theory of environmental liability without proof of damage

**José Juan González**

## 1. INTRODUCTION

Since the Rio Declaration on Environment and Development was signed in 1992, many Latin American states have enacted new environmental protection legislation.[1] In some jurisdictions, such as Brazil and Venezuela, legislation has specifically addressed harm caused to the environment, whereas in others, liability and compensation for environmental damage are included in a wider regime aimed at protecting the environment and natural resources. However, few of these environmental laws establish rules governing environmental liability as it is considered here. In many cases, the legal instruments confuse environmental damage in its own right with damage caused to natural resources, persons and goods, and consequently attempt to apply traditional civil liability to damage caused to the environment in its own right. This approach fails to recognise that environmental damage is quite different from civil damage and thus civil liability cannot deal with it effectively. Accordingly, recent developments in Latin American environmental laws relating to liability could be moving in the wrong direction.

This chapter analyses recent trends in Latin American environmental legislation with respect to environmental damage and proposes an alternative approach to deal with it, namely 'liability without proof of damage'.

## 2. ENVIRONMENTAL DAMAGE IN LATIN AMERICA

The initial reaction of international as well as national legal systems to environmental damage consisted in applying civil liability,[2] particularly 'objective' or 'strict' liability.[3] For instance, in the United States, apart from the classic common law damage mechanisms,[4] a broad system for attributing civil liability was established by the Comprehensive Environmental Response, Compensation and Liability Act 1980 (CERCLA),[5] and by the Oil Pollution Act 1990 (OPA). In Canada, the Fisheries Act 1985 (ss 34–42) the Canadian Shipping Act 1985, (ss 673–727) the Canadian Environmental Protection Act 1999, (ss 39–103) the British Columbian Waste Management Act 1996 (ss 26–28) and the Ontario Environmental Protection Act 1990 (ss 92–97) refer to damage from a similar perspective.

Latin America, Uruguay, Ecuador and Mexico approach environmental damage by applying civil codes. In Bolivia and Honduras, however, civil liability is complemented by a number of rules on collective legal standing. In countries such as Argentina, Brazil, Colombia, Costa Rica and Chile, environmental law regimes have incorporated a series of innovative principles and rules directed towards environmental restoration.

In Brazil, the Civil Action of Responsibility for Damage Caused to Environment, Consumer, Goods and Rights of Historic, Aesthetic and Landscaping Value Act of 1985 provides for: economic compensation for environmental damage; procedures to file actions for environmental damage (Arts. 20, 30, 6–9); judicial ordering of precautionary measures (Art. 4); determinations that have effects *erga omnes* (Art 16) and establishing an Environmental Fund whose objective is provide sufficient economic resources for environmental restoration (Arts. 13 and 20). This legislation made Brazil one of the first countries to recognise collective legal standing in environmental issues through two innovative mechanisms: the *inquérito civil* (Art. 80(1)) and the *açâo civil pública* (Art. 9). The *inquérito civil* (Ferraz and Augusto, 1995) is an administrative procedure conducted by a specialised prosecutor, aimed at collecting the necessary proof to file an *açâo civil pública*. The *açâo civil pública* (Celso, 1995) facilitates protection of the collective environmental interest by providing for actions for environmental restoration on behalf of the people.

In Chile, the General Environmental Law 1994 incorporated a concept of environmental damage as well as differentiating civil actions from environmental actions.[6]

In contrast, in Mexico, progress in this respect remains limited. Until recently, the most relevant legal provisions on liability for environmental harm were found in the 1996 reform of the General Act for Ecological Balance and Environmental Protection. The Act states, in Art. 203, that any person who contaminates or causes deterioration of the environment or adversely affects natural resources or biodiversity is obliged to repair it under the terms of the civil code. Apart from the aforementioned provision, Art. 151 of the General Act establishes three confusing rules in regard to liability for damage caused by hazardous waste management:

(a) First, liability for the management and final disposition of hazardous waste lies with the generator of such waste;

(b) Secondly, when the generator hires the management and disposal services of a company authorised by the Ministry (of Environment) and such wastes are handed over to them, they will accept liability for the waste management;

(c) Finally, notwithstanding the second rule, the liability of the company is independent of the liability of the generator.

This provision is based on the general application of the strict liability system, but does not introduce a specific rule to adapt it to cases involving hazardous waste.

More recently, in Mexico, the General Act for Wildlife of 2000 introduced a chapter regarding damage to the natural elements that comprise wildlife but this is of limited utility in addressing liability for environmental damage. The introduction in 2003 of a new General Act for the Prevention and Integral Management of Waste of 2003 conflates civil liability with the system of administrative sanctions applicable to those who disobey administrative regulations, by failing to take into account whether or not such illegal behaviour causes damage (see Art. 68).

Subsequently several bills have been drafted that aim to establish an environmental liability regime for Mexico, but they are still dominated by civil liability, and none have yet been passed by Congress. For example, the Act on Civil Liability for Damage and Environmental Degradation was approved by the House of Representatives in 2005 but its approval by the Senate is still pending.[7]

Applying civil codes in cases of environmental damage by simply referring to general rules, as in Mexico, or by adapting such rules through specific laws, as in most Latin American countries, is not the best approach to address the problem of liability for environmental damage. The particular nature of environmental damage brings new challenges for jurisprudence (Catalá, 1998, p. 247), including determining:

(a) Who has standing to file a legal action to restore the environment?

(b) What time limit should apply for filing an environmental damage action?

(c) Who should be responsible for environmental damage?

(d) Who has the burden of proof?

(e) What constitutes reasonable restoration?

(f) What should the effects of the legal decision be?

These problems have been analysed in numerous legal studies, published in a range of languages (Perales, 1980; Prieur, 1991; Church and Nakamura,

1993; Prati, 1997; Marqués-Sampaio, 1998; Barriga, 2000; Hutchinson, 2000; Mosset and Hutchinson, 2000; González, 2002) but reflections from scholars have not yet provided the basis for a new and original theory of liability for environmental damage.

In the same way, research shows that while a few Latin American environmental laws try to engage with such problems, none have established a comprehensive system for environmental liability, and the laws that have been made ignore the particular nature of environmental damage.

## 3.　ENVIRONMENT AND ENVIRONMENTAL DAMAGE

Environmental damage is distinct from civil damage, not only because it affects the environment rather than the interests of people or corporations, but also because it has particular characteristics that are absent from civil damage. In consequence, liability and compensation regimes in this field demand a clear legal definition of both the environment and damage to it.

### The Environment as a Subject of Legal Protection

Although from the scientific point of view it has been assumed that the environment is the sum of all the natural elements – water, soil, air, flora and fauna (Nabel and Wright, 1996, p. 672), from a legal perspective, especially a theoretical one, the environment is a subject of legal protection that differs from its constituent elements (Díaz, 1996; Giampiero, 2000, p. 145).[8] Natural resources can be viewed from at least two perspectives. On the one hand, they have a traditional utilitarian value as economic inputs to production processes. On the other hand, they play a major environmental role as suppliers of environmental services, such as waste disposal provided by water and air, and as outputs derived directly from nature, such as recreational and ecological services (Sève, 2002–2003). Moreover, as one scholar has argued, where natural resources interact, they develop new environmental properties that they do not possess in isolation (Brañes, 2004). Such properties, known as 'environmental functions' or 'environmental services' are themselves in constant interaction and thus constitute a new legal subject – the environment. So it can be seen that, while environment and natural resources are related, they are different legal subjects, though for a long time legal science has ignored this difference. As a consequence, most modern environmental legal regimes have been built on the fallacy that the environment can be protected by simply protecting natural elements. That explains why the first generation of environmental laws, those enacted after the Stockholm Conference[9] and before the Rio Earth Summit,[10] laid down regimes closely linked to traditional branches of law, such as administrative and civil law, which had regulated property and the use and exploitation of natural resources for centuries (Robinson, 2003, p. 28).

Nevertheless, environmental protection requires more sophisticated and less orthodox legal instruments, aimed at protecting the equilibrium of environmental functions, rather than natural elements as such. In fact, the process through which legal systems recognise differences between natural resources and environment, and in consequence, start building new legal categories, such as environmental damage and environmental liability, constitutes part of the evolution of environmental law as a new and independent branch of law, whose objective is to protect the environment as a whole. Unfortunately, it is not possible to say that either international law or national regimes in the field of environmental law are moving in that direction.

Specifically in the field of environmental liability, comparative analysis of environmental laws shows a trend toward the regulation of liability for environmental damage, but in most cases the difference between environment and natural resources is not clearly established. Instead, such laws typically apply civil liability rules when the environment is damaged. A review of Latin American environmental laws further shows that, although the majority of relevant laws in the region include a definition of environment, this does not mean that the environment – as distinct from natural resources – is clearly recognised as a specific subject for legal protection.

Recognition of the environment as a specific subject for legal protection presupposes not only that it is defined by environmental legislation, but also demands that environmental law is built on two premises. First, it requires a set of rules aimed at avoiding environmental damage. This is the preventive side of environmental law and it is pursued by command and control mechanisms such as environmental impact assessment, environmental standards, licenses and permits. Second, when preventive instruments fail, complementary rules are required to ensure environmental restoration. This is the restorative side of environmental law and the core of the environmental liability system.

An analysis of Latin American environmental laws shows that, while preventive mechanisms have developed independently to a considerable degree, liability for and compensation of environmental damage have been dealt with in a fashion closely linked to traditional civil liability. This is so despite the fact that environmental damage and civil liability refer to different things. The former deals with damage that affects the collective legal interest in protecting the environment, including the human right to a healthy environment; the latter is aimed at protecting individual interests affected when natural resources are damaged, even in cases where those resources are public property and public trust is involved.

Having differentiated environmental and civil damage, the second fundamental question lies in determining what constitutes environmental damage.

## The Nature of Environmental Damage

It is not easy to define environmental damage because, in contrast to what happens in the event of civil damage, when the environment is injured harm is not necessarily tangible, and thus the consequences thereof are often not immediately perceptible

However, frequently both scholars (Sanchez, 1994)[11] and policy makers[12] wrongly identify environmental damage as synonymous with civil damage, whose negative effects on natural resources are more easily perceptible. Two factors contribute to this confusion. First, environmental damage and civil damage share some characteristics; both require injury, notwithstanding that, in environmental damage, the injury is to the environment itself, and to people's right to a healthy environment, rather than to any individual's legal interest.

Secondly, civil damage and environmental damage are sometimes associated. Civil damage may result from environmental harm. For instance, climate change affects human health and conversely, the environment can be affected by civil damage (Prieur, 2001, p. 868).[13] This may occur due to two different causes; first, environmental damage could be provoked by a catastrophic event, as in the case of major industrial accidents. The explosions that occurred in Seveso, Italy in 1976 and Bhopal, India in 1984 (Ruiz and Scovazzi, 2005) are dramatic examples. Secondly, environmental damage may be a consequence of a series of actions over time, as in cases of historic or cumulative pollution.

Nevertheless, the connections between civil and environmental damage do not mean that they can be dealt with from the same perspective as, in addition to similarities, there are also major differences between them. As a result, we have to distinguish between 'pure environmental damage' and 'civil damage that arises from environmental incidents'. The second situation is physically evident and clearly fits into the category of civil damage, and civil liability is clearly applicable to it. 'Pure environmental damage' on the other hand is much more complex, due primarily to the fact it applies to an immaterial legal subject that becomes a legal issue as a result of a series of interactions of environmental functions. Such an injury may be difficult to identify immediately, since environmental damage often only becomes evident when environmental functions are affected in such a way that ecological imbalance occurs, compromising life support functions (Hutchinson, 2001, p. 37).[14] In addition, identifying environmental damage involves complex scientific challenges that are not as common in the case of civil damage. This has been observed by a United Nations Environment Programme report, which stated that environmental damage is 'a change that has a measurable adverse impact on the quality of a particular environment or any of its components, including its use and non-use values, and its ability to support and sustain an acceptable quality of life and a viable ecological balance' (UNEP, 2003, p. 12). Thus defined, environmental damage does not include civil damage to public or private property.

'Pure environmental damage' has a number of characteristics that distinguish it from civil damage: (a) it is uncertain because its causes, effects and magnitude are not easily ascertainable, but particularly because a number of scientific limitations apply to determining the moment when environmental damage has occurred; (b) it also has a collective character, usually affecting huge numbers of people and often resulting from multiple causes; and finally, (c) the temporal effects of such damage cannot easily be determined, as it is sometimes made manifest only after many years. Regardless, such distinctions between pure environmental damage and civil damage are not recognised either by international or comparative law.

At the international level, neither soft nor hard law instruments have defined environmental damage. Most instruments refer to damage in terms of 'property' and 'health', excluding damage to the environment in its own right. Exceptions include the liability regimes set out in the 1993 Lugano Convention[15] and the 1999 Basel Protocol[16] which make specific reference to environmental damage. Article 2.7 of the Lugano Convention defines 'damage' as follows:

(a)    loss of life or personal injury;
(b)    loss of or damage to property other than to the installation itself or property held under the control of the operator, at the site of the dangerous activity;
(c)    loss or damage by impairment of the environment in so far as this is not considered to be damage within the meaning of sub-paragraphs (a) or (b) above provided that compensation for impairment of the environment, other than for loss of profit from such impairment, shall be limited to the costs of measures of reinstatement actually undertaken or to be undertaken;
(d)    the costs of preventive measures and any loss or damage caused by preventive measures.

It can be noted, however, that 'loss or damage by impairment of the environment' under Art. 2.7(c) is limited to the costs of measures of reinstatement. Article 18 sets out the possibility for an order to be made 'that the operator be ordered to take measures of reinstatement'. This is a limited acknowledgement that there is a distinction between civil damage (that is the loss of profit from the impairment) and damage to the environment itself, and that that damage can addressed in terms of the measures for reinstatement.

The Basel Protocol has a more limited focus in terms of costs reinstatement. However, neither instrument establishes any specific regulation in regard to the mechanics of reinstatement.

At a national level in the Latin American region, the laws of Chile, Brazil, Costa Rica, Cuba, Nicaragua, Argentina and Mexico all define the concept of environmental damage. However, in most of the cases this is identified with damage to natural elements and such definitions are not always complemented by a specific liability regime.

For instance, under Art. 2 of the Chilean General Environmental Law of 1994, environmental damage is 'all loss, diminution or significant reduction affecting the environment or one of its components'. The environment is 'the global system constituted by natural and artificial elements of a physical, chemical or biological nature, socio-cultural elements and their interactions, in permanent modification by human or natural action and that governs and conditions the existence and development of life in its multiple manifestations'.

In Brazil, the Environmental Crimes Act N° 9,605 of 1998 refers to environmental damage frequently (Art. 40, Art. 40, § 2, Art. 58, I, Art. 54, § 3, Art. 17, Art. 14, II, Art. 28, I, Art. 20) but neither defines it nor distinguishes it from traditional civil damage.

In Costa Rica, the Environment Act allocates to the Environmental National Technical Secretariat the function of 'Taking care of the environment and of investigating petitions regarding environmental degradation or environmental damage' (Art. 84, (c)). The Biodiversity Act indicates that '[W]hen environmental damage occurs to an ecosystem occurs, the state will be able to take measures to restore it, to recover it and to rehabilitate it' (Art. 54). However, neither law defines the concept we are discussing.

In Cuba, Law No. 81 on the Environment of 1977 defines environmental damage as 'all loss, diminution, deterioration or significant reduction, incurred by the environment or one or more of its components that take place because of disobeying a regulation or legal provision' (Art. 8).

In Nicaragua, Art. 5 of the General Act on the Environment and Natural Resources defines environmental damage as 'All loss, diminution, deterioration or damage that is caused to the environment or one or more of its components'.

In Argentina, the Constitution states that environmental damage will mainly generate the obligation of restoration but the difference between civil and environmental damage is not clear-cut. In addition, Art. 27 of the Argentinean General Act on the Environment defines environmental damage as 'all significant alteration that negatively modifies the environment, its resources, the balance of the ecosystems, or the collective resources or values'.

In Mexico, the General Act on Ecological Balance and Environmental Protection does not define environmental damage, but its Regulation on Environmental Impact Assessment refers to ecological damage, stating 'Damage to ecosystems is the result of one or more adverse impacts on one or several natural elements or processes of ecosystems that triggers an ecological imbalance'. Nevertheless, no specific regime to deal with such damage is laid down by that statute.

Further, as a result of inappropriately equating civil damage and environmental damage, Latin American legal systems attempt to apply traditional civil law to environmental damage by adapting the traditional procedural rules on legal standing, time limits for filing an action, causation, the burden of proof, restoration and scope of the legal decision, aiming to make the allocation of liability more flexible. Nevertheless, the application of civil liability to environmental damage remains difficult because, in all cases, proving the existence of the damage is a fundamental requirement for allocating liability and, as mentioned above, environmental damage is often neither easily nor immediately identifiable.

## 4.   INAPPLICABILITY OF CIVIL LIABILITY TO ENVIRONMENTAL DAMAGE

In Latin American civil law tradition, there are two types of civil liability (as distinct from criminal liability): fault liability and strict liability. Fault liability is based on the existence of three elements: damage, fault and a causal link between that conduct and the damage. Strict liability on the other hand does not require proof of fault, though causation must still be established. The strict liability system has always been linked to dangerous activities, involving a considerable level of risk; it is potentially applicable to environmental damage. However, this may be problematic for a number of reasons. First, when the environment is compromised, legally proving causation can pose major difficulties. Although some Latin American environmental laws attempt to address this by reversing the burden of proof, proving the occurrence of the damage remains a major challenge. For instance, in Chile, Art. 52 of the General Environmental Law states that the 'perpetrator of environmental harm is presumed to be liable in cases where he has not complied with regulations on environmental quality, standards of emissions, prevention or decontamination plans, special regulations for cases of environmental emergency or standards of protection, environmental preservation or conservation, established by this law or other legal or regulatory provisions'. Similarly, in Argentina, Art. 29 of the General Act on the Environment states: 'Where infringement of environmental regulations exists, then the responsibility of the author of the environmental damage is *iuris tantum* presumed'. Finally, in Mexico, the Environmental Act for the Sustainable Development of the State of Colima provides that 'it is presumed that damage is imputable to a pollution source if, because of the characteristics of the processes it develops, the substances or materials it handles or the residues it generates, have the ability to produce such damage'. This provision in effect reverses the burden of proof, which is appealing in that it enables the victim to avoid a significant part of the cost of a trial. In addition, this rule is justified because the defendant generally has more technical and scientific information about the activities causing the damage than the victim.

An additional problematic consideration lies in the collective character of environmental damage, which makes it difficult to determine who can bring a claim. Three types of approach can be identified. The first is demonstrated in Brazil, Cuba and Mexico, where locus standi is granted to a public agency. The second features in Argentina, El Salvador and Ecuador, where legal standing to file an action for environmental restoration is vested in non-government organisations. Under the final approach, adopted in Bolivia, Brazil, Colombia, Costa Rica, El Salvador, Nicaragua and Panama, any person is able to commence such an action.

Further problems arise from the continuing nature of environmental damage, which makes it difficult to determine an appropriate limitation period for bringing an action. Continuity of environmental damage means that it is generated by a succession of acts which make it difficult to determine when time starts to run. Normally, the cause of environmental damage is complex, consisting of a series of acts occurring over an extended period. Time may be calculated as running from at least three different moments: (a) when the cause is produced, as in the case of the General Act on Ecological Balance and Environmental Protection of Mexico; (b) when the damage is evident, as in Chilean and Panamanian regimes; or (c) when the effects of damage have ceased, as in the case of the Mexico's City Environmental Law.

Even if the other obstacles are overcome, determining restoration requirements remains problematic. While general civil law considers that damage can be addressed by paying compensation or returning the damaged object to its previous condition, in the environmental field, restoration *in natura* must be the priority. That is, the aim is to return the environment to its previous condition. Case law and a number of legislative instruments have recognised the pre-eminence of restoration *in natura* over economic compensation, as seen in Argentina, Brazil, Cuba, Chile, Ecuador, El Salvador, Honduras, Mexico, Nicaragua and Panama.

Nevertheless, in this context, restoration *in natura* and economic compensation present almost insurmountable practical difficulties, as full and accurate scientific data is required to calculate the required level of restoration for the harmed environment. This approach must be underpinned by law in order to ensure its effective application. A review of Latin American environmental laws shows that none of them have included rules directed to determining appropriate restoration. If restoration of the harmed environment is impossible, then economic compensation should to be paid. However, the legal systems should address questions of quantification and who should receive compensation. Thus far, the most popular solution in Latin America has been establishing environmental funds that collect and manage economic compensation ordered by the courts in cases where restoration *in natura* is impossible.

Even if these problems can be solved, the application of civil liability to environmental damage will always leave cases where there is no prospect of restoration. This could occur because, when the damage to the environment became evident, two things may have happened: the time limit to file an action has elapsed, or the person who was liable has disappeared. In consequence, the requirement under civil liability of proving the existence of the damage becomes a real constraint to the allocation of liability for environmental damage.

The characteristics of uncertainty and the continuous and progressive nature of environmental damage demand that liability be attributed before the damage becomes evident. Because of this, an adequate environmental liability system has to be sufficiently flexible to allow for allocation of liability to those who contribute to future injury to the environment. This is the liability without proof of damage proposed in this study.

Thus it is necessary to build a new liability system to specifically address environmental damage. Such a system must be independent of the traditional strict liability system that requires proof of damage and causation. The liability system proposed here should be designed on the basis of recognising that those responsible for high-level risks to the environment are liable for the future damage to which they contribute. In consequence, the system must allocate to such contributors the obligation to pay for the restoration of future damage even though that damage has not yet occurred.

## 5. LIABILITY WITHOUT PROOF OF DAMAGE

As demonstrated above, a number of factors ensure that the restoration of environmental damage through the application of civil liability is not always possible. In recent times, however, under the influence of principles laid down by the Rio Declaration,[17] a transformation of the environmental policies in several Latin American countries has begun, which may address this limitation.[18] These new environmental policies pursue a double objective: on the one hand, they oblige the polluter to assume the cost of its polluting activity, and on the other, they aim to amass sufficient resources to restore environments damaged by a non-identifiable polluting agent.[19] However, there are limits to the application of the polluter pays principle. These include:

- the financial magnitude of environmental damage;
- the difficulty in attributing responsibility to defendants and causation issues that necessitate developing restorative mechanisms with a collective character, based on the principle of solidarity; and
- the spreading of liability for environmental damage among all possible contributors to its occurrence.

This does not require that the damage has become evident, but merely proof of the potential of certain activities to contribute to it; consequently, this new approach does not require proof of damage as a requirement of the attribution of liability.

There are three mechanisms that allow allocation of liability without proving the occurrence of the damage: environmental insurance, environmental taxation and environmental restoration funds.

## 6. NEW MECHANISMS TO ATTRIBUTE LIABILITY FOR ENVIRONMENTAL DAMAGE

Economic instruments make it possible to allocate liability more efficiently than a strict liability system. Appropriate implementation of environmental insurance, environmental taxation and environmental restoration funds allows governments to collect enough revenue from potential contributors to future environmental damage and to direct such revenues to restoration without either proving causation – and in consequence without proving damage – or facing all the procedural inconvenience that civil liability entails.

**Environmental Insurance**

Applying insurance to environmental harm could make it possible to spread liability more broadly without proving the existence of damage. However, insurance could be considered as an alternative means to make companies pay the costs of future environmental damage only if, first, environmental legislation prescribes mandatory insurance for those who conduct activities that involve a considerable level of risk for the environment; and, secondly, insurance companies are obliged by law to pay the cost of environmental damage generated by such activities without inquiring who among the group of polluters has caused the damage.

Most recent environmental legislation in Latin America imposes obligatory insurance for activities or processes associated with latent risk. For example, in Chile, according to the General Environmental Law 1994, companies are allowed to commence activities submitted for environmental impact assessment before an authorisation is issued, on condition that environmental insurance is in place covering the risk of environmental damage. In Colombia, in accordance with Article 60 of Act No. 99, the concessionaire of a mining project is obliged to guarantee the future restoration of the soil through insurance. In Mexico, Article 35 of the General Act on Ecological Balance and Environmental Protection establishes that the Ministry of the Environment can demand the arrangement of insurance or guarantees in respect of the fulfilment of the conditions of an environmental impact authorisation where the works undertaken can cause serious ecosystem damage.

Insurance may alleviate the burden of paying for environmental restoration. In addition, in such cases, by paying for insurance, polluters make provision for the potential negative consequences of their polluting activities, thus transforming insurance into an anticipatory instrument for collecting economic resources to build capacity to remedy environmental damage before it occurs.

Nevertheless, in most of the aforementioned cases, environmental insurance is linked to the civil liability system which, as discussed, is not readily applicable in cases of environmental injury. Thus it is necessary to set out a new legal approach where insurance is considered as a way to collect money from polluters, and that the insurance companies would then be obliged to restore future environmental damage caused by the activities of those who hold insurance without involving the system of civil liability.

## Environmental Taxation

Where environmental damage is associated with diffuse pollutants, determining causation is almost impossible. In these circumstances, environmental taxes could provide a potential instrument through which polluters pay for future environmental damage they may generate. Many countries have passed fiscal legislation that, besides contributing to revenue generation, aims to regulate polluting activities. For instance, in 1980, the United States of America established the Oil Crude Tax, the Chemical Feedstock Tax, the Imported Chemical Derivatives Tax and the Corporate Environmental Income Tax to provide the Superfund programme with a financial base, securing site cleanup where polluters cannot be located, are bankrupt, or refuse to take action (Milne, 2004).

Certainly, environmental taxation is still not universally endorsed among Latin American countries. For instance, in Chile and Mexico, environmental taxation is mentioned in environmental legislation but neither has as yet imposed such a tax. Moreover, in those countries where environmental taxes have been introduced, they are still imposed for revenue purposes and not aimed at environmental restoration, as for example with the forest conservation tax contained in the Costa Rican Forest Act of 1986 (Arts. 42, 43).

However, environmental taxation offers a significant possibility of building a new liability system for environmental damage because revenue from environmental taxes could be used to restore damaged environments without the necessity for attributing liability to a perpetrator under civil codes.

## Environmental Restoration Funds

Environmental restoration funds could also help to spread responsibility among all potentially liable persons, while avoiding the problem of proving the existence of environmental damage. A review of environmental law in Argentina,[20] Bolivia,[21] Brazil,[22] Chile,[23] Costa Rica,[24] Cuba,[25] Salvador[26] and Nicaragua[27] shows that all have established restoration funds, comprised of revenue from a variety of sources, including court-ordered damages in civil liability and administrative fines imposed for violations of environmental protection law. Such funds are useful restoration mechanisms where a polluter cannot be identified or causation is problematic, but they must be applied on the basis of a connection with insurance and taxes that are established by legislation. Unfortunately, in the Latin American context such a connection does not yet exist.

In summary, an adequate combination of insurance, environmental taxes and restoration funds could help in the process of building a new environmental liability system that eliminates the requirement of proving damage as a condition precedent of ensuring the restoration of the damaged environment.

Under such a new liability system, all possible contributors to environmental damage would be obliged to pay a tax, channelled to an environmental fund to restore environmental damage. Remediation would be conducted directly by the government and no action would be required to attribute liability because it would already be allocated by tax law. In the same way, activities generating environmental risk would be obliged to have insurance to face any future environmental damage restoration. In this case, payments collected by insurance companies would have to be deposited into the environmental restoration fund, and in the event of the occurrence of environmental harm, the fund would undertake restoration without inquiring about causation.

## 7.   CONCLUSION

Attempts by Latin American environmental law to adapt civil liability to address environmental damage show that, while some steps have been taken, these are at present insufficient. Despite innovation in many countries to reverse the burden of proof, establish longer limitation periods and recognise wider locus standi, the core problem remains: the difficulty of proving environmental damage. One aspect of the problem requires addressing liability for future environmental damage. In the same way that the incorporation of strict liability regimes around the world meant a revolution for legal science, dealing with environmental damage demands the evolution of a new theory of responsibility, in which liability does not require proof of damage. This cannot be addressed through the system of civil liability but must instead rely on collective mechanisms such as environmental insurance, taxes and restoration funds. Some Latin American jurisdictions have been moving in this direction but, as yet, there is not a sufficient connection between the requisite elements to enable the articulation of a new system of attributing liability for environmental damage. It is high time scholars and international organisations laid down a legislative agenda that guides policy makers in the task of constructing an adequate environmental liability system aimed at restoring damage inflicted on the environment.

# NOTES

1. These include Bolivia, General Act on the Environment (1992); Venezuela, Criminal Environmental Act (1992); Honduras, General Act on the Environment (1993); Chile, Environment Act (1994); Costa Rica, Organic Act on the Environment (1995); Paraguay, Environmental Crimes Act (1995); Nicaragua, General Act on the Environment and Natural Resources (1996); Mexico, General Act on Ecological Balance and Environmental Protection Act (1988 as amended in 1996), General Act on Wildlife (2000), General Act on Prevention and Comprehensive Management of Waste (2003); Cuba, Act on Environment (1997); El Salvador, Environmental Act (1998); Panama, General Act on the Environment (1998); Brazil, Environmental Crimes Act (1998); Colombia, Environment Act (1993); Dominican Republic, General Act on the Environment and Natural Resources (2000); Uruguay, General Act for Environmental Protection (2000); and Argentina, General Act on the Environment (2002).

2. Nuisance, trespass, negligence and strict liability comprise the key legal mechanisms for civil actions to protect the environment.

3. In civil law countries, strict liability is known as objective liability.

4. See note 2 and the rule in *Rylands v Fletcher* (1868) LR 3 HL 330 which initiated the system of strict liability, together with the doctrines of the public trust and riparian rights.

5. See also Superfund Amendments and Reauthorization Act of 1980 (SARA).

6. Article 53 of the Environment Act states that when environmental damage has been suffered, it is possible to file a legal action to obtain the restoration of the environment harmed which does not constrain the possibility of filing the civil action by the person directly affected.

7. The original Bill included a number of innovations aiming to build a robust environmental liability system but it was completely modified by Chamber of Representatives.

8. This is not a novel idea; in 1987 the Supreme Court of Justice of Italy established such a distinction in its decision 210/87 and in 1995 the Supreme Court of Justice of Spain held that the environment cannot simply be reduced to the sum of its natural elements, but that it constitutes a complex tapestry of the relations established among all such elements.

9. The United Nations Conference on the Human Environment (UNCHE) was held in Stockholm, Sweden from 5 June to 16 June, 1972.

10. The United Nations Conference on Environment and Development (UNCED) was held from 3 June to 14 June, 1992 in Brazil, Rio de Janeiro.

11. Cabanillas Sanchez argues: 'the patrimonial injury that the owner of a property suffers, or the disease that a person contracts, or even death are consequences of environmental pollution. The environmental damage includes both injuries to the environment as such and personal injury to the owner or person who contracts a disease or dies. Environmental damage must be analysed from that double perspective'.

12. For instance, one of the most recent initiatives regarding liability for environmental damage, the 'Directive 2004/35/CE of the European Parliament and the Council of the 21 of April of 2004 on environmental liability with regard to the prevention and remedying of environmental damage', was based on the idea of associating civil damage with environmental damage.

13. Michael Prieur asserts that the concept of ecological damage was used for first time by M. Despax (1980) in his work 'Droit de l'environnement' to insist on the specificity of indirect injuries resulting from transgressions against the environment.

14. Tomás Hutchinson (2001) defines environmental damage as 'all injury to collective or individual interests in preserving the natural conditions of life'.

15. Convention on Civil Liability for Damage resulting from Activities Dangerous to the Environment, at http://conventions.coe.int/.

16. Basel Protocol on Liability and Compensation for Damage Resulting from Transboundary Movements of Hazardous Wastes and their Disposal, at http://www.basel.int/pub/protocol.html.

17.   Principle 16 of Rio Declaration on Environment and Development (A/CONF.151/26 (Vol. I) states: 'National authorities should endeavour to promote the internalization of environmental costs and the use of economic instruments, taking into account the approach that the polluter should, in principle, bear the cost of pollution, with due regard to the public interest and without distorting international trade and investment'.
18.   The polluter pays principle provides a foundation for a new liability system for environmental damage.
19.   The polluting agent may not be identifiable because it is impossible to establish causation or because by the time the damage becomes evident the polluting agent has disappeared.
20.   Fund for Environmental Compensation established by Art. 34 of the General Act on the Environment.
21.   National Fund for the Environment established by Art. 87 of the Act on the Environment.
22.   National Fund for the Environment established by Act No. 7.797.
23.   Fund for Environmental Protection, established by Art. 68 of the General Act on the Environment and Fund for Forest Financing established by Art. 46 of National Forest Act.
24.   National Environmental Fund established by Art. 93 of the Organic Act of the Environment.
25.   National Fund of the Environment established by Art. 81 of the Environmental Act.
26.   Environmental Fund of El Salvador established by Art. 11 of the Environment Act.
27.   National Environmental Fund established by Art. 48 of the General Act on the Environment and Natural Resources.

# REFERENCES

Barriga, Mercedes Campos Díaz (2000), *La Responsabilidad Civil por Daños al Medio Ambiente. El Caso del Agua en México* (Civil Liability for Environmental Damages: The case of water in Mexico), Mexico: UNAM.

Brañes, Raúl (2004), *Manual de Derecho Ambiental Mexicano* (Mexican Environmental Law Handbook), México: Fondo de Cultura Económica, pp. 17–23.

Catalá, Lucía Gomis (1998), *Responsabilidad por Daños al Medio Ambiente* (Liability for Environmental Damage), Navarra: Aranzadi.

Celso, A. (1995) 'A ação civil pública e a defensa dos direitos constitucionais difusos' (The Public Civil Action and protection of diffuse constitutional rights) in Edis Milaré (ed.), *Ação Civil Pública* (Public Civil Action), São Pablo: Editora Dos Tribunais, pp. 163–167.

Church, Thomas W. and Robert Nakamura (1993), *Clearing Up the Mess: Implementing Strategies in Superfund*, Washington, DC: The Brookings Institution.

Despax, M. (1980), *Droit de l'environnenment*, Paris: Litec.

Díaz, Manuel Piñar (1996), *El Derecho a Disfrutar del Medio Ambiente en la Jurisprudencia* (The right to a healthy environment in judicial decisions), Granada: Comares.

Ferraz, Mello de Camargo and Antonio Augusto (1995), 'Inquèrito Civil: Dez Anos de um Instrumento de Ciudadania' (Inquèritocivil: Ten Years of a Citizen's Action Instrument), in Edis Milaré (ed.), *Ação Civil Pública* (Public Civil Action), São Pablo: Editora Dos Tribunais, pp. 62–69.

Giampiero, Di Plinio (2000), *Principi di Diritto Ambientale* (Principles of Environmental Law), Milano: Giuffrè Editore.

González, José Juan (2002), *La Responsabilidad por el Daño Ambiental en México: El Paradigma de la Reparación* (Liability for environmental damage in Mexico: Paradigm of restoration), Mexico: Miguel Angel Porrua.

Hutchinson, Tomás (2000), 'Responsabilidad pública ambiental' (Public Environmental Liability), in Jorge Mosset Iturraspe and Tomás Hutchinson, *Daño Ambiental* (Environmental Damage), Buenos Aires: Rubinzal-Culzoni Editores.

Marqués-Sampaio, Jose (1998), *Responsabilidade Civil e Reparacao de Dannos ao Medio Ambiente* (Civil Liability and Restoration of Damage to the Environment), Rio de Janeiro: Editora Lumen Juris.

Milne, Janet (2004), 'What has the United States done? A Diagnosis of Federal Environmental Taxes', in Lawrence Kreiser (ed.), *Critical Issues in International Environmental Taxation: Insights and Analysis for Achieving Environmental Goal through Tax Policy*, United States of America: CCH, pp. 403–439.

Mosset Iturraspe, Jose and Tomás Hutchinson (2000), *Daño Ambiental* (Environmental Damage), Buenos Aires: Rubinzal-Culzoni.

Nabel, Bernad and Richard T. Wright (1996), *Environmental Science: The Way the World Works*, New Jersey: Prentice Hall.

Perales, Carlos De Miguel (1980), *La Responsabilidad Civil por Daños al Ambiente* (Civil Liability for Environmental Damage), Madrid: Civitas.

Prati, Luca (1997), 'La ripartizione delle responsabilità ambientali all'interno delle organizzazioni imprenditoriali e dei gruppi societari' (Allocation of environmental liability into economic organization and social group), *Rivista Giuridica dell'Ambiente*, **13**(1), 29.

Prieur, Michel (1991), *Droit de l'Environnement* (2nd edition), Paris: Dalloz.

Prieur, Michel (2001), *Droit de l'Environnement* (4th edition), Paris: Dalloz.

Robinson, Nicholas (2003), 'Challenges Confronting the Progressive Development of a Second Generation of Environmental Laws', in Lin-Heng Lye and Maria Socorro Z. Manguiat (eds), *Towards a 'Second Generation' in Environmental Laws in the Asia Pacific Region*, Switzerland and Cambridge, UK: IUCN.

Ruiz, José Juste and Tullio Scovazzi (eds) (2005), *La Práctica Internacional en Materia de Responsabilidad por Accidente Industriales Catastróficos* (International Practice on Liability for major industrial accidents), Valencia: Tirant lo Blanch.

Sanchez, Antonio Cabanillas (1994), 'El daño ambiental' (Environmental damage), *Revista de Derecho Ambiental*, **12**, 11–12.

Sève, Juan (2002–2003), IRG, 'A Discussion Paper on Environmental and Natural Resources Accounting and Potential Applications in African Countries', available at www.irgtd.com/resources/publications/africa/2002–03.

United Nations Environment Programme (UNEP) (2003), *Environmental Liability and Compensation Regimes: A Review*, Nairobi: UNEP Division of Environmental Policy Implementation.

# 12. Diffuse damages in environmental torts in Brazil

## Arlindo Daibert

## 1. INTRODUCTION

This chapter takes as a given that the core of sustainable development is that human activities must be constrained by the capacity of the environment to sustain those activities. This is consistent with the *chapeau* to Article 225 of the Brazilian Federal Constitution as well as evolving environmental legal doctrine and jurisprudence in Brazil, to the effect that the right to an ecologically balanced environment is a fundamental right of a diffuse nature.[1] Therefore, any human action that may disrupt such balance must be regarded as a violation of society's fundamental right, and hence conduct which is at odds with the notion of sustainable development. It follows that the essential role of environmental law in promoting sustainable development must be to ensure that human activities do not affect the ecological balance of the environment.

In the light of this, environmental torts can be regarded as the outcome of human conduct that law itself acknowledges as illicit, based on the adverse effects of that conduct on the environment. As such, environmental torts represent the antithesis of sustainable development, challenging law to provide not only for the complete restoration of the environment's ecological balance, but also for the full compensation for each of the interests potentially impaired by environmental wrongdoing. In that endeavour, the specific interests that may be affected by harmful actions against the environment require careful juridical identification of the full spectrum of rights and the persons affected, as well as of the nuances in the nature of the damage caused. This calls for an analysis beyond ordinary tort liability schemes. The award of damages for injuries caused to individual/private rights, to collective rights, and to public corporations/entities' rights, even when remediation or recovery of the harmed natural resources in question may be achieved, is but a part of the redressing equation, as society's interests, in their own right, are not considered.

This chapter argues that in order to ensure full and complete compensation through the award of damages, and thus to discourage environmentally unsustainable actions, both material and moral[2] damage to society's right to an ecologically balanced environment must be acknowledged, economically appraised, and appropriately redressed.

The importance of balancing human activities with the carrying capacity and resilience of the natural environment is a relatively recent concern, at least on a global scale (Hunter et al., 2002). One result of this has been the emergence of sustainable development as the proper means of associating economic development and the satisfaction of basic human necessities with the maintenance of a sound environment. While applying the notion of sustainable development has proved difficult, as social, economic and environmental views rarely converge, the intention of the present work is not to discuss the conceptual intricacies and flaws of sustainable development.

The chapter is underpinned by the conviction that social or economic interests cannot override the importance of environmental values, as the latter are the quintessential expression of life and human needs can only exist while there are living human beings able to have and to express them. Thus, for the purpose of this work, sustainable development is viewed primarily in environmental terms, to be assessed according to the likelihood of an action to interfere with society's right to a sound and ecologically balanced environment. Such a rationale, far from aspiring to be the final word in a necessarily disputed discussion, merely provides a logical premise upon which these ideas are built. They entail two principles. The first is that the right to an ecologically balanced environment is a fundamental societal and, therefore, an *indivisible* right, which can neither be relinquished by its several (although undetermined) holders, nor disposed of by anyone in particular (Daibert, 2007; Silva, 2008). Society's right to the environment, so expressed, has total autonomy from and no basis whatsoever in property, be it public or private, either in natural resources or on the land where they are located (Daibert, 2008). Hence, whatever use a property owner (be it public or private) may wish to make of natural resources, land, environmental services or commons, in order to bring benefits to an individual or a group of individuals, shall only be permissible to the extent it does not cause harm to any essential quality of the environment. The second principle underpinning the present discussion is that the right to an ecologically balanced environment belongs to future as much as to present generations[3] and that, therefore, in this context intergenerational equity is as much an ethical as an economic imperative (Robinson, 2008). If past generations could speak now, they might argue that they promoted depletion of natural resources in ignorance of the negative, cumulative, environmental effects their actions would have for the present generation. This argument does not, however, hold for the present generation which is well aware that taking more than what is needed to survive today with dignity is not only environmentally unsustainable, but also, looking to the interests of future generations, ethically unacceptable (Robinson, 2008). The environmental capital of future generations can neither be used today to finance our generation's economy nor to pay our social debt to the destitute, which must instead be funded by existing financial resources acquired from our generation's fair share of the environment and our inheritance of riches extracted from nature by past generations.

## 2.   ENVIRONMENTAL TORTS AND SUSTAINABILITY

Ensuring that the promotion of environmentally sustainable development permeates every possible aspect of today's life is most certainly the major challenge of modern environmental law. It is thus obvious that nothing could be less environmentally sustainable than an action that law itself considers harmful to the environment. Therefore, an effective regime of environmental torts is fundamental to promoting environmentally sustainable development, in order to set limits on activities and impose consequences for infringing them. In this context, securing satisfactory redress for all parties potentially harmed by an environmental tort poses particularly complex problems. Failure to grasp and address all of the nuances that environmental damage implies will result in insufficient redress for the full spectrum of interests affected. From the perspective of diffuse damage this also allows wrongdoers to accrue assets at society's expense, further spurring a vicious cycle of unsustainability.

## 3.   CURRENT ENVIRONMENTAL LAW SCHEMES FOR TORTS

Current law, in simply applying common torts schemes to environmental torts, does not provide full compensation in environmental tort cases (Cavalieri Filho, 2002; Steigleder, 2004).[4] To do so, it must develop and enforce its own complementary, specific system of redress, that considers the peculiarities of environmental damage and the societal interests involved. To develop this idea, it is necessary first to recall the key concepts and notions of tort law, in order to contrast them with those that this chapter considers essential to address the specific aspects of environmental torts.

The generally accepted elements of liability may be described as follows: (a) a party's unlawful action; (b) actual damage caused to another party's assets; and (c) a causative link between the one party's unlawful action and the damage suffered by another party.

In terms of the parties involved, it is usually recognised that damage can be inflicted on (a) an individual; and/or (b) a set of individuals (a group, category or class,[5] hereinafter referred to as a 'collectivity', sustaining what will be referred to as collective damage).

The damage in question is normally categorised as material and/or moral (immaterial). Material damage comprises two types. The first is emergent damages (i.e., economically quantifiable injuries *immediately resultant* on the injured party from the wrongdoer's unlawful conduct, estimated on the economic value necessary to compensate for losses of property or any other concrete, tangible assets instantly impaired or destroyed by the wrongdoer's action at the time it took place) (Cavalieri Filho, 2002, p. 81). The second is loss of profits (i.e., economically quantifiable benefits or profits the aggrieved party may have reasonably expected to earn in the future, had the damage not occurred) (ibid.). Moral damage, on the other hand, should be understood as harming immaterial, abstract, intangible, non-tradable assets that are, nonetheless, highly prized values such as honour, peace of mind, tranquillity, quality of life, and worth, etc. Although their economic value is difficult to quantify, interference with them by a wrongdoer's action requires (to the extent possible) significant financial compensation. Moral damages are usually estimated by the courts, but statutes can also stipulate fair amounts (Cavalieri Filho, 2002). They also have a punitive character, deterring potential future wrongdoing.

The above provides the starting point for assessing environmental liability in torts, and developing a specific scheme to apply in environmental cases that is additional or complementary to the general torts perspectives. Such a scheme must address the impact of a given wrongdoing on the environment, considered as a whole, and take into due account the following: enlarging the class of rights' holders in order to include society (as the sole holder of the right to an ecologically balanced environment) in the list of potentially aggrieved parties; and amplifying the general torts approach to damages by aiming to provide compensation to the full extent of the damage, material and moral, that environmental wrongdoing implies to society's right.

Dealing firstly with the matter of rights holders, environmental liability schemes, following the prevalent approach in torts, normally only entertain claims in respect of damage due to environmental harms caused to individuals.[6] Thus, on proof of causation of loss by unlawful conduct of the wrongdoer, individuals may be entitled to recover emergent damages[7] and compensation for loss of profits.[8]

Following the same thread, there is no difficulty in according public entities the same status as individuals, whenever they must spend money on remediation and recovery in respect of publicly owned natural assets (such as a publicly owned forest) and/or they face losses of natural resources found in public lands and other resources. They are just as entitled to recoup such emergent damages as private parties are. However, in order to seek compensation for loss of profits, public entities may have to produce evidence that the land and/or natural resources impaired by the wrongdoing would have been legitimately subjected to an economic use, if the unlawful conduct had not taken place.[9]

The award of damages in respect of environmental torts encapsulating the negative effects of environmental harm perpetrated against the rights of a collectivity is not problematic in principle either, because the rights of a collectivity will always be the standard rights of its members jointly considered. This also explains why, in essence, collective damage can be of both a material and moral nature where collective interests are concerned. A few examples will illustrate this.

For instance, in terms of material damage we can consider the economic losses of a fishing community. If the fishermen can no longer catch and sell fish because of environmental contamination of the body of water where they fish, the general loss of income sustained can be considered collective material damage. In that case, a fishermen's association, for instance, would be able to submit a single claim for redress on behalf of its members. Based on the same rationale, individual and group emotional distress and loss of self-esteem caused by the suppression (whether temporary or permanent) of their livelihood, are aspects of moral damage that must be also acknowledged and collectively redressed.

Where payment of damages is concerned, from the perspective of the assets affected in environmental cases, the focus has usually been on the best way to direct the perpetrator of an environmental wrongdoing to pay for the following: remediation of the affected natural resources, or the costs of equivalent action taken toward that end by another party, plus material and moral damage caused to individuals and/or collectivities.

By and large, this is as far as the ordinary environmental torts regime goes, both in terms of identification of rights holders and of definition of the objects for which they might be entitled to receive compensation. This is precisely why such a legal scheme does not provide enough protection to the whole spectrum of rights and assets that may be violated by an environmental tort, as discussed below.

## 4. SOCIETY'S DIFFUSE RIGHTS TO AN ECOLOGICALLY BALANCED ENVIRONMENT

One of the principles this work is based on states that society has an autonomous right to an ecologically balanced environment. In ideal terms, this should be acknowledged as a fundamental right, if not on its own at least insofar as it is a critical element of the right to life, as life in a poor, low-quality, unhealthy environment is effectively the denial of life itself.[10] In this respect, it seems that the Brazilian Federal Constitution has created a very comprehensive and useful provision aiming at determining the essentials of society's environmental rights:

> Art. 225. *All* have the *right to an ecologically balanced environment*, which is *an asset of common use* and essential to a sound quality of life, and both the Government and the community shall have the duty to defend and preserve it for present and future generations [Emphasis added].

Some of this provision's many merits will now be considered. First, the provision demonstrates that the ordinary environmental tort liability scheme fails to give protection to society's autonomous rights respecting the environment, as it neglects the rights that society holds as a whole; rights that belong to all members of society. Nevertheless, these rights, in principle, can be invoked by anyone, as long as this is done on behalf of all.[11] These rights are indivisible and not subject to exclusive use or private appropriation; they bind their holders by means of a factual, legitimate, fundamental interest in an asset which inspires its legal recognition and protection; and they are neither individual nor collective, but rather of a trans-individual nature, as they are beyond any possibility of individualisation; in other words, they are diffuse rights.[12]

The Brazilian constitutional provision also opens an opportunity for posing a practical question: does anyone own the environment? Should diffuse rights be interpreted as meaning that society is the rightful 'owner of the environment'? Concerning this matter, the constitutional provision under analysis is hugely important in facilitating an assertion that has already been touched upon in the introduction of this chapter: that society's right to a balanced environment is not dependent on any discussion about ownership of natural resources or of the lands where they might be located. That is so because the right that society holds is not to property in the environment itself, therefore it is neither subject to any sort of change in scope deriving from, nor does it interfere with (in private property law terms, at least) individual ownership rights.[13] The same societal rights are neither rights of property of, nor privilege in, the use of natural resources or lands where they might be found. Society's rights instead represent a common prerogative to ensure the ecological balance of the environment so that it can be used for its essential purpose, maintaining a sound quality of life.

Despite the irrelevance of ownership for the assertion of its environmental diffuse rights, society is nonetheless entitled to demand that the use of property (whether public or private) guarantees that it will not hinder, impair or endanger the common goal of ensuring the ecological balance of the environment. That is implicit in Article 225 and made quite clear in other parts of the Brazilian Constitution (Daibert, 2008).[14] Potential conflicts involving the use of property and environmental rights should be assessed on the basis of whether property rights are being exercised according to the social function that the Constitution requires from the property, which includes the duty of the property owner to protect the environment. Hence, the only relevant aspect to be addressed involving property in land or natural resources in light of society's environmental rights, is whether ownership rights are being properly exercised in order not to interfere in the environmental balance. That, of course, does not imply that property rights would vanish from private or public hands and become subject to communal management. This is so precisely because society need not invoke or dispute any sort of property rights to assert or protect its right to a balanced environment. Second, it is because no public or private ownership right may be subjected to any kind of societal control concerning environmental matters, as long as the proprietors' rights are exercised without interfering with that same balance. In addition it is, to a limited extent, open to the property rights' holder to contest society's environmental claims based on proprietary rights (in addition to possible claims based on the reach or validity of a given environmental regulation). Regulatory takings doctrine serves to assess whether environmental protection burdens imposed on the property owner on behalf of society render the use of the property impracticable and, therefore, require compensation to be paid by taxpayers in exchange for the affected property.[15]

On the other hand, society's diffuse rights to the environment are commonly confused with collective rights or even with rights that a public entity may hold as the owner of natural resources and lands. Collective rights, as discussed, are, however, akin to a summation of individual rights that can be exercised or claimed by an entity on behalf of a set of individuals whenever indivisible rights are trans-individually held by a group, class or category. The fact that greater or lesser numbers of individuals may enjoy rights as part of a collectivity – as well as the connection such rights may have with an environmental tort – does not, however, convert them from collective to diffuse. Furthermore, the rights of the public entity over its properties differ from diffuse rights, as the latter should not be seen as belonging to any public corporation, for they are not subject to any kind of individual appropriation or divisibility.

The following question could be posed: what if, by collecting damages as an individual from a wrongdoer, a public entity may achieve the restoration of an affected environment by means of merely obtaining the recovery of its harmed assets? Would that not show the diffuse nature of the public entity's action? As far as this goes, if compensation for lost assets was the sole goal of the public entity's claim, the resultant restoration of the environment would be merely an incidental, although advantageous, result of its course of action.[16] However, in systems like that in Brazil, a public entity can submit a claim for redress of damage against its own property rights (over natural resources and lands it owns) as well as a claim for redress for injuries to diffuse rights. Nevertheless, the latter does not mean that the public entity is 'the holder' of the diffuse right it is claiming. On the contrary, to the limited extent the public entity will be arguing in favour of diffuse rights, it will only be speaking on behalf of society, not in its own right as a public entity, as it acts purely as the party granted locus standi to raise diffuse rights in court.

Yet there are other kinds of damage to diffuse rights that must be redressed on behalf of society and go beyond the restoration of the balance of the environment. So, if a public entity's claim, such as the one initially posed in the previous paragraph, fails to obtain redress for the complete array of damage society can be subjected to by an environmental tort, other persons may be entitled to seek proper compensation for the aspects of diffuse rights that were disregarded because that would have been nonetheless an individual rights-based lawsuit.

Nuisance cases, where a property owner complains of damage caused to his or her own property by the improper use of a neighbour's property, raise further questions. In a number of legal systems, this may grant the right to an injunction or to seek individual redress, even if the environment is also affected. A successful lawsuit, under such terms, would usually stop the wrongdoer's conduct and perhaps remedy the adverse impact on the injured party's property. However, the plaintiff would neither have standing to sue for the remediation of the wrongdoers' property nor for the protection of other affected areas, in order to promote environmental balance. The right is limited to the protection only of the owner's property (albeit connected to an environmental issue), exclusively based on the ownership of the land and only legitimate to the extent that such land was affected by the neighbour's wrongdoing. In other words, it would never be as broad a claim as one based on diffuse environmental rights.

In spite of all arguments presented, the truth is that the legal debate usually overlooks the important distinctions[17] that exist in such situations, making it very difficult to achieve full compensation for society in environmental torts, which generally result only in compensation for damage to individual and, to a lesser extent, collective interests.

Ultimately, the acknowledgment of diffuse environmental rights and of the entitlement of society, as the holder of such rights, to receive compensation for their violation must be addressed, in order to guarantee that the sustainability balance disrupted by an environmental tort is always properly and adequately remedied. This is not just a rhetorical problem, but rather a question of fairness in ensuring complete compensation of the full spectrum of aggrieved interests. As a result, legal regimes that do not establish clear schemes to protect diffuse rights must be deemed incomplete. Such regimes err in leaving society's interests unprotected in their failure to understand diffuse rights as an autonomous category of rights, independent of those of any other sort of public entity or private rights.

## 5. ADDRESSING COMPENSATION FOR DIFFUSE RIGHTS VIOLATIONS

Reflecting on the nature of the interests motivating the parties involved in litigation in this area, it could be argued that damage caused to individuals' assets and rights is not 'environmental' in nature. Indeed, while invoking such rights may perhaps indirectly contribute to remediation of the affected environment, this will only be an oblique result of measures targeted on the satisfaction of individual interests, which are ordinarily not fully coincident with those of society. This is even the case when a public entity claims for redress of the loss of its assets; as such a claim can only be based on its ownership rights.[18] In other words, a tort first directly impacts the environment adversely; and only then indirectly to individuals, perhaps prompting litigation. Thus, the problems regarding the actual quality and the ecological balance of the environment itself need to be addressed elsewhere – under a specific regime applicable to diffuse rights.

There are, however, practical benefits in treating individuals' torts claims, only indirectly related to damage to the environment, as environmental damage claims, as they may then benefit from strict liability or other special approaches that environmental law may deem applicable to environmental torts. Such a method could systematically combine consideration of indirect adverse effects on individuals with the direct adverse impacts of the same tort on the environment, as both generate environmental impacts. Such an approach recognises that the effects triggered by environmental damage on individual rights and those on the environment (and hence, to society) may have common ground. Nonetheless, the way that the law deals with them must ultimately be differentiated and independent, albeit characterised by a good measure of consistency.

Genuine environmental tort is the product of the direct, adverse impacts on the environment in its own right, affecting the environment's ecological balance and representing a perfectly discernible violation of society's autonomous diffuse rights thereon. Let us consider, for example, where a forest has been felled. In terms of restoring the ecological balance and satisfying society's rights, the ownership of the trees and/or the land in question is irrelevant, as society's interest in the balance of the environment remains a totally autonomous diffuse right. This being the case, environmental liability is to be understood not only in terms of the precise right in question (the diffuse right to an ecologically balanced environment) and its holder (society or 'all'), but also in the recognition that the violation of such a right entitles its holder to redress, like any other party in an ordinary tort situation. In this context, environmental liability should be founded on two additional pillars: environmental remediation needed to restore the ecological balance that has been disrupted; and compensating society for the particular, identifiable consequences it will bear as a result of the damage, in terms of the time that it will be deprived of an ecologically balanced environment, together with its services and functions. In addition, in order to address fully the compensation component of damage caused to society's environmental diffuse rights, it must be acknowledged that damage to such rights can also be of both a material and a moral nature. First, we must consider what is encapsulated by material diffuse damage. Will it extend to emergent damages resulting from damage to diffuse environmental rights when we know that society does not own the environment? What impact does this have on determining damages awards?

In relation to the loss of profits, can society's diffuse right to a balanced environment accommodate a right to profit from nature, providing for redress for reasonably expected earnings that a tort may have frustrated for the future?

With regard to emergent damages associated with harmed diffuse rights, the first issue is the lack of ownership of the environment by society. The problem is: if society does not own the environment, how can it ever be entitled to seek compensation for the devaluation of such assets? Let us initially keep in mind that not every natural resource constitutes a commodity or tradable good, nor is subject to an ownership regime. Does that absence of ownership of the environment make environmental protection in cases of tangible, although not tradable, environmental assets impossible? Does this also preclude imposing a duty on a defendant to fully compensate for interference with intangible values? The answer must in both cases be no, as lack of ownership of the environment cannot in any sense mean that the right to its ecological balance is empty or unenforceable. The fact that the right to an ecologically balanced environment is intangible and impossible to appropriate (as are its elements such as air quality, water quality, etc.) does not make it less of a right. Nor does this render its elements less legally recognisable, legitimately enjoyable or subject to juridical protection in order to safeguard the array of purposes that serve the common goal of assuring a sound quality of life.[19] If the ecosystems are no longer able (whether temporarily or permanently) to provide such services and functions, is there an alternative? Even if this were feasible, what would be the cost? If such impacts are wrought on the environment, the legal consequences, including the financial costs of addressing the whole range of problems experienced, must be imposed on the wrongdoer. That is why it is irrelevant to inquire about ownership of natural resources, land or nature; at the same time it is essential to acknowledge a discernable, legally protected and justiciable diffuse right to an ecologically balanced environment.

A second aspect regarding material compensation for diffuse rights violations is that one should recall that compensation based on rights other than diffuse rights can eventually achieve the restoration of certain environmental assets, though this may or may not bring about the complete remediation of the affected ecological balance of the environment. This circumstance alone would entail the recognition that such claims are unlikely to suffice to redress material damage caused to diffuse rights. Moreover, they could never result in full compensation for all aspects of diffuse rights violation, at most providing possible, incidental benefits to the harmed environment. None of this would be problematic if it is recognised that diffuse rights claims need never be based on any kind of assertion of property in the environment or the natural resources that it comprises. The relevance of the discussion is not to realise the market value of the affected resources or land where they stand, but to aim to restore the environment's ecological balance. Material compensation for diffuse rights violations does not, however, stop here, because such compensation shall be deemed incomplete if society does not receive redress for losses that are quantifiable in economic terms, based on the actual value of environmental functions and services harmed as a consequence of the environmental damage, which also represents a distinct head of emergent damage (Findley, 1999, pp. 567–568).[20]

In relation to the loss of profits, under the current regime it is quite difficult, if not impossible, to envision diffuse rights implying any sort of notion capable of visualising profits that society could possibly have earned, should the environmental damage not have occurred. However, in theory, would it not be possible to construct a legal scheme (whether national or international) instituting and regulating the payment for ecological services rendered, for example, by whole, large-scale, widespread ecosystems (such as the Brazilian portion of the Amazon Forest) to other parts of Brazil and/or to the global community (Appleton, 2002)?[21] While questions of the ownership of such funds (which could be extended to diffuse rights holders)[22] would need to be resolved, they could certainly represent a reasonable expectation for profits derived from the environment.

The fact that the current, prevailing view is reluctant to ascribe a market value to environmental services/functions (Scherr, et al., 2004, p. 3; Ranganathan, 2008, pp. ii, 38) does not mean that such services and functions do not have an economically appraisable value. One of the reasons that environmental services/functions are subject to little consideration from the market lies in the difficulties encountered by law in grasping the diffuse nature of the rights existent over them and in developing an effective regime for their protection. Law generally makes it problematic for society to assert its rights, making them subservient to other rights held by more organised and easily acknowledgeable interest groups (Robinson, 2004, p. 3). This also helps explain why it is still so difficult nowadays to find consensus about whether obvious, valuable, essential, environmental services and functions like water and air purification, climate and microclimate control, pollinating, etc., should have a price tag, whereas it is so easy to accept that individuals may profit from the actions that may result in their impairment.

It is important that environmental law evolves to ensure that those who impair such environmental services and functions through wrongdoing pay for the damage caused to society, compensating for emerging damage based on the cost of services and functions at stake, and also taking into account the time that society will be deprived of them. This will be aided by improvements in science and economics on the appraisal of such effects (Ranganathan, 2008). It is unquestionable that damage exists; the issue of how much it represents in monetary terms is either a matter of technical estimation or of judicial arbitration, or both. What cannot be accepted is that the indisputably aggrieved society remains deprived of proper redress because our legal system is incapable of delivering justice in this context.

In addition, it should be pointed out that problems with environmental services and functions will most certainly and dramatically adversely affect public health and welfare. That will generate loss in terms of additional expenditure of public funds in order to offset or diminish those impacts for the public. These negative effects will, however, fall within the realm of individual rights, not diffuse rights, as they will be borne by the expenditure of public entities, although this proportional increase in public expenditure may well help to estimate the value of the environmental services and functions that the wrongdoer must pay for. With a material diffuse damage legal scheme thus delineated, a question remains: is it possible that an environmental tort challenges compensation, based on moral diffuse damage? The answer, by all means, should be in the affirmative.

Although society's diffuse rights are not based on the consideration of individuals' interests, society is but the sum of all individuals and comprised by them. Therefore, if individuals can suffer from emotional distress or loss of self-esteem indirectly resulting from the negative effects caused by wrongful damage to their environment, why then may not the ultimate amalgam of individuals also agglomerate its members' interests and entitlements as a whole in order to seek compensation for the violation of diffuse moral rights on the same basis? For this reason, moral environmental diffuse damage should be assessed, in parallel with that of a material nature, aiming to compensate for losses not easily economically quantifiable, but nonetheless always resulting from wrongful environmental damage. These include: negative psychological impacts directly caused to society by perceived environmental degradation; emotional distress resulting during the time that society is deprived of the entirety of the impaired or destroyed environment; emotional distress and deterioration in quality of life during the time that society cannot benefit from environmental services and functions that the same suppressed or degraded environment would otherwise render; consequent negative impacts of that state of affairs on values such as society's self-esteem, psychological integrity and aesthetic enjoyment.

Compensation for moral diffuse damage has been the subject of litigation in Brazilian courts several times and is gaining momentum in legal commentary (Sampaio, 2003, pp. 188–189; Steigleder, 2004). The first case discussing moral environmental diffuse damage took place in the State of Rio de Janeiro Court of Appeal.[23] It involved a piece of land of about 4,000 square metres where vegetation was seriously interfered with by the property owner, causing severe environmental damage. The City of Rio de Janeiro, invoking environmental diffuse rights on behalf of society, filed a Public Civil Action[24] seeking complete restoration of the degraded vegetation, asking the court to direct the wrongdoer to replant 2,800 saplings of native species, according to a plan approved by the municipal environment department. In addition, the plaintiff sought compensation for the moral diffuse damage that society would suffer as a result of the tort (for the time society would be deprived of the degraded ecosystem and its full environmental capacity to provide for services and functions), as well as in respect of the negative aesthetic impacts and harmful consequences for quality of life. The trial judge granted the remediation measures, but did not award the moral diffuse damages. The Court of Appeal, however, in addition to upholding the remedial measures, also ordered that the defendant pay a fine equivalent to 200 minimum wages in Brazil.[25] It did so asserting that: restoration of the degraded environment did not hinder the award of compensation for moral diffuse damages; that the material damage, represented by the restoration of the degraded ecosystem, was distinct from the moral damage resulting from 'the loss of environmental values' by society. The Court further held that society was entitled to receive moral compensation for the time it would take for the affected ecosystem to completely recover its original characteristics and functionality, because during that time, quality of life would be affected as well. The Court noted that the numbers of cases involving environmental torts was increasing and that an award of compensation for moral damage should be granted in part to deter others. Finally, the Court also highlighted that, although there is no statutory provision as to the size of moral diffuse damages awards, it could itself determine an amount, based on reasonableness and proportionality.[26]

However, a higher court[27] in a second case[28] essentially held that moral damages must be linked 'to the notion of pain, of suffering, [which are] of individual character'. The court added that granting compensation for moral diffuse damage would be incompatible with the 'notion of trans-individuality' that diffuse rights embodied, mainly when the effects of the wrongdoing and the compensation awarded are indivisible. This case considered misconduct by a municipality that had unlawfully remained inactive in face of a notorious illegal subdivision that was being carried out by a private investor, causing severe environmental damage. The majority view was that only individuals could be compensated by moral damages, on the basis that there is no such thing as 'moral damage to seas, rivers, the Atlantic Rain Forest or even a moral aggression to a collectivity or a non-identified group of people'[29] and that it would always have to be granted to 'a person, bearer of proper individuality'.[30]

It is significant however, that the case was decided by a majority of three to two. Furthermore, one of the majority, while taking the view that there was no basis for awarding moral damages in the instant case, added: 'there will be situations in which the [moral] damage may be compensated with objective measures of physical remediation or of financial compensation for the moral collective and diffuse damage'.[31]

A subsequent case reached the same court and happened to be decided by the very same panel of judges that participated in the previous opinion.[32] This time, though, the outcome was different: the court unanimously upheld an opinion of the State of Rio Grande do Sul Court of Appeal that had granted compensation for moral diffuse damage in a case of noise pollution, signalling a possible change in the Superior Court of Justice's view on the matter.

Thus, the award of moral diffuse damages has been accepted by the Brazilian Courts and other systems may be expected to follow suit. In fact, this issue should have been less controversial than it was in Brazil, given that statutory environmental law[33] clearly provides for the right to such moral compensation in cases of damage to the environment, to aesthetic and scenic values, and to 'any other collective or diffuse interest'.

## 6.  CONCLUSION

Acknowledging the autonomy of society's diffuse right to an ecologically balanced environment and recognising the legal consequences that such autonomy implies are only initial steps that environmental law must take in order to ensure that environmental damage is properly addressed. In addition, compensation for both material and moral damage caused to society as a result of the violation of that diffuse right is imperative to guaranteeing that the environment and sustainability are effectively protected. In this situation, material and moral diffuse damages should be coupled with individual/collective rights compensation, administrative penalties and criminal enforcement. All of these tools must be used and the law must be enforced to its full extent if we are to act consistently with what we preach, in recognising the value of the environment.

At the same time, acknowledging diffuse rights also requires extending standing to sue to facilitate stronger societal control of actions interfering with the environment and the maintenance of sustainability, as rights are illusory if citizens cannot enforce them in court (Thornton, 2007, pp. 38–46). Here, once again, Brazil provides a good example in its Public Civil Suit, under Federal Law No. 7,347, of 24 July, 1985. According to this statute, several entities are entitled to sue on behalf of society in order to assert diffuse rights (these are not limited to environmental matters): (state and federal) offices of public prosecution; all levels of government and their attached legal entities (including private companies held by the administration). Furthermore, private entities, such as foundations or civil associations (NGOs), also have standing to sue if they satisfy certain requirements, including having environmental protection as one of their institutional purposes in their constitutive documents.

Acknowledging society's diffuse environmental rights and securing compensation to society as the sole legitimate rights holder is a prerequisite for sustainability. It is also a requirement of morality and justice. Finally, a proper legal scheme for environmental torts is a key element of environmental protection, as it provides a clear disincentive to potential environmental wrongdoers. Moreover, it provides an essential tool for environmental practitioners and judges to better address environmental malfeasance and thus to promote sustainable development.

# NOTES

1. The concept of diffuse rights in the present work is not exclusive to, but is adopted from, the Brazilian legal system. The meaning of the term is discussed below.
2. The material and moral nature of damage is also a notion that, although not exclusive to, is borrowed from Brazilian legal doctrine, for the purpose of this article; see further below.
3. Art. 225, *chapeau* Brazilian Constitution 1988.
4. Although equivalent conceptual structures exist in legal systems generally, the focus here is on Brazilian law.
5. Defined by the *Brazilian Consumer's Code*, Brazilian Law 8,078 of 11 September, 1990. Art. 81, II as: a determined collectivity of persons bound to one another and to the adverse party by a standard juridical relationship.
6. As of this point, the plural 'individuals' will be used as simultaneously, although indifferently, referring to an isolated individual; or a group of individuals having homogeneous rights arising from the same environmental tort, but not organised as a *collectivity*.
7. For example, the costs of restoration or remediation of assets destroyed or impaired, including compensation for privately owned natural resources or land, health care costs, and other personal, direct harm suffered by the injured parties as an immediate consequence of the wrongdoing. See Apelação Cível (Appeal) No. 257.636-1 – Cubatão – 9ª Câmara de Direito Privado do TJSP (9th Panel of Private Law Court of Appeal of the State of Sao Paulo Judiciary) – Relator (Judge) Ruiter Oliva – 15.10.96, for a case of illness (resulting from the intoxication by benzene) caused by an industry's risky activity with regard to an employee.
8. For example, the market price of natural resources or land that belonged to them, which could have been legitimately committed to an economic use, as well as the money they might have earned for the time they ended up being incapable of carrying out their professional activities, should the tort have not taken place. See Apelação Cível (Appeal) No. 2002.001.16035, 7a Câmara Cível do TJRJ (7th Panel on Civil Law of the Court of Appeal of the State of Rio de Janeiro Judiciary), Relator (Judge) Luiz Roldão, 19.08.2002, on the right of a fisherman to collect from the polluter the monthly income he no longer could earn from fishing in the Guanabara Bay, as a result of an oil spill in 2000.
9. Whether or not a public entity could seek compensation for moral damage in its own right is an interesting point, but beyond the scope of this chapter.
10. See, for example, the Supreme Court of India ruling in *Subhash Kumar v State of Bihar* (AIR 1991 SC 420).
11. In spite of that, Brazilian Federal Law No. 7,347 for the Public Civil Suit, enacted in 1985 apparently does not allow everyone to file law suits on the grounds of diffuse environmental damage (Art. 5 of the statute and Conclusions, below), limiting standing to sue to certain entities etc. However, the Brazilian Constitution of 1988 arguably revoked that limitation, providing that 'all' have the right to an ecologically sound environment. Further, Art. 5, No. XXXV, given that, for every right in Brazil, there must be an action to seek judicial protection.
12. Brazilian Consumer's Code, Brazilian Law 8,078 of September 11, 1990. Art. 81, I, defines them as trans-individual rights of an indivisible nature, whose holders are undetermined persons linked by factual circumstances.
13. Limitations applicable to all sorts of property are found in environmental regulations; these constrain the way property rights are exercised, but do not, in principle, change the juridical relationship between the asset and its owner.
14. See Arts 5, XXIII, and III and VI, combined with Art. 182, §20 and Art. 186, I and II of the Brazilian Constitution, on the social function of property.
15. In Brazil, administrative limitations (including those of an environmental nature) on property rights are likely to be upheld by Courts as long as they are equally applicable to

all properties in a similar situation; see Recurso Extraordinário (Constitutional Appeal) No. 102847, Segunda Turma do (Second Panel), Supremo Tribunal Federal (Brazilian Supreme Court), Relator (Justice) Aldir Passarinho, 12.03.85. Thus far no court has upheld property rights as an obstacle to environmental protection claims based on lawful administrative limitations.

16. The rationale may be derived and reinforced, in Brazil, from the ruling in the Special Appeal (Recurso Especial) No. 706.449, 4th Panel (4a. Turma) of the Superior Court of Justice, *Proquigel Química S/A v. Associação dos Moradores do Jardim Cristal e Jardim Marambaia*. Opinion issued on 26 May, 2008, delivered by Judge Fernando Gonçalves. Here the Court separates individual rights claims from diffuse rights claims.

17. See note 28 for a case that clearly misses such important nuances.

18. Keeping in mind that the participation of a public entity in a lawsuit that claims diffuse rights is solely based on the specific standing law grants to that entity to act on behalf of society.

19. See Art. 225, *chapeau*, of the Brazilian Constitution; it states that the right to an ecologically balanced environment is an 'asset of common use and essential to a sound quality of life'.

20. See, for example Section 1006(d)(1)(B) of the 1990 Oil Pollution Act (OPA), 33 USCA §2706.

21. This hypothetical situation should not be confused with regimes where individuals have been paid to conserve private natural resources or land that they own, which are necessary for specific ecosystems to render their inherent ecological services.

22. To be managed perhaps through the creation of a specific fund for that purpose, such as in the case of the Fund for the Defence of Diffuse Interests (Fundo de Defesa dos Interesses Difusos), established by Art. 2(I), of the Federal Executive Order (Decreto) No. 1306/94, based on Art. 13 of Federal Law No. 7,347/85.

23. Appeal (Apelação Cível) No. 2001.001.14586, Second Court of Appeal (Segunda Câmara Cível), *City of Rio de Janeiro v. Artur da Rocha Mendes Neto*; opinion issued on 6 March, 2002, delivered by Judge Maria Raimunda T. de Azevedo.

24. See Brazilian Federal Law No. 7,347, of 24 July, 1985.

25. A minimum wage in Brazil is roughly equivalent to US$300 per month, so the compensation awarded was approximately US$60,000.

26. Another ruling in the same State Appellate Court, but by a different panel, acknowledged the right to redress in the same terms; see Appeal (Apelação Cível) No. 2007.001.57524, Thirteenth Panel of Appeal (Segunda Câmara Cível), *Germano Pereira da Silva v. Ministerio Publico do Estado do Rio de Janeiro*; opinion issued on 13 February, 2008, delivered by Judge José Azevedo Pinto.

27. The Superior Court of Justice (Superior Tribunal de Justiça), the highest court for non-constitutional matters.

28. Special Appeal (Recurso Especial) No. 598.281, 1st Panel (1a. Turma) of the Superior Court of Justice, *Public Prosecution of the State of Sao Paulo v Municipality of Uberlandia*. Opinion issued on 2 May, 2006, delivered by Judge Teori Albino Zavascki.

29. Ibid.

30. Ibid.

31. Ibid.

32. Special Appeal (Recurso Especial) No. 791.653, 1st Panel (1a. Turma) of the Superior Court of Justice, *Public Prosecution of the State of Rio Grande do Sul vs. Agip do Brasil S/A*. Opinion issued on 6 February, 2007, delivered by Justice José Delgado.

33. Art. 1 *chapeau*, I, III, and IV, of the same provision of Law No. 7,347, of 24 July, 1985.

# REFERENCES

Appleton, Albert F. (2002), *How New York City Used an Ecosystem Services Strategy Carried out Through an Urban–Rural Partnership to Preserve the Pristine Quality of Its Drinking Water and Save Billions of Dollars* (A paper for Forest Trends), at www.forest-trends.org/documents/meetings/tokyo_ 2002/NYC_H2O_ Ecosystem_ Services.pdf.

Cavalieri Filho, Sérgio (2002), *Programa de Responsabilidade Civil* (Tort Liability Program), São Paulo: Malheiros Editores, pp. 84–113.

Daibert, Arlindo (2007), 'An Overview of the Environment and the Constitution in Brazil', in Isabelle Larmuseau (ed.), *Constitutional Rights to an Ecologically Balanced Environment*, Belgium: VVOR – Vlaamse Vereniging voor Omgevingsrecht.

Daibert, Arlindo (2008), *Notas Sobre Proteção Ambiental e o Direito de Propriedade no Direito Brasileiro* (Notes on Environmental Protection and the Property Right in the Brazilian Law), Brazil: Editora Fórum, pp. 150–155.

Findley, Roger W., Daniel A. Farber and Jody Freeman (1999), *Cases and Materials on Environmental Law*, St Paul, Minnesota: West Group.

Hunter, David, James Salzman and Durwood Zaelke (2002), *International Environmental Law and Policy*, New York: Foundation Press, pp. 178–184.

Ranganathan, Janet (2008), *Ecosystem Services, A Guide for Decision Makers*, Washington, DC: World Resources Institute, pp. 29–44.

Robinson, Nicholas A. (ed.) (2004), *Strategies Toward Sustainable Development: Implementing Agenda 21*, Dobbs Ferry, New York: Oceana Publications, pp. 347–366.

Robinson, Nicholas A. (2008), 'Imperatives in Environmental Law', in Arlindo Daibert (ed.), *Notas Sobre Proteção Ambiental e o Direito de Propriedade no Direito Brasileiro* (Notes on Environmental Protection and the Property Right in the Brazilian Law), Belo Horizonte: Editora Fórum.

Sampaio, Franciso José Marques (2003), *Evolução da Responsabilidade Civil e Reparação dos Danos Ambientais* (Tort Liability Evolution and Redress of the Environmental Damages), Rio de Janeiro: Editora Renovar.

Scherr, Sara, Andy White and Arvind Khare (2004), *For Services Rendered – The Current Status and Future Potential of Markets for the Ecosystem Services Provided by Tropical Forests*, International Tropical Timber Organization, at http://www.forest-trends.org/documents/files/doc_123.pdf.

Silva, Vasco Pereira da (2008), *Verde Direito: o Direito Fundamental ao Amiente* (Green Law: the Fundamental Right to the Environment), in Arlindo Daibert (ed.), *Direito Ambiental Comparado* (Comparative Environmental Law), Belo Horizonte: Editora Fórum, pp. 17–46.

Steigleder, Annelise Monteiro (2004), *Responsabilidade Civil Ambiental – As Dimensões do Dano Ambiental no Direito Brasileiro* (Environmental Torts – The Dimensions of Environmental Damage in the Brazilian Law), Brazil: Livraria do Advogado

Thornton, James (2007), 'Can lawyers save the world?', *The Ecologist*, June, 38–48.

PART THREE

Natural resources and sustainability

# 13. Transboundary aquifers: towards substantive and process reform in treaty-making

## Joseph W. Dellapenna and Flavia Rocha Loures

## 1. INTRODUCTION

This chapter discusses the final shape, scope and text of the Draft Articles on the Law of Transboundary Aquifers and Aquifer Systems of the International Law Commission ('2008 ILC Draft Articles').[1] The goals are to assess whether and to what extent the 2008 ILC Draft Articles conform to Agenda 21 and the Rio Declaration, and to propose appropriate adjustments to address the instances where they do not.

The International Law Commission (ILC) – the United Nations body charged with the codification and development of customary international law – initiated the study on the law of transboundary aquifers in 2000, upon a request by the UN General Assembly.[2] In 2006, the ILC adopted a first set of draft articles and invited states to present comments by January 2008. Based on states' comments, the ILC prepared a revised draft and submitted it to the UN General Assembly in 2008, as the basis for negotiating and possibly adopting a global instrument on international groundwater law. In December 2008 the UN General Assembly considered the draft articles and: (a) took note of their final text; (b) commended them to the attention of governments without prejudice to the question of their future adoption or other appropriate action; (c) encouraged the states concerned to make appropriate bilateral or regional management arrangements, taking into account the draft articles; and (d) decided provisionally to examine the question of the draft articles' final form at its 66th Session, in 2011.[3]

The draft articles aim to codify and develop the customary international rules that, for the ILC, currently govern the utilisation, management and protection of water flowing underneath the territories of two or more countries, and of the geological structure containing such water.

The chapter argues for the adoption of a protocol to the United Nations Convention on the Law of the Non-Navigational Uses of International Watercourses ('UN Watercourses Convention'),[4] taking into account the 2008 ILC Draft Articles as a means to advance integrated water resources management in international law, in line with Agenda 21. The expectation is that, in the future, the two instruments combined may serve as a binding, coherent, systematic and global framework for improved freshwater governance, especially in the case of their widespread ratification. Such a framework would better integrate the management of surface and underground waters, as compared to the scenario of two separate and independent treaties. The protocol in question would go further than the ILC Draft Articles by fully incorporating the principles of sustainability and prevention/precaution, and have an expanded scope.

On the latter issue, the 2008 ILC Draft Articles cover only aquifers that are in themselves transboundary. However, domestic aquifers may actually be part of a larger transboundary system, whether they are connected to international watercourses or have recharge zones within states not overlying the formation. The draft articles should thus apply to aquifer systems in all aspects through which transboundary harm may be caused and should regulate the rights and duties of all states with a significant relationship to those aquifers.

Finally, the chapter discusses the final text of the draft articles, which, to a significant extent, neglect two important principles of the Rio Declaration: sustainable development and precaution. The draft articles fail: (a) to apply fully the principle of sustainable development to recharging aquifers, which are renewable resources, by authorising extractions to exceed recharging rates; and (b) to incorporate the precautionary principle among the fundamental norms guiding the draft articles, limiting its application to pollution, even though precaution should also guide groundwater extraction.

The chapter begins with a brief analysis of the UN Watercourses Convention. The convention counts 20 parties in October 2010 – 15 short of the number required for entry into force (Art. 36). The chapter then examines the relationship between the convention and the draft articles, which attempt to build on and adjust the former to the specifics of groundwater resources.[5] The next section makes the case for expanding the scope of the 2008 ILC Draft Articles to cover all aquifers of relevance to international law, including domestic aquifers connected to international watercourses, and to govern the rights and obligations of all states concerned, including those not overlying the formation, but with recharge zones or connected surface waters within their territories. The chapter moves next to the content of the ILC Draft Articles, showing how they fail to give due regard to key principles of the Rio Declaration and proposing the necessary amendments and adjustments.

## 2. THE UN WATERCOURSES CONVENTION

The UN Watercourses Convention codifies and progressively develops the law governing the use, protection and management of international watercourses. The UN General Assembly adopted the convention with 106 approving votes and the sponsorship of 38 states,[6] after nearly 30 years of legal study and political negotiations. In this period, a large number of countries submitted comments and had countless opportunities for making statements, and the process was open to participation by virtually all United Nations' member states.

The UN Watercourses Convention is the first and only global codification of the law on the non-navigational uses of international watercourses endorsed under the auspices of the UN General Assembly. The convention reflects customary law, particularly in its provisions on equitable and reasonable utilisation, transboundary harm prevention, and notification and consultations on planned measures (McCaffrey, 2001, pp. 250, 259).

Highlighting the need for an integrated approach to systems of surface and groundwaters, the UN Watercourses Convention applies to rivers and lakes and to any connected aquifers (Art. 2(a)–(b)). The introductory section determines the convention's scope, sets out key definitions, clarifies its relationship with existing and future watercourse agreements, and establishes the rights of states in the negotiation of those agreements.

The convention's cornerstone is the principle of equitable and reasonable utilisation and participation, requiring states to consider all relevant factors in their mutual relations and to endeavour to attain the optimal and sustainable utilisation of international watercourses, consistent with their adequate protection. The convention also incorporates a duty of due diligence in the prevention of significant transboundary harm. Moreover, states are subject to a general duty to cooperate, which includes the regular exchange of relevant information.

Special dispute prevention procedures apply to planned activities in a basin that may have significant negative effects across borders. When states fail to reach an agreement through those procedures, they may resort to the convention's well-developed dispute settlement mechanisms.

The UN Watercourses Convention also governs the protection, preservation and management of international watercourses. Article 20 requires that states, individually and, where appropriate, jointly, protect and preserve aquatic ecosystems, including against any harmful effects from land-based activities within the basin (Tanzi, 2000, pp. 10–11).[7] States must act diligently in dealing with water pollution, preventing the introduction of potentially harmful invasive species, protecting the marine environment as it may be affected through freshwater inflow, and dealing with harmful conditions and emergencies. At the request of any watercourse state, riparians must enter into consultations concerning transboundary water management.

The UN Watercourses Convention offers the world what comparable treaties have accomplished regionally, as a universally agreed and formal negotiation and exchange platform in the field of international water law.[8] Already it has served as the basis for negotiating the ILC Draft Articles. Once in force and widely ratified, the convention would offer a better foundation for the development of global treaty law on emerging water issues. Moreover, the convention's implementation would facilitate the detection of relevant areas calling for international regulation through amendments and protocols – public participation in transboundary negotiations, for example. Such amendments and protocols would, as appropriate, supplement, reform and adjust the mother convention, enabling the coherent and progressive development of treaty law in the field.

The debates on the final shape of the 2008 ILC Draft Articles offer an opportunity to spur the ratification process of the UN Watercourses Convention. Bringing the convention into those discussions would also draw attention to a fundamental problem with the draft articles, which develop international groundwater law in a manner that is unlikely to facilitate the integrated management of surface and underground waters. The next section discusses how the draft articles are fundamentally isolated from the framework of the law of international watercourses, rather than nicely fitting into it as a specific application of the general rules of the convention.

## 3.  RELATIONSHIP BETWEEN THE 2008 ILC DRAFT ARTICLES AND THE UN WATERCOURSES CONVENTION

The UN Watercourses Convention addresses groundwater only insofar as it is connected to surface waters, leaving fossil aquifers out of its scope.[9] Moreover, albeit covering connected aquifers, the convention does not address the special characteristics of groundwater systems. In view of these regulatory gaps, the UN General Assembly asked the ILC in 2000 to study the law governing transboundary groundwaters in the context of its work on shared natural resources.[10]

While the results embodied in the 2008 ILC Draft Articles are progressive, they fail in several respects to address fully the concerns as developed in the Rio Declaration[11] and in Agenda 21.[12] It is so in part because the draft articles do not address all hydrogeologic structures that affect transboundary groundwater and, in part, because they do not account for the relationship between the law of transboundary aquifers and that of international watercourses, as codified in the UN Watercourses Convention.

## The Hydrologic Cycle and Integrated Water Resources Management

States have considered the possibility of adopting the 2008 ILC Draft Articles at a later stage, as a separate, independent convention. As we discuss below, this approach would run counter to Agenda 21, which clearly calls for the integrated management of surface and underground waters:

> The widespread scarcity, gradual destruction and aggravated pollution of freshwater resources in many world regions, along with the progressive encroachment of incompatible activities, demand integrated water resources planning and management. Such integration must cover all types of interrelated freshwater bodies, including both surface water and groundwater (Ch. 18, para 18.3).

For good reasons, the call in Agenda 21 should be accepted and the 2008 ILC Draft Articles and the UN Watercourses Convention should serve as interrelated, mutually supportive stepping-stones in the progressive development of international water law. It is possible to achieve this by recasting the draft articles as a protocol to the convention, which would also call for a revision of some of its key provisions. This approach would better reflect the physical links between surface and underground waters, without overlooking the special vulnerabilities of transboundary aquifers.

Aquifers and surface waters are commonly interconnected, forming single natural systems. With rare exceptions, therefore, the UN Watercourses Convention and the 2008 ILC Draft Articles deal with the same natural resource at different stages of the hydrologic cycle. As such, 'human intervention at one point in the system may have effects elsewhere within it'.[13] This means that polluting or overexploiting watercourses may have effects underground and vice-versa. For example, water may seep from a river into an aquifer under the riverbed and further downstream re-emerge to recharge a lake. In such a case, contamination of the river could affect the aquifer and eventually a lake that lacks a surface connection to the river, just as excessive extractions from the aquifer could compromise the levels of the interconnected lake.

Watercourse and aquifer states, through their policy-makers and water managers, ignore such hydrological interactions between surface and underground waters only at their peril. 'Sovereignty over groundwater must be restricted in the same way as it is over surface water .... [T]he hydrologic, economic, and engineering variables involved are essentially the same' (Dellapenna, 2001).

It makes no sense to apply two independent legal instruments to intimately interconnected components of one single process – the hydrologic cycle. Just as groundwaters are often related to surface waters, a global treaty governing transboundary aquifers must somehow be integrated into the UN Watercourses Convention – proposed as the overall global legal framework for international watercourses and their aquifers. It is only through the framework convention/protocol approach that international water law would adequately account for the need to manage freshwater systems as hydrological units, requiring conjunctive management of surface and underground waters.[14]

Even for non-renewable aquifers,[15] comprehensive planning must consider all available water sources within a border region and manage them together in an integrated fashion, with a view to attaining their optimal and sustainable development and protection. Yet, 'the vulnerability of groundwater, especially fossil groundwater, to depletion and pollution calls for the development of norms of international law that contain stricter standards ... than those applied to surface waters'.[16] Hence, the UN Watercourses Convention and its protocol, serving as one single international regime for both surface and underground waters, would best reflect the hydrologic cycle, while adequately addressing the policy implications of the special characteristics of underground water resources.

### Linking the Law of International Watercourses with that of Transboundary Aquifers in Treaty-Making

From the beginning, the ILC sought to adapt the general principles of the UN Watercourses Convention to the special needs of groundwater. In this sense, the convention has been described as 'the basis upon which to build a regime for groundwaters'.[17] At the General Assembly's 61st Session, many delegations 'noted with approval that the draft articles had been largely modeled on the [convention] and reiterated the value of that instrument'.[18]

In their final version, nonetheless, the 2008 ILC Draft Articles focus so excessively on aquifers that they almost completely fail to provide for the situations where surface and groundwaters form a single unit and should be managed as such – situations in which aquifer and watercourse states would have correlated obligations and rights. Ultimately drafted to become an independent instrument, the draft articles often:

- Overlook the relations between aquifer states and non-aquifer states that are nonetheless hydrologically interconnected within a system of surface and underground waters. For example, the draft articles do not extend to those other states the obligations and rights regarding data generation, which are far more detailed than those in the UN Watercourses Convention.
- Unnecessarily reiterate certain provisions of the convention, which would apply equally to surface and underground waters. This is the case with Draft Article 18, on the protection of transboundary aquifers in time of armed conflict. In such instances, the draft articles take attention away from their very own provisions that aim to address the specifics of groundwater resources. Such overlapping provisions containing rules that should apply to surface and groundwaters alike, from a legal point of view constitute an unnecessary distraction that serves only to make implementation more difficult.
- Mix together provisions of the UN Watercourses Convention, sometimes failing to include key aspects contained in that instrument. For example, Draft Article 5(2) attempts to condense into one provision Articles 6(3) and 10(2) of the convention, but fails to clarify the relationship between groundwater uses other than those needed to address vital human needs. The convention, on the other hand, makes clear that no water use enjoys inherent priority over others, including existing activities. This principle lies at the core of the convention's approach to balancing the interests of all watercourse states in the application of the principle of reasonable and equitable use. Draft Article 5(2) also fails to require aquifer states to consult with each other in applying the principle of reasonable and equitable use, when needed, in the absence of joint management arrangements.
- Instead of advancing the law by taking the principles applicable to watercourses as minimum starting points, create less strict provisions for aquifers. For example, as we shall see below, the provision on planned measures deviates from the UN Watercourses Convention by failing to include a duty on the notifying state to suspend implementation during consultation and negotiation procedures. Under the draft articles, we have the absurd situation in which international law deals with activities threatening surface waters with greater caution than for those that may affect aquifers, which are far more vulnerable to irreversible harm.

Therefore, a protocol to the UN Watercourses Convention, taking into account the positive developments reflected in the 2008 ILC Draft Articles, would address the greater environmental vulnerability of groundwater within the framework of the mother treaty. Implemented in an integrated fashion, the convention and its protocol would better support transboundary freshwater cooperation while avoiding the unnecessary overlapping provisions and the danger of subtle inconsistencies and gaps that have arisen between them as stand-alone documents. The dual applicability of independent and separately evolving international conventions would create confusion, increasing the potential for interstate conflict, while failing to support and guide states in applying integrated river basin management in a transboundary context.

From a practical viewpoint, the protocol approach would facilitate the elaboration and implementation of transboundary integrated river basin management plans, in the interest of national focal points in charge of applying both instruments. One single regime would also represent an economy in costs for the holding of meetings of the parties, if, in the future, the parties to both instruments decided to create such governance mechanisms. This position becomes even stronger if one considers the desire of most states to limit the number of multilateral environmental agreements and to focus on the implementation of the existing ones.

The unified legal treatment of surface waters and groundwater would thus consider their interconnections and distinctive features and govern them under a coherent and integrated international legal system.

In conclusion, as currently drafted, the 2008 ILC Draft Articles miss the point of creating special rules for groundwater without overlooking their connections with surface waters and the legal relations emerging from hydrological connections between watercourse states and aquifer states. In other words, the draft articles inadvertently create a gap between the law of international watercourses and that of transboundary aquifers, making it harder for states to promote their integrated management. The adoption of a carefully crafted protocol to the UN Watercourses Convention would aid in addressing those problems. Nonetheless, the fact that the convention is not yet in force has likely represented an obstacle for states to consider that alternative.

## 4.   PROBLEMS IN THE SCOPE OF THE 2008 ILC DRAFT ARTICLES

Certain problems with the 2008 ILC Draft Articles would seriously limit their utility regardless of whether they become a protocol or stand alone as another international agreement. While space does not allow a full development of all of the problems we have identified in the draft articles, we consider two key omissions from the draft articles relative to the goals of the Rio Declaration – the failures to embrace the principle of sustainability and to fully incorporate the prevention/precautionary principles.

In turn, we discuss a central problem in the 2008 ILC Draft Articles that impedes their accomplishment of the Rio goals: their limitation to groundwater systems with a geological structure intersected by international boundaries, without encompassing other types of groundwater systems through which transboundary harm may be caused.[19] Even for transboundary aquifers, the draft articles do not clarify sufficiently the role of states not overlying the aquifer, but with recharge zones or connected surface waters within their territories. The limited scope of the draft articles undermine the goals set forth in the Rio Declaration, in particular the principle of sustainable development (Principles 3–5, 8, 9, 12), the obligation to cooperate on environmental challenges (Principles 12, 14), the obligation to apply the precautionary approach (Principles 15, 17), and the obligation to promote the internalisation of environmental costs (Principle 16).

Let us look at the problem in more detail. As mentioned before, the 2008 ILC Draft Articles cover transboundary aquifers. They also apply to aquifers with transboundary hydraulic connections to other aquifers. Hence, certain groundwater systems through which transboundary harm might be caused fall outside the draft articles' scope. Below we attempt to describe these different situations:

(a) *Transboundary aquifers*: single aquifers with transboundary geological structures;
(b) *Aquifers with transboundary hydraulic connections to other aquifers*:[20] a series of interconnected aquifers underlying the territories of two or more countries;
(c) *Transboundary aquifer systems*: single aquifers or interconnected aquifers with recharge zones located outside the territory of the state(s) underlain by the geological formation(s); and
(d) *Domestic aquifers connected to transboundary freshwater systems*: domestic aquifers connected to internationally shared river basins, lakes, or wetlands.

Below we analyse situations (c)–(d), which the 2008 ILC Draft Articles do not cover:

## Transboundary Aquifer Systems

Activities in states that do not overlie an aquifer, but with recharge zones within their territories, pose a threat to aquifer states as they may affect the integrity of the system. The draft articles do not reflect that reality. They artificially treat countries that are home to recharge zones but have no direct access to an aquifer as 'non-aquifer states'.[21] This is so because, while science defines an aquifer as a system formed by its geological formation, the water it contains, *and* its recharge and discharge zones (Eckstein, 2005, p. 7), the draft articles do not include those zones in their own definition of the term 'aquifer' (Dellapenna and Loures, 2006).

This is a serious failure, as recharge zones connect different components of a larger natural system. Hence, all states within the system are vulnerable to unilateral mismanagement of portions of the shared aquifer system located outside their respective territories. For example, a state could suffer impacts from groundwater pollution in an aquifer resulting from pesticides used in agricultural activities within or around recharge areas outside that state's territory.

Notwithstanding their limited definition of an aquifer – and thus of an aquifer state – the 2008 ILC Draft Articles impose on states overlying recharge zones a duty of cooperation to protect transboundary aquifers dependent on such zones (Art. 10). Hence, the draft articles impose duties on 'non-aquifer states' without securing their rights over natural resources within their own territories. This could lead those states to resist approval of the draft articles. In order to mitigate this risk, the rights and duties toward freshwater and related resources should be established for all states within an aquifer system, within a legal framework for benefit-sharing and regional cooperation.

Countries in whose territory recharge zones are located properly speaking *are* aquifer states. The reciprocal rights and duties of aquifer states must be balanced, just as in the case of basin states sharing a transboundary basin that includes a system of domestic tributaries. All aquifer states are entitled to utilise and develop in a reasonable and equitable manner the portions of an aquifer system (including their recharge zones) within their territories, just as they are under a duty to participate equitably in the management and protection of those resources.

Therefore, a future protocol to the UN Watercourses Convention should expand the 2008 ILC Draft Articles' definition of aquifer states, establish the rights and duties of all states within the aquifer system, and cover wholly even those domestic aquifers with recharge zones located beyond the borders of the state overlying the resource. Otherwise, such a protocol would fail to address a gap in treaty law with respect to the global regulation of aquifers with recharge areas[22] in another state's territory, as the draft articles do.

## Domestic Aquifers Connected to Transboundary Freshwater Systems

An aquifer located entirely within one country's territory, but connected to an international river basin, although not a transboundary resource per se, is part of a larger hydrological unit that is physically shared among different states. For example, a domestic aquifer is vulnerable to pollution originating outside the aquifer state in an international river that discharges into such an aquifer. Similarly, if a watercourse state not overlying the aquifer diverts excessive amounts of water from a river upstream of an aquifer's recharge zones, it may interfere with an aquifer's recharge process and disrupt its hydrological balance. In the reverse situation, overexploitation of an aquifer may significantly reduce its discharge into surface waters and have effects on dependent ecosystems and water uses downstream in the territories of co-riparians beyond the borders of the aquifer state.

Under the regime proposed in the 2008 ILC Draft Articles, domestic aquifers linked to international watercourses would remain subject to the UN Watercourses Convention, but would not receive the same level of protection as under the draft articles. For example, the draft articles go as far as to require an aquifer country to develop groundwater utilisation plans (Art 4). No such obligation exists under the convention. Therefore, states with aquifers located exclusively within their territories, but connected to international watercourses, would be subject to a less stringent regime than those states sharing transboundary aquifers. This is despite the fact that the threat of transboundary harm is present in both cases.

Hence, a protocol to the UN Watercourses Convention should apply to all aquifers connected to international watercourses and better clarify the role of watercourse states within the system. In this sense, such a protocol would state clearly that watercourse states are entitled to protect, manage and utilise equitably areas within their own territories where such international watercourses are located. In so doing, the protocol would require watercourse states to take into account the right of aquifer states to utilise, equitably and reasonably, the portions within their own territories of those aquifers associated with such watercourses. Another duty the protocol would spell out would be for watercourse states to prevent diligently the causing of significant harm to aquifer states when undertaking activities that had or were likely to have an impact on aquifers connected to their watercourses. Finally, the proposed protocol would call on aquifer and watercourse states to cooperate with each other, to the extent necessary to ensure the aquifer's protection from detrimental effects originating in connected international watercourses or vice-versa.

## 5.   FAILURE TO CONSIDER ADEQUATELY THE PRINCIPLE OF SUSTAINABILITY

Draft Article 4 sets forth the rule of equitable and reasonable utilisation as applicable to groundwater. It determines that aquifer states 'shall not utilise a recharging transboundary aquifer or aquifer system[23] *at a level that would prevent continuance of its effective functioning*'.[24] The Report of the Working Group that prepared Draft Article 4 indicates that, 'this paragraph does not imply that the level of utilisation must necessarily be limited to the level of recharge'.[25] Furthermore, Draft Article 4 requires aquifer states to 'aim at maximising the long-term benefits derived from the use of [ground]water' (Draft Art. 4(1)(b)), all the while crafting 'individually or jointly a comprehensive utilisation plan, taking into account present and future needs of, and alternative water sources for, the aquifer States' (Draft Art. 4(1)(c)).

Hence, Draft Article 4 does not directly embrace the principle of sustainability in the case of recharging aquifers, and its several specific provisions at best refer only indirectly and somewhat confusingly to that principle. As the draft articles' Rapporteur explains:

> In most cases, the quantity of contemporary water recharge into an aquifer constitutes only a fraction of the main body of water therein.... If we impose a strict rule of sustainable utilization and limit the amount of extraction of water to that of the current water recharge, it would in reality deny aquifer States the right to utilize the valuable water resource, accumulated over the years.... [T]he aquifer should be kept in a condition to maintain its function ... not [constrained by] ... a strict rule of sustainable use.[26]

Therefore, the 2008 ILC Draft Articles disregard the capacity of certain groundwater systems for natural renewal. If this approach were to develop progressively into a general rule of international groundwater law, it would be fostering the gradual exhaustion of recharging aquifers. The draft articles thus depart in a major respect from the principle of sustainable development or use of water resources. The International Law Association's Berlin Rules express this point with clarity, requiring states to 'give effect to the principle of sustainability in managing aquifers, taking into account natural and artificial recharge' (Art. 40(1)).

If sustainability is a priority, overall extraction and discharges should not normally exceed overall recharge within a reasonable period. Sustainable management of groundwater depends on maintaining a balance between extraction and discharge rates and rates of natural or artificial recharge. Additional drawdowns that may take place under extraordinary circumstances during drought should be made up during wet years.

The closest the 2008 ILC Draft Articles come to embracing sustainability is in Draft Article 4(1)(d), which, as mentioned above, requires the aquifer to be kept in a condition to maintain its effective functioning. But is it possible to know for sure the amount of water we can extract above recharge levels before the aquifer collapses? Unlike the situation with surface waters, the impacts of overexploitation on the geological structure of an aquifer may take a long time to reach neighbouring states. Such impacts may lead to unexpectedly falling water tables, soil subsidence, or other problems across the border, yet not for a very long time. As the International Law Association explains, 'rapidly falling water tables might not appear until some years after a serious overdraft begins, by which time it might be too late to do much about it' (Art. 4(1)(d), p. 387). Hence, Draft Article 4 allows great latitude for discretion and potential abuses. Moreover, once the infrastructure is in place for over-extraction, it becomes almost impossible to enforce sustainability in periods reserved for recharge.

In view of the above, departure from the principle of sustainability should not have become a rule under the 2008 ILC Draft Articles; if it is to be allowed, overexploitation of recharging aquifers should be an exception applicable to cases of water scarcity, combined with a lack of sustainable and feasible alternatives. In other words, countries generally should only be allowed to exceed actual recharge rates in emergency situations, conditioned upon compensation for the period of overexploitation after the emergency ceases. Nonetheless, there must be a threshold of how much overexploitation can sustainably occur; that threshold relates to the hydro-geo-climatological dimensions of the landscape. Moreover, states should be responsible for ensuring adequate compensation between dry and wet periods, and between emergency and ordinary usage, through effective monitoring and enforcement strategies and institutions.

## 6.   FAILURE TO CONSIDER ADEQUATELY THE PRECAUTIONARY PRINCIPLE

The precautionary principle as set out in Principle 15 of the Rio Declaration, states:

> In order to protect the environment, the precautionary approach shall be widely applied by states according to their capabilities. Where there are threats of serious or irreversible damage, lack of full scientific certainty shall not be used as a reason for postponing cost-effective measures to prevent environmental degradation.

The precautionary principle also receives special emphasis under the Berlin Rules, Article 23. In line with that principle, ILC Draft Article 12 refers to pollution that '*may* cause significant harm to other aquifer states' (emphasis added). The language chosen invokes a preventive approach that covers situations in which an aquifer state pollutes a transboundary aquifer, without necessarily causing immediate significant transboundary harm. 'This could occur where the pollution remains in the original state over a long period of time, or where other states are not presently utilising the aquifer and where their environment is not reliant on it'.[27] Draft Article 12 goes on to state, 'Aquifer States shall take a precautionary approach in view of uncertainty about the nature and extent of a transboundary aquifer or aquifer system and of its vulnerability to pollution'.

Draft Article 12 takes an important step in incorporating a preventive approach and specifically referring to precaution. However, it does so only with respect to groundwater quality issues. The principles of prevention and precaution should apply to transboundary groundwater management in a broad sense, due to the characteristic vulnerabilities of these water systems, and not only under rules governing pollution. International law should require countries to address problems involving groundwater overexploitation, lowering of the water table, and soil subsidence with the same level of caution as for pollution. Just as with pollution, the impacts on groundwater systems resulting from overexploitation may take a long time to reach neighbouring states and actually become transboundary, as discussed above.

As underscored by some states during discussions on the 2008 ILC Draft Articles, the precautionary principle is 'well recognised as a general principle of international environmental law and [needs] to be stressed in the draft articles'.[28]

In light of the vulnerability of aquifers to irreversible harm caused by both pollution and overexploitation, countries may wish to consider whether to include the preventive and precautionary principles among the other general principles of law applicable to transboundary aquifers when negotiating specific aquifer agreements. Such a provision could read, for example, 'In view of uncertainty about the nature and extent of aquifer systems and of their special vulnerability to detrimental impacts from human activity, aquifer states shall take a precautionary approach'[29] and apply a preventive approach, as appropriate.

Another instance in which the draft articles fail to require preventive state conduct with respect to transboundary groundwater systems is Draft Article 15. This provision establishes the principles and procedural rules applicable in the case of planned measures that may affect a transboundary aquifer and, thereby, potentially result in significant adverse effects upon another state.

Unlike its equivalent in the UN Watercourses Convention (Arts. 14(b) and 17(3)), this provision fails to include a duty on the notifying state to suspend the project's implementation during consultation and negotiation procedures. This omission contradicts the preventive and precautionary approaches incorporated into Draft Article 12. In fact, allowing the continuation of implementing activities while the potential for significant transboundary harm is discussed among the aquifer states concerned hampers the efficacy of all provisions regulating an aquifer's protection, preservation and management.

Under the UN Watercourses Convention, the international community agreed to address potentially harmful planned measures with caution in regard to international watercourses. The same approach is even more warranted in the case of underground freshwater systems, which are far more vulnerable to irreversible harm than surface bodies of water (Eckstein, 2005, p. 8).[30]

## 7. CONCLUSIONS

Viewing the 2008 ILC Draft Articles through the lens of Agenda 21 and the Rio Declaration reveals some serious faults, particularly regarding the likelihood that the draft articles would not enable the full integration of the management of transboundary groundwater with other waters to which it is related and to other resources with which it is interdependent. The draft articles also fail to embody adequately the principles of sustainability, prevention and precaution.

In order to address the above problems, the UN General Assembly should consider adopting a protocol to the UN Watercourses Convention, taking into account the positive legal developments incorporated into the basis of the 2008 ILC Draft Articles, to create a strong foundation for international water law. The convention has served as the primary basis for elaborating the draft articles and thus for developing international groundwater law. The convention is the solid framework from which international groundwater law has emerged, and should be the mother treaty to the future instrument resulting from the draft articles. Unifying the law on international watercourses and on transboundary aquifers into a single treaty regime would reflect sound science, simplify implementation of international law and promote integrated water resources management in a transboundary context.

In addition, promoting the adoption of such a protocol might actually spur interest in the UN Watercourses Convention's entry into force, especially now with the active engagement by other actors in the global community towards that goal.[31] This is important since states have not discussed thoroughly the idea of adopting the 2008 ILC Draft Articles as a protocol to the convention exactly because the latter remains ineffective.

Such a protocol should address all the aquifers and aquifer systems through which transboundary harm may be caused. It should also define the rights and duties of all states with a significant relationship to the aquifer, including those with recharge zones within their territories, or drained by international watercourses to which aquifers are connected. The protocol should also fully embrace the principles of sustainability, prevention and precaution.

Finally, when negotiating their aquifer agreements, the world's governments should keep in mind the 2008 ILC Draft Articles and consider how they can be best applied to foster the cooperative management of groundwater systems shared with neighbouring nations. In so doing, states are advised to take into account both the weaknesses and strengths of the draft articles – some of which we have endeavoured to highlight in this chapter.

## NOTES

1.  International Law Commission, Draft Articles on the Law of Transboundary Aquifers, in Official Records of the General Assembly, 63rd Session, Supplement No. 10 (A/63/10) ('2008 ILC Draft Articles').
2.  UN General Assembly, 55th Session, Resolution A/RES/55/152 (19 January 2001).
3.  UN General Assembly, 63rd Session, Resolution A/RES/63/124 (15 January 2009), p. 2.
4.  Convention on the Law of Non-Navigational Uses of International Watercourses, UN Doc. A/51/869 (signed 21 March 1997) ('UN Watercourses Convention').
5.  Report of the International Law Commission on the Work of its 58th Session [2006] 61 UN GAOR Supp. No. 10, UN Doc. A/61/10 ('2006 ILC Report'), 194.
6.  UN General Assembly, 51st Session, 99th Plenary Meeting, UN Doc. A/51/PV.99, (1997), p. 2, 7–8.
7.  See www.unece.org/env/water/publications/documents/conventiontotal.pdf.
8.  For example, the UNECE Water Convention paved the way for a protocol on water and health and another on civil liability: Convention on the Protection and Use of Transboundary Watercourses and International Lakes, http://www.unece.org/env/water/pdf/watercon.pdf (signed 17 March 1992, in force 6 Oct. 1996); Protocol on Water and Health, 17 June 1999 (in force 4 Aug. 2008), http://www.unece.org/env/documents/2000/wat/mp.wat.2000.1.e.pdf; Protocol on Civil Liability and Compensation for Damage Caused by the Transboundary Effects of Industrial Accidents on Transboundary Waters, 21 May 2003 (not in force), http://www.unece.org/env/civil-liability/documents/protocol_e.pdf.
9.  Under the UN Watercourses Convention, a watercourse means 'a system of surface waters and ground-waters constituting by virtue of their physical relationship a unitary whole and normally flowing into a common terminus'; UN Watercourses Convention, note 4, Art. 2(a).
10. UN General Assembly, see note 2.
11. Rio Declaration on Environment and Development, UN Doc. A/CONF.151/5/Rev.1, (1991), at http://www.unep.org/Documents.Multilingual/Default.asp?documentid =78& articleid=1163Principle 10.

12. Agenda 21, UN Doc. A/Conf.151/26) (1991), at http://www.un.org/esa/dsd/agenda21/res_agenda21_00.shtml.

13. International Law Commission, Draft Articles on the Law of the Non-Navigational Uses of International Watercourses (with Commentaries), GA Res. 49/52, at 90, UN Doc. A/RES/49/52 (9 Dec. 1994) ('1994 ILC Draft Articles'), http://untreaty.un.org/ilc/texts/instruments/english/commentaries/8_3_1994.pdf

14. Berlin Rules on Water Resources, Arts. 5, 37, in International Law Association, Report of the 71st Conference (2004), p. 334 ('Berlin Rules').

15. 2008 ILC Draft Articles, note 1, Art. 2(e), defining a 'recharging aquifer'. Non-recharging aquifers are aquifers whose exploitation does not interfere with, or depend upon, any dynamic water balances. Such aquifers may receive negligible amounts of contemporary recharge or be completely isolated from the hydrologic cycle.

16. Chusei Yamada, 1st Report on Shared Natural Resources: Transboundary Groundwaters, UN Doc. A/cn.4/533 (30 Apr. 2003), p. 3.

17. See Chusei Yamada, 2nd Report on Shared Natural Resources: Transboundary Groundwaters, UN Doc. A/cn.4/539 (9 Mar. 2004), p. 3; see also 2006 ILC Report note 5, p. 194.

18. United Nations General Assembly, 61st Session, Topical Summary of the Discussion held in the Sixth Committee, prepared by the Secretariat, UN Doc. A/cn.4/577, (19 Jan. 2007) 5–6 ('2007 Topical Summary'). See also 'Statement of the Delegation of Mexico to the UNGA 6th Committee' (30 Oct. 2006) (on file with authors), qualifying the convention as an indispensable source of reference for the 2008 ILC Draft Articles.

19. See 2008 ILC Draft Articles, note 1, Art. 2(a) & (c), determining the draft articles' scope of application through the following definitions: aquifer means a 'permeable water-bearing underground geological formation underlain by a less permeable layer and the water contained in the saturated zone of the formation'; 'transboundary aquifer' means 'an aquifer…, parts of which are situated in different states'.

20. The 2008 ILC Draft Articles apply the expression 'aquifer system' to 'a series of two or more aquifers that are hydraulically connected': 2008 ILC Draft Articles, note 1, Art. 2(b). In this chapter, however, we refer to a series of aquifers as 'aquifers with transboundary hydraulic connections to other aquifers'. We do so to avoid confusion with the expression aquifer system, understood herein as an aquifer, together with its discharge and recharge areas.

21. See 2008 ILC Draft Articles, note 1, Art. 2(a), (d).

22. According to the ILC, 'a recharge zone contributes water to an aquifer and includes the zone where the rainfall water directly infiltrates the ground, the zone of surface runoff which eventually infiltrates the ground and the underground unsaturated zone of infiltration. The discharge zone is the area through which water from the aquifer flows to its outlet, which may be a river, a lake, an ocean, an oasis or a wetland. Such outlets are not part of the discharge zone itself'. 2006 ILC Report, note 5, p. 201.

23. A recharging aquifer is an aquifer 'that receives a non-negligible amount of contemporary water recharge'. 2008 ILC Draft Articles, note 1, Art. 2(e).

24. Note 23. Draft Article 4(1)(d) (emphasis added).

25. International Law Commission, Working Group on Shared Natural Resources, 'Report of the Working Group', UN Doc. A/CN.4/L.681, (2005), p. 4.

26. Chusei Yamada, '3rd Report on Shared Natural Resources: Transboundary Groundwaters', UN Doc. A/CN.4/551 (2005), p. 9. This understanding was later reiterated in the commentaries that accompany the draft articles. See International Law Commission, 'Draft Articles on the Law of Transboundary Aquifers, with Commentaries', *Yearbook of the International Law Commission*, vol. II, part II, 2008.

27. 3rd Report on Transboundary Groundwaters, note 26, p. 15.

28. See Report of the International Law Commission to the General Assembly, 60 UN GAOR Supp. No. 10, UN Doc. A/60/10 (2005) ('2005 ILC Report'), p. 38.

29.    Study Group on the International Law Commission's Draft Articles on the Law of
       Transboundary Aquifers, International Law Association (2007), p. 9, http://www.ila-
       hq.org/en/committees/study_groups.cfm/cid/1020.
30.    Groundwater 'generally flows at much slower rates …, which causes contamination … to
       manifest at slower rates …. [Decontamination] … can be extremely difficult and
       expensive, if at all possible ….'.
31.    See    webpage   of   the   UN   Watercourses   Convention   Global   Initiative,
       http://wwf.panda.org/what_we_do/how_we_work/policy/conventions/water_conventions/
       un_watercourses_convention/.

# REFERENCES

Dellapenna, Joseph W. (2001), 'The customary international law of transboundary
    fresh waters', *International Journal of Global Environmental Issues*, **1**, 264, 274.
Dellapenna, J.W. and Loures, F.R. (2007), 'Forthcoming developments in
    international groundwater law: proposals for the way ahead', *Water 21* (Aug.
    2007), at http://www.iwapublishing.com/pdf/W21Aug07%20groundwaterlaw.pdf.
Eckstein, Gabriel E. (2005), 'Protecting a hidden treasure: the UN International Law
    Commission and the international law of transboundary ground water resources',
    *Sustainable Development Law & Policy*, **5**, 7.
McCaffrey, Stephen (2001), 'The contribution of the UN Convention on the law of
    the non-navigational uses of international watercourses', *International Journal of
    Global Environmental Issues*, **1**, 250, 259.
Tanzi, Attila (2000), 'The Relationship between the 1992 UNECE Convention on the
    Protection and Use of Transboundary Watercourses and International Lakes and
    the 1997 UN Convention on the Law of the Non-Navigational Uses of
    International Watercourses', Report of the UNECE Task Force on Legal and
    Administrative Aspects (Geneva).

# 14. Achieving sustainability: plant breeders' and farmers' rights

## Mekete Bekele Tekle

## 1. INTRODUCTION

This chapter focuses on the question of plant breeders' and farmers' rights in the context of the requirements for the achievement of sustainability pursuant to Agenda 21[1] and the implementation of the Convention on Biological Diversity.[2] Agenda 21 provides a blueprint for sustainable development. It emphasises that sustainable development involves the responsibility of national governments, the promotion of international cooperation, and broad public participation. It also canvasses the role of communities in sustainable development, particularly in the conservation and sustainable utilisation of biodiversity. It stipulates the need for the involvement of communities in the conservation and sustainable use of ecosystems and the need to encourage traditional methods of agriculture, agro-forestry, forestry, range management and wildlife management, all of which are useful to maintain or increase biodiversity. In addition, it stipulates that communities must share the economic and other benefits derived from the utilisation of their biological and genetic resources. Agenda 21, para 15.1 in particular is relevant to the issue of plant breeders' and farmers' rights; it states that the objectives and activities of that chapter are intended to improve the conservation of biological diversity and the sustainable use of biological resources, as well as to support the Convention on Biological Diversity.

The Convention on Biological Diversity (CBD) is the first legally binding international instrument to address comprehensively concerns of biological diversity. The objectives of the CBD are the conservation of biodiversity, the sustainable use of its components, and the fair and equitable sharing of the benefits arising out of their utilisation. It also recognises and provides for community rights, as one of the conditions necessary for the realisation of its objectives. Article 8 (j) of the convention provides:

> Subject to its national legislation, respect, preserve and maintain knowledge, innovations and practices of indigenous and local communities embodying

traditional lifestyles relevant for the conservation and sustainable use of biological diversity and promote their wider application with the approval and involvement of the holders of such knowledge, innovations and practices and encourage the equitable sharing of the benefits arising from the utilization of such knowledge, innovations and practices.

This provision recognises the rights of communities to allow the use of their knowledge, and to share the benefit arising out of the utilisation of that knowledge. In addition, Art. 10(c) of the CBD provides for the rights of communities to continue the traditional practices of using biodiversity that are compatible with conservation or sustainable use requirements.

The rights of farmers are derived from the past, present and potential future contributions of farmers and to the conservation, improvement and supply of plant genetic resources for food and agriculture. This was recognised in a resolution of the Food and Agriculture Conference in 1989. The conference defined farmers' rights as 'rights arising from the past, present and future contribution of farmers in conserving, improving and making available plant genetic resources, particularly those in the centres of origin/diversity'.[3]

The eventual recognition process of this right took many years. The International Treaty on Plant Genetic Resources for Food and Agriculture (ITPGRFA) was finally adopted in 2001. It emphasises the necessity of promoting and protecting farmers' rights at both national and international levels. It provides that national governments are responsible for implementing farmers' rights according to their needs and priorities, as appropriate and subject to national legislation (Feyissa, 2006, p. 1).

With the objective of protecting Africa's common biodiversity and livelihood system with a common tool, the Organization of African Union (OAU), now the African Union (AU), developed a model law in 2000 to facilitate the respective rights of communities, farmers and breeders. It is entitled African Model Legislation for the Protection of the Rights of Local Communities, Farmers and Breeders, and for the Regulation of Access to Biological Resources, or in short, the African Model Law (OAU Model Law, 2000, p. 1).[4] This model law was recommended by the Organization of the African Union (OAU) in 1998. The objectives of this law include recognising the inalienable rights of local communities and breeders; provision of appropriate systems of access to biological resources, community knowledge and technologies subject to the prior informed consent of the state and the concerned local communities; promotion of conservation, evaluation and sustainable utilisation of biological resources and ensuring that biological resources are utilised in an effective and equitable manner towards strengthening the food security of the nation (OAU Model Law, 2000, p. 2). It recognises 'the need to implement the relevant provisions of the Convention on Biological Diversity, in particular Art. 15 on access to genetic resources, and Art. 8(j) on the preservation and maintenance of knowledge, innovations and practices of indigenous and local communities'.

The primary purpose of the model law is to help African countries develop their national biodiversity laws.[5] The model law recognises and provides for the rights of communities over biodiversity and the innovations, practices, knowledge and technologies associated therewith. The elements of community rights recognised by the model law include the right to regulate access to their biological resources and their traditional knowledge; the right to use their knowledge on the conservation and sustainable use of biological diversity; the right to collectively benefit from the use of their biological resources and knowledge; and the right to exercise collective rights as legitimate custodians and users of their biological resources.

The model law states that the rights of communities to regulate access include the right to refuse access where such access is likely to be detrimental to socio-economic life, or the cultural or natural heritage of the communities. Furthermore, it provides that communities shall obtain at least 50 per cent of the benefit to be shared from the utilisation of biological resources and traditional knowledge. The African Model Law recognises the rights of plant breeders and details how to regulate the relationship between the breeders and other stakeholders relating to biological resources. The document thus provides African countries with a model document for their national laws concerning such rights. Many African countries are expected to use the model law to enact similar national laws of their own.

Ethiopia is a country with diverse farming systems and with a range of farmers' needs and objectives to be met. There is a need to accommodate conflicting interests of different stakeholders. With a view to recognising the effort and contribution of plant breeders, it has become necessary and appropriate to ensure the rights of the farming and pastoral communities, who have been conserving the agricultural biodiversity resources used to develop new plant varieties, in order to continue their old customary practice of use and exchange of seeds.[6] It is in the interests of the plant breeders' on the one hand, and those of farmers and pastoralists, on the other hand, that the Ethiopian law tries to solve the conflict of interest of these groups. The Ethiopian legislation of 2006 is based directly on the African Model Law (OAU Model Law, 2000). In the context of progress in the uptake of concepts of ecological sustainability, the 1997 Ethiopian *Environmental Policy*[7] adopts the definition of sustainable development as found in the Brundtland report, *Our Common Future* (World Commission on Environment and Development, 1987):

The overall policy goal is to improve and enhance the health and quality of life of all Ethiopians and to promote sustainable social and economic development through the sound management and use of natural, human-made and cultural resources and the environment as a whole so as to meet the needs of the present generation without compromising the ability of future generations to meet their own needs.

Through its environmental policy, Ethiopia recognised the need for *in situ* and *ex situ* conservation of its genetic resources. The environmental policy also states that it is committed to ensuring the safeguarding of community and national interest while fulfilling its international obligations. Further commitments were made to legally control the importation and use of biological materials including genetically engineered ones.[8] It is on the basis of such national and international commitments that the country issued a new plant breeders' rights law in 2006.[9] Article 27 of the Ethiopian Plant Breeders' Right Proclamation recognises in principle that the rights of farmers emanate from the contribution for the continued conservation and sustainable use of plant genetic resources. One of the main purposes of Ethiopian plant breeders' rights law, in addition to the protection of the rights of plant breeders, is the promotion of investment in the genetic resources sector, as stated in the preamble. The law aims at striking a balance between the potentially conflicting interests of the communities, the farmers and breeders. While the interests may not always conflict, there is a potential for conflict of interest between the plant breeders and the farmers when there appears to be a borderline case between the 'protected variety' and 'farmers variety' as defined under Art. 2, sub-articles 7 and 8 of the Ethiopian plant breeders' proclamation.

In line with the objectives of Agenda 21, the Ethiopian plant breeders' law provides for the proper management of biotechnology and attempts to harmonise the interests of different groups of users of the biological resources. The law fits into the basic objectives of Agenda 21 which focuses on increased food availability, enhanced protection of the environment and human health and establishment of appropriate mechanisms for a sound management of biotechnology.[10] The law endeavours to create harmony among the stakeholders of the resources and to ensure their sustainable use by all within the scope permitted by the international conventions and guiding environmental law principles.

## 2.   BREEDERS' RIGHTS: CONCEPTUAL FRAMEWORK

The plant breeders' right is a type of intellectual property protection designed to fit the nature of inventions in the field of developing new plant varieties.

The plant breeders' right is accorded to a plant breeder who has developed a new plant variety, which is *new, distinct, uniform and stable*. The plant breeders' right grants an exclusive right to exploit the new plant variety. The scope of the protection varies, depending on the protection system. The scope of protection of the plant breeder's right under the 1978 version of International Convention for the Protection of New Varieties of Plants (UPOV), for example, is limited to the commercialisation of the reproductive material of the variety. However, the 1991 version of UPOV[11] extends the scope of protection to all production and reproduction of the variety. It has restricted the farmers' privilege to use harvested seed from their own holdings only, and prohibited the exchange of seed from previous harvests (Redgwell and Bowman, 1996, p. 165).

The Ethiopian Science and Technology Policy of 1993 (ESTC, 1993), specifies the directions and strategies to be followed in the various sectors of science and technology. Intellectual property is one of the sectors that the policy addresses. It provides for the creation of favourable conditions that will encourage scientists and researchers, as well as the private sector and providers of capital to participate in science and technology. Accordingly, it provides for the establishment of an effective patent and technology transfer regime that encourages and enhances technological innovation and invention. Nonetheless the patent system does not cover the issue of plant breeders. However, the 1992 Ethiopian National Seed Industry Policy recognises alarming local genetic erosion due to improved exotic varieties, and notes the need to minimise such impacts through the implementation of balanced development strategies in conservation, seed production and supply of plant genetic resources. It also recognises the active participation of farmers in the seed industry for the promotion of sustainable use of local cultivars.[12]

The policy stated that a law that provides for plant breeders' rights will be enacted. However, it did not specify the nature of the plant breeders' regime to be developed.

The 1995 Constitution of Ethiopia recognises and provides for the protection of intellectual property rights. The Proclamation on 'Inventions, Minor Inventions and Industrial Designs' issued in 1995 provides for the protection of patent rights. The Proclamation was enacted to encourage local inventive activities and build national technological capability, and encourage the transfer and adoption of foreign technology.

As this proclamation excludes plant or animal varieties and essential biological processes from patentability, new plant varieties could not have been protected by Ethiopian patent law. As a legal gap-filling measure in this respect, a new law to regulate breeders' rights was enacted in 2006. The Plant Breeders' Right Proclamation No. 481 of 2006 now serves as the main legal instrument regulating plant breeders' rights and related matters. According to the definition given under the Proclamation, a 'breeder' is a person who:

(a) has bred and developed a new plant variety; or (b) has employed or commissioned the work of the person who has bred or developed a new plant variety; or (c) is a successor in title of the person mentioned in (a) or (b) of this Sub-Art.; (Art. 2(3)).

On the basis of this definition, a breeder could be only a natural person who has to undertake the breeding activity personally as envisaged under the breeder's right proclamation. But a breeders' right could be granted to any person. What is the scope of the plant breeder's right? According to Abbott, Cottier and Gurry, the plant breeder's right may extend to seven acts that need the proper authorisation of the plant breeder: (1) production or reproduction (multiplication); (2) conditioning for the purpose of propagation; (3) offering for sale; (4) selling or other marketing; (5) exporting; importing; and (7) stocking for any of the purposes mentioned above (Abbott et al., 1999, p. 67).

A plant breeder's bred variety has to qualify for the protection of this right if the requirements of a new plant variety definition under the law are satisfied. A 'new plant variety' is defined as a variety that:

- by reason of one or more identifiable characteristics, is clearly distinguishable from all other varieties, the existence of which is a matter of common knowledge at the date of application for a plant breeders' right;
- is stable in its essential characteristics, in that after repeated reproduction or multiplication, at the end of each cycle, it remains true to its description;
- having regard to its particular features of sexual reproduction or vegetative propagation, it is sufficiently homogenous or is a well-defined multi-line; and
- its material has not been sold or otherwise disposed of to others by the breeder for purposes of commercial exploitation of the variety (Art. 2(5)).

A breeder must ascertain that the claimed new variety has not been sold in Ethiopia at least one year prior to the date of application for protection; or has not been sold in other territories earlier than six or four years of date of application, depending on the plant variety in question (Art. 2(5)).

The proclamation also draws a distinction between the 'protected variety' and the 'farmers' variety'. The former is a plant variety that is protected by the plant breeders' right granted by the relevant authority. A 'farmers' variety' is a plant variety having specific attributes and which has been discovered, bred, developed or nurtured by Ethiopian farming communities or a wild relative of a variety about which the Ethiopian farming communities have common knowledge (Art. 2(9)). Farmers have selected, bred, improved and conserved the crop biodiversity that constitutes the basis of food and agricultural production in Ethiopia today.

The farmers' right is recognised as emanating from the recognition of the contribution that local and indigenous farming communities of all regions of the world, particularly those in the centres of origin and crop diversity, have made and will continue to make for the conservation and development of plant genetic resources which constitute the basis of food and agricultural production throughout the world. The concept of the farmers' right seeks to ensure the conservation of agrobiodiversity while supporting people's livelihood.[13] The *in situ* conservation of agrobiodiversity makes it imperative that the concept of farmers' rights be evolved and implemented to enable farming communities to effectively conserve local biodiversity.

## 3.   THE SCOPE OF THE PLANT BREEDERS' RIGHT

The scope of breeders' rights under the legislation is limited to the new genera and species to be determined by the competent authority to list the varieties subject to licensing. Each breeder shall be granted a plant breeders' right in respect of his/her new variety under Art. 4 of the Proclamation. The breeder has rights of use and exploitation of the variety by his or her own or through anyone to be designated by him or her. These rights include the right to produce, sell, license, distribute or delegate these rights and powers to other persons (Art. 5). The right of propagating material is an exclusive right of the breeder and no one shall exercise such an act without being duly authorised by the breeder. All rights of commercial exploitation of the breeder's right shall rest with breeders and it is only with their knowledge and permission that others can be involved in such activities.

## 4.   EXEMPTIONS TO THE PLANT BREEDERS' RIGHT

There are exemptions to plant breeders' rights which apply regardless of the fact that the new plant varieties of the breeders are accorded legal protection. Art. 6 of the Proclamation exempts any other persons or farming communities from propagating, growing and using a protected variety for purposes other than commerce. Anybody can sell plants or the propagating material of the protected variety for use as food or for any other use that does not involve growing the plant or the propagating material of the protected variety. However, farmers cannot sell farm-saved seed or propagating material of a protected variety in the seed industry on a commercial scale. All normal and traditional transactions by farmers are tolerated under these circumstances. This could be seen as upholding the principle of protecting the local community's right to use their genetic resources according to the Access to Genetic Resources and Community Knowledge, and Community Rights Proclamation 2006.

According to Art. 8 of that Proclamation:

(1)   Local communities shall have an inalienable right to use or exchange among themselves their genetic resources or community knowledge in the course of sustaining their livelihood systems in accordance with their customary practices and norms.

(2)   No legal restriction shall be placed on the traditional system of local communities on the use and exchange of genetic resources and community knowledge.

Protected plant varieties could be sold as they are within a farm or any other place and could be used as an initial source of variation for the purpose of developing another new plant variety by other person. But there is an exception to the rule where a person makes repeated use of plants or propagating material of the variety for the commercial production of another variety.

The use of a protected variety as food for home consumption and for the market, and for the purpose of furtherance of breeding, research or teaching is allowed (Art. 6(e)). Any person may request and be permitted to obtain a protected variety from the gene banks or plant genetic resources centres. Proper requests should be made to the appropriate government agencies to acquire protected varieties. There are various Ethiopian institutions that deal with genes and saved seeds.[14]

## 5.   RESTRICTIONS ON THE PLANT BREEDERS' RIGHT

Apart from exemptions to the breeders' right, there are also restrictions imposed by law with regard to the problems that may arise due to competitive practices of the rights holders. The restrictions would be imposed whenever the interest of the public so requires. Article 7(1) (a)–(e) of the Plant Breeders' Rights Proclamation provides for the list of the grounds for the restriction of such a right as follows:

- problems related to competitive practices of holders;
- problems of food security, nutritional or health needs or biological diversity are found adversely affected;
- where a high proportion of a protected variety offered for sale is being imported;
- where the requirements of the farming community for propagating material of a particular protected variety are not met; and
- when it is important to promote the public interest for socio-economic reasons for developing indigenous and other technologies.

When the rights of a breeder are restricted by the Ministry of Agriculture and Rural Development, the holder of the right will be served with a notice stating the particulars of the restrictions and the extent of the compensation to be paid. The public will also be informed about the restrictions. If the holder of the right is aggrieved by a decision of the Ministry, the appellant has a right to appeal to a court. The appellant must bring the grievance within 60 days from the date of the decision that imposed the restriction and should state the relief sought (Art. 30).

## 6.  COMPULSORY LICENSING

There are conditions under which the compulsory licensing could be granted upon application of interested parties. If a holder of rights refuses to authorise others to use his protected variety or offers authorisation on unreasonable terms or if the public interest so requires, then an application may be made to the Ministry of Agriculture and Rural Development for a compulsory license (Art. 8). The Ministry could consider the application for compulsory licensing if the holder of the right fails to satisfy the market need of the protected variety and is not selling sufficient amounts or when such person refuses to license other persons to produce or sell the propagating material, or when the holder of the right is under no circumstances expected to give permission for the protected variety. On the basis of any one of these reasons a compulsory license might be given to the applicant.

The duration of a compulsory license is limited to a minimum period not shorter than three years and with a maximum of five years. This period may be extended if duly requested and approved by the Ministry provided that the conditions warranting extension prevail. Persons who are granted a compulsory license shall pay the amount of compensation to the holder of the right. The amount to be paid shall be determined by the Ministry of Agriculture and Rural Development. Those to whom a compulsory license has been granted shall have a non-exclusive right to perform all of the activities for which the authorisation of the holder of the right would have been required. However, this does not in any way affect the rights of the holder from using the variety or to grant its use right to others as regulated under the law (Art. 8(3)–(5)).

## 7.   APPLICATION FOR A PLANT BREEDERS' RIGHT

A breeder who wants to be granted a plant breeders' right in respect of a new plant variety must present a written application to the Ministry of Agriculture and Rural Development. The application must be made by a person who has bred or discovered and developed the variety, or a successor in title to the breeder. A rights holder could be any person, whether an Ethiopian national or foreigner as well as a resident or non-resident, irrespective of the place of breeding – local or abroad (Art. 10(1)). It does not matter whether the plant variety is bred in Ethiopia or elsewhere. A breeder's right can be secured through an application lodged with the Ministry of Agriculture and Rural Development. Any person who qualifies as an applicant and who wishes to be granted a plant breeders' right in respect of a new plant variety shall apply to the Ministry. Plant breeding can be a joint activity of two or more persons or they can be joint successors to a plant breeder's right abroad (Art. 10).

A plant breeders' right could also be granted to either a public or private institution. Such institutions shall be considered as right holders for all practical purposes to implement the law. Where a plant variety has been bred or claimed to have been bred as a new variety by two or more persons independently of each other, the entitlement shall belong to the person who first applied to the Ministry of Agriculture and Rural Development (Art 10(4)). If a person who is not entitled to a plant breeders' right has applied for the holder of a right, the entitled person can apply to the Ministry for the assignment of the plant breeders' right to him or her. The Ministry shall grant a plant breeders' right if satisfied that the plant variety is new and when it finds no ground to refuse the grant as regulated under the proclamation. It must be ascertained that plant breeders' right has not been granted to other persons before making the decision (Art. 14).

Any person may lodge a protest with regard to the granting of a plant breeders' right by the Ministry if he or she reasonably believes that a plant breeders' right is against the public interest. Such a protest could also be lodged if the complainant considers that the plant variety for which an application to acquire a breeders' right does not fulfil the requirements for the granting of such a right. A protest may also be lodged by a person who considers that the applicant is not entitled to a plant breeders' right. The applicant must set out the grounds for the opposition to the grant of the requested plant breeders' right. The conditions and procedures pursuant to which opposition shall be lodged, examined and resolved are expected to be provided by a regulation to be issued by the Council of Ministers (Art. 13). Such regulations will facilitate the proper implementation of the breeders' right and other stakeholders' rights.

## 8.   DURATION OF A PLANT BREEDERS' RIGHT

Article 9 of the Proclamation specifies a maximum period of 20 years with respect to annual crops and 25 years in the case of trees, vines and other perennial trees. Under normal circumstances, the counting period for the duration starts from the date when the application for a plant breeders' right is accepted. In the interim period when the Ministry of Agriculture and Rural Development receives the application and considers either granting or refusing the request for a plant breeders' right, the applicant would be the holder of the right. The provisional protection lasts until the Ministry makes a decision on the application submitted by the breeder. The Ministry must take the necessary measures to prevent the use of the genetic material of such variety for non-research purposes (Art. 12).

## 9.   TRANSFER AND REVOCATION OF PLANT BREEDERS' RIGHTS

The holder of the breeders' right is free to transfer such a right by contract provided that all legal requirements are complied with.[15] There are procedural requirements for a registration of contract of transfer of breeders' right to have legal effect. A breeder has the option of surrendering the right by informing the Ministry of Agriculture and Rural Development. The Ministry shall register and thereby give public notice of the fact of the right being surrendered. If the transfer of a breeders' right is requested by another person through a court procedure, the Ministry shall only register the surrender of the right by leave of court or by the consent of the parties in the court proceedings. Where a plant breeders' right is erroneously granted to a person who is not entitled to it, the Ministry may transfer the breeders' right to the rightful person (Art. 21).

Breeders' rights can be revoked upon the request of any person affected by the granting of the right. The application for revocation of a breeders' right shall be submitted to the Ministry (Art. 23).

## 10. REMEDIES AND PENALTIES FOR INFRINGEMENTS OF THE BREEDERS' RIGHT

Any act in respect of a protected variety for which the authorisation of the holder is required and which is done without such authorisation shall constitute an act of infringement of a plant breeders' right under the proclamation. Article 25 of the proclamation entitles a person whose plant breeders' right has been infringed to institute an action in court to require the cessation of the act of infringement and claim compensation for damage. The court shall order the cessation of the infringement and payment of compensation unless the defendant proves himself to be the rightful holder and thereby counterclaim the revocation of the plaintiff's right in accordance with Art. 23.

The enforcement measures provided under the proclamation include imprisonment and fining of the infringer of the right. According to Art. 29 any person who infringes a plant breeders' right shall, in addition to the confiscation of the seed or propagating material of the protected variety which are the proceeds of the infringement, be punished with imprisonment not exceeding three years or a fine of 5000 Ethiopian Birr (approximately US$500), or both.

## 11. THE FARMERS' RIGHT

Farmers are recognised as the original breeders and they continue to be the major contributors to conservation, breeding and utilisation of diverse species and crop varieties. Farmers' rights have been conceived as a counter to commercial breeders' rights. They are based mainly on the idea that farmers also contribute to agricultural innovations and deserve equal recognition and rewards as those of commercial breeders. In a developing country like Ethiopia, there is not much difference at first glance between a farmer and a breeder. Farmers are the main suppliers of seed and seed exchange transactions in many developing countries. What rights do farmers have? The farmers rights may differ from country to country but most of the guiding principles and some of the basic rights are accepted by many of them. According to Anitha Ramanna (2003, pp. 5–6) there are three basic aspects of farmers' rights:

(1) *Farmers' Privilege*: Referred to as the farmers' exemption under Art. 5 of the 1978 UPOV Convention, it essentially provides an exemption for farm-saved seeds by farmers under plant breeders' rights. Originally, plant breeders' rights under UPOV were only for commercial production

and marketing, and since the use and exchange of saved seeds was considered non-commercial, the activity was considered outside the scope of plant breeders' rights. It thus allowed farmers to save, use and exchange seed but not sell seed without penalty and under plant breeders' right systems. In the 1991 UPOV revision, the farmer's exemption was reduced to an optional clause leaving it to states to decide on the extent of farmers' rights to save and exchange seed.

(2) *Benefit Sharing*: With the completion of the Convention on Biological Diversity in 1992, the concept of benefit sharing emerged and was applied by some to farmers' rights.[16] The Convention led to a shift in viewing genetic resources not as common heritage (shared by all) but rather as the sovereign right of nations. Benefit sharing was formulated as a means to assert this sovereign right. In this context, benefit sharing refers to the compensation to farmers and their communities who contribute to the creation of a new variety or the development and conservation of existing varieties. It essentially refers to the rights and rewards that farmers deserve for contributing to agricultural innovation and growth.

(3) *Farmers' Rights to Ownership*. Farmers' rights here refer not to exemptions or to benefits but to the rights of farmers to claim ownership over their varieties in a similar fashion to that of breeders. It represents the extension of the ideology of intellectual property rights to farmers' varieties. Farmers' rights differ from breeders' rights in that they were intended to be vested in the 'International Community' rather than with individuals. However, by not specifying what genetic materials were covered or who could claim ownership, the Food and Agricultural Organisation definition created a problematic category. Farmers' rights have remained an elusive goal. Their early association with the anti-breeders' rights agenda, and their ambiguities regarding materials and holders of the rights, thwarted its acceptance as an international principle or programme. Following the negotiation of the International Treaty for Plant Genetic Resources for Food and Agriculture (ITPGRFA) in 2001, as Brush indicates, the fate of Farmers' Rights fell to be determined at the national level (Brush, 2007).

Chapter 32.3 of Agenda 21 recognises farmers as one societal group that may contribute to sustainable agricultural development. It states:

A farmer-centred approach is the key to the attainment of sustainability in both developed and developing countries and many of the programme areas in Agenda 21 address this objective. A significant number of the rural population in developing countries depend primarily upon small-scale, subsistence-oriented agriculture based on family labour. However, they have limited access to resources, technology, alternative livelihood and means of production. As a result, they are engaged in the overexploitation of natural resources, including marginal lands.

Accordingly, Agenda 21 underscores the need to strengthen the role of farmers to ensure sustainability of agricultural production systems. To this end, it stipulates the need to develop environmentally sound farming practices and technologies; help farmers to share expertise in conserving resources; encourage self-sufficiency in low-input and low-energy technologies; encourage research on equipment that makes optimal use of human labour and animal power; make prices reflect environmental costs; and make price structure, trade policies and farm support payments encourage sustainable use of natural resources.

The International Treaty on Plant Genetic Resources for Food and Agriculture is also important in establishing the farmers' right. The treaty was adopted by the conference of the Food and Agricultural Organisation in November 2001. The objectives of the treaty are 'the conservation and sustainable use of plant genetic resources for food and agriculture and the fair and equitable sharing of the benefits arising out of their use, in harmony with the Convention on Biological Diversity, for sustainable agriculture and food security' (Art. 1 of the International Treaty on Plant Genetic Resources for Food and Agriculture). It recognises farmers' rights as one of the means to realise its objectives, emanating from the 'enormous contribution that the local and indigenous communities and farmers of all regions of the world, particularly those in the centres of origin and crop diversity, have made and will continue to make for the conservation and development of plant genetic resources, which constitute the basis of food and agriculture production throughout the world' (Art. 9). The elements of farmers' rights include: the right to protection of traditional knowledge on plant genetic resources; the right to participate in sharing the benefits arising from the utilisation thereof; the right to participate in making decisions at national level on matters related to the conservation and utilisation of plant genetic resources; and the right to save, use, exchange and sell farm saved seed/propagating material (Art. 9).

The Organisation of African Unity Model Law discussed earlier also recognises the rights of farmers and specifies their basic elements. These include: an exclusive right to commercialise farmers' varieties, the right to the protection of traditional knowledge; the right to obtain an equitable share from the benefits arising from utilisation of genetic resources; the right to participate in decision making pertaining to agrobiodiversity; the right to save, use, exchange and sell farm-saved seed of farmers' varieties; the right to use a new breeder's protected variety to develop farmers' varieties; and the right to collectively save, use, multiply and process farm-saved seed of protected varieties (Arts. 25 and 26). The Model Law regulates the farmers' right in a similar manner to that under the International Treaty on Plant Genetic Resources for Food and Agriculture.

Many countries have policies and regulatory laws and institutions for the protection of their communities and farmers' rights. Ethiopia has recently joined this group of countries with regard to the protection of its farmers' rights. Protection of farmers' and communities' traditional knowledge is recognised in all relevant Ethiopian policies (Bekele, 2007, p. 117). Farmers and communities have the right to decide on access and use of their traditional knowledge, including the right to share benefits derived from the use of this knowledge. Accordingly, Ethiopia brought a case against the Starbucks Coffee Company of the United States for the protection of intellectual property rights for sun-dried-coffee beans from one of Ethiopia's coffee-growing regions. The coffee company's objection was to Ethiopia's choice of intellectual property protection. Trade marking is an unusual, though not unprecedented, choice for a geographic region. It gives the holder the exclusive right to use the name in branding, but it does not place any requirements on the product. Instead, Starbucks argued, Ethiopia would be better served by another form of protection, called geographic certification, used for such products as Idaho potatoes, Roquefort cheese and Florida oranges. It guarantees that the product comes from the stated region but allows others to use the name in their branding. The case was brought before the US Patent and Trademark Department and it was agreed by the Ethiopian Government and the Company that Starbucks should pay a certain amount of the proceeds to the Ethiopian farmers. Ethiopia claimed an intellectual property right of her farmers and managed to strike a deal to benefit her farmers' right for an entitlement to a certain percentage of Starbucks' profit from the sale of the coffee brand developed by Ethiopian farmers. A pound of coffee fetched farmers a benefit of $1.45. In the US, however, that same pound of coffee commands a much higher price: $26 for a bag of Starbucks' roasted as Shirkina Sun-Dried Sidamo (Ethiopian) brand. The conflict began in March 2005, when Ethiopia filed with the US Patent and Trademark Office to trademark the names of three coffee-producing regions: Yirgacheffe, Harrar and Sidamo. The last region's claim was successful.[17]

The need for national laws for the protection of intellectual property rights is of paramount importance, as is manifest from the issues that arise in the process of using the products. Ethiopia needs detailed regulations and well-organised enforcement bodies to protect the interests of its communities. However, there are no administrative regulations so far to facilitate the implementation of these rights, although there are expectations that such rules and procedures will be prepared, as the 2006 Plant Breeders' Rights and the Access to Genetic Resources, Community Knowledge, and Community Rights proclamations envisage the need for the issue of implementing regulations.

Article 27 of Plant Breeders' Rights Proclamation recognises the farming communities as the custodians of plant genetic resources of the country, as farmers are the main actors and contributors with respect to conservation and sustainable use. The farmers' rights in relation to use of plant variety are stated (Art. 28) as:

- to save, use, exchange and sell farm-saved seed or propagating material of farmers' varieties;
- to use protected varieties including material obtained from gene banks or plant genetic resource centres to develop farmers' varieties; and
- to save, use, multiply, exchange and sell farm-saved seed or propagating material of protected varieties.

Restrictions are imposed on the sale of farm-saved seeds or propagating material if the source of such seeds is a protected variety and certified by a seed industry.

## 12. IMPLEMENTATION OF THE FARMERS' AND BREEDERS' RIGHTS

The proclamation on Access to Genetic Resources and Community Knowledge and Community Rights 2006 recognises communities' rights over the genetic resources and knowledge they have developed, but limits community decision-making powers to decisions on access to their knowledge only. Access to genetic resources is to be decided by the state, although communities may appeal if the access decision negatively affects them. According to Feyissa (2006, p. 22) such discrepancies were created due to lack of comprehensive knowledge of the structure of farmers and communities in Ethiopia, and on the scope of their rights. A major problem has been lack of awareness of the conceptual frameworks, issues, trends and challenges of farmers' rights among the relevant stakeholders, including policy makers and farmers themselves.

Most of the stakeholders are not informed about the objectives and concepts of farmers' rights, while farmers as a whole are totally unaware of the issues. As about 85 per cent of Ethiopia's people live in the rural environment, most communities in Ethiopia are recognised as farming communities – be it pastoralists or those involved in mixed crop–livestock agriculture. There are also small-scale farmers that have varying and immediate interactions and who are considered as members of 'local communities' as identified in Art. 8(j) of the Convention on Biological Diversity. These farmers do not depend on a single crop or crop variety for their subsistence, but grow several varieties of crops, and continue to harvest and domesticate semi-wild and wild plant species. The other problem area of implementation is the definition of farmers and communities in the context of Ethiopia. The Plant Breeders' Rights Proclamation does not define or explain what is meant by 'farmers' and 'farmers' rights', and does not sufficiently articulate the customary and custodianship rights of farmers.

The land tenure system of Ethiopia is also another obstacle for the implementation of the farmers' right. According to Art. 40(1) of the 1995 Constitution of Ethiopia, land is owned by the state and the people, and the scope of farmers' land ownership is limited to usufruct rights. The current land tenure law, as regulated by the Federal Democratic Republic of Ethiopia Rural Land Administration and Use Proclamation of 2005, is also restrictive in terms of tenure security, for it gives the state an immense power over the farmers. For these reasons, the farmers' property rights over land and related rights are not adequately appreciated in terms of motivating the farmers to achieve the sustainable use of land and land-related resources.

However, the proper implementation of the Access to Genetic Resources and Benefit Sharing Proclamation and the Plant Breeders' Rights Proclamation appears to be practically impossible without having regulations in place to balance the interests of plant breeders and farmers.

## 13. CONCLUSIONS

The Ethiopian statutes on plant breeders' rights and on access and benefit sharing are based on the existing internationally recognised principles in these fields. The African Model Legislation for the Protection of the Rights of Local Communities, Farmers and Breeders and for the Regulations of Access to Biological Resources has also been used as a guiding model for the drafting of the two proclamations. As a result, the country can claim a national law that balances and protects the respective rights of the communities, farmers and breeders in line with most of the international treaties and soft laws of both international and regional nature. The Rio Declaration and the Convention on Biological Diversity have yet to be seen in light of the respective development of similar national laws in other countries.

The Ethiopian plant breeders' law adequately provides for the mutual protection of the rights of both the breeders and farmers in line with relevant paragraphs of Agenda 21 by providing for articles on the exemptions and restrictions of the respective rights and duties of these two groups. The provisions of the law are compatible with the Convention on Biological Diversity and could be used in advancing the principles of sustainable development enshrined in the Rio Declaration.

## NOTES

1. Agenda 21, UN Doc. A/CONF. 151/26 (1992), available at http://www.un.org/esa/dsd /agenda21/.
2. (1992) 31 ILM 818.
3. Twenty-fifth Session of the FAO Conference – Rome, 1989 Resolution 5/89; see http://www.fao.org/docrep/x0255e/x0255e03.htm.
4. OAU Model Law, Algeria – 2000, Rights of Communities, Farmers, Breeders and Access to Biological Resources, http://www.cbd.int/doc/measures/abs/msr-abs-oau-en.pdf p.1.
5. Part 1 begins: 'The main aim of this legislation shall be to ensure the conservation, evaluation and sustainable use of biological resources, including agricultural genetic resources, and knowledge and technologies in order to maintain and improve their diversity as a means of sustaining all life support systems'.
6. Preamble of 'Plant Breeders' Right Proclamation No. 481/2006', *Federal Negarit Gazeta of the Federal Democratic Republic of Ethiopia*, 11th Year No. 58, p. 3181 (hereafter 'Plant Breeders' Right Proclamation').
7. See Environmental Protection Authority in collaboration with the Ministry of Economic Development and Cooperation (1997), *The Federal Democratic Republic of Ethiopia Environmental Policy*, Addis Ababa.
8. Note 7, p. 9.
9. See http://www.grain.org/brl/?docid=965&lawid=3042.
10. Agenda 21, para 16.1.
11. See http://www.upov.int/en/publications/conventions/1991/act1991.htm.
12. Ethiopian National Seed Industry Policy, 1992, para 3.01–3.07.
13. For background see Report of the Ad Hoc Technical Expert Group Meeting on The Potential Impacts of Genetic Use Restriction Technologies on Smallholder Farmers, Indigenous and Local Communities and Farmers' Rights, http://www.cbd.int/doc/meetings/sbstta/sbstta-09/information/sbstta-09-inf-06-en.pdf
14. Some of these institutions are: Ethiopian Seeds Enterprise, Ethiopian Institute of Biodiversity Conservation and the Gene Bank.
15. A transfer of plant breeders' right by a contract may have no effect unless entered in the register of plant breeders' right (Art. 19 of the Plant Breeders' Right Proclamation).
16. See for example, Report of the Ad Hoc Technical Expert Group Meeting on the Potential Impacts of Genetic Use Restriction Technologies on Smallholder Farmers, Indigenous and Local Communities and Farmers' Rights, http://www.cbd.int/doc/meetings/sbstta/sbstta-09/information/sbstta-09-inf-06-en.pdf .
17. See, http://www.wipo.int/export/sites/www/academy/en/ipacademies/educationalmaterials /cs4_sidamo.pdf for a summary of the case.

## REFERENCES

Abbott, Frederick, T. Cottier and C. Gurry (1999), *The International Intellectual Property System: Commentary and Materials* (Part One), The Hague: Kluwer Law International.

Bekele, Mekete (2007), 'Community Rights to Genetic Resources and their Knowledge: African and Ethiopian Perspectives', in N. Chalifour, P. Kameri-Mbote, Lin Lye Heng and J. Nolan (eds), *Land Use Law for Sustainable Development*, Cambridge: Cambridge University Press.

Brush, Stephen B. (2007), 'Farmers' right and protection of traditional agricultural knowledge', *World Development*, **35** (9), 1499–1514.

Ethiopian Science and Technology Commission (1993), *National Science and Technology Policy*, December, Addis Ababa.

Feyissa, Regassa (2006), 'Farmers' Rights in Ethiopia: A Case Study', Background Study No. 5, The Fridtjof Nansen Institute, at www.fni.no/doc&pdf/FNI-R0706.pdf.

Ramanna, Anitha (2003), 'India's Plant Variety and Farmers' Right Legislation: Potential Impact on Stakeholder Access to Genetic Resources', Washington, DC: International Food Policy Research Institute, EPTD Discussion Paper.

Redgwell, C. and M. Bowman (1996), *International Law and the Conservation of Biological Diversity*, The Hague: Kluwer Law International.

World Commission on Environment and Development (1987), *Our Common Future*, Oxford: Oxford University Press.

## PART FOUR

Energy, climate change and sustainability

# 15. International law and sustainable energy: a portrait of failure

## David Hodas

## 1. INTRODUCTION

Energy is central to society's well-being. The availability of high quality energy is necessary to maintain and expand technology, to grow, distribute and cook food, to provide potable water, to prevent wastes from polluting our environment, to heat, cool and light our living spaces and to both maintain and expand economic prosperity. Sadly, about 1.6 billion people in the world lack access to electricity; most living in South Asia (930 million) and Africa (554 million) (IEA, 2007a, pp. 567–572). About 2.5 billion people use, at an unsustainable rate, traditional inefficient biomass fuels (such as wood, charcoal, agricultural waste and animal dung) for cooking and heating, therefore harming their health, the environment and their economic prospects (see Modi et al., 2006; IEA, 2007a, p. 10).[1] In some African nations, for example, an inadequate supply of reliable, high quality energy has reduced economic growth by 2 per cent (Wine, 2007). Moreover, if energy needs are supplied from fossil fuels (coal, petroleum, natural gas), global emissions of greenhouse gases will soar, as will the adverse effects of pollution from mining, drilling and transporting fuels, and the emission of sulphur dioxide, nitrogen dioxide, particulates, mercury and other air pollutants. According to the International Energy Agency:

> The world is facing twin energy-related threats: that of not having adequate and secure supplies of energy at affordable prices and that of environmental harm caused by consuming too much of it. ... Yet the current pattern of energy supply carries the threat of severe and irreversible environmental damage – including changes in global climate. Reconciling the goals of energy security and environmental protection requires strong and coordinated government action and public support. The need to curb the growth in fossil energy demand, to increase geographic and fuel-supply diversity and to mitigate climate-destabilising emissions is more urgent than ever (IEA, 2007a, p. 1).

Fossil fuels are reservoirs of high quality energy assembled by natural systems over long stretches of geological time. These fuels, petroleum, coal and natural gas, have been the foundation of the industrial revolution and continue to be the essential support of modern society. However, the use of these fuels poses significant sustainable development challenges. First, using fossil fuels creates enormous pollution and environmental problems. Second, the amount of fossil fuels is finite, and in the case of petroleum we have probably already consumed about half of the world's supply (Deffeyes, 2001; Goodstein, 2004, pp. 24–25). Scarcity has made petroleum significantly more expensive – over the last decade the price per barrel has risen over 900 per cent from just under US$16 on 1 January 1998 to about $144 in mid-July 2008 (Energy Information Agency, 2010).[2] With demand (86.8 mbbl/day) slightly higher than supply capacity (86.6 mbbl/day) prices will not fall, but could rise steeply if any supply is lost due to storms, domestic unrest, or any other reason. Present consumption also prejudices future generations and we are presently consuming about 86.8 million barrels of petroleum per day (IEA, 2008).[3] At this rate we will use the remaining 1.5 trillion barrels in around 45 years. Third, the availability of these marvellous fuels is not equitably apportioned. Some countries, such as the OPEC nations, the United States, United Kingdom, Canada, Russia and others, have been blessed with large reserves, while others have little or no oil (IEA, 2008, pp. 22–29). Given the end of the age of low-priced oil, nations without oil reserves and nations that use oil inefficiently will face enormous economic and development challenges (Hodas, 2005, p. 59). Growing global demand for fossil fuels and associated global warming threatens global security (Stuhltrager, 2008).[4] Finally, most of the anthropogenic causes of global warming are directly attributable to fossil fuel use (IPCC, 2007a).

It is then evident that there is an urgent need for the world to address sustainable energy issues. At an economic development level, the gap between global demand and supply of petroleum is razor thin (IEA, 2007b).[5] As the Chinese and Indian economies grow, demand for petroleum to fuel cars, trucks, airplanes, boilers and electric generators will grow rapidly. The price of oil will soar, hobbling economic development in developing nations. Moreover, our energy system will be ever more vulnerable to storms in areas such as the Gulf of Mexico and the North Sea, and political and labour unrest in oil producing countries around the world. Even very modest supply disruptions can dramatically raise the price of petroleum (Hodas, 2007, p. 46).

The urgency is also environmentally driven. Global warming is rapidly approaching dangerous levels. Recent studies have indicated that sea levels are rising more rapidly than the tempered IPCC models predicted they would (LLNL, 2008).[6] Warming may be accelerating – displaying levels at the upper range of IPCC estimates and suggesting rapid movement towards dangerous anthropogenic climate change (Hansen et al., 2007). Impacts already manifesting themselves include shrinking glacier-supported freshwater supplies in India, China and South America as glaciers retreat[7] and in California's Sierra Mountains, as the snow pack shrinks.[8] Melting glaciers in China and India present a major threat to food security (Brown, 2010, p. 6).

So, the world faces a great sustainable development challenge – it must simultaneously provide billions more people with access to high quality energy and also investigate and adapt to the effects of global warming. Meeting the capital requirements to maintain and expand the world's energy system will also be a staggering challenge. The International Energy Agency estimates that to follow a business-as-usual path will require capital investment over the next decade or two of over $20 trillion dollars (IEA, 2007a, p. 40)

It is hard to imagine a more daunting and important sustainability challenge than energy. One would therefore have thought that the international sustainable development project would put the need for sustainable energy and for energy to support sustainable development at the top of its agenda. However, as this chapter demonstrates, energy is not part of the international sustainable development paradigm – all efforts to address sustainable energy at the international level have been failures.

## 2.   ENERGY AND THE SUSTAINABLE DEVELOPMENT FRAMEWORK

The international process seeking to address both sustainable energy and global warming has been charitably characterised as ossified (Depledge, 2006, p. 1), but as shown here, it is more realistically described as 'mostly dead' (Goldman, 1999, p. 276).[9] Perhaps this was to be expected – from the inception of the sustainable development idea, energy issues have always been treated as an unwanted step-child. The story begins in 1972. The Stockholm Declaration[10] makes no mention of energy. Of course, in 1972 energy was very cheap – oil prices were very low, nuclear power was still the hoped-for 'too cheap to meter' source of electricity, air pollution was a matter of poor combustion in car engines, lead was the miracle octane booster in gasoline, and global warming was an idea quietly discussed in a few, small scientific circles (Christianson, 1999).

The 1982 World Charter for Nature[11] mentions energy in its prologue, but only in the most general terms: 'Mankind is part of nature and life depends on the uninterrupted functioning of natural systems which ensure energy and nutrients'. None of its substantive statements or principles mentions energy.

In 1992, the leaders of the nations of the world met at the United Nations Conference on Environment and Development ('UNCED') in Rio de Janeiro to adopt principles of sustainable development and to sign two treaties – The Convention on Biodiversity[12] and the United Nations Framework Convention on Climate Change.[13] These treaties, which seek to address economic development, the environment, present and future generations, and equity, were the first legal documents seeking to address sustainable development. UNCED also produced the Rio Declaration on Environment and Development[14] and Agenda 21,[15] a book-length treatment of sustainable development problems and general policy prescriptions for how they should be addressed. Both the Rio Declaration and Agenda 21 were official, approved outcomes adopted by all the world's nations. Taken together, these documents comprise the world's adoption of sustainable development as the common goal of humankind, defining its basic principles, and providing a road map for proceeding toward that goal. To further the implementation of the principles contained in Agenda 21 and the Rio Declaration, the Commission on Sustainable Development was established within the UN system.[16]

However, the Rio Declaration contains no reference to energy. Similarly, Agenda 21, which is 40 chapters long, includes sections on Social and Economic Dimensions, Conservation and Management of Resources for Development, Strengthening the Role of Major Groups, and Means of Implementation, but does not include a specific chapter on energy.

This omission was not an oversight or inadvertent. In preparation for the UNCED, the IUCN (International Union for Conservation of Nature), the United Nations Environment Programme and WWF (the World Wide Fund for Nature) published *Caring for the Earth: A Strategy for Sustainable Living* (IUCN, UNEP, WWF, 1991) which recognised the central role energy plays in defining human welfare and devoted a full chapter to energy (IUCN, UNEP, WWF, 1991, Ch. 10). Proposed priority actions included: 'long-term energy strategies for all countries; increased efficiency in energy generation from fossil fuels, and increased use of alternative, particularly renewable, energy sources; increased efficiency in the distribution of energy; reduced energy use per person in all sectors, and major increases in the efficiency of energy use in the home, industry, business and transport' (IUCN, UNEP, WWF, 1991, p. 90). *Caring for the Earth* further urged the adoption of 'explicit policies and laws to ensure that the price of energy covers the full social costs, that taxes or fees are used to encourage greater efficiency, and that laws set standards for energy production, distribution and use, stressing environmental protection' (Robinson, 1993). Unfortunately, as Nicholas

Robinson reports, '[d]isputes over fuels, especially between oil exporting and importing nations, made it difficult at UNCED to negotiate a comprehensive or meaningful chapter in Agenda 21 regarding energy' (Robinson, 1993).

Instead, discussion of energy issues was sparingly sprinkled among several Agenda 21 chapters, and even then appeared only in general terms. Energy is mentioned twice, obliquely, in the human health chapter: health impact assessments should be part of the development of new industries and energy facilities (Agenda 21, 6.41(j)(i)); and 'health educational campaigns should also be used to tell poor persons about the indoor air pollution from burning biomass and coal indoors' (Agenda 21, 6.41(b)(ii)), as if these poor people do not realise that their huts are filled with smoke. The use of substitute, clean energy sources is not, however, mentioned in Agenda 21.

In addressing human settlement, Agenda 21 also states that developed countries need to promote renewable sources of energy and more efficient modes of transportation (Agenda 21, 7.47, 7.48, 7.52) and 'energy-efficiency technology' (Agenda 21, 7.49). Agenda 21 further proposes that: 'A comprehensive approach to human settlements development should include the promotion of sustainable energy development in all countries' (Agenda 21, 7.51). Sustainable energy development as defined, with respect to developing countries, requires only: (a) forestry programmes to provide the poor with sustainable biomass energy, and (b) 'programmes to promote ... solar, hydro, wind and biomass' technologies, promote technology transfer of renewable energy technologies, and develop information and training programmes to promote energy efficiency.

Energy is briefly mentioned in two other parts of Agenda 21: Chapter 9, Protection of the Atmosphere, urges research, development, transformation and use of improved energy-efficiency technologies (Agenda 21, 9.12(c)). Chapter 14, Promoting Sustainable Agriculture and Rural Development, has a short subsection urging states to promote rural communities shifting to more productive, sustainable sources of energy (Agenda 21, 14.93–14.104).

As mentioned above, the CSD was created to foster the development of Agenda 21. Its activities are divided into nine clusters, which reflect the chapters of Agenda 21. Since there is no chapter on energy in Agenda 21, there is no energy cluster. Although not mentioned in Agenda 21 or the Rio Declaration, energy remained the elephant in the room. In response, the CSD announced that it would devote its ninth meeting, in the spring of 2001, to energy. It created an ad hoc specialists process to gather facts, develop ideas and propose specific policy ideas for CSD-9[17] and invited participation from a wide range of civil society: business/industry; scientific and technological communities; workers and trade unions; local authorities; and nongovernmental organisations.[18] At the same time, however, the UNDP engaged in a major effort to produce a World Energy Assessment, a comprehensive work identifying the range of sustainable energy issues the world faces, and recommending policy approaches to address them (Goldemberg and Johansson, 2000). Thus, CSD-9 was well informed on sustainable energy. However, neither the preparatory process, nor CSD-9 itself, was to address climate change or greenhouse gas emissions from burning fossil fuels. Other than the absence of discussion of greenhouse gas emissions from fossil fuels, CSD-9 produced a fairly specific consensus policy document as a road map towards sustainable energy.[19] CSD-9 concluded with an agreement to return to energy at CSD-15 in 2007 to press forward on implementing the policies agreed upon at CSD-9.

In May 2006, CSD-14 began its two-year 'implementation cycle' to review progress in energy for sustainable development, industrial development, air pollution/atmosphere, climate change, and cross-cutting issues among these topics. The first year (the 'Review Year') was to focus on information gathering and progress evaluation with respect to implementing Agenda 21, the Johannesburg Plan of Implementation, and the United Nations Millennium Development Goals. CSD-14 was to develop the information base for policy action at CSD-15 (the 'Policy Year').[20] As expected, work at CSD-14 was dominated by energy – energy security, rising oil prices, and the relative roles of fossil fuels and renewable energy – because, as the Chair noted, these issues 'are unparalleled in their importance for achieving sustainable development goals'.[21] CSD-14 was valuable in the range of its discussions, and because it provided delegates with a 'wealth of presentations, case studies, "lessons learned" and practical ideas' (CSD-14 (2006, p. 12) about energy for sustainable development. All CSD-14 participants stressed repeatedly how critical energy was for sustainable development and that energy security (although variously defined) was necessary. Overall, 'CSD-14 performed a frank and sobering scrutiny of energy challenges ... and managed to erect bridges (albeit shaky ones) to CSD-15' (CSD-14, 2006, p. 12). CSD-14's lengthy consensus report expressed 'a greater sense of urgency, and demonstrated that the cost of inaction is becoming steep indeed' (CSD-14, 2006, p. 13). Thus the stage was set for CSD-15 to choose the policy measures necessary to meet these sustainable energy challenges.

From 30 April to 11 May 2007 CSD-15 convened at the United Nations in New York to consider sustainable energy problems, including, for the first time, global warming and greenhouse gases from fossil fuels. The stage was set for concrete steps to shift the world's energy system towards sustainability. Tragically, CSD-15 not only failed to meet its objectives, but hosted the collapse of international efforts to promote sustainable energy (CSD-15, 2007, p. 2).[22] It was also a harbinger of how fragile, if it is not already broken, the international climate change negotiation process is.

Although there was 'broad agreement that the issues of energy for sustainable development ... and climate change are of fundamental importance to achieving the goals of sustainable development and the Millennium Development Goals. ... the delegates remained divided on key points in the energy and climate change chapters'.[23] At CSD-15, there was no agreement on any sustainable energy topic, prior consensus principles dissolved, no CSD report was issued, and there was not even any agreement on when or how the CSD should review energy in the future or follow up on the interlinked issues of energy for sustainable development, air pollution and climate change.

## 3.  THE COLLAPSE OF CONSENSUS AND THE ABANDONMENT OF SUSTAINABLE DEVELOPMENT PRINCIPLES

To the casual observer, the breakdown at CSD-15 might not appear to be particularly significant – it was just another international meeting that did not produce any results. However, on closer examination, the nature of the disagreements and the specific subjects in which they appeared are significant in understanding the failure of the world to advance sustainable development and negotiations over global warming. For instance, several of the disagreements, discussed below, were over central ideas and principles that had been accepted as the norm since at least 1992. The depth of the failure of international law here can only be appreciated by examining the specific disagreements, all of which concerned principles central to the sustainable energy enterprise, and by natural extension, the effort to address global warming.

### Common but Differentiated Responsibilities – Preamble

The common but differentiated responsibilities principle had been a central feature of international environmental law for decades. This principle provides that all states have common responsibilities to protect the environment and promote sustainable development, but because of varying economic, social and ecological conditions each state will carry a different level of responsibility that corresponds to its ability to act. This equitable principle places greater responsibility for environmental problems on wealthier nations and those more responsible for the problem. Most significantly, the principle of common but differentiated responsibilities 'presents a conceptual framework for compromise and cooperation in meeting ... environmental challenges' (Hunter et al., 2007, p. 495).

Although not denoted as such, the principle can be traced to the 1972 Stockholm Declaration, Preamble paragraph 7: 'To achieve this environmental goal will demand the acceptance of responsibility by citizens and communities and enterprises and institutions at every level, all sharing equitably in common efforts', and Principle 23, which elaborates: 'it will be essential in all cases to consider the system of values prevailing in each country, and the extent of the applicability of standards which are valid for the most advanced countries, but which may be inappropriate and of unwarranted social cost for the developing countries'.

In 1992, Principle 7 of the Rio Declaration specifically reaffirmed the doctrine: 'In view of their different contributions to global environmental degradation, states have common but differentiated responsibilities'.

This principle was first made operative as a matter of international law in 1987 by the Montreal Protocol on Substances that Deplete the Ozone Layer Art. 5, Special Situations of Developing Countries.[24] In 1992, the United Nations Framework Convention on Climate Change ('UNFCC') reaffirmed this doctrine: 'The Parties should protect the climate system in accordance with their common but differentiated responsibilities'.[25]

The Kyoto Protocol to the UNFCC followed the principle in allocating different emission reduction targets to different nations, ranging from 8 per cent below 1990 levels (European Community) to 10 per cent above 1990 levels (Iceland), with the overall goal of reducing carbon dioxide emissions by 5 per cent from 1990 levels.[26] In 2001, the doctrine, as stated in Rio Declaration Principle 7, was included in the treaty on persistent organic pollutants.[27]

However, at CSD-15, the participants refused to include the common but differentiated responsibilities doctrine even in the CSD report preamble. First, the United States objected to highlighting only common but differentiated responsibilities.[28] On the other hand the least developed countries, the G-77 countries and China wanted language on countries emerging from conflict, foreign occupation, and new and additional resources to be included. The US proposed language noting significant progress in reducing indoor air pollutants and leaded gasoline, Norway and Switzerland sought a reference to the most recent assessment report of the Intergovernmental Panel on Climate Change (IPCC, 2007b).[29] The European Union sought language that would support an increased target of 0.7 per cent of GNP for development assistance, but the United States and Australia wanted to delete the use of 'targets'. Faced with these disagreements delegates abandoned their efforts to draft a Preamble.

## Energy for Sustainable Development

With respect to energy, there was general agreement at a broad, rhetorical level on the critical importance of energy to sustainable development and that access to reliable, affordable, economically viable, socially acceptable and environmentally sound energy services is crucial, particularly for developing countries.[30] The Chair's summary also noted the 'general acceptance of the need to further diversify energy supply by developing advanced, cleaner, more efficient, affordable and cost-effective energy technologies, including advanced and cleaner fossil fuel technologies and renewable energy technologies'.[31] Delegates broadly agreed that these goals could be achieved by phasing out harmful subsidies and promoting investment in energy services, energy efficiency improvements,[32] cleaner fossil fuel technologies and supporting development of renewable sources of energy such as hydro power, geothermal, wind, solar and bioenergy.[33] However, once any specific issue was raised with respect to energy for sustainable development, chasms of disagreement emerged.

For instance, the considerable discussion of the role of fossil fuels revealed deep disagreement as to the role that these fuels should play. Saudi Arabia wanted language recognising the 'dominant' role of fossil fuels in the future, but the G-77 and China argued for a balanced approach, and still other nations that the world's priority should focus on significantly increasing renewable energy sources and diminishing reliance on fossil fuels (CSD-15, 2007, p. 7).[34] After all this wrangling, the delegates agreed that fossil fuels 'will continue to play an important role' in the future, but the world will endeavour to diversify the energy mix. However, delegates, after lengthy negotiations, could not agree on what this proposition meant (ibid.).

In trying to decide what this diversification into renewable energy should mean, the EU stressed the urgent need to substantially increase the global share of renewable energy sources. To assure progress, the EU and others insisted that a move beyond simply recognising the role of national and voluntary regional targets and initiatives to establish concrete 'time-bound' targets at CSD-15 for significantly increasing renewable energy sources, energy efficiency and reducing the number of people without access to modern, clean sources of energy was required. However, Azerbaijan, Japan, the Russian Federation and the United States, among others, strongly opposed the EU's idea. The G-77/China objected that the 'role' of voluntary targets would only be 'recognised' (CSD-15, 2007, p. 7). However, the EU, adamant in its insistence on concrete timetables, rejected the counter-proposals during the negotiations.[35] The attempt by the CSD-15 Chair to broker a compromise by simply referring to the idea of targets in the Chair's proposed compromise text was rejected by the EU. In consequence, the mere 'mention of time-bound targets proved to be one of the areas where agreement could not be reached' (CSD-15, Chair Summary, 2007, p. 11).

Nor could the delegates find any consensus with respect to specific actions to improve energy efficiency, a supposedly uncontroversial subject. First, the EU proposed language promoting national and international energy efficiency standards, consumer participation and energy efficient transportation (CSD-15, 2007, p. 1). However, Russia opposed the language proposed, countering with a supply-side proposal that did not mention energy efficiency but urged 'encouraging open and competitive markets for energy production, supply, use and transit' (ibid.). Australia proposed text on energy efficiency to specify policies, regulations and standards 'at the national level' (ibid.).

The delegates could not even agree on how to begin talking about energy efficiency. The EU proposed language to 'initiate' instead of language from other nations to 'consider initiating' a process for an international agreement on energy efficiency whereas the US, supported by Japan and the Republic of Korea, suggested that the text 'promote international efforts on energy efficiency' (CSD-15, 2007, p. 1).[36] No consensus could be reached (CSD-15, 2007, Chair Summary, p. 18).

The EU also proposed that the CSD-15 establish a monitoring and review mechanism to evaluate real progress towards energy for sustainable development. While there was general recognition that a CSD review of energy issues would be useful to evaluate progress and policy effectiveness, Japan and others did not agree[37] on any details such as who would engage in the review, when it would be done, how it would be done, what would be reviewed, or how focused and measured the review would be. EU member nations proposed formal and detailed review arrangements. According to the Chair's summary of events, despite the 'recognition of the desirability of a specific review of energy issues within the context of CSD in the coming years, there was a considerable divergence regarding who, how, when and in what detail such a review should be conducted. Some were of the view that one or two days in 2010 and 2014 should be devoted to monitor and follow up the implementation of decisions on energy for sustainable development, and its means of implementation. Other countries proposed more formal and detailed review arrangements, but no decision could be reached on undertaking such a review or its modalities' (CSD-15, 2007, Chair Summary, p. 20). The end result according to the Chair: '*No* consensus was reached on review and follow-up on the inter-linked issues of energy for sustainable development, industrial development, air pollution/atmosphere and climate change' (CSD-15, 2007, Chair Summary, p. 42)[38] (emphasis added). In other words, as of the conclusion of CSD-15 energy for sustainable development was indefinitely removed from the CSD agenda (and work).

**Air Pollution/Atmosphere**

The delegations agreed broadly on air pollution issues, including the need to accelerate the transition from inefficient utilisation of biomass to cleaner energy sources, technology, and appliances for cooking and heating; develop strategies for sustainable urban and land-use planning; promote the establishment of country and regional air quality standards; improve control of emissions through the establishment of emission limit values from different sources to mitigate air pollution; improve urban air quality through utilisation of cleaner fuels and technologies; promote less polluting public and mass transport systems; encourage the switch to more fuel/energy-efficient vehicles; encourage improved inspection and maintenance requirements for vehicles; improve fuel and vehicle efficiency and the use of technologies that reduce emissions; improve information on sources and health impacts of indoor air pollution; improve collection, compilation and analysis of data; provide financial and other resources to support programmes that address adverse health impacts and increase successful approaches and best practices and partnerships to reduce indoor air pollution (CSD-15, 2007, Chair Summary, p. 26).

Agreed approaches to reduce air pollution included: sharing information on adopting and replicating best practice from around the world; accelerating the shift from biomass to cleaner energy; and using cleaner fuels and vehicles (CSD-15, 2007, Chair Summary, pp. 25–26). But the devil was in the details. Despite recognising the urgency of addressing air pollution problems, the action agreed upon was, at best, minimal: supporting, 'as appropriate', international monitoring efforts and sharing, 'on a voluntary basis', regional and sub-regional experiences that address transboundary air pollution (CSD-15, 2007, p. 8). The delegations also agreed to invite donor nations to contribute to the next replenishment of the Multilateral Fund under the Montreal Protocol, and to help developing countries address naturally occurring air pollution, particularly dust, sandstorms, smoke from forest fires and volcanic ash.

However, when it came to actual air quality standards and real, measurable steps to reduce air pollution, consensus disappeared. For instance, the EU proposed that World Health Organisation global air quality guidelines should be used as minimum air pollution standards (CSD-15, 2007, p. 8). India and others objected, arguing that air pollution standards should not be universal (ibid.). The issue was resolved by the weak phrase, 'taking into account WHO guidelines as appropriate' (ibid.).

Another area of disagreement was the problem of pollution from aviation and maritime sources. Delegates disagreed on whether relevant measures should be taken only through the International Maritime Organization and the

International Civil Aviation Organization, as the US and the G-77/China suggested, or through 'other relevant international frameworks' as well, as the EU insisted (ibid.). The EU also supported the establishment of voluntary guidelines for the aviation and maritime sectors; however the broader EU language was strongly opposed by the US, the Russian Federation and several other countries (ibid.). Efforts to resolve the issue continued until the very end of the session, but delegates failed to reach agreement.

**Climate Change**

At a broad level, 'climate change was recognised as a global sustainable development challenge with strong social, economic and environmental dimensions' (CSD-15, 2007, Chair Summary, p. 28). Many states viewed the recent IPCC assessment of impacts of climate change on sustainable development as a cause for concern. Despite general agreement on the importance of climate change, and that CSD-15 should defer generally to the UNFCCC process, significant disagreements also emerged here. Notably, the delegates could not agree on whether to or how to include references to post-2012 commitments under the UNFCCC and the Kyoto Protocol in the CSD-15 text (CSD-15, 2007, pp. 8–9). Nor was there agreement with respect to even mentioning: the principle of common but differentiated responsibilities; the findings of the IPCC; identifying new and additional financial resources for mitigation of or adaptation to climate change; the use of market-based mechanisms, or carbon capture and storage technology; developing insurance schemes by developed countries for minimising impacts of climate change on developing countries; and making reference to sustainable production and consumption patterns and enhancing dialogue between the Kyoto Protocol and Montreal Protocol on ozone-depleting substances that are also greenhouse gases (CSD-15, 2007, Chair Summary, p. 29).

So long as the details were vague, the delegates readily and broadly agreed on the need for the development and dissemination of advanced energy technologies, including cleaner fossil fuels, energy efficiency and renewable energies that contribute to the reduction of greenhouse gas emissions, particularly if this could be achieved via the private sector and market-oriented approaches. Another uncontroversial idea was that the world should move towards (though how fast and how close was unsaid) 'a longer-term strategy and a comprehensive response to climate change by promoting sustainable economic growth, accelerating the transition to a lower greenhouse gas-emitting economy, and enhancing adaptive capacities and response measures to cope with the impacts of climate change' (CSD-15, 2007, Chair Summary, p. 34).

## Industrial Development – Revisiting Sustainable Development and Principle 2 of the Rio Declaration

Countries also disagreed over whether to emphasise 'development' or 'sustainable' development. For instance, Switzerland wanted language on 'sustainable' economic growth and industrial development 'within the natural resource base', whereas the G-77/China wanted the language to emphasise the importance of industrial development to poverty alleviation (CSD-15, 2007, p. 9). There were even disagreements over references to Principle 2 of the Rio Declaration on states' sovereign rights to exploit their own resources. The G-77/China language would emphasise the rights of each country to decide their own industrial development, environmental protection and environmental management strategies (ibid.). Instead, Australia, Switzerland and the US sought language emphasising the responsibility of states to ensure that activities within their jurisdiction and control do not cause damage to the environment of other states or to areas beyond the limits of national jurisdiction (ibid.). Agreement could not be reached.

The *Earth Negotiations Bulletin* also reported that the EU proposed adding the phrase 'building on the principle of sustainability and good governance', to national policy frameworks language (CSD-15, 2007, p. 9). But the G-77/China group of developing countries questioned whether any such principle existed and also opposed any conditionality being placed on national policymaking (ibid.). In the area of innovative environmental management systems, such as life-cycle analysis, eco-design and green procurement, the G-77/China expressed concern over eco-labelling and its restrictions on trade. It proposed deleting 'certification' from the list of trade-related capacity building, and using the term 'technical knowledge' in place of 'intellectual property' (ibid.).

Further disagreements appeared in addressing basic infrastructure issues. The G-77/China suggested 'scaling up resource flows' but the US rejected that phrasing, preferring instead 'promoting resources' (CSD-15, 2007). Hoping to break the deadlock, the CSD-15 Chair offered 'mobilising' resources instead; Australia, the EU and the US agreed, but the suggestion was opposed by the G-77/China, which countered with the phrase 'enabling environment that facilitates foreign direct investment' (ibid.).

Disagreement was also present in respect of technological cooperation: the EU and Japan suggested deleting a reference to 'sharing of intellectual property and know how', while Botswana called for 'equitable sharing' (CSD-15, 2007). As to capacity building, the G-77/China opposed the EU proposal to promoting education and skills development 'on a non-discriminatory basis' (ibid.).

## 4.   THE FINAL COLLAPSE OF CSD-15

Despite negotiation sessions lasting late into the night throughout CSD-15, by the time the closing plenary convened on the final day of the meeting, the list of significant unresolved issues remained lengthy, particularly in the energy for sustainable development and climate change sections of the document (CSD-15, 2007, p. 10).[39] In an effort to save CSD-15 from failure, at 5:45 p.m. the Chair presented the meeting with a compromised CSD-15 Report text on a 'take it or leave it' basis – delegations could not 'change a word' (ibid.). The Chair announced that if they rejected the text,[40] the only outcome from the session would be a Chair's Summary of the discussions. The energy section of the Chair's compromise noted that fossil fuels 'will continue to play a dominant role in the energy supply in the decades to come'. It offered targets (without timelines) on increasing access to energy, energy efficiency and renewable energy, but they would be voluntary targets, which nations should make greater use of 'as appropriate'. (CSD-15, 2007, p. 3). There was no mention of a progress review mechanism or arrangement. Nor did nuclear power appear as part of the energy mix (CSD-15, Chair Summary, 2007, Annex).

Delegates reconvened at 8:05 p.m. after regional consultations on the Chair's compromise text (CSD-15, 2007, p. 10).[41] The EU rejected the text because it neither addressed the identified challenges nor met international expectations (ibid.). For the EU, robust targets and timetables for renewable energy, energy efficiency and access to energy sit at the heart of combating climate change and achieving sustainable development. Switzerland rejected the text because it did not add value, and weakened previous language (CSD-15, 2007, p. 10). As a result, since consensus is required, CSD-15 did not adopt a decision text. Energy for sustainable development, already homeless within the UN system, was effectively banished from the international sustainable development agenda.

CSD-15 was declared closed at 8:55 p.m. and the process for CSD-16 began with – a new controversy. The new chair, from Zimbabwe, was narrowly elected over strong opposition because of the lack of rule of law and good governance in Zimbabwe (CSD-15, 2007, p. 10).

The *Earth Negotiations Bulletin* assessment of CSD-15 is discouraging:

> CSD-15 proved to be a sobering reminder that fundamental disagreements exist between states on the nature, scope and ambition of the sustainable development agenda – particularly the issues of energy and climate change – and the role, relevance and value of the CSD itself (CSD-15, 2007).

It is apparent that at CSD-15 the EU was dissatisfied with the pace of progress in both climate change negotiations and the failure of the CSD to give high priority to energy efficiency and renewable energy as central, cost-effective means to advance sustainable development and reduction of greenhouse gas emissions. It is equally apparent that the United States was correspondingly resistant to calls for energy targets and timetables of any sort, concrete standards and any increased responsibility under the rubric of common but differentiated responsibilities. Others, such as the G-77/China were displeased with the lack of additional financial assistance and with the potential that international sustainable development doctrines could interfere with domestic economic policy. CSD-15 therefore sent ominous signals for the success of future climate change negotiations.

Even though the EU, after difficult negotiations, was willing to ease up on its ambitious climate change positions at the CSD, those concessions made it far more important to the EU that concrete, measurable progress be made by CSD-15 on sustainable energy issues. The EU wanted the CSD to be more than a feeble 'talk shop' (CSD-15, 2007, p. 11).

The swift death of the Chair's last-minute 'take it or leave' text was significant as an indicator of how unyielding contending views of sustainable energy and climate change have become. One observer noted that the CSD follow-up to its abandonment of energy issues by turning, only minutes after CSD-15 failed, to address the third cycle on agriculture, Africa and other land-related issues in CSD-16 was like 'rearranging the deck chairs on the Titanic' (CSD-15, 2007, p. 12).

## 5.   SUSTAINABLE ENERGY AND CLIMATE CHANGE: LESSONS FROM CSD-15's FAILURE

It is now crystal clear that there is no global commitment to energy as part of sustainable development, energy for sustainable development, sustainable energy, or any serious energy-based responses to climate change. The rhetoric is broadly and blandly supportive of the need for sustainable energy, but no important details were subject to consensus. This is starkly clear in the range of topics where there was disagreement:

- Whether the principle of common but differentiated responsibilities should apply to sustainable energy or to climate change;
- Targets and timetables for an increased role of renewable energy, efficiency and access to energy;

- How, whether and when to review progress in achieving sustainable energy goals;
- Whether WHO guidelines for should constitute minimal air quality standards;
- What standards should govern aviation and maritime air pollution;
- The most recent IPCC climate change findings; Post-Kyoto 2012 greenhouse gas emissions; technical and financial assistance; and the role of market instruments;
- Principle 2 of the Rio Declaration;
- Whether pure economic development takes priority over and should be separated from sustainable development principles that development must be balanced by environmental needs and equity;
- Sharing intellectual property; increased money for financial assistance to developing countries for infrastructure, capacity building in the realm of education and skills development;
- Sustainable Patterns of Production and Consumption;
- Setting a target 0.7 per cent of donor nation GNP for development assistance;
- Measures to support Africa; and
- Whether the next review of the interconnected issues of energy for sustainable development, air pollution, industrial development, and climate change should limited be a one or two day meeting in 2010 and 2014 or whether there should be detailed evaluation and measurement of progress.

It is all too apparent that, within the framework of sustainable development, energy remains an outsider. The international negotiation process is not proving up to the task of addressing energy or climate change. International talks and meetings can proceed apace, exhausting all the participants who must scurry around the globe to attend these assemblies, but, until the United States, the EU and China (and perhaps India) reach agreement on greenhouse gas emission targets and timetables and on specific goals, policies and timetables for sustainable energy, no climate change agreement will be reached and energy for sustainable development will remain, at the international level, a homeless orphan. Until that day arrives, it makes little sense to focus on international institutions and treaty negotiations as vehicles for addressing climate change or sustainable energy.

Instead, we must focus on domestic law and policy. As the author has observed elsewhere (Hodas, 2008), with the correct policies in effect in domestic law, enormous steps can be taken to advance energy efficiency and cost-effectiveness. More efficient biomass stoves can dramatically reduce indoor air pollution and reduce the amount of fuel that must be burned for the same level of cooking. Appliance efficiency standards, building codes, low energy light bulbs, and a myriad of new efficient power-generating technologies can all serve to decrease the need for inefficient, dirty power and enable renewable energy to provide significantly greater energy services at lower cost.

To make the most of this approach we must consider best practices, policies and laws throughout the world, honestly evaluating them and looking to see how they can be improved and adapted for use in other jurisdictions. We must also examine existing energy and environmental laws and regulations to identify which obstruct efficiency investments, or promote emitting greenhouse gases. We must work in the trenches, building laws and policies from the ground up, that will make it profitable for the private sector to invest in energy efficiency. If investors can make money investing in energy efficiency technologies and renewable energy, huge reservoirs of capital will become available. Instead of the ineffective top-down approach of the CSD, we must make the law sustainable-energy friendly; build the right policies in law, and sustainable energy investments will follow.

## 6. POSTSCRIPT

Since this chapter was first drafted, the international impasse it describes has not been resolved. The terms and forum of the debate have shifted from the CSD to the UNFCCC, where little progress has been made. The December 2007 Bali Conference of the Parties produced an Action Plan that would be the 'roadmap' for negotiations that might lead to a substantive climate change agreement at the Copenhagen COP in December 2009.[42] As the Bali Roadmap journey proceeded, the International Energy Agency, in a remarkably candid and blunt report, urged the nations to address the world's profound sustainable energy and climate change challenges:

> The world's energy system is at a crossroads. Current global trends in energy supply and consumption are patently unsustainable – environmentally, economically, socially. But that can – and must – be altered; there's still time to change the road we're on. It is not an exaggeration to claim that the future of human prosperity depends on how successfully we tackle the two central energy challenges facing us today: securing the supply of reliable and affordable energy; and effecting a rapid transformation to a low-carbon, efficient and environmentally benign system of energy supply. What is needed is nothing short of an energy revolution.

Preventing catastrophic and irreversible damage to the global climate ultimately requires a major decarbonisation of the world energy sources (IEA, 2008, p. 3).

The International Energy Agency's conclusions were stark and sobering, unlike any past annual assessment:

The energy future will be very different. [I]t is becoming increasingly apparent that the era of cheap oil is over. It is within the power of all governments, of producing and consuming countries alike, acting alone or together, to steer the world towards a cleaner, cleverer and more competitive energy system. Time is running out and the time to act is now (IEA, 2008, p. 16).

But no formal agreement was achieved following the Bali Roadmap to Copenhagen, where negotiations stalled. Informal discussions among several major nations produced a political agreement, the so-called 'Copenhagen Accord', which the COP, after lengthy, contentious debate, agreed only to 'take note' of.[43] The Copenhagen Accord called for nations to make non-binding pledges for greenhouse gas emission reductions and mitigation activities, which would be the basis for further negotiations that hopefully would conclude successfully at COP 16 in Cancun, Mexico in late November 2010. While over 80 nations submitted pledges, the Cancun preparatory meetings were largely unproductive.[44] The Cancun COP itself produced several agreements including REDD (Reducing Emissions from Deforestation and Degradation), technology, mitigation and finance, but 'most participants acknowledged that it was a relatively small step in combating climate change'.[45]

Internationally, not a single substantive issue left hanging after CSD 15 has been resolved. Concepts and principles of sustainable energy have not appeared on any formal meeting agenda. For instance, a phase out of fossil fuel consumption subsidies, $557 billion in 2008, could cut carbon dioxide emissions by 6.9 per cent (2.4 gt) by 2010 (about the current emissions of France, Germany, Italy, Spain and the UK combined).[46] Tragically, as UNFCCC meetings avoid concrete discussion about how to shift to a more sustainable, low carbon world economy, international talks increasingly become disconnected from real-world policy, science and law.

# NOTES

1. The health impacts can be severe: 'about 1.3 million people – mostly women and children – die prematurely every year because of exposure to indoor air pollution from biomass' (International Energy Agency, 2007a, p. 10).
2. See http://www.eia.doe.gov/emeu/international/crude1.html.
3. See, http://omrpublic.iea.org/currentissues/full.pdf.
4. National Commission on Energy Policy and Securing America's Energy Future, Oil shock wave: Oil Crisis Executive Simulation (2005), at http://www.energycommission.org /files/contentFiles/oil_shockwave_report_440cc39a643cd.pdf.
5. See http://omrpublic.iea.org/.
6. See https://publicaffairs.llnl.gov/news/news_releases/2008/NR-08-06-07.html.
7. UN Environment Programme. 'Glaciers Are Melting Faster Than Expected, UN Reports' (18 March 2008), at http://www.unep.org/Documents.Multilingual/Default.asp? DocumentID=530&ArticleID=5760&l=enhttp://www.unep.org/Documents.Multilingual/ Default.asp?DocumentID=530&ArticleID=5760&l=en.
8. California Climate Change Center, *Climate Warming and Water Supply Management in California*, CEC-500-2005-195-SF (March 2006), at http://www.energy.ca.gov/2005 publications/CEC-500-2005-195/CEC-500-2005-195-SF.PDF.
9. See Goldman (1999), where Miracle Max, when asked to revive the hero, explains the difference between 'mostly dead' and 'dead': if the hero is mostly dead, then he is partly alive and could possibly be revived; but if he is completely dead, he is dead forever, at p. 276.
10. Stockholm Declaration of the United Nations Conference on the Human Environment (UN Doc. A/CONF. 48/14/Rev.1), (1973) 11 ILM 1416.
11. World Charter for Nature (UN Doc. A/37/51), (1983) 22 ILM 455.
12. UNEP/Bio. Div./CONF/L.2, (1992) 31 ILM 818.
13. UN Doc. A/CONF.151/26, (1992) 31 ILM 849.
14 Rio Declaration on Environment and Development (13 June 1992) (UNCED Doc. A/CONF. 151/26 (Vol. 1)), (1992) 31 ILM 874.
15. Agenda 21, UN Doc. A/CONF.151/26, Vols I–IV (1992), at http://www.un.org/ esa/sustdev /documents/agenda21/english/agenda21toc.htm.
16. See http://www.un.org/esa/sustdev/csd/csd_mandate.htm.
17. Report of the Ad Hoc Open-ended Intergovernmental Group of Experts on Energy and Sustainable Development, New York, 26 February–2 March 2001 (UN Doc. E/CN.17// 2001/15), at http://www.un.org/esa/sustdev/documents/docs_csd9.htm.
18. See Documents for the Multi-stakeholder Dialogue Segment on Energy and Transport, http://www.un.org/esa/sustdev/documents/docs_csd9.htm.
19. Commission on Sustainable Development, Report on the ninth session (5 May 2000 and 16–27 April 2001) (UN Doc. E/CN.17/2001/19), http://www.un.org/esa/sustdev/ documents /docs_csd9.htm.
20. IISD; *Earth Negotiations Bulletin CSD-14 Final: Summary of the Fourteenth Session of the Commission on Sustainable Development: 1–12 May 2006* (15 May 2006), at http://www.iisd.ca/csd/csd14.
21. Commission on Sustainable Development, Report on the fourteenth session 22 April 2005 and 1–12 May 2006 (UN Doc. E/2006/29(SUPP) E/CN.17/2006/15 (SUPP) 19, http:// daccessdds.un.org/doc/UNDOC/GEN/N06/377/66/PDF/N0637766.pdf?OpenElement.
22. Evaluations of CSD-15 ranged from 'this whole conference is a joke' (reportedly said by a minister), to 'reality has finally caught up with us' (an observation by an old CSD hand), at http://www.iisd.ca/download/pdf/enb05253e.pdf.
23. Chairman's Summary, Fifteenth Session of the Commission on Sustainable Development, (May 2007), at http://www.un.org/esa/sustdev/csd/csd15/documents/chair_summary.pdf.
24. Montreal Protocol on Substances that Deplete the Ozone Layer 1522 UNTS 3, (1987) 26 ILM 1541 (concluded at Montreal 16 September 1987; entered into force 1 January 1989).

25. United Nations Framework Convention on Climate Change (1992) (UN Doc. A/CONF.151/26), (1992) 31 ILM 849 (entered into force 21 March 1994) Art. 3, 1. The Preamble also notes 'that the global nature of climate change calls for the widest possible cooperation by all countries and their participation in an effective and appropriate international response, in accordance with their common but differentiated responsibilities'.

26. Kyoto Protocol to the United Nations Framework Convention on Climate Change. Adopted at Kyoto Japan 11 Dec. 1997 (UN Doc. FCCC/CP/1997/I.7/Add.1), 37 (1998) ILM 32 (entered into force, 16 Feb. 2005). Art. 3 para. 1; Annex B.

27. Stockholm Convention on Persistent Organic Pollutants. Concluded at Stockholm 22 May 2001 (entered into force, 17 May 2004). UN Doc. UNEP/POPS/CONF 2, (2001) 40 ILM 278. Preamble, Art 10 and Art. 11: 'each Party shall, within its capabilities'.

28. These summaries of the negotiating failures are based on the Chairman's Summary and the *Earth Negotiations Bulletin*, Summary of the Fifteenth Session of the Commission on Sustainable Development: 30 April–11 May 2007 (14 May 2007), at http://www.iisd.ca/download/pdf/enb05254e.pdf.

29. See http://ipcc-wg1.ucar.edu/wg1/wg1-report.html.

30. Chairman's Summary, 15th session of the Commission on Sustainable Development, para. 2, 9, 25.

31. Note 31, para 9.

32. Some countries proposed 'initiating a process that would lead to an international agreement on energy efficiency', but 'no consensus could be reached on initiating a formal agreement process;' note 31, para 18.

33. Note 31 paras 14–17.

34. The role of nuclear energy was ignored. Pakistan, Algeria, Chile and Argentina and other delegations proposed language that would have added nuclear power in the sustainable energy mix. EU and others opposed that reference to nuclear power. No agreement could be reached on addressing nuclear energy, so it was not addressed.

35. The EU also proposed the idea of a mechanism or arrangement to review progress towards sustainable development. The US, Japan, Canada, Australia and others objected. No agreement was reached.

36. See http://www.iisd.ca/download/pdf/enb05249e.pdf.

37. The EU proposed a review arrangement for energy for sustainable development, progress reports facilitated by UN-Energy, and a review of Johannesburg Plan of Implementation commitments and CSD decisions on energy in 2010/2011 and 2014/2015. Japan expressed uncertainty about the EU's proposed review mechanism. IISD, *Earth Negotiations Bulletin*, CSD-15 #6 (7 May 2007) 2, http://www.iisd.ca/ download /pdf /enb05249e.pdf.

38. The Chair's proposed compromise text had suggested a one or two day meeting in 2010 and 2014.

39. See http://www.iisd.ca/csd/csd15.

40. Commission on Sustainable Development, Report on the fifteenth session (12 May 2006 and 30 April–11 May 2007), Annex, Decision text proposed by the Chairperson (UN Doc. E/2007/29 E/CN.17/2007/15), at http://daccessdds.un.org/doc/UNDOC/GEN/N07/363/23/PDF/N0736323.pdf?OpenElement.

41. See http://www.iisd.ca/csd/csd15/.

42. See http://unfccc.int/meetings/cop_13/items/4049.php.

43. See http://unfccc.int/files/meetings/cop_15/application/pdf/cop15_cph_auv.pdf.

44. Earth Negotiations Bulletin SB32 Final, Summary of Bonn Climate Change Talks 31 May – 11 June 2010 (Monday 14 June 2010), www.iisd.ca/climate/sb32

45. *Earth Negotiations Bulletin* Vol. 12 No. 498 (Monday 13 December 2010) p. 1 http://www.iisd.ca/download/pdf/enb12498e.pdf.

46. Office of the Chief Economist, International Energy Agency, 'Energy Subsidies: Getting the Prices Right' (7 June 2010).

# REFERENCES

Brown, Lester R. (2010), *Plan B 4.0 Mobilizing to Save Civilization*, Earth Policy Institute, New York and London: Norton and Co.

Christianson, Gail E. (1999), *Greenhouse: The 200-Year Story of Global Warming*, New York: Penguin Books.

Commission on Sustainable Development (CSD) (2006), *Earth Negotiations Bulletin, CSD-14 Final*, International Institute for Sustainable Development (IISD).

Commission on Sustainable Development (CSD) (2007), *Earth Negotiations Bulletin, CSD-15* Vol. 6, International Institute for Sustainable Development (IISD).

Deffeyes, Kenneth S. (2001), *Hubbert's Peak: The Impending World's Oil Shortage*, Princeton, New Jersey: Princeton University Press.

Depledge, Joanna (2006), 'The opposite of learning: ossification in the climate change regime', *Global Environmental Politics*, **6**, 1–22.

Energy Information Agency (2010), 'Selected Crude Oil Spot Prices', *Oil Market Report*, at http://www.eia.gov.

Goldemberg, José and Thomas B. Johansson (2000), 'World Energy Assessment: Energy and Challenge of Sustainability', in Jose Goldemburg (ed.) UN Department of Economic and Social Affairs, and World Energy Council, New York: UNDP.

Goldman, William (1999), *The Princess Bride*, London: Bloomsbury

Goodstein, David (2004), *Out of Gas: The End of the Age of Oil*, New York: W.W. Norton & Company Inc.

Hansen, James, M. Sato, R. Reudy, P. Kharecha and A. Lacis (2007), 'Dangerous human-made interference with climate: A GISS modelE study', *Atmos Chem Phys*, **7**, 2287–2312.

Hodas, David (2005), 'The Challenge of High-Priced Oil', *Natural Resources & Environment*, **20**, 59–61.

Hodas, David, (2007) 'Climate Change and Land Use in Africa', in Nathalie J. Chalifour et al. (eds), *Land Use Law for Sustainable Development*, Cambridge: Cambridge University Press.

Hodas, David (2008), 'Imagining the unimaginable: reducing United States greenhouse gas emissions forty percent', *Virginia Environmental Law Journal*, **26**, 271–290.

Hunter, D., James Salzman and Durwood Zaelke (2007), *International Environmental Law and Policy*, 3rd edn, New York: Foundation Press.

Intergovernmental Panel on Climate Change (IPCC) (2007a), 'Summary for Policymakers', *Climate Change 2007: The Physical Basis; Contribution of Working Group I to the Fourth Assessment Report of the IPCC*, at http://www.ipcc.ch/publications_and_data/publications_ipcc_fourth_assessment_report_wg1_report_the_physical_science_basis.htm.

Intergovernmental Panel on Climate Change (IPPC) (2007b), *The IPCC Fourth Assessment Report: The Physical Science Basis of Climate Change*, at http://www.ipcc.ch/ipccreports/ar4-wg1.htm.

International Energy Agency (IEA) (2007a), *World Energy Outlook 2006*, available at http://www.worldenergyoutlook.org/2007.asp.

International Energy Agency (IEA) (2007b), *Oil Market Report* (17 September), available at http://omrpublic.iea.org.

International Energy Agency (IEA) (2008), *Oil Market Report* (10 June), available at http://omrpublic.iea.org/omrarchive/10jun08full.pdf.

IUCN, UNEP, WWF (1991), *Caring for the Earth: A Strategy for Sustainable Living*, at http://coombs.anu.edu.au/~vern/caring/care-earth3.txt.

Lawrence Livermore National Laboratory (LLNL) (2008), 'Ocean Temperatures and Sea Level Increases 50 per cent Higher than Previously Estimated', News Release (18 June 2008) (LLNL).

Modi, V., S. McDade, D. Lallement and J. Saghir (2006), *Energy and the Millennium Development Goals*, New York: Energy Sector Management Assistance Programme, United Nations Development Programme, UN Millennium Project, and World Bank.

Robinson, Nicholas A. (ed.) (1993), *Agenda 21: Earth's Action Plan*, New York: Oceana Publications.

Stuhltrager, James (2008), 'Global climate change and national security', *Natural Resources & Environment*, **22** (3), 36.

Wine, Michael (2007), 'Toiling in the Dark: Africa's Power Crisis', *The New York Times*, 29 July.

# 16. Cross-border gas pipelines and sustainability in southern Africa

## Willemien du Plessis

## 1. INTRODUCTION

The Rio Declaration on Environment and Development[1] of 1992 sets out a framework for environmental regulation worldwide, emphasising the promotion of developing new technologies, reducing pollution and developing effective environmental legislation (not least environmental impact assessments, including engagement with cross-border issues).[2]

The world faces a multi-dimensional energy crisis: fossil fuels generate adverse environmental impacts, prompting the development of alternatives; energy security is a pressing issue[3] and new energy markets are emerging. Agenda 21[4] refers briefly to the need to address energy generation and consumption,[5] while the United Nations Framework Convention on Climate Change[6] targets greenhouse gases. As a result, greater reliance is being placed on gas as an energy source. The Energy Charter Treaty and its subsequent Energy Charter Protocol (ECS, 2004)[7] sought to ensure safe and environmentally friendly transfer of gas in Eurasia. While no African country has signed the Treaty as yet, it may nonetheless provide lessons for cross-border gas transfer in Africa.

South Africa has long relied primarily on coal-generated electricity for both domestic supply and export of energy. Export energy demand in the South African Development Community (SADC) has grown substantially and South Africa has indicated that it would not be able to sustain energy export to its neighbouring countries. Accordingly countries such as Mozambique investigated the viability of gas fields as an alternative source of energy. Sasol, a major South African petroleum company, decided to import gas from Mozambique as an alternative to oil and coal-based petroleum products and in response to stricter enforcement of environmental legislation in South Africa. This presents a number of legal challenges, as South Africa and Mozambique have distinct general and environmental legal regimes and use different languages (English and Portuguese respectively).

In concluding a legal agreement between the two countries to facilitate gas transfer in addition to compliance with law applicable to African Union and SADC members, two different environmental impact assessment regimes applied. Additional conditions were specified in terms of a World Bank agreement.[8] Furthermore, at the time, South Africa had only draft legislation on gas transfer via pipelines, while Mozambique had none.

In examining the contribution of post-Rio regulation of cross-border transfer of gas, applicable international and regional instruments are discussed alongside the relevant Mozambican and South African legislation.

## 2.   INTERNATIONAL AND REGIONAL INSTRUMENTS

Various international and regional instruments, rooted in the Rio Declaration, make provision for the safe and environmentally friendly transfer of gas. Instruments such as the Energy Charter and Protocol (9.11–12 and 34.19); (Nanda and Pring, 2003) refer explicitly to sustainable development and environmental protection principles (Birnie et al., 2009, pp. 485–488).

### The Rio Declaration

The Rio Declaration includes a range of sustainable development principles (e.g., Principle 3) and requires tackling 'unsustainable patterns of production and consumption' (Principle 7); improving use of science and technology (Principle 9); adopting effective environmental legislation and standards (Principle 11); and addressing trans-boundary environmental issues (Principles 12 and 19), notably through environmental impact assessment (in Principle 17).

Furthermore, Agenda 21 also explicitly promotes the development of sustainable energy,[9] in particular through regional and sub-regional plans (para. 9.12(g)).

The Johannesburg Plan of Implementation,[10] adopted by the World Summit on Sustainable Development, further addresses sustainable energy issues. It advocates, amongst other things, promoting cleaner and more efficient use of natural gas and introducing cleaner fossil fuel technologies. It also commits states to strengthening and facilitating regional cooperation agreements to promote cross-border transfer of energy (including via natural gas pipelines (para. 20(v)). The Energy Charter with its Protocol is one such instrument.

## The Energy Charter and Protocol, and Related Developments

The Energy Charter is a binding multilateral framework for inter-governmental energy cooperation[11] unique in international law, which supports efforts to develop global energy security (Art. 2) (Bamberger et al., 2000), based on open, competitive markets and sustainable development.

Two of the aims of the Energy Charter and its 1994 Protocol on Energy Efficiency and Environmentally Related Aspects are improved energy efficiency and reduced environmental impact. Under the Charter, states may regulate energy in accordance with their own legislation (Art. 18(3)), subject to the requirement to minimise environmental impacts. Obligations include: taking the precautionary principle into account; accepting the polluter pays principle with regard to trans-boundary pollution (Art. 19(1)); taking environmental considerations into account in energy policy; introducing international environmental energy efficiency standards (Art. 19(3)(c)); and developing and sharing information on cleaner fuels etc. (Art. 19(1)(a)–(k)).

To give effect to the Energy Charter and to promote free trade in energy, two model agreements were formulated to provide guidelines and facilitate negotiations on cross-border pipleines (para. 11, 15–16). The Intergovernmental Agreement (IGA) concerns construction and operation of pipelines between states. The Host Government Agreement (HGA) applies between host governments and project investors and includes provision on environmental and other standards and liability (paras 20–23). It further refers in its Appendices to a variety of Codes of Practice and international law provisions that may be relevant. The HGA (Art. 1(35)), applies to evaluation, development and design to operate, repair, extension, replacement (Art. 1(17)), and abandonment or rehabilitation plans (Art. 36 and Part III of Appendix 1). Environmental and safety standards appropriate for the specific biosphere must be agreed upon and described in the HGA in Article 13, and state assistance must be provided where material environmental damage or risks to health and safety exist.[12] Project investors are required (Art. 13) to take immediate remedial action for spillages/leaks and to pay compensation on a strict liability basis. If the operation of the pipeline 'creates a serious threat to public health and safety, property or the environment', it may be halted only for such length of time as is needed to remove the threat (Art. 8(4) of IGA). States should provide that governments are obliged to ensure effective regulation (Arts. 6(2) and (3) and (9)), including requiring that all necessary authorisations[13] are obtained (Art. 9(2) and to provide access to all supporting documentation on request (Art. 26(1)).

A further interesting development in this area is ongoing discussion of the 2003 draft Energy Charter Transit Protocol which seeks (Waern, 2002)[14] to regulate, in an environmentally sound manner, the transit of energy materials and products (hydrocarbons and electricity), across at least two international boundaries.[15] The Energy Charter Secretariat published a report on the transit of natural gas in April 2007[16] which found that historically most countries relied on agreements rather than legislation in this area (developments in the latter area tend to be recent). Significantly, though, this report did not refer to environmental matters.

There is some scepticism about the implications of the Charter Treaty on nation states. Stevenson, for example, argues that its provisions are biased in favour of investors who take direct action and that the treaty restricts state actions, possibly preventing the application of domestic environmental laws. Stevenson also criticises the effectiveness and inclusiveness of the treaty's dispute resolution mechanism (Stevenson, 2001).

**African Union and SADC**

As the African states have not signed the Energy Charter, it is important to consider whether there are other measures that are in place that ensure environmentally friendly transfer of natural gas. Both South Africa and Mozambique are members of the African Union (AU). Its objectives include promoting sustainable development and the integration of African economies.[17] The functions of the AU's Executive Council include coordinating and taking decisions regarding environmental protection (Art. 13(1)(e). The AU promotes interstate cooperation, harmonisation of policies and integration of programmes among contracting parties (Art. 3). In order to further its objectives it must seek to develop harmonious economic activities, strengthen regional economic communities (Art. 4(2)(a)) and harmonise and coordinate environmental protection policies (Art. 4(2)(o)).

A specialised technical committee may be constituted under the Constitutive Act of the AU to deal with industry, science and technology, energy, natural resources and the environment (Art. 14(1)(d)). Its role includes harmonising and coordinating projects within Africa (Art. 15(c)). Member states still will be allowed to regulate the protection of their environment (Art. 35(1)(c)) and to control their strategic products (Art. 35(1)(h)); however, they must inform the Secretariat of the Commission on Industry, Science and Technology, Energy, National Resources and Environment of their activities in this regard. Under Article 49, member states must ensure the development of basic industries, such as energy, to ensure self-reliance and modernisation. Member states also must 'strengthen their scientific and technological capabilities' to ensure socio-economic transformation (Art. 51). Under Article 54, member states are obliged to coordinate and harmonise their energy policies and must ensure effective development thereof and harmonise their national energy development plans.

Article 55 covers cooperation on nuclear energy as well as new and renewable energy.

Both South Africa and Mozambique subscribe to the African (Banjul) Charter on Human and People's Rights.[18] It provides that everyone has the right to cultural, social and economic development and states should ensure the exercise of their right to development (Art. 22). According to Article 24, 'All people shall have the right to a generally satisfactory environment favourable to their development.'

South Africa and Mozambique are both signatories to the 1992 SADC Treaty[19] which explicitly states that, in the exploitation of natural resources, the environment must also be protected. Various protocols were formulated to give substance to the Treaty and the 2002 SADC Protocol on Energy[20] states as its objective that member states should cooperate to harmonise their national and regional energy policies, strategies and programmes as well as the development and utilisation of energy (including natural gas) (Art. 3). Member states also should ensure that the 'development and use of energy is environmentally sound' (Art. 2(8)). Guidelines were developed for various energy sectors, including gas (Annex 1). A Commission (Art. 4) (comprising a committee of ministers, senior officials and a technical unit) is tasked with giving effect to the Protocol, through harmonising laws, regulations and agreements governing exploration programmes and ensuring an emphasis on environment, health, safety and security (Item 2(a)(iv)) (Cao et al., 2007).

The question is whether South African and Mozambican legislation adheres to the principles contained in these instruments.

## 3.   THE LAW OF SOUTH AFRICA AND MOZAMBIQUE

### Constitutional Provisions

The Constitutions of South Africa[21] and Mozambique[22] each provide for the protection of the environment and human health, though in somewhat different terms. Under the Mozambican Constitution (Art. 90(1)), every citizen has the right to live in a balanced environment as well as a duty to defend this right. The corresponding South African right is phrased negatively, in section 24(a), namely that everyone has a right to an environment that is not harmful to his or her well-being.

The Mozambican Constitution places an obligation on the state to 'promote efforts to guarantee the ecological balance and the conservation and preservation of the environment for the betterment of the quality of life of its citizens' (Art. 117). The ownership of all natural resources vests in the state (Arts. 98 and 102). The Mozambican Constitution places a further obligation on government to adopt policies to ensure environmental protection and the rational use of natural resources (Arts. 90(2) and 117(2)). Under the South African Constitution, the government is similarly obliged to ensure that the environment is protected for present and future generations (s. 24(b)), and the right is to be balanced against justifiable economic and social development.

In Mozambique all land belongs to the state.[23] Individuals and juristic persons may only acquire a right to land use and benefit and the state determines the conditions of land use (Arts. 109 and 110). In contrast, South African law provides for private ownership of land (s. 25 of the Constitution) (Badenhorst et al., 2006, pp. 521–583), though the South African National Environmental Management Act 107 of 1998 (NEMA) in section 2(4)(o) states that 'the environment is held in public trust for the people, the beneficial use of environmental resources must serve the public interest and the environment must be protected as the people's common heritage'. Mozambicans (Art. 45(f)-(g)) 'have the duty to protect and conserve the environment', while the Constitution does not place such a duty on its inhabitants. Section 24(a) of the South African Constitution is phrased in such a manner that the fundamental right may be enforced against both private and public institutions (Ferreira, 1999).

The right of access to information is guaranteed in article 48 of the Mozambican Constitution and in section 32[24] of the South African Constitution.

**Environmental Framework Laws**

To give effect to the constitutional provisions and the international law obligations discussed above (Art. 4 Decree 20/1997; s. 2 NEMA), the Environment Law (Salomao, 2006)[25] was promulgated in Mozambique and the NEMA in South Africa. It is important to note from the outset that the Environment Law of Mozambique is regarded as a framework law and therefore other legislation must be adapted to it (Art. 32(1) Decree 20/1997)). In contrast, in South Africa, there is uncertainty as to the role of NEMA vis-à-vis other sectoral specific legislation (Nel and Du Plessis, 2001).

Both acts have as their aim the achievement of sustainable development (Art. 2 Decree 20/1997; s. 2 NEMA), and bind both private and public sectors (Art. 3 Decree 20/1997; ss. 2, 23, 24 and 28 of NEMA). Shared principles in both jurisdictions include: promotion of the quality of life of people; protection of culture and traditional knowledge; conservation of biodiversity and ecosystems; the precautionary principle; the polluter pays principle; public participation (including participation of women) and a holistic approach to the environment. The Mozambican principles also include a reference to international cooperation to ensure solutions to cross-border and global environmental problems, while the South African provision refers only to discharging of national and international obligations. Section 2 of NEMA refers to several additional principles that are not present in the Mozambican legislation, for example: environmental justice; environmental impact assessment; integrated environmental management; access to information; the right of workers to refuse to do work harmful to the environment; equitable access to natural resources; recognition of the needs and values of communities; and environmental education (s. 2(4)).

Under article 5 of the Mozambican Environment Law, the government must prepare a national programme for environmental management to be implemented by the National Council for Sustainable Development.[26] This Council is the counterpart of the Environmental Advisory Forum established under the NEMA (Arts. 3–6). Local government is responsible for the implementation of the Environment Law at the local level in Mozambique (Art. 7), in South Africa, on the other hand, NEMA refers to all spheres of government.[27]

Both Acts provide for a public participation process, specifically in South Africa with regard to the environmental impact assessment process (s. 24(4)(d) NEMA), and in Mozambique empowering civil society to participate in the preparation of legislation and policies (Art. 8).

The laws of both jurisdictions refer to pollution. The Mozambican law places a prohibition on pollution, while the NEMA refers to a duty of care when there is pollution or a possibility thereof and also applies the polluter pays principle.[28] The Mozambican law provides for the introduction of environmental quality standards to ensure sustainable use of the nation's resources,[29] while the South African law is silent in this regard (du Plessis and Nel 2006).[30]

Both countries regulate environmental impact assessment. In Mozambique an environmental license (Art. 15 Decree 20/1997) is issued, while the NEMA (s. 24) refers to environmental authorisations. Both pieces of legislation specify the minimum content of an environmental impact study but the detail of the EIA procedures are dealt with by regulations issued in terms of the framework acts.[31] In Mozambique a developer must obtain an environmental license before applying under any other legislation (Art. 15(2) Decree 20/1997)), which is not the case in South Africa. In South Africa this leads to many disputes as developers regard the issuing of the one license as a *sine qua non* for the issuing of the other license. Under the South African regime, regulation is triggered if the activities in question are listed in NEMA. In the Mozambique Environment Law, on the other hand, regulation is focussed on affected environmental media and the different types of infrastructure involved.[32] The law also provides for environmental education (Art. 20/1997; s. 2(4)(h) NEMA), access to justice (Art. 21 Decree 20/1997;

s. 32 NEMA) (Neethling et al., 2001),[33] a right of access to information,[34] environmental inspectors[35] and for cooperation between officials.[36] The Mozambican law also provides for the possibility to appoint community supervisors (Art. 30 Decree, 20/1997). Although South African law does not provide for community supervision, it is sometimes included as a condition in authorisations (du Plessis and Nel, 2006).

The Mozambican law specifically provides for the possibility of including market-based instruments, such as incentives to encourage the introduction and use of environmentally sound technology and productive processes in the legal process. The South African Environmental Conservation Act 73 of 1989 introduced the notion of market-based instruments and the National Treasury published a discussion document in this regard (Paterson, 2005; du Plessis and de la Harpe, 2007a).

Mozambique specifically provides for environmental auditing in terms of Decree 32/2003.[37] South Africa does not have specific environmental audit regulations but the EIA regulations and the Mineral and Petroleum Resources Development Act 28 of 2002 provide that relevant officials may order that an environmental audit be done in case of non-compliance or as an authorisation condition.[38] The Mozambican audit regulations[39] are applicable to both private and public activities and may be conducted either by a state organ or by a private entity.[40] The scope of the environmental audit is wide and includes not only the impacts of routine activities, but also the degree of compliance with the environmental licensing process and other laws and the conditions of operation, as well as measures taken to rehabilitate the environment and to protect human life (Art. 4). The costs of an audit are carried by the entity that is audited.[41] The recommendations of an audit report are binding on the audited entity and non-compliance is regarded as an offence.[42] Only registered auditors may be used.[43] Auditors are subject to potential criminal and civil liability in respect of the information contained in the report (Art. 13; Kidd, 2004; du Plessis and de la Harpe, 2007b).

**Gas Pipeline Regulation**

When the Mozambican–South African pipeline was negotiated, neither of the countries had any legislation pertaining to gas in place, although such legislation was subsequently promulgated.

In Mozambique all petroleum resources, including natural gas (Art. 1(m) Decree 3/2001), are regarded as natural resources that belong to the state (Art. 6).[44] A gas pipeline contract[45] is regarded as authorisation to construct and operate a gas pipeline[46] and is approved by the Mozambican Council of Ministers.[47] This right should not be in conflict with other rights to use natural resources (Art. 20(1) Decree 24/2004). Any such conflicts that arise must be dealt with by ministers with relevant portfolios (Art. 20(2) Decree 24/2004).

South Africa has no choice but to import gas from its neighbouring countries as it has no large-scale domestic gas fields.[48] It has a dedicated Gas Act 48 of 2001 (Gas Act), one of the objectives of which is to promote the efficient, effective, sustainable and orderly development and operation of gas transmission, storage and distribution. A license is needed to construct and operate gas transmission facilities (s. 15(1)). An application must, amongst other things, include a description of the administrative, financial and technical abilities of the applicant, a description of the proposed facility including maps and diagrams as well as plans and ability to comply with all applicable labour, health, safety and environmental legislation (s. 16). An EIA must be undertaken in both jurisdictions.[49]

The South African minister must take the following criteria into account before deciding on the granting of a license: the national interest and the promotion of regional growth or any other social objective (s. 19(2)). Licenses may be issued subject to conditions pertaining to, *inter alia*, construction, operation and access of third parties to uncommitted capacity in the pipelines.[50]

Under Mozambican law, the contract must include a gas pipeline development plan,[51] together with details of infrastructure to be used: the status of applicable land use permits; a technical description of the facilities and the pipeline route;[52] quality standards that will be implemented; safety objectives and risks; an EIA;[53] and the main implementation, operating and maintenance policies.[54] An estimate of operation and decommissioning costs also must be provided along with details of how closure will be financed (Art. 30(4)(m)–(n) Decree 24/2004). Two years before closure, a decommissioning plan must be submitted which includes an EIA of the effects of the termination of operations (Art. 32 Decree 24/2004).

Similarly, the operator in South Africa must submit a closure plan to the National Energy Regulator but in this case only six months prior to closure or dismantling. An environmental impact assessment must also be carried out with regard to the decommissioning activities, site clean-up and disposal of dangerous material and chemicals. Alternatives for further use or disposal of installations must also be addressed.[55] License conditions may include the provision of environmental performance bonds for rehabilitation purposes and an independent consultant must certify that the site is properly rehabilitated before the financial security can be released.[56]

The holder of the authorisation or right in Mozambique must conduct its operations in accordance with the law and good oilfield practice, prepare a development and decommissioning plan and should compensate injured parties for any loss or damage that result from the gas pipeline operations.[57]

The operator must 'develop, implement and update policies, strategies, execute evaluations, plans and technical solutions' to ensure that the operation of the gas pipeline is in accordance with safety and environmental objectives.[58] Operators as far as possible must avoid environmental pollution, pollution of water resources and waste of natural energy.[59] Operators also must introduce a management system to ensure the 'systematic management and implementation of its activities'. It should include, amongst other things, requirements pertaining to safety; environmental protection; resource management; third party liability; decommissioning; rehabilitation; and damage to facilities (Art. 35(3) Decree 24/2004). The facilities and worksites must comply with international good oil or gas pipeline-related practices, which must be referred to in the development plan (Arts. 40, 41 and 89 Decree 24/2004). Risk analyses with regard to the gas pipelines operation which may impact on the health and safety of people as well as on the environment must be undertaken as set out in the operating manuals (Art. 42, Decree 24/2004). In contrast, the South African Gas Act does not regulate any of these issues.

Under the Mozambican regime, the operator is 'jointly and severally liable with the concessionaire' for, *inter alia*, establishing safety objectives and to conduct risk assessments and to pay compensation for damages.[60] Provision must be made for emergency and contingency plans to limit, for example, loss of life, injuries, pollution and damage to property. The operator must develop contingency plans to prevent and minimise the impact of emergency situations and should be able to rehabilitate the environment in the case of accidents (Arts. 86–87 Decree 24/2004).[61] Again these issues are not regulated by the South African Gas Act. However, emergency incidents must be dealt with under section 30 of the NEMA, and if water resources are threatened or polluted, section 20 of the National Water Act 36 of 1998 must also be adhered to. In NEMA an 'incident' is defined as 'an unexpected sudden occurrence including a major emission, fire or explosion leading to serious danger to the public or potentially serious pollution of or detriment to the environment, whether immediate or delayed' (s. 31(1)(a) NEMA) which relates to risks associated with gas pipelines.

In Mozambique a holder of a right must transport the gas of third parties if capacity is available in the gas pipeline and if there are no unsolvable technical problems (Art. 18(1)–(2) Decree 3/2001).[62] In South Africa such an obligation may be imposed by license conditions (s. 21 (1)(d) Gas Act). In both jurisdictions, the state (or in South Africa's case the National Energy Regulator) may inspect operations at any time.[63] The Mozambican holder of the right to operate a gas pipeline must conduct his or her operations in accordance with the relevant legislation and accepted technical and economic practices and standards.[64] He or she also must give due regard to the health and safety of personnel and the protection of the environment (Art. 3(5) Decree 24/04). The object of the South African Gas Act is to 'ensure the efficient, effective, sustainable and orderly development and operation of gas transmission' and 'to ensure the safe, efficient, economic and environmentally responsible transmission … of gas' (s. 2(c)) but it does not contain the same level of detail as the Mozambican legislation.

In Mozambique the operating company must ensure that no ecological damage is caused by its operations and operate in accordance with internationally accepted standards (Art. 23(1)(a) Decree 3/2001). If the company causes damage to crops, soils, buildings or improvements, it must compensate the legal user or the occupant for harm caused (Art. 20(4) Decree 3/2001). In South Africa operations are regulated by the license and EIA conditions.

As all land belongs to the state in Mozambique, companies operating gas pipelines must obtain rights to land use and benefit as well as a right of way (Art. 20(5) Decree 3/2001),[65] in accordance with land use laws.[66] In South Africa, land may be expropriated by the National Energy Regulator on behalf of a licensee for gas transmission (Badenhorst et al., 2006, pp. 553–578).[67] The duration of the Mozambican contract specifies the period of the land use granted (Art. 20 Decree 3/2001), while licenses are granted for a period of 25 years (renewable) (s. 23 Gas Act). Contracts already in existence at the time of the 2004 Petroleum Law remain in force.[68] In contrast, in South Africa gas pipeline operators had to apply for a license under the new Act within six months of it coming into operation (s. 35 Gas Act). However, the Mozambique Gas Pipeline Agreement regulates gas transmission between Mozambique and South Africa for ten years after its conclusion (s. 36). The National Energy Regulator must issue licenses based on the agreement and may impose other conditions that are not contrary to the agreement (s. 36(4)).

Disputes between Mozambique and foreign investors should, under the Petroleum Law, be settled by conciliation, arbitration or mediation (Art. 27 Decree 3/2001). In South Africa, section 30(2)–(3) of the Gas Act provides that disputes may be resolved either by the National Energy Regulator or by an arbitrator or mediator appointed by it. Decisions of arbitrators are binding on the parties.

In Mozambique the ministry responsible for petroleum may undertake inspections of all facilities and sites. The operator must cooperate and assist the inspector (Art. 93 Decree 24/2004). Similarly the National Energy Regulator may undertake investigations in South Africa (s. 31 Gas Act). Non-compliance with administrative provisions or orders is an offence in both countries and may render offenders liable to a fine.[69]

## 4.  CONCLUSION

The principles of the Rio Declaration, Agenda 21 and the Johannesburg Plan of Implementation are reiterated in other international documents such as the Energy Charter, the African Charter, the SADC Treaty and the SADC Energy Protocol. The national environmental and gas-related legislation of Mozambique and South Africa includes the same principles, notably: the precautionary and polluter pays principles; EIAs; reducing unsustainable production and consumption; improved use of scientific and technological knowledge and effective environmental legislation. Not all of the relevant provisions address cross-border environmental issues, though they do state that regional cooperation in this regard is necessary. Insofar as energy issues are concerned, it is clear that governments world-wide make use of partnerships in an effort to cooperate to find environmentally sound and energy-efficient energy sources and systems and that gas is regarded as one such medium.

Most countries regulate their own environment and develop domestic gas-related legislation and policies, but the African Union and SADC clearly state that these policies and laws should be harmonised to ensure an environment that is both protected and conducive to development. One of the focus areas of SADC is to create an enabling legal and fiscal framework to promote and facilitate cross-border transfer of and trade in gas.

The Energy Charter in many ways represents the gold standard in this area; how do the South African and Mozambican regimes measure up?

The Energy Charter, South African and Mozambican legislation all include the rule that environmental considerations should be integrated into energy policies. The Charter allows the state to regulate aspects of energy relevant to their own environment and safety and this approach is taken in South African and Mozambican law. Parties to the Energy Charter must strive to minimise their environmental impacts and like provision is included in the South African and Mozambican framework and energy laws. It is also clear that, under the Charter, the minimisation of impacts should be cost-effective, though only the Mozambican legislation refers to the cost aspect.

In common with the Energy Charter, the two countries' framework laws refer to the precautionary and polluter pays principles, although their relevance is curtailed by the fact that they do not necessarily pertain to cross-border issues. According to the Energy Charter, third parties must be able to gain access to the transmission of gas via the pipeline, an area addressed in the Mozambican legislation, but is only achieveable through a permit condition under the South African regime. The Energy Charter Treaty and Mozambican legislation introduce reference to international standards. On the other hand, the Energy Charter states clearly that energy efficiency must be improved, while the Mozambican legislation is silent in this regard. In South Africa, energy efficiency is regulated by the National Energy Act 2008.

The Energy Charter Treaty further provides that information should be shared with regard to economic energy policies. Only the African Union Treaty and the SADC Energy Protocol make reference to information sharing between countries and no such provision is to be found in the legislation of the two countries.

The promotion of environmental awareness, transparent decision-making and public participation processes feature in the Energy Charter and the Mozambican and South African regimes. Under the Energy Charter, provision is made to address cross-border disputes by a Charter Conference. Although both the South African and Mozambican legislation provide for alternative dispute resolution mechanisms, these are not related to cross-border issues. By implication all cross-border issues will have to be dealt with by way of diplomacy. Otherwise the parties will have to make proper provision for dispute resolution mechanisms in their agreements.

The Energy Charter Treaty serves as an example of how the SADC Treaty and Protocol on Energy could be extended, for example, to include draft contracts, regulating matters pertaining to cost and liability and cross-border arbitration. However, this should not enable operators of gas pipelines to evade national and regional law.

As stated above, cross-border pipelines may give rise to various political, financial and legal issues. One such matter is, for example, the control of land, which may complicate matters. On the Mozambican side, public participation and decision-making can be addressed swiftly, while on the South African side the process may be long and drawn out as each and every owner is regarded as an interested and affected party that has to be consulted during the EIA process. On the Mozambican side, the government may decide to relocate communities from the land they occupy while expropriation on the South African side again will result in long drawn-out procedures. The legal and property regime on the South African side may cause delays and may have severe cost implications that could impact on the eventual decision to proceed with a project.

The harmonisation of laws is going to be a challenge in the SADC. In the case of the Mozambican–South African gas pipeline the question already arises as to which laws the parties to the contract will adhere to when the contract lapses after 10 years. If the legislation has not been harmonised after the lapse of the 10-year period, it is possible that the existing contract may be renewed and that the laws of each country will still regulate the pipeline in its territory. In view of the lack of harmonised laws, the contractual parties could also draft their own rules according to one or the other country's legislation, whichever is the more stringent. If no contractual agreement is reached, the South African counterpart will have to re-apply for a licence in terms of the Gas Act and its requirements. At an interview in Maputo a Mozambican official indicated that Mozambique is bound by the South African–Mozambican Agreement and that the applicant (in this case Sasol) will not have to re-apply for a licence on the Mozambican side.

According to the Regional Indicative Strategic Development Plan of SADC[70] the energy sector still faces a wide range of challenges ranging from funding and gender issues to technological problems: 'overcoming these challenges would not only add momentum to the longer term vision of full economic integration, but would also contribute towards increased economic growth and poverty reduction' (para 3.3.2.3). At a meeting of the Ministers responsible for Environment and Natural Resources Management in July 2010 at Victoria Falls, Zimbabwe, the Ministers re-affirmed their commitment 'to sustainable management of the environment and natural resources, and called upon all stakeholders to undertake development activities in a sustainable manner'.[71]

It is clear that since Rio the sustainability principles have developed and are continuing to be included in international, regional and national legal instruments wherever there is political buy-in. The question that still needs to be addressed is whether the goals of Rio and the subsequent documents, such as those intended to promote sustainable cross-border gas pipelines, are going to be effectively implemented and enforced, especially on the African continent and SADC.

## NOTES

1. Rio Declaration on Environment and Development, UN Doc. A/CONF.151/26 (Vol. I) at http://www.unep.org/Documents.Multilingual/Default.asp?documentid=78&articleid=1163.
2. Report of the United Nations Conference on Environment and Development, Rio de Janeiro, 3–14 June 1992, Principles 7, 9, 11–13, 17–19.
3. First Edition of the Model Intergovernmental and Host Government Agreements for Cross-Border Pipelines Annex to CC252 Explanatory Note para. 7, www.encharter.org/index.php?id=40.
4. Agenda 21, UN Doc. A/CONF. 151/26 (1992), available at: http://www.un.org/esa/dsd/agenda21/.
5. See note 4 at chapter 7, especially paras 7.46.754.
6. UNFCCC, 31 (1992) ILM 849; Kyoto Protocol to the United Nations Framework Convention on Climate Change, Kyoto, 11 December 1997.
7. See www.encharter.org/fileadmin/user_upload/document/en.pdf.
8. Cobus van der Walt, 'Sasol–Mozambique Pipeline', unpublished paper delivered at a Sanpad Workshop, Potchefstroom, South Africa, 26 August 2005 (on file with author).
9. See http://www.un.org/esa/sustdev/documents/agenda21/english/agenda21chapter9.htm.
10. United Nations Report of the World Summit on Sustainable Development, Johannesburg, South Africa, 26 August–4 September 2002, Chapter 1.2.

11. It also creates a multilateral policy forum to discuss energy issues.
12. Article 9 IGA and 1(4) HGA. If the project investor fails to take action, the host government may recover the costs from the project investor – Art. 11(5) HGA.
13. Article 26(1)(j) and Art. 30 on *force majeure*.
14. See www.encharter.org/index.php?id=37.
15. See also Art. 4(1) of the draft Protocol and Energy Charter Secretariat *The Energy Charter Treaty and Related Documents A Legal Framework for International Energy Cooperation* 15, at www.encharter.org/fileadmin/user_upload/document/en.pdf.
16. At http://www.encharter.org/fileadmin/user_upload/document/Oil_Monitoring_Report.pdf.
17. Constitutive Act – Art. 3(j).
18. African [Banjul] Charter on Human and Peoples' Rights, adopted 27 June 1981, OAU Doc. CAB/LEG/67/3 rev. 5, (1982) 21 ILM 58, entered into force 21 October 1986, at http://www.africa-union.org/official_documents/Treaties_%20Conventions_ %20Protocols /Banjul%20Charter.pdf.
19. The Treaty of the Southern African Development Community, as amended, Windhoek, 17 August 1992.
20. Protocol on Energy, Maseru, 24 August 1996.
21. Constitution of the Republic of South Africa, 1996.
22. Constitution of Mozambique, 2004.
23. Article 109.
24. This should be read with the Promotion of Access to Information Act 2000.
25. Law 20/97. For commentary on Mozambican Environmental law see Alda Salomão, *Lei do Ambiente Comentada* (Centro de Formação Jurídica e Judiciária 2006).
26. Instituted under Art. 6 Decree 20/1997.
27. Section 2. Section 152 of the Constitution, read with the Local Government: Municipal Systems Act 32 of 2000, specifically states that local government is responsible for environmental protection.
28. Article 9 Decree 20/1997: s. 28 NEMA. See also s. 19 of the South African National Water Act 36 of 1998.
29. Other issues dealt with in the Mozambican law are the protection of cultural heritage resources (Art. 11); biodiversity (Art. 12), environmental protection zones (Art. 13), waste and the protection of the coast and other ecologically sensitive zones (Art. 14).
30. Water quality standards are published under the National Water Act 1998 and air quality standards under the National Environmental Management: Air Quality Act 2004.
31. Mozambique Decree 78/98 of 29 December; Government Notice R543–547 Government Gazette 33306, 18 June 2010.
32. The construction of gas pipelines is listed in the Mozambican regulations in Appendix 1 as item 1(m) and the underground and surface storage of gas is listed as item 4.7(b). The South African regulations do not list gas pipelines as such but reference is made to the bulk transportation of dangerous goods outside an industrial complex using pipelines – Government Notice R544–545, note 31.
33. The Mozambican law provides for damages (Art. 21(2)) while in South Africa damages are regulated by the common law. In Mozambique specific provision is made to apply for suspension (Art. 22), while the South African common law remedy of an interdict is available. In terms of Art. 25 of Decree 20/1997 developers must take out civil liability insurance – no such obligation exists in South African law. Article 26 Decree 20/1997 introduces strict liability where environmental damage is caused, though such an approach is not well-known in South African law. In *Bareki NO v. Gencor Ltd* 2006 1 SA 432 (T) 440H–I, however, it was decided that s. 28 of NEMA (duty of care and polluter pays principle) relies on strict liability (though notably this was introduced by legislation, not the common law).
34. Article 19 Decree 20/1997; s. 31 NEMA, Promotion of Access to Information Act and s. 32 of the South African Constitution.
35. Article 28 Decree 20/1997, read with Decree 11/2006 of 15 June; ss 31A–Q NEMA.

36.   Article 29 Decree 20/1997 places a duty to cooperate. Like provision exists under Chapter 3 of the South African Constitution and Chapter 2 of NEMA. See also the Intergovernmental Relations Framework Act 2005.

37.   Of 12 August, issued in terms of articles 18 and 33 of the Environmental Law Decree 20/1997.

38.   Government Notice 527 *Government Gazette* 26275, 23 April 2006.

39.   Environmental audit is defined in Art. 2 of Decree 32/2003.

40.   Article 3 read with articles 6 and 7 describing the nature of public and private audits.

41.   Article 9 – the translation in this regard is unclear as it states that the costs must be carried by the applicant. From reading the regulations, it seems that the above interpretation is more viable. The contents of the environmental audit report are described in Art. 10 Decree 32/2003.

42.   It is, however, unclear in terms of which law the offence will be committed; Decree 32/2003 does not prescribe a penalty.

43.   Article 11. The obstruction or hindrance of an environmental auditor is an offence. The fines collected for offences in terms of Decree 32/2003 are allocated in the following manner – 60 per cent to the state budget and 40 per cent to the Environmental Fund (FUNAB).

44.   The state may at any time participate in the construction and operation of gas pipelines according to the terms of the contract: Art. 8. Foreigners, such as the South African Petroleum Company, Sasol, with technical competence and financial resources may obtain a right to conduct petroleum operations: Art. 9 Decree 3/2001.

45.   The gas pipeline concession contract contents are prescribed in Art. 11 Decree 3/2001 – significantly no reference is made to the environment.

46.   Article 11 read with Art. 14 Decree 3/2001. An application is to be submitted to the minister with the portfolio for petroleum products (Art. 10(1) Decree 24/04). The contents of the application are described in Art. 10(2) – at this stage no mention is made of the environment.

47.   Article 10 Decree 3/2001, read with Art. 12 of Decree 24/04 with regard to the duration of contracts. Articles 14–18 of Decree 24/2004 deal with the termination of contracts – a contract may be rescinded if the operations are not conducted in terms of legislation – Art. 16(3) Decree 24/2004.

48.   Ocean exploration operations revealed small quantities of gas but importation will continue in the absence of large-scale domestic production.

49.   Article 23(1)(a) Decree 3/2001. Personnel safety must be ensured and accidental discharge, leakage and waste must be declared to the competent authority – Art. 21(1)(g) Decree 3/2001. See 3.2 for EIA regulations in South Africa.

50.   Ibid., s. 21 read with Government Notice R321 Government Gazette 29792, 20 April 2007 (the Gas Pipeline Regulations).

51.   Article 14(2) Decree 3/2001. A gas pipeline development plan is defined in Art. 1(q) Decree 3/2001.

52.   See also Art. 55 Decree 24/2004. Under Art. 54 the selection of the pipeline route should be assessed in the EIA report.

53.   An EIA must be done in accordance with Art. 90 Decree 24/2004.

54.   Article 30(4)(a)–(l) Decree 24/2004. The design of the gas pipeline must be done in accordance with Art. 52 Decree 24/2004 and provision should be made for safety measures: Art. 53.

55.   Regulation 11 of *Government Notice* R321.

56.   Regulation 11 of *Government Notice* R321.

57.   Article 17 Decree 3/2001. The Act must be read with the Petroleum Operations Regulations Decree 24/04 of 20 August issued in terms of Art. 28(1)(d) of Law 3/2001. The purpose of the regulations is to ensure that petroleum operations are conducted in a systematic manner and to ensure comprehensive and coordinated supervision.

58.   Article 34(1)(a); Articles 62–74 deal with safety systems and control of safety issues.

59. Article 34(1)(a), (e), (g) and (i) Decree 24/04. All personnel must be informed of the contents of the plans, laws and regulations: Art. 34(2).
60. Ibid., Art. 23(1)(a) and (d). The operator must have insurance to cover damage caused to the environment, third party liability, decommissioning and rehabilitation as well as damage to facilities: Art. 39.
61. The minister responsible for the petroleum industry must coordinate the measures in the contingency plan if other authorities are also involved.
62. If there is not sufficient capacity, the holder of the right must increase the pipeline's capacity to accommodate third parties: Art. 18(3).
63. Article 22 Decree 3/2001; s. 29 Gas Act read with Government Notice 963 Government Gazette 29259, 29 September 2006, that describes the duties, rights and obligations of inspectors.
64. National standards are to be supplemented by international standards such as ISO, the American Society of Mechanical Engineers and the American Petroleum Institute – Art. 101. All information gathered in terms of the gas pipeline contract is regarded as confidential: Art. 5(1).
65. Ibid., Art. 20(5): compensation must be paid.
66. Land Act Decree 19/97.
67. Section 32(1) Gas Act. The expropriation must comply with s. 25 of the Constitution. The obligations in terms of the use of the land are dealt with by s. 33 and a servitude will normally be registered.
68. Contracts conclude in terms of Law 3/81 of 3 October: Art. 26.
69. Article 95 Decree/2004,. 50 per cent of the fine so paid is to be transferred to the National Petroleum Institute. Under s. 26 of Gas Act the National Energy Regulator may fine a licensee that ignores a compliance notice at a rate of up to R2 million per day for period of the contravention.
70. See www.sadc.int/key_documents/risdp/chapter3.php. See also the SADC Energy Cooperation Policy of 1996, the SADC Energy Sector Action Plan of 1997 and the SADC Energy Activity Plan of 2000.
71. See www.sadc.int/index/browse/page/778. At a meeting of Energy Ministers on 25 April 2007, the Mozambican President indicated that Mozambique is investigating alternative sources for the production of clean energy such as natural gas – Valy Bayano, 'African energy ministers call for cooperation', *Southern African News Features* (22 April 2007), at www.sardc.net/editorial/newsfeature/07220407.htm.

# REFERENCES

Badenhorst, P.J., H. Mostert and J.M. Pienaar (2006), *Silberberg and Schoeman's Law of Property*, 5th edition, Durban: Butterworths.
Bamberger, Craig S., Jan Linehan and Thomas Wälde (2000), 'Energy Charter Treaty in 2000: in a new phase', *Journal of Energy & Natural Resources Law*, **18** (4), 331–352.
Birnie, Patricia W., A. Boyle and C. Redgwell (2009), *International Law and the Environment*, Oxford: Oxford University Press.
Cao, C.F., S. Baik, J.B. Choi and Y.J. Kim (2007), 'Protection of underground gas pipelines from third party damage by on-line monitoring using piezoelectric accelerometers', *Journal of Process Mechanical Engineering*, **221** (1), 61–65.
du Plessis, W. and S. de la Harpe (2007a), 'Recent Developments in the Use of Environmental and Energy Taxes in South Africa', in K. Deketelaere et al. (eds),

*Critical Issues in Environmental Taxation*, Volume IV, Oxford: Oxford University Press.

du Plessis, W. and S. de la Harpe (2007b), 'The duty to disclose and the right to refuse: undefined dilemma of environmental practitioners', *South African Journal of Environmental Law and Policy*, **14**, 83–103.

du Plessis, W. and J. Nel (2006), 'Driving Compliance to and Enforcement of South African Legislation by Means of a Hybrid of "New" Environmental Governance Instruments', Paper delivered at the 4th Colloquium of the IUCN Academy of Environmental Law, Pace Law School, New York, October, 2006 (on file with author).

Energy Charter Secretariat (ECS) (2004), *The Energy Charter Treaty and Related Documents: A Legal Framework for International Energy Cooperation*, ECS, 13.

Ferreira, G.M. (1999), 'Omgewingsbeleid en die fundamentele reg op 'n skoon en gesonde omgewing', *Journal of South African Law*, 90–113.

Kidd, M. (2004), 'Environmental audits and self-incrimination', *Comparative International Law of South Africa*, **37** (1), 84–95.

Nanda, V.P. and G. Pring (2003), *International Environmental Law and Policy for the 21st Century*, Ardsley, New York: Transnational Publishers, pp. 90–119.

Neethling, J., P.J. Potgieter and P.J. Visser (2001), *Law of Delict*, Durban: Butterworths.

Nel, Johan and Willemien du Plessis (2001), 'An evaluation of NEMA based on a generic framework for environmental framework legislation', *South African Journal of Environmental Law and Policy*, **8** (1), 4, 27–28.

Paterson, A. (2005), 'Tax incentives – valuable tools for biodiversity conservation in South Africa', *South African Law Journal*, **1**, 182–216.

Southern African Development Community (SADC) (1996), *Energy Cooperation Policy of 1996*.

Southern African Development Community (SADC) (1997), *Energy Sector Action Plan of 1997*.

Southern African Development Community (SADC) (2000), *Energy Activity Plan of 2000*.

Stevenson, R.J. (2001), 'Energy Charter Treaty: Implications for Australia', *Journal of Energy & Natural Resources Law*, **19**, 113–131.

Waern, Karl Petter (2002), 'Transit provisions of the Energy Charter Treaty and the Energy Charter Protocol on transit', *Journal of Energy & Natural Resources Law*, **20**, 172–191.

# 17. Is EU climate change policy legally robust?

## Javier de Cendra de Larragán

## 1. INTRODUCTION

Climate change has been among the top priorities of world leaders for some years now.[1] The EU has for a long time sought to play a leading role in the development of international climate change policy (Gupta and Grubb, 2000; Oberthür and Roche Kelly, 2008), and has worked hard to ensure that a new climate change international agreement for the post-2012 period was adopted at COP-15 at Copenhagen in December 2009. In the run-up to that conference, Commissioner Stavros Dimas declared:

> Over the past two months the EU has set out a comprehensive vision for the Copenhagen agreement. We now look to our partners to support our positions or to propose constructive alternatives.[2]

However, the fact was that, during the negotiations that took place at Copenhagen, the EU struggled to have its voice heard, and the final deal – known as the Copenhagen Accord – was negotiated by the US, China and a reduced number of developed countries without the active involvement of the EU. Moreover, the Copenhagen Accord neither supports the EU position in the international negotiations nor does it propose a constructive alternative as the Commission wished. That is because the EU position was premised on a comprehensive and legally binding international agreement, while the Copenhagen Accord is a non-legally binding and rather vague political document, which moreover opens up the way for the possible dismantling of the current international climate change regime without clearly articulating a new one. Despite the wide gulf between its wishes and the reality, the EU has kept its spirits high by welcoming the Copenhagen Agreement as a useful starting point for further negotiations towards a 'robust and legally binding agreement under the UNFCCC' (European Commission, 2010a).

This notwithstanding, the EU made clear its disappointment with the outcome of the Copenhagen Summit,[3] and following its conclusion the

Commission came up with two policy documents: one laying down a strategy for the post-Copenhagen negotiations in order to reinvigorate global action on climate change (European Commission, 2010a), and another examining options to increase its 2020 mitigation target from 20 to 30 per cent (European Commission, 2010b).

In order to back up its leadership role at the international level, the EU, over the last 20 years, has developed a rather elaborate domestic climate change regime. The Commission has recently gone as far as to affirm that, at a global level, 'only the EU has adopted the legislation required to guarantee the delivery of its 2020 reduction target' (European Commission, 2010a, p. 9). This claim speaks directly about the effectiveness of the legal regime. However, there is consensus in the literature that, while looking rather impressive on paper (de Cendra de Larragán, 2010a), the EU climate change regime has not yet demonstrated its effectiveness in reducing greenhouse emissions, and moreover faces similar implementation and enforcement challenges as the rest of EU environmental policy (Jordan et al., 2010).

Moreover, the Commission's claim also assumes that the EU climate change regime is robust, in the sense that it is capable, if fully implemented and adequately enforced, of achieving its mitigation goals. This is certainly a far-reaching claim that deserves closer investigation.

While this chapter will not examine whether the EU climate change regime is being properly implemented at Member State level, or whether it can be adequately enforced (Jordan et al., 2010), it will, however, seek to assess, from a legal perspective, the claim implied in the Commission's statement regarding the robustness of the climate change regime. There are both legal and political reasons to do so, as will be shown, but first it is necessary to clarify what is understood here by robustness. A web search of the term 'robust' brings forward the following definitions: (1) the characteristic of being strong enough to withstand intellectual challenge;[4] (2) the quality of being able to withstand stresses, pressures, or changes in procedure or circumstance;[5] (3) the ability of a system to continue to perform satisfactorily under load.[6] All these definitions are particularly relevant to the study of the EU climate change regime, but this chapter will focus primarily on the first one, which is the closest to a legal analysis. Nevertheless, some connections between the different levels of robustness will be suggested in the next paragraph.

Robustness can be understood in a legal sense as the capacity of a regulatory framework to withstand challenges, whether they come from legislators, parties to proceedings in a court of law, the courts themselves, and academics. One of the most fundamental challenges that can be raised against a regulatory framework concerns its degree of (in)consistency with the fundamental legal principles of the legal system in which it is embedded.

A regulatory framework which conflicts with those principles might struggle to resist legal challenges brought against it. It is therefore important to examine whether the EU climate change regulatory framework is indeed in line, and if so to what extent, with the relevant legal principles of EU law, because doing so will provide an indication of the degree of robustness of the regime. Moreover, without a robust EU climate change regime, the promotion of a robust international climate change regime as desired by the EU (European Commission, 2010a) will lack credibility.

There are additional political reasons to conduct this analysis: first, a regulatory framework that is robust from the perspective of legal principles of international and EU law is more likely to withstand pressures coming from states participating in the international negotiations and foreign private actors seeking to challenge certain elements of that regime. This can contribute to the sense of confidence that EU policy makers need when negotiating at international level. Moreover, a robust framework is also more likely to be acceptable to all actors regulated by it, and therefore has a higher chance of being respected and of achieving mitigation targets. In addition, a robust framework offers a solid foundation on which to build further, while refining the architecture in order to cope with new challenges. For all these reasons, the degree of coherence between the climate change regime and legal principles determines to some extent the degree of robustness in the sense given by the second definition provided above. Last but not least, a climate change regime that is in line with legal principles might have a higher capacity to perform (in this context perform can be understood in the sense of achieving its goals) than one that is not (or less) in line with legal principles, therefore providing robustness in the third sense conveyed above. This chapter will not, however, attempt to demonstrate empirically the relationship between the three dimensions of robustness provided above; it will rather assume that all dimensions of robustness are related to the intellectual quality of the regime. One corollary is that the more robust the internal EU climate change regime is, the more robust its position in the international climate change regime will be, thereby adding to the policy leadership of the EU amidst the current situation of uncertainty regarding the future shape of the international climate change regime.

## 2. METHODOLOGY

This chapter does not attempt to assess the entire EU climate change regime, but will rather focus on distributional choices made therein.[7] In addition, it will not examine issues of implementation and enforcement, although these are key determinants of its effectiveness. Distributional choices are here defined as those decisions made by the legislator and the executive (and sometimes by courts as a result of their decisions in particular cases brought before them) that aim primarily at shaping the distribution of burdens and benefits, and of environmental damages and benefits, stemming from climate change policies between generations, between countries and within countries.

Five types of distributional choice in the context of climate change policy can be identified:

(1)   Distribution between generations;
(2)   Distribution between countries at international level;
(3)   Impacts of internal climate policies on foreign countries;
(4)   Distribution of the burden between EU Member States; and
(5)   Distribution of the burden between sources within the EU.

The difference between choices (2) and (3) is as follows: whereas (2) refers to choices regarding rules for burden sharing among states, (3) refers to collateral distributional impacts of internal choices on foreign countries. The difference between choices (4) and (5) is to be found in the subjects of the distribution. Whereas (4) refers to EU Member States, (5) refers to private sources located within those Member States. This distinction is necessary because there is EU law directly regulating burden sharing among private sources located within the EU.

The legal perspective adopted to examine these distributional choices is built on the view that law can be understood as a search for a rational proportionality among three dimensions:

- In the relationship between ends and means;
- In the distribution of benefits and burdens; and
- In the participation of interested members of society in the law-making process.

If law is understood as a search for rational proportionality among these three dimensions, then those dimensions can be understood to form part of what can be termed the 'meta-principle of proportionality'. This would include all the principles of practical rationality that form part of a particular legal system. Given that these principles are not only norms of practical reasoning (Thomas, 2005), but also the fundamental pillars of law and legal systems (Tridimas, 2006), they can play a role not only in guiding the activity of courts, but also the activity of law makers and scholars. The scheme that is presented in Table 17.1 shows an overview of the meta-principle of proportionality and the way in which existing legal principles fit into it.

*Table 17.1    The meta-principle of proportionality*

Position of legal principles within the meta-principle of proportionality

| First dimension of the meta-principle of proportionality | Suitability | Intensity | Focus on one single area, constant monitoring, adequacy to reality |
|---|---|---|---|
| | | Quality | Sustainable development, integration, precaution, prevention, polluter pays principle, rectification at source |
| | | Probability | Legal certainty, legitimate expectations, penalties, effectiveness (in the sense of adequate enforcement) |
| | Necessity | Principle of attribution | |
| | | Principle of subsidiarity | |
| | | Principles of environmental and cost-effectiveness | |
| Second dimension of the meta-principle of proportionality | Proportionality between countries | Principles of common but differentiated responsibilities, solidarity, loyal cooperation | |
| | Proportionality between private parties | Principle of intergenerational equity Principle of proportionality (suitability, necessity, proportionality in the narrow sense Fundamental rights and fundamental freedoms Principle of equality | |
| Third dimension of the meta-principle of proportionality | Access to information | | |
| | Public participation | | |
| | Access to justice | | |
| | Environmental justice | | |

All legal principles can be placed within the meta-principle of proportionality in order to explore their meaning and legal nature. Elsewhere, this author has found that four principles of EU law contain a relatively well-defined core: proportionality, equality, legitimate expectations and legal certainty.[8]

All the other principles included in the meta-principle of proportionality are either too vague or lack a clear core except for, perhaps, the precautionary principle (da Cruz Vilaça, 2004; de Sadeleer, 2006)[9] and, following a recent strand of case law from the ECJ and several opinions of Advocate General Kokott,[10] the polluter pays principle. This ambiguity applies in particular to environmental principles such as integration and rectification at source, and suggests the limitations that many legal principles have when used as tools to test distributional choices. Nevertheless, it remains the case that most principles have a sufficiently defined core that enables them to usefully guide choices made by policy makers and to structure academic debate.

However, because the ECJ affords a very large margin of appreciation to the European Community (EC) policy maker when making complex policy choices, it is very unlikely that the Court will declare that EC climate change policy is in breach of principles of EC law. Nevertheless, it is more likely that the ECJ may decide that certain decisions taken by the European Commission are in breach of one or more legal principles. In fact, a number of ECJ judgements have already annulled Commission decisions taken in this context for being in breach of legal principles.

## 3.   ASSESSMENT OF DISTRIBUTIONAL CHOICES VIS-À-VIS LEGAL PRINCIPLES

**Are Distributional Choices Made in EU Climate Policy in Line with the Relevant Legal Principles?**

This author has assessed this issue in detail elsewhere, by performing an extensive assessment of the fit between the principles within the different dimensions of the meta-principle of proportionality and each of the distributional choices identified above (de Cendra de Larragán, 2010a). From that assessment, a large number of observations have arisen, which have led to some policy recommendations. However, for reasons of space, this section will present only the most relevant observations while updating them in several respects.

## Burden Sharing Between Generations

To the extent that dangerous climate change is not averted, future generations will have to shoulder a higher burden than they would if current generations would mitigate their emissions to a sufficient extent, and it can be argued that such an outcome would be unfair. So the question arises as to how the EU has dealt with this problem, and which principles, if any, are guiding its response. To start with, it is generally accepted in the literature that the Kyoto target adopted by the EU does not bear any logical relation to the (non-legally binding) long-term target endorsed by the EU. This long-term target seeks to avoid an increase in global average temperature above 2°C in comparison with pre-industrial levels. Neither is the 20–30 per cent mitigation target in 2020 consistent with that long-term goal. The European Parliament sought to adopt a legally binding obligation to reduce emissions annually in accordance with a linear path towards the long-term target, but the Council refused to do so. Instead, a non-legally binding reference has been made to the need to move the EU into a highly energy-efficient and low GHG-emitting economy.[11]

In the light of these observations, one can ask whether the EU contribution towards the long-term target is proportional to its responsibility for creating the problem, and therefore consistent with the polluter pays principle. The EU has justified its contribution on the basis of a number of principles in addition to the polluter pays principle, such as capacity to pay, mitigation potential, early action and population trends, which leads to a lower burden for the EU than would arise if the only principle followed was the polluter pays principle (European Commission, 2009b, p. 4).

One should also ask to what extent explicit concern for future generations has influenced the EU targets. The EU has sought to justify the adoption of the long-term target on the basis of a cost–benefit analysis, concluding that for higher increases in global mean temperature, costs will outweigh benefits, both at global level and within the EU. However, the EU has neither made explicit the assumptions found therein nor the rationale, and has not discussed alternative approaches that could have led to very different results. In particular, the Commission has not systematically discussed the substantial body of literature on economic modelling of climate change, and thus the analysis underpinning the adoption of the long-term target appears to be incomplete, if not defective. Hence, the final choice – regardless of its material correctness – does not appear to have been based on a rational balancing of all the available scientific evidence (Tol, 2007). Moreover, considerations of an ethical nature have not been discussed in any detail. For instance, while considerations of the rights of future generations are clearly very relevant in justifying an ethical duty to adopt such a target, they have not played any explicit role. The Commission has sought to offer an additional justification based on public support, by noting that the majority of participants involved in various workshops on international climate policy support the target of 2°C. While that is true, those workshops took place a number of years after the initial target was adopted, hence raising doubts as to the ultimate rationale for it. Of course, the fact that it is not mentioned can mean that it is implicit, but the question is whether this approach grants sufficient protection to the rights of future generations.

From a legal perspective, it has to be noted that the rights of future generations are currently not expressly recognised in EU law, although it can be argued that they are implicit in the concept of sustainable development. The Lisbon Treaty includes, as one of the tasks of the EU, the promotion of solidarity between generations, but there are no specific mechanisms to ensure that the interests of future generations are represented in the law-making process. The Preamble of the Charter of Fundamental Rights says that 'the enjoyment of these rights entails responsibilities and duties with regard to other persons, to the human community and to future generations'.

The question can be raised whether establishing legal mechanisms to protect the rights of future generations could add anything of value to the principle of sustainable development. It has been argued in the literature that this could indeed be done, in particular by introducing a provision dealing explicitly with obligations to future generations, establishing organs that are entrusted with producing assessments of the long-term sustainability of certain policies, and granting some people or organisations the right – on an ad hoc or a permanent basis – to challenge regulatory choices when they feel that the interests of future generations in sustainability are being ignored (Ekeli, 2007). Introducing these or similar clauses in constitutions would allow courts, constitutional and otherwise, to assess whether particular laws sufficiently respect the rights of future generations.

## The EU Position on Burden Sharing Between Countries at International Level

The position of the EU on burden sharing at international level can be examined by considering its approach to the principle of common but differentiated responsibilities (CBDR). In fact, over time, the EU understanding of the CBDR principle has become more complex, nuanced and constructive. The EU is moving away from a focus on sharing burdens to one of sharing efforts.[12] Arguably, the difference is not merely one of semantics. Effort sharing is premised on the principle of solidarity among countries and generations and on promoting mutual advantage rather than on how to share losses.[13] Therefore it is underlined by a more optimistic view of regime building. While the EU still advocates the need for developed countries to adopt absolute mitigation commitments, it now places a stronger focus on the need to establish objective criteria to ensure comparability of efforts among developed countries and developing countries, in particular the most advanced ones.[14] Moreover, all developing countries, except for the Least Developed Countries (LDCs), should commit to low-carbon development strategies. According to the EU, those strategies should set out a credible pathway to limit developing countries' emissions, and should identify the external support needed to implement actions that are too expensive for the countries themselves. The credibility of those strategies should be determined by means of independent technical analyses. Furthermore, the EU has also proposed, in line with the CBDR principle and with the value of solidarity, that all developed countries should contribute, in accordance with the polluter pays principle, to the funding of adaptation policies in developing countries.

The EU does not accept the view put forward by some developing countries[15] that historical responsibility should play a central role in burden sharing. This view is based on the observation that the process of industrialisation that has taken place in the past few centuries in developed countries has been the main contributor to climate change. The EU holds the view that the United Nations Framework Convention on Climate Change (UNFCCC) does not endorse the principle of historical responsibility. Other developing countries consider that the main principle for burden sharing should be equal allocation of emission rights per capita. The per capita approach is based on the idea of sharing fairly the absorptive capacity of the atmosphere. Its application would lead to a huge redistribution of the emission rights between developed and developing countries, and would force the former to purchase from developing countries most of the entitlements they need to maintain current production and consumption patterns. Not surprisingly, the EU has not endorsed the principle of equal allocation of emission rights per capita either. Rather, the EU position resembles to some extent the Contraction and Convergence (C&C) approach, which requires long-term convergence of per capita emissions, while affording countries with per capita emissions below the global average the right to increase their emissions further before reducing them in line with the required global average. Nevertheless, the EU approach does not completely reflect the spirit of C&C for two reasons. First, the EU rejects the equal per capita dimension on which C&C is founded. While the EU position would lead to some global redistribution of public funds, it would still fall short of the large redistributions that would be required under the equal per capita approach. Second, while equal per capita allocation and C&C would give rise to an unconditioned redistribution of emission rights, the EU position favours a conditional redistribution subject to developing countries adopting monitorable, reportable and verifiable (MRV) low-carbon development strategies. But a more fundamental difference exists between the approach of the EU and of developing countries to burden sharing (Müller, 2009). The EU has adopted a burden-sharing paradigm pursuant to which all countries need to engage in mitigation activities according to their responsibility and capacity. According to this paradigm, it would be possible to exempt some parties from contributing to the policy objectives if they have no or very little capacity to contribute. But what would not seem acceptable within this paradigm is that some countries may profit from doing nothing to mitigate their emissions. Hence, having 'hot air' would not be acceptable. Moreover, it would be even less acceptable to benefit from selling 'hot air' in the global carbon market.[16] But, as some have pointed out, the burden-sharing paradigm is not the only possible one and, in fact, many developing countries support a very different paradigm, based on the allocation of property rights to a natural resource among countries – the 'right to natural resources' paradigm.

Under the 'right to natural resources' paradigm, concepts such as 'ecological space' and 'equal per capita allocation' become meaningful principles to guide the allocation of the absorptive capacity of the atmosphere, because within that paradigm it is possible to defend the position that all human beings have a right to a sufficient share of that absorptive capacity. Given the current overuse of that absorptive capacity, some citizens, regardless of where they live in the world, should reduce their emissions to a sufficient extent so that others may increase theirs while remaining within 'safe' aggregate levels (Hayward, 2006). The paradigms of burden sharing and the right to natural resources are not only very different, but also very entrenched within the negotiating positions of different parties to the international negotiations.

When considering the findings discussed in the previous paragraph from the perspective of legal principles, and in particular from the perspective of the CBDR principle, the conclusion seems sobering. As international law currently stands, burden sharing at international level remains essentially a political exercise, informed by a number of elements including self-interest and normative views. The CBDR would be at most a conglomerate of an indeterminate number of principles of distributive justice, but neither their meaning nor the precise combination that should be implemented to determine individual contributions enjoy widespread agreement among states. Fundamentally, the position of the EU itself does not seem to be entirely consistent with any particular set of principles: it can best be described as a rather balanced and pragmatic position, and in that sense it may offer some grounds to build a future agreement on the meaning and consequences of the CBDR. This is because the EU position, at its core, reflects an acceptance of the role of many principles, some of which have the effect of increasing the EU burden. Nevertheless, it should be noted that the EU's proposed contribution to burden sharing remains short of what would be required if the polluter pays principle, based on historical responsibility for past emissions, or if the principle of equal per capita allocation, were to be used as the main principles for burden sharing at international level.

Particular elements of the EU climate change regime that may have negative distributional impacts beyond the EU borders, and particularly among the most vulnerable individuals and communities are: (1) the use of flexible mechanisms and reduced emissions from deforestation and forest degradation plus conservation (REDD-plus), (2) the use of biofuels, and (3) the issue of carbon leakage. An analysis of each of these issues indicates some important tensions.

Regarding the use of credits from flexible mechanisms, while the EU has sought to reduce its reliance on credits that fail to ensure additionality, environmental integrity and sustainable development, it still relies on them to a significant extent to ensure compliance with its mitigation target. Regarding the use of biofuels, the EU legislator has justified the adoption of a legally-binding target of 10 per cent for the use of biofuels in transport, which can come either from the EU or from other countries, on the basis that it is necessary to reduce emissions in the short term. The use of biofuels is contentious, with many saying that it does not contribute to mitigation while having negative impacts on water, biodiversity and food production. The use of imported biofuels in the EU is not subject to quantitative limits, even if it is difficult to imagine how the EU will be able to control the social and environmental impacts of imported biofuels in foreign countries. The EU has required that biofuels, in order to be used for the purpose of complying with the legally-binding target, must be produced in a sustainable manner. One relevant question is whether this requirement can be enforced for imported biofuels, particularly considering the difficulties in inspecting production conditions abroad. The EU proposes a dual solution to this problem: first, to accept only biofuels fulfilling sustainability criteria; second, to assess *ex post* potential negative impacts of biofuels. Two criticisms seem in order: first, the EU legislator has paid more attention to the potentially negative environmental impacts than to the social ones; second, the question of whether imported biofuels should be allowed at all and whether there are other alternatives that would achieve a better proportion between means and ends does not seem to have been seriously considered by the EU legislator.

Third, leakage remains one of the most important hurdles for the adoption of stringent climate policy. Whether it is a real issue or not is difficult to prove empirically, but the EU legislator is making a huge effort to ensure that *ex post* empirical analyses do not need to be conducted by substantially reducing the burden upon companies subject to international competition. Moreover, the EU's approach to burden sharing in the international negotiations seems inconsistent with the approach it followed during the negotiations of the first EU burden-sharing agreement. Consistency would have required considering, also at international level, equal per capita allocation as a guiding principle for the distribution of the efforts within sectors not exposed to international competition.

Another element of EU climate change law that can have important impacts abroad is the unilateral inclusion of aviation in the EU Emission Trading Scheme (ETS) (Directive 2008/101/EC), and the likely inclusion of shipping in the near future. By taking the decision to unilaterally include these sectors into the EU ETS, the EU risks facing legal challenges in a number of international fora due to the extra-territorial effects of its legislation. The literature is not in agreement on the legality of those measures (Kaminskaite-Salters, 2009), which could obviously backfire if a legal challenge is successfully made.

Last but not least, although the EU has attached a key role to the technology known as carbon capture and storage, it has not yet considered formally the panoply of measures known collectively as geoengineering. It might yet be forced to do so, either because the international negotiations prove unable to deliver the kind of emission reductions that would avoid dangerous climate change, or because some other countries will start to seriously consider it as a tool within their instrument mix. Acting with foresight in this matter would seem to be required by the precautionary principle. One of the most quoted definitions of the principle states that:

> Where there are threats of serious or irreversible damage, lack of full scientific certainty shall not be used as a reason for postponing cost-effective measures to prevent environmental degradation.[17]

In relation to geoengineering, this definition could be interpreted as requesting that, in the face of potentially catastrophic climate change-related impacts, lack of full scientific certainty about the consequences of geoengineering should not be used as a reason to consider the need of undertaking geoengineering-related research with a view to eventually deploying some forms of geoengineering in order to avert climate change impacts. In order to consider this interpretation of the principle a legitimate one, it would be necessary to show that geoengineering is not only a cost-effective measure to prevent environmental degradation, but also that it will not cause substantial environmental degradation itself. This argument would gain purchase if it could be demonstrated that measures geared to reduce greenhouse gas emissions directly are not *in practice*[18] cost-effective. In order to arrive at such a conclusion, it is clearly necessary to increase the political and economic resources currently devoted to explore geoengineering as a climate change mitigation tool.[19]

## Burden Sharing Among EU Member States

As noted above, the EU has adopted two consecutive burden-sharing agreements in order to share the Kyoto target[20] and the unilateral 2020 mitigation commitment among its Member States.[21] The second burden-sharing agreement was termed 'effort sharing', in an effort to place more emphasis on the opportunities that arise from climate change policy, and less on the costs. The second 'effort-sharing' agreement is a more rational instrument than the first in respect of all dimensions of the meta-principle of proportionality. In particular, it achieves a better proportion between ends and means, by scoring higher on the three tests of intensity, quality and probability. It is, moreover, well justified under the principle of necessity and provides a central role for the principles of solidarity and common but differentiated responsibilities (de Cendra de Larragán, 2010a). Nevertheless, some tensions do remain.

First, the EU targets are not yet in line with the ultimate objective of EU climate change policy, since a direct link between the mid-term and the long-term targets is still missing.

Second, effort sharing within the EU seems to be subject to power relations to the extent that certain countries have clearly benefited from past inaction. That outcome goes against the core of the polluter pays principle, and could weaken the credibility of the EU in the international negotiations, particularly because the EU is pressing 'advanced' developing countries to take on targets as soon as possible. If Member States that miss their targets are not punished under EU law, developing countries may legitimately conclude that failure to comply with their own targets – if they accept them at all – should not carry any negative consequences at international level.

Third, the principle of loyal cooperation could turn out – *a posteriori* – to be very relevant for effort sharing among Member States. In particular, it could mean that Member States that over-comply with their targets are forced to place excess Assigned Amount Units (AAUs) in the hands of the EU, or otherwise purchase AAUs from other countries to ensure the compliance of the EU with its own target (de Cendra de Larragán, 2010a).

Last but not least, it must be noted that neither the burden-sharing agreement nor the effort-sharing agreement mention the size and distribution of adaptation costs within the EU, although it is clear that they will be considerable and very asymmetrically distributed. Adaptation has only recently been tackled within EU climate change policy,[22] but depending on the extent of damages and their distribution, the EU might need to consider a burden-sharing approach to adaptation, just as the EU has proposed to distribute among developed countries the costs of financing adaptation in developing countries. While the EU proposed to use the polluter pays principle and capacity to pay as the main guiding principles for sharing those costs among developed countries, it has not yet determined which principles will be used to share the financial commitment for developing countries among Member States. It would be logical to think that the same principles proposed for effort sharing in mitigation would be used in this context, in addition to giving attention to the vulnerability of each country to climate change impacts.

**Burden Sharing Within the Internal Market**

The test of quality asks to what extent distributional choices are in line with the integration principle, the polluter pays principle and the principle of rectification at source. EU climate change policy is progressing towards a fuller application of these three principles. Integration can be seen particularly in the fact that the EU institutions have declared that, from 2013 onwards, all sectors and gases will be included within the EU climate change regime. The polluter pays principle has been advanced particularly with the move from grandfathering[23] to auctioning as the core allocation method in the EU Emissions Trading Scheme, despite the fact that the negotiation of the directive amending the EU ETS (Directive 2009/29/EC) introduced a number of delays and complexities in the transition phase (Weishaar, 2008; Cló, 2009). Regarding the principle of rectification at source, it is clear that the EU ETS does not properly implement it, and actually goes against it, although this is justified in the context of climate change mitigation both by environmental and economic reasons. Two principles that are crucial in the context of burden sharing within the internal market are proportionality and equality. The issue of coverage of the EU ETS, as well as the choices of different allocation methods for different sectors, need to be carefully justified in order to be in compliance with these two principles. The principle of equality particularly was at issue in the *Arcelor* case,[24] where the ECJ ruled that, although different sources of greenhouse gas emissions are in principle in a comparable situation, since all emissions are liable to contribute to climate change and all sectors of the economy that emit greenhouse gases can contribute to the functioning of the EU ETS, differential treatment is nevertheless allowed if it is appropriately justified. In this, it adopted a different approach from the French Council d'Etat, which, in making a preliminary reference to the ECJ on this case, considered that the

EU ETS could be in violation of the principle of equality by excluding certain economic sectors from its coverage.

Another area where important tensions remain is the consumption side of the internal market. The European Environment Agency (EEA) has shown that while EU climate change law has paid a great deal of attention to the production side, the consumption side remains largely unaddressed (EEA, 2009, p. 44). While it is to be expected that price signals may progressively influence, at least to some extent, consumption decisions, the EEA shows that those signals are not enough to generate substantial changes, and additional measures will be needed. The EU has argued for some time that eco-labelling is an effective way of encouraging consumers to consider the emissions of their purchasing and consumption choices, but the fact is that it is not capable of generating significant emission reductions (Mahmoudi, 2006). Hence, further measures are urgently needed here.

Regarding the specific tests of attribution, subsidiarity and proportionality, a number of potential legal tensions stem from the highly political process through which EU climate change policy – and particularly the 2008 EU climate change and energy package – has evolved. Indeed, in order to strike a deal on relatively ambitious EU mitigation targets, the distribution of the effort in the context of the abovementioned package has been negotiated at the highest political level. As a consequence, the legal procedure to adopt it – co-decision under Art. 175 EC – has had less relevance than in other instances of EU environmental law. While this more political approach has probably been necessary in order to approve a very complex package, it may have limited the possibility to consider in detail the potential future consequences for all stakeholders, including competent regulators within Member States. Indeed, it has been said that given the complexity of the climate change and energy package – including the interactions among the different instruments – many of its consequences, including those of a legal nature, will only be discovered over time (Deketelaere, 2009). At a minimum, this calls for a constant and careful monitoring of its impacts in order to detect which elements conflict, which are mutually supportive, which can be added and which can be streamlined or eliminated.

The third dimension of the principle of meta-proportionality is concerned with the legal rules governing the access of interested stakeholders to the law-making process and to courts of law. The Commission, as the institution in charge of initiating the lawmaking process, is responsible for promoting public participation. But a tension exists between promoting participation and expediency, as the Commission has acknowledged explicitly on a number of occasions (Lee, 2005, p. 134 *et seq.*). Climate change is a matter where expediency may be of the essence, and wide public participation may delay the adoption of important measures. The pathway selected by the EU has been to push quickly for a comprehensive and far-reaching regime, where even the European Parliament has at times accepted the highly political level of the negotiations and has sought to support the balance developed by Member States at the Council. The EU institutions have justified this expedient approach on the basis of the urgency of the problem and of the broad support given by EU citizens to EU climate change policy. Nevertheless, there are particular areas where public participation might have been restricted to an extent that may cause legal tensions; Directive 2009/29/EC amending the EU ETS is a case in point. Indeed, this Directive requests the Commission to develop a large number of measures to implement it. Those measures will be developed following the applicable comitology procedures (see Robinson, 2007, p. 85), which are not characterised by their transparency. Therefore, private parties who might feel aggrieved by those measures may seek to challenge them before the European courts.

This takes us to the issue of access to justice. As EU law currently stands, private parties lack the standing to challenge general legal measures before the ECJ. However, given the very high level of harmonisation achieved in the EU ETS, and therefore the relatively reduced margin of discretion afforded to national authorities to take further decisions, private parties could be deprived of their right to seek protection in domestic courts. Therefore there is a case to be made for the ECJ to consider broadening their very narrow stance to access to justice in order to allow private parties to challenge decisions made by the Commission in the context of the EU ETS. Such a change in approach by the ECJ could, *ex post*, compensate to some extent for the limited participation of private parties in the decision-making process, by allowing parties to have measures examined by the European courts.

## 4.   FINAL REMARKS

The most significant conclusion of this chapter is that burden sharing within the EU climate change regime has increased, over time, its degree of consistency with the relevant legal principles. This would support the view that legal principles can provide and have in fact provided guidance in structuring and rationalising bargaining processes in EU climate change law and policy, thereby contributing to enhance its robustness. Of course, this conclusion should be interpreted with care, due to the ongoing lack of agreement about the core content of some important legal principles, particularly the polluter pays principle, the integration principle and CBDR. Whether agreement can be achieved about the meaning of these principles is unclear, particularly given the fact that some of them are closely related to the always conflictive and elusive concepts of justice and fairness.

Nevertheless, the main conclusion of this chapter attests to the robustness of the substantive legal foundations of the EU climate change policy edifice, regardless of its actual effectiveness in delivering emission reductions. It also suggests that the EU climate change regime can provide a model for countries in other regions to follow when developing their own climate regimes, as well as providing a blueprint for the international regime, although more firmness on this observation clearly requires further research. Notwithstanding this, there are a number of areas where tensions have been identified:

- The EU legislator does not seem to have considered alternatives to the use of biofuels that would reduce the need to import them, particularly given the existing controversy about the potentially negative impacts of first and second generation biofuels.
- The EU might do well to pay more attention to the 'natural resources' paradigm, and should keep searching at international level for a bridge between that paradigm and the currently preferred burden-sharing paradigm.
- The EU needs also to start considering the pros and cons of geoengineering in a formal manner.
- The possibility that some old Member States profit from past inaction in the area of mitigation sends a contradictory message to developing countries and may reduce the credibility of the EU approach in the international negotiations.
- The principle of solidarity may give rise to surprises in relation to potential liabilities of Member States towards the EU in the context of burden sharing, and might prove very relevant in the context of adaptation in ways that are yet to be discovered. The consumption side has not yet been addressed satisfactorily in EU climate change policy, and instruments such as EU-wide personal carbon trading could be explored as a possible alternative (de Cendra de Larragán and Peeters, 2010).

## NOTES

1. See, for instance, the meeting of the G-8 that took place in July 2009 in L'Aquila, Italy. There, the members of the G-8 issued a joint declaration entitled 'Responsible Leadership for a Sustainable Future', where they 'recognise the broad scientific view that the increase in global average temperature above pre-industrial levels ought not to exceed 2°C', and accept that this requires that global emissions fall by 50 per cent by 2050, and that

emissions from developed countries should fall by 8 per cent or more by 2050 'compared to 1990 or more recent years'.

2.    Climate change: Commissioner Dimas calls for tangible progress towards global deal in next UN negotiations, IP/09/488, 27 March 2009.

3.    See the statement of President Barroso on the Copenhagen Climate Accord, 19 December 2009, at http://europa.eu/rapid/.

4.    wordnetweb.princeton.edu/perl/webwn.

5.    See http://en.wikipedia.org/wiki/Robustness.

6.    See http://www.peopleandplace.net/media_library/text/2009/5/19/glossary_of_climate_adaptation_ and_decision-making

7.    The next sections are largely based on de Cendra de Larragán and Peeters (2010).

8.    However, even the structure and mode of application of these principles is not completely settled. European courts do not always apply the principle of proportionality in the same manner; sometimes they distinguish between the three tests of suitability, necessity and proportionality *stricto sensu*, while on other occasions they combine the first two tests, and this may have impacts on the outcome of the decision. Likewise, the principle of equality can be interpreted in different ways depending on the type of case, particularly whether it deals with the internal market or with fundamental rights. Other principles that have also been developed with a remarkable degree of sophistication by the European courts are legal certainty and legitimate expectations.

9.    Nevertheless, even this principle is subject to strong controversies regarding its meaning and legal consequences in different settings. For an analysis of the role of the precautionary principle in determining liability of private parties for climate change damages, see Miriam Haritz (2010).

10.   The most important opinion in this regard is that of AG Kokott in Case C-254/08, *Futura Immobiliare srl Hotel Futura, Meeting Hotel, Hotel Blanc, Hotel Clyton, Business srl v. Comune di Casoria*, delivered on 23 April 2009. The ECJ issued its ruling on 16 July 2009. Case C-254/08 *Futura Immobiliare srl Hotel Futura, Meeting Hotel, Hotel Blanc, Hotel Clyton, Business srl v. Comune di Casoria*, 16 July 2009, not yet reported. See also Case C-188/07 *Commune de Mesquer v. Total France SA, Total International Ltd*, 24 June 2008.

11.   See Decision No. 406/2009/EC of the European Parliament and of the Council of 23 April 2009 on the effort of Member States to reduce their GHG emissions to meet the EC's GHG emission reduction commitments up to 2020, OJ L 140, 5.6.2009, Recital 4.

12.   'European Parliament legislative resolution of 17 December 2008 on the proposal for a decision of the European Parliament and of the Council on the effort of Member States to reduce their greenhouse gas emissions to meet the Community's greenhouse gas emission reduction commitments up to 2020' (COM(2008)0017 – C6-0041/2008 – 2008/0014(COD), www.europarl.europa.eu/sides/getDoc.do?pubRef=-//EP//TEXT+TA+ P6-TA-2008-0611+0+DOC+XML+V0//EN&language=EN#BKMD-16.

13.   Nevertheless this chapter uses the term 'burden sharing' instead of 'effort sharing' for convenience, except in the context of burden sharing between EU Member States, where the distinction is kept.

14.   The Council has considered that developing countries as a group need to achieve a substantial and quantifiable deviation below the currently predicted emissions growth rate. See Conclusions of the Council of the European Union, Brussels 3 March, at www.register.consilium.europa.eu. See also European Commission (2009b, p. 5).

15.   Including, for example, Brazil, China and Saudi Arabia.

16.   It should nevertheless be noted here that several Member States of the EU have purchased 'hot air' in the international carbon market in order to comply with their mitigation targets under the Kyoto Protocol. For instance, according to the environmental data service ENDS, the Czech Republic has agreed to sell 8.5 million AAUs (Assigned Amount Units) to Spain (5 million) and Austria (3.5 million). Emissions in the Czech Republic are expected to be about 17 per cent below the country's target. The total amount of the Czech Republic's AAUs available for sale is 100 million, including those already sold.

See ENDS Europe Daily (2009) and press releases from the Ministry of the Environment of the Czech Republic (2009a, 2009b). In both cases, the AAUs sold are linked to a green investment scheme, a mechanism through which proceeds from the sale of AAUs are invested by the Czech Republic in activities that ensure GHG emissions reductions.

17. Principle 15 of the 1992 Rio Declaration on Environment and Development.
18. I emphasise the term 'in practice' because although many measures can be considered by economic models to be cost-effective, their implementation in practice may not be so; one widely accepted example of those type of measures are energy efficiency-enhancing measures in the building sector; see Sorrell et al. (2004).
19 The United Kingdom, for instance, is undertaking substantial multidisciplinary research on geoengineering. See for instance, The Royal Society (2009). See also House of Commons Science and Technology Committee (2010).
20. Council Decision 2002/358/EC of 25 April 2002 concerning the approval, on behalf of the European Community, of the Kyoto Protocol to the United Nations Framework Convention on Climate Change and the joint fulfilment of commitments thereunder, OJ L130, 15.5.2002.
21. Decision No 406/2009/EC of the European Parliament and of the Council of 23 April 2009 on the effort of Member States to reduce their greenhouse gas emissions to meet the Community's greenhouse gas emission reduction commitments up to 2020, OJ L140, 5.6.2009.
22. The European Commission elaborated a 'green' concluding chapter on adaptation to climate change in 2007 (European Commission, 2007). This led to the publication of a white paper (European Commission, 2009a).
23. Grandfathering in this context refers to the gratis allocation of allowances on the basis of historical emissions. This has been the dominant method of allocation in the first and second trading periods of the EU ETS. In the third trading period, starting on 1 January 2013, auctioning will become the default method, although grandfathering will still be used in several instances.
24. European Court of Justice, Case 127/07 *Societé Generale Arcelor Atlantique et Lorraine and Others v Premier Ministre, Ministre de l'Écologie et du Développement durable, Ministre de l'Economie, des Finances et de l'Industrie,* 16 December 2008.

# REFERENCES

Cló, S. (2010), 'Grandfathering, auctioning and carbon leakage: assessing the inconsistencies of the new ETS Directive', *Energy Policy*, **38**, 2420–30.

da Cruz Vilaça, J.L. (2004), 'The precautionary principle in EC law', *European Public Law*, **10** (2), 369–406.

De Cendra de Larragán, J. (2010a), *Distributional Choices in EU Climate Change Policy: Towards a Principled Approach?*, The Netherlands: Kluwer Law International.

De Cendra de Larragán, J. (2010b), 'United we stand, divided we fall: the potential role of the principle of loyal cooperation in ensuring compliance of the European Community with the Kyoto Protocol', *Climate Law*, **1** (1) 159–76.

De Cendra de Larragán, J. and Marjan Peeters (2010), 'Distributional Choices in EU Climate Change Policy Seen through the Lens of Legal Principles', in P. Martens and C. Chang (eds), *The Social and Behavioural Aspects of Climate Change*, Sheffield: Greenleaf Publishing, pp. 216–38.

Deketelaere, K. (2009), 'Concluding Remarks', at the *Conference on European Greenhouse Gas Emissions Trading: Lessons to be Learned*, Maastricht, 29–30 January 2009.

de Sadeleer, N. (2006), 'The precautionary principle in EC health and environmental law', *European Law Journal*, **12** (2), 139–172.

Ekeli, K.S. (2007), 'Green constitutionalism: the constitutional protection of future generations', *Ratio Iuris*, **20** (3), 378–401.

ENDS Europe Daily (2009), 'Czechs sell 8.5 million AAUs to Spain, Austria', 14 October 2009, www.endseurope.com/22382?referrer=search.

European Commission (2007), *Green Paper from the Commission to the Council, the European Parliament, the European Economic and Social Committee and the Committee of the Regions. Adapting to Climate Change in Europe: Options for EU Action* (COM/2007/0354 final; Brussels: European Commission Publications Office, 29 June 2007).

European Commission (2009a), *Adapting to Climate Change: Towards a European Framework for Action* (White Paper COM/2009/147 final; Brussels: European Commission Publications Office, 1 April 2009).

European Commission (2009b), *Communication from the Commission to the European Parliament, the Council, the European Economic and Social Committee and the Committee of the Regions: Towards a Comprehensive Climate Change Agreement in Copenhagen*, 28 January 2009 (COM/2009/39 Final) Brussels: European Commission Publications Office.

European Commission (2010a), *Communication from the Commission to the European Parliament, the Council, the European Economic and Social Committee and the Committee of the Regions: International Climate Policy Post-Copenhagen: Acting now to Reinvigorate Global Action on Climate Change* (COM/2010/86 Final), Brussels: European Commission Publications Office.

European Commission (2010b), *Communication from the Commission to the European Parliament, the Council, the European Economic and Social Committee and the Committee of the Regions: Analysis of Options to Move Beyond 20% Greenhouse Gas Emission Reductions and Assessing the Risk of Carbon Leakage* (COM/2010/265 Final) Brussels: European Commission Publications Office.

European Environment Agency (2009), *Greenhouse Gas Emission Trends and Projections in Europe 2009: Tracking Progress in Europe towards Kyoto* (Report No. 9/2009, Copenhagen: European Environment Agency).

Gupta, J. and Michael Grubb (eds) (2000), *Climate Change and European Leadership*, The Netherlands: Kluwer Law International.

Haritz, M. (2010), 'Climate Change Liability and the Application of the Precautionary Principle', in P. Martens and C. Chang (eds), *The Social and Behavioural Aspects of Climate Change*, Sheffield: Greenleaf Publishing, pp. 216–238.

Hayward, T. (2006), 'Global justice and the distribution of natural resources', *Political Studies*, **54** (2), 349–64.

House of Commons Science and Technology Committee (2010), 'The Regulation of Geoengineering', *Fifth Report of Session 2009–2010*, London, www.publications.parliament.uk/pa/cm200910/cmselect/.../221.pdf.

Jordan, Andrew et al. (2010), *Climate Change Policy in the European Union: Confronting the Dilemmas of Mitigation and Adaptation?* Cambridge: Cambridge University Press.

Kaminskaite-Salters, G. (2008), 'Expansion of the EU ETS: the Case of Emissions Trading for Aviation', in Michael Faure and Marjan Peeters (eds), *Climate Change and European Emissions Trading: Lessons for Theory and Practice*, Cheltenham, UK and Northampton, MA, USA: Edward Elgar, pp. 322–42.

Lee, M. (2005), *EU Environmental Law: Challenges, Change, and Decision-making*, Oxford: Hart Publishing.

Mahmoudi, S. (2006), 'Integration of Environmental Considerations into Transport', in R. Macrory (ed.), *Reflections on 30 Years of EU Environmental Law: A High Level of Protection?* Groningen: Europa Law Publishing, pp. 185–95.

Ministry of the Environment of the Czech Republic (2009a), 'Czech Republic and Spain conclude an agreement on the sale of 5 million Kyoto Units', 14 October 2009, www.mzp.cz/en/news_pr091014aau_spain.

Ministry of the Environment of the Czech Republic (2009b), 'Austria has purchased an additional 3.5 million Czech emission credits', 13 October 2009, www.mzp.cz/en/news_pr091013aau_Austria.

Müller, B. (2009), 'Additionality in the clean development mechanism: why and what?' *Oxford Institute for Energy Studies* EV44 (March), Oxford, at http://www.oxfordenergy.org/pdfs/EV44.pdf.

Oberthür, S. and Claire Roche Kelly (2008), 'EU leadership in international climate policy: achievements and challenges', *The International Spectator*, **43** (3), 35–50.

Robinson, J. (2007), *Climate Change Law: Emissions Trading in the EU and the UK*, London: Cameron May.

Sorrell, S., E. O'Malley, J. Schleich and S. Scott (2004), *The Economics of Energy Efficiency: Barriers to Cost Effective Investment*, Cheltenham, UK and Northampton, MA, US: Edward Elgar.

The Royal Society (2009), *Geoengineering the Climate: Science, Governance and Uncertainty*, London: The Royal Society, at http://royalsociety.org/geoengineering-the-climate/.

Thomas, E.W. (2005), *The Judicial Process – Realism, Pragmatism, Practical Reasoning, and Principles*, Cambridge: Cambridge University Press.

Tol, R. (2007), 'Europe's long-term climate target: a critical evaluation', *Energy Policy*, **35** (1), 424–32.

Tridimas, T. (2006), *The General Principles of EC Law*, Oxford: Oxford University Press.

Weishaar, S. (2008), 'The European Emissions Trading System: Auctions and their Challenges', in Michael Faure and Marjan Peeters (eds), *Climate Change and European Emissions Trading: Lessons for Theory and Practice*, Cheltenham, UK and Northampton, MA, USA: Edward Elgar, pp. 343–64.

# 18. Combating climate change in Uganda

## Emmanuel Kasimbazi

## 1. INTRODUCTION

Climate change means a change of climate that is attributed directly or indirectly to human activity that alters the composition of the global atmosphere and which is in addition to natural climate variability, observed over comparable time periods.[1] It is a problem with unique characteristics. It is a global long-term problem (extending over several centuries) and involves complex interactions between environmental, economic, political, institutional, social and technological processes (Metz et al., 2001, p. 50). As a result of these concerns, the international community has taken legal steps to combat climate change. The United Nations Framework Convention on Climate Change, whose objective is to achieve stabilisation of greenhouse gas concentrations in the atmosphere at a level that would prevent dangerous anthropogenic interference with the climate system,[2] and the Kyoto Protocol,[3] which sets binding numerical targets for the limitation and reduction of greenhouse gas emissions for the industrialised and transition countries[4] and other related instruments,[5] are all legal instruments to which Uganda is a party.[6] Available scientific information reveals that climate change poses a serious environmental problem with far-reaching social, political and economic consequences, particularly in developing countries such as Uganda. Therefore, developing and implementing Kyoto Protocol mechanisms, such as the Clean Development Mechanism (CDM), are fundamental to environmental sustainability in a least developed country like Uganda (Akiiki, 2002). This chapter reviews the laws, principles, standards and guidelines that have been developed to combat climate change and to implement the Kyoto Protocol and assesses their strengths and weaknesses in Uganda.

### Climate Change Trends in Uganda

Uganda is a signatory to both the United Nations Framework Convention on Climate Change (UNFCCC) and its Kyoto Protocol. As a state party to the two agreements, Uganda is required to enact effective environmental legislation and formulate cost-effective programmes to improve the quality of local emission factors.

Uganda is a land-locked country in eastern Africa with an area of 241,038 square kilometres, of which open water and swamps constitute 43,941 square kilometres or 17 per cent (Ministry of Agriculture, Animal Industry and Fisheries (MAAIF), 2002, p. 15). Most parts of the country lie at an average altitude of 1200m above sea level. By virtue of its location across the equator, two rainy seasons are experienced annually, although the two seasons merge as you move away from the equator (Waiswa, 2003). Mean annual rainfall varies from 750 to 2000 mm between different parts of the country, shaping the geographic distribution of social and economic activities (Orindi and Eriksen, 2005, p. 22).

The country is pleasantly cool, with mean temperatures ranging from a minimum of 15°C in July to a maximum of 30°C in February and a long-term mean temperature of 21°C. In the highlands and around mountains, the elevated landmass exerts a local influence on the climate, producing rainfall and temperature patterns that are distinct from those of the lowlands (Republic of Uganda, 2005, p. 3).

Climate in Uganda, particularly rainfall, has been erratic since the early 1990s. The incidence, duration and amount of rainfall have all exhibited abnormal departures from long-term means. While rainfall in some years was far short of long-term means, thereby causing droughts, in other years it was excessive and produced catastrophic floods. The heaviest rains in recent years were recorded in 1994 and were associated with the El Niño phenomenon. The rains led to sharp rises in lake levels, widespread flooding, washing away of roads and bridges, extensive soil erosion and landslides (Republic of Uganda, 2005, p. 3).

In addition to the variability in rainfall amounts, there have been confusing shifts in the seasons since the early 1990s, with heavy rains falling in the months expected to be dry and persistent desiccating sunshine experienced in the months that are normally wet and cold (Republic of Uganda, 2005, p. 3). Since Uganda's agriculture is heavily dependent on rainfall, the erratic swings in the seasons caused an increase in the frequency of food and water shortages in the country, with the worst-hit area being the dry cattle corridor that stretches from the Uganda–Tanzania border to the Karamoja region. Several deaths from starvation have been recorded in the Karamoja and Teso regions in recent years (ibid.).

## 2.  THE APPROACHES UNDER UNFCCC AND KYOTO PROTOCOL TO COMBAT CLIMATE CHANGE

The United Nations Framework Convention on Climate Change

One of the major principles of the Convention is the precautionary principle, which imposes an obligation on states to take measures to prevent and minimise the causes of climate change and mitigate its adverse effects (UNFCCC, Art. 3). The Convention emphasises that, where there are threats of serious or irreversible damage, lack of full scientific certainty is not to be used as a reason for postponing such measures (UNFCCC, Art. 3). The precautionary principle is important in climate change because it provides that activities threatening serious or irreversible damage should be restricted or even prohibited before there is absolute scientific certainty about their impact. Therefore the precautionary principle is usually associated with taking regulatory measures in situations of scientific uncertainty to prevent environmental damage. Ironically, however, regulatory action is not necessarily the first thing required of states when applying the precautionary principle, as usually, further research to collect more and new types of data and monitor the status of a particular environment is a priority. This aims to reduce the uncertainties involved before adopting regulatory action. Thus, the precautionary principle is potentially controversial and does not sit particularly comfortably with established legal values, as more emphasis is placed on research than established regulation. One possible explanation for states' reluctance to use the precautionary principle may be a concern that it may lead to the imposition of stricter and more inflexible obligations (de Sadeleer, 2002).

As one of the means to monitor climate change, the parties to the Convention undertake to periodically update, publish and make available to the Conference of the Parties, in accordance with article 12, national inventories of anthropogenic emissions by sources and removals by sinks of all greenhouse gases not controlled by the Montreal Protocol, using comparable methodologies to be agreed upon by the Conference of the Parties (UNFCCC, Art. 4(1)(a)). The Convention requires parties to take climate change considerations into account, to the extent feasible, in their relevant social, economic and environmental policies and actions. They are also required to employ appropriate methods, for example, impact assessments, formulated and determined nationally, with a view to minimising adverse effects on the economy, on public health and on the quality of the environment, of projects undertaken by them to mitigate or adapt to climate change (UNFCCC, Art. 4(1)(f)).

It can be observed that the UNFCCC is not specific insofar as reduction targets are concerned. In the Convention, the industrialised nations committed themselves to reduce their greenhouse gas emissions to 1990 levels (UNFCCC, Art. 4(2) (b)), but there was no specified time period for fulfilling this commitment. This commitment does not compel the industrialised countries to take swift action for the immediate realisation of the Convention objectives. Further, there are no such commitments for the developing countries, even though the cost of reducing emissions may be considerably lower than in the industrialised countries. Nevertheless, the formulation of the UNFCCC is to a significant step towards climate change mitigation in that it provides the general regulatory framework (Baumert et al., 1999).

## The Kyoto Protocol

As stated above, the commitments under the UNFCCC were not specific. The parties to the Convention decided in 1995 to convene to establish a protocol that would set emission reduction targets for the developed nations. This led to the meeting in Kyoto, Japan, 1–11 December, 1997 that produced the Kyoto Protocol.[7] The Kyoto Protocol, adopted at the Third Session of the Conference of the Parties to the UN Framework Convention on Climate Change (COP 3), sets binding numerical targets for the limitation and reduction of greenhouse gas emissions during the period 2008–2012.[8] The term greenhouse gases (GHGs) refers to chemicals present in the atmosphere that have certain radiation-blocking properties that trap the sun's energy in the earth's atmosphere, creating a type of insulation (UNIDO, 2007). These gases include carbon dioxide, methane, nitrous oxide, hydrofluorocarbons, perfluorocarbons and sulphur hexafluoride.[9] These are defined by UNFCCC as those gaseous constituents of the atmosphere, both natural and anthropogenic, that absorb and re-emit infrared radiation (UNFCCC, Art. 1, para. 5).

The Kyoto Protocol obliges the parties included in Annex I, which are mostly developed countries, to implement elaborate policies and measures, in accordance with their national circumstances, to achieve their quantified emission limitation and reduction commitments under Article 3. These measures include: enhancement of energy efficiency; enhancement of sinks and reservoirs of greenhouse gases not controlled by the Montreal Protocol; promotion of sustainable forest management practices; afforestation and reforestation; research on, and promotion, development and increased use of new and renewable forms of energy, of carbon dioxide sequestration technologies and of advanced and innovative environmentally sound technologies (Art. 2 (1)).

At the Conference of the Parties held in December 2007 in Bali (UNFCCC/COP-13, 2007), countries acknowledged that tackling deforestation and forest degradation through conservation can promote the objective of the Convention and complement other relevant international conventions and agreements. The Bali COP enjoined all parties to further strengthen and support efforts to reduce emissions from deforestation and forest degradation (REDD) on a voluntary basis and encouraged all parties to support capacity building, technical assistance, and transfer technology to improve data collection, estimation of emissions, monitoring and reporting, and address the institutional needs of developing countries in estimating and reducing emissions from deforestation and forest degradation (ibid.). The Bali COP also encouraged all parties to explore a range of actions, options and efforts as well as demonstration activities in relation to reducing emissions due to deforestation and degradation, and enhancing carbon stocks due to sustainable forest management (ibid.). The adoption of the REDD scheme at the Bali Conference promised an option of reducing deforestation as well as promoting carbon credits as an alternative income-generating activity within forest countries. These deliberations were taken up at the Copenhagen COP in December 2009, finding expression in Article 6 of the Copenhagen Accord,[10] and will no doubt be further elaborated in the negotiations for the adoption of a new or amended instrument in subsequent meetings.

The Kyoto Protocol defines three international policy instruments (Kyoto mechanisms) which provide opportunities for Annex 1 parties to fulfil their commitments cost effectively. These are the Clean Development Mechanism (CDM), International Emissions Trading (IET) and Joint Implementation (JI). Of these three mechanisms, it is CDM that applies to developing countries like Uganda because JI and IET are generally meant for industrialised countries. The next section analyses how Uganda has applied the CDM to combat climate change.

**The Clean Development Mechanism**

Article 12(2) of the Kyoto Protocol defines the purposes of the Clean Development Mechanism as being to assist developing countries in achieving sustainable development, contributing to the ultimate objective of the UNFCCC and assisting industrialised countries in achieving compliance with their quantified emission limitation and reduction commitments. The CDM allows governments or private entities in industrialised countries to implement emission reduction projects in developing countries and then receive credits in the form of 'certified emission reductions' (CERs) which they may count against their own national reduction targets. The CDM also offers the opportunity to mobilise additional funds for developing countries, especially in the field of renewables and energy efficiency.

In order to participate in the CDM there are three eligibility criteria that must be met by participating countries. These are: voluntary participation in the CDM, the establishment of a national CDM authority and ratification of the Kyoto Protocol (Art.12(5)).[11] For a project to be eligible the following conditions must also be satisfied: the designed project must assist Non-Annex I parties (developing countries) 'in achieving sustainable development and contributing towards ultimate objectives of the Convention';[12] it must result in 'real, measurable and long-term benefits related to the mitigation of climate change';[13] and projects must result in 'reductions in emissions that are additional to any that could occur in the absence of the certified project activity.'[14] Uganda is eligible to apply the CDM because it satisfies the necessary requirements. Therefore, a number of projects, policies and laws have been implemented and others have been proposed in order to implement the CDM.

## 3. THE SIGNIFICANCE OF UGANDA'S NATIONAL POLICY AND LEGAL FRAMEWORK FOR THE IMPLEMENTATION OF CDM

Uganda has developed national capacities to implement the CDM. These include the development of a comprehensive legal and policy framework that facilitates the implementation of CDM. This section reviews the policies, laws and projects that have been proposed and developed to implement the CDM in various sectors of the economy.

### The Forestry Sector

Uganda has about 49,500 km$^2$ of forests, consisting of tropical high forests and savannah woodlands (99 per cent) and plantations (1 per cent). The western region of the country, comprising Kibale, Kabarole and Bundibugyo districts, has more than 60 per cent of the country's closed forests, while the central region has a little more than 20 per cent. The forest and woodland resources of Uganda are found both within and outside protected areas according to the National Environmental Management Authority (NEMA, 2000/2001, p. 5). Apart from a few large blocks of intact forests, the rest of the forest and woodland estate consist of small, scattered patches and are therefore difficult to manage centrally (ibid.). Better forest management has a key role to play in mitigating climate change. Climate change and forests are intrinsically linked. On the one hand, changes in global climate are already stressing forests, through higher mean annual temperatures, altered precipitation patterns and more frequent and extreme weather events. At the same time, forests trap and store carbon dioxide, playing a major role in mitigating climate change. Forests store enormous amounts of carbon: in total, the world's forests and forest soils currently store more than one trillion tons of carbon – twice the amount found floating free in the atmosphere (FAO, 2006). On the other side of the coin, when destroyed or over-harvested and burned, forests will become sources of carbon dioxide (ibid.).

To realise the potential of the forests in carbon sequestration, better forest management practices are necessary and this is effected through various policies and laws which are also relevant for the implementation of the CDM.

**The policy framework for implementing the CDM in the forestry sector**

A number of policies and programmes support the implementation of the CDM in the forestry sector. The *Uganda Vision 2025* (MFPED, 1998) was launched in 1998 as a strategic framework for National Development and is one of the policy framework documents relevant in the implementation of the CDM. The Vision promotes strategies to limit greenhouse gas emissions which include: improving energy efficiency so as to reduce demand and hence the amount of carbon dioxide generated during energy production; using cleaner energy sources and technologies to reduce emissions of carbon dioxide and pollutants that cause acid rain and other environmental problems; improving forest management; expanding forest areas and encouraging tree planting to increase the size of carbon sinks in the country; and adopting agricultural practices which reduce emissions of methane and nitrous oxide (MFPED, 1998, p. 283). These strategies indicate Uganda's commitment to apply CDM mechanisms.

The Uganda Forestry Policy 2001 (MWLE, 2001), whose objective is to establish an integrated forestry sector that achieves sustainable increases in the economic, social and environmental benefits from forests and trees by the people of Uganda, especially the poor and vulnerable, is also relevant for the implementation of the CDM in Uganda (ibid.). The policy provides for the protection of the Permanent Forest Estate (PFE) under government trusteeship and the development and sustainable management of natural forests on private land (ibid.). It also provides for a wide cross- section of stakeholder participation in the management of the forests. The policy further encourages partnerships with the local forest communities to develop sustainable management of forests (MWLE, 2001, p. 10). This partnership provides an opportunity for foreign companies to work with the local communities to implement CDM projects through reforestation and afforestation.

The 1994 National Environment Management Policy (NEMP, 1994) is also important for the implementation of the CDM. The overall goal of the NEMP is to establish sustainable social and economic development, which maintains or enhances environmental quality and resource productivity on a long-term basis that meets the needs of the present generations without compromising the ability of future generations to meet their own needs, consistent with the prescriptions of the Brundtland Report, *Our Common Future* (WCED, 1987).[15] The Policy contains guiding principles that are relevant in the implementation of CDM projects in Uganda. The policy recognises that Uganda's forests provide a wide range of environmental services and values such as the amelioration of climate and stabilisation of soils, which are critical to national development (MWLE, 1994, p. 31). The policy also recognises that private forestry should be encouraged by appropriate incentives, extension services, marketing assistance and increased security of land and tree tenure (MWLE, 1994). Private forestry is important in encouraging private individuals and civil society organisations to participate in the implementation of CDM projects in the forestry sector.

The policy also has relevant strategies for the implementation of CDM. For instance, it calls for improvement of the local capacity to manage protected and gazetted forest reserves by encouraging people's participation in forest planning and management (MWLE, 1994). The development of local capacities ensures the viability of CDM projects initiated in the forestry sector. The policy also calls for economic incentives and the necessary legal framework and technology to encourage and facilitate rural communities, wood fuel-using industries and institutions, and the private sector to be self-sufficient in forest product requirements (ibid.). The economic incentives under the policy may include financial support from CDM supporting countries.

### The legal framework for the implementation of CDM in the forestry sector

The 1995 Constitution of Uganda has provisions regulating forestry resources that are relevant for the implementation of the CDM in Uganda. Under the Constitution, it is the duty of Parliament to enact laws to protect and preserve the environment from abuse, pollution and degradation and also to promote measures intended to manage the environment for sustainable development and to promote environmental awareness.[16] The state has the duty to protect important resources, including land, water, wetlands, oil, minerals, fauna and flora on behalf of the people of Uganda.[17] Under article 237 (2)(b), the government or, where appropriate, local government, is required to hold in trust for the people and protect natural forest reserves and any land to be reserved for ecological and tourism purposes for the common good of all citizens. The trust obligation imposed on the state facilitates the implementation of the CDM in two ways. First, CDM projects can be more easily implemented by the government than would have been the case if the forestry resources were subject to private ownership, which would involve a lengthy process of land acquisition for the realisation of projects. Second, the trust obligation bars the government from leasing out or otherwise alienating the forests referred to, (fortified by s. 44(4) of the Land Act, Uganda, 2000). This ensures subsistence of CDM forest projects.

The National Environment Act 2000,[18] the main purpose of which is to provide for sustainable management of the environment and which establishes the National Environment Management Authority (NEMA) as a coordinating, monitoring and supervisory body, is also relevant in the implementation of CDM projects. NEMA is the main institution responsible for the operation of the Environmental Impact Assessment (EIA) regime (National Environment Act, 2000, 'NE Act', s. (1)(f)). Projects that must undergo the EIA process include forestry-related activities such as reforestation and afforestation.

Under the Act, NEMA is required, in consultation with the lead agency, the National Forestry Authority, to issue guidelines and prescribe measures for the management of all forests in Uganda (NE Act, s. 45(1)). These guidelines must take into account forests in protected areas, including forest reserves, national parks and game reserves, and forests on lands subject to interests held by private persons (NE Act, s. 45(2)).

NEMA, in consultation with the National Forestry Authority, is given powers to expressly exclude human activities in any forest area by declaring it a specially protected forest (NE Act, s. 45). The establishment of NEMA and the obligations imposed on it in relation to forest management ensure that the implementation of CDM projects is integrated into the overall environmental legal framework of Uganda. This is advantageous to the extent that such integration guarantees facilitation of the implementation process by the government.

The National Forestry and Tree Planting Act, 2003 (NFTP Act) is the main Act dealing with forestry resources management in Uganda. The objective of this Act is to promote the conservation, sustainable management and development of forests for the benefit of the people of Uganda. The Act promotes tree planting and management of forest produce. This provision can be utilised for afforestation for CDM purposes. The Act also provides a legal framework for the declaration of forest reserves for purposes of protection and management of forests and forest produce, and for the sustainable use of forest resources, and promotes enhancement of the productive capacity of forests.[19] A key provision of the Act requires that every project or activity that may, or is likely to have a significant impact on a forest shall undergo EIA (NFTP Act, s. 38). The Act further makes provision for the collaborative management of forests, whereby a responsible body may enter into a collaborative forest management arrangement with a forest user group for the purposes of managing a central forest or a local forest reserve (NFTP Act 2003, s. 15). The provision allowing ordinary citizens to own private forest plantations encourages investment in the forestry sector for the implementation of CDM projects.

A number of CDM projects are being implemented in the forestry sector. These are:

(1) The Nanga Farms Ltd project, aiming to establish a quality industrial pine plantation by 2021(1,000 ha);

(2) The FACE (Forest Absorbing Carbon Emissions) Foundation of the Netherlands, in conjunction with Uganda Wildlife Authority (UWA), Mt. Elgon and Kibale Afforestation Projects aiming to rehabilitate degraded forests in the two National Parks (25,000 ha);

(3) The first phase of a sustainable plantation by the new Forests Company Ltd in the Namasa Central Forest Reserves in Mubende District (ultimately 6,500 ha) and the active management of Assisted Natural Regeneration (ANR) of a further 500 ha;

(4) The National Forestry Authority's Nile Afforestation Project in Rwoho Central Forest Reserve in South Western Uganda (about 2,000 ha);

(5) The Busoga Forest Company Ltd commercial forest plantation in Bukaleba Forest Reserve in Mayuge District;

(6) The Global Woods (U) Ltd reforestation project in the Kikondwa forest Reserve in Kiboga District;

(7) The Bakojja New Wood County Project, a mixed soft/hard wood plantation forest in Buwekula County of Mubende District; and;

(8) The Sango-Bay Estates Ltd project which intends to add 12,800 ha to its existing 20,000 ha (CERA Uganda, 2010).

**The Energy Sector**

Energy consumption is crucial in climate change and the implementation of the Kyoto Protocol. In Uganda, energy use is still dominated by wood fuels, followed by petroleum and hydroelectricity. Wood fuels alone account for over 94 per cent of total energy consumption. Petroleum accounts for about 5 per cent, while hydroelectricity accounts for only about 1 per cent. All petroleum products used in the country are imported (MWLE, 1995 p. 38). Taken as a whole, the nature of energy consumption in Uganda is likely to increase carbon dioxide concentrations in the atmosphere. Reliance on wood fuels and petroleum products produces more carbon dioxide than is the case with hydroelectricity. Policies, laws and projects therefore need to target reduction in the use of wood fuels and petroleum products in favour of hydroelectricity. Uganda has a policy and legal framework that can be used to achieve the above goals. The next section reviews how these policies, laws and programmes are relevant for the implementation of CDM projects.

**The policy framework for the implementation of the CDM in the energy sector**

The National Energy Policy, 2002 adopts the goal of meeting the energy needs of Uganda's population for social and economic development in an environmentally sustainable manner (MEMD, 2002), and is the main policy relating to energy use in Uganda. This policy seeks to meet the following broad objectives: to establish the availability, potential and demand of the various energy resources in the country; to increase access to modern, affordable and reliable energy services; to improve energy governance and administration; and to stimulate economic development and manage energy-related environmental impacts (MEMD, 2002 p. 35). The policy proposes to develop the use of renewable energy resources (including solar) on both small and large scales (MEMD, 2002 p. 19). Uganda is endowed with a plenty of sunshine, yielding solar radiation of about 4–5 $kWh/m^2/day$ (MEMD, 2002, p. 20). This level of insolation is quite favourable for all solar technology applications. Solar energy applications in Uganda include solar photovoltaic (PV), water heating, cooling and crop drying (MEMD, 2002).

Solar Energy Uganda Ltd has obtained Global Environment Facility funds to install 72,000 solar household systems in rural Uganda. This is expected to reduce household kerosene use by 28,630 tons by 2010, ultimately delivering a carbon dioxide emission reduction of 18,000 tons per annum, worth approximately US$50,000 (Kasimbazi, 2005). The National Environment Management Policy (NEMP, 1994) in relation to energy strives to meet national energy needs through increased use of hydropower, improved efficiency of energy use, increased use of alternative energy sources, increased production of both plantation and on-farm trees and promotion of exploration and production of fossil fuels. The policy can be viewed as harbouring a weakness when it seeks promotion of exploration and production of fossil fuels, as most anthropogenic carbon dioxide comes from burning of fossil fuels such as oil, coal and gas (Kerr, 2002, p. 2).[20] Nonetheless, the policy lays down guiding principles for the energy sector that are relevant for the implementation of the CDM. The policy, for instance, calls for promotion of private woodlots, especially in wood-deficit areas, and for private sector involvement in energy exploration, development and distribution, including hydroelectric power and fuel wood (including peri-urban) plantations (NEMP, 1994, p. 39). This widens the range of potential participants in CDM projects to include sectors that may be more efficient in this regard than the government. The policy also calls for the decentralisation of energy planning to district and local levels to take into account local needs and opportunities (NEMP, 1994). This ensures public participation in the implementation of CDM projects at all levels of development. This is useful insofar as it cuts implementation costs, encourages public participation and promotes public awareness of climate change.

The policy lays down strategies for the energy sector in order to realise its objectives. Of relevance to the CDM is encouraging the private sector to generate and distribute hydro-electricity by removing the monopoly in generating, transmitting and distributing electricity by the Uganda Electricity Distribution Company Limited (UEDCL) (NEMP, 1994). It is thought that this will increase the amount of hydropower generated, thereby reducing the level of reliance on fossil fuels and pressure on the forest resources.

### The legal framework for the implementation of CDM in the energy sector

As in other sectors, the Ugandan Constitution[21] provides some guidance on the implementation of the CDM in Uganda in the energy sector. Under the National Objectives and Directive Principles of State Policy, it is provided that the state shall promote and implement energy policies that will ensure that people's basic needs and those of environmental preservation are met.[22] The fulfilment of this obligation may require the government to take a number of steps, including the implementation of CDM projects, for example, developing solar energy and enhancing hydropower generation.

The Electricity Act[23] provides for the establishment of the Electricity Regulatory Authority (ERA) (Electricity Act, s. 4), whose functions include: issuing licenses for the generation, transmission, distribution or sale of electricity; controlling activities in the electricity sector; and liberalising of and bringing competition to the electricity sector (Electricity Act, s. 10). This Act is important for CDM projects because it provides for rural electrification, under which most of the CDM projects in Uganda are implemented. Section 62 provides that the government shall undertake to promote, support and provide rural electrification programmes through public and private sector participation in order to achieve equitable regional distribution and access to electricity; maximise the economic, social and environmental benefits of rural electrification subsidies; promote expansion of the grid and development of off-grid electrification; and stimulate innovations within suppliers.

A number of rural electrification projects under CDM have been implemented in Uganda. For instance, the West Nile Electrification Project, with financial support from the Prototype Carbon Fund (PCF), is part of the Government of Uganda's Energy for Rural Transformation (ERT) Scheme, supported by the World Bank and various bilateral partners. The project involves the construction of two small hydropower stations, efficient diesel backup facilities, and the rehabilitation of the mini-grid in the region. The initiative will tackle emissions from highly inefficient diesel and petrol-fuelled generators and engines in the district of Arua and Nebbi in north-western Uganda (Kasimbazi, 2005, p. 305). Another significant project is the Kilembe Grid Extension Project. The objective of this project is to extend the transmission and Low Voltage (LV) distribution lines from a current hydro facility (originally built to provide power to a now-closed copper mine) to nearby villages and trading centres that are not connected to the grid (Kasimbazi, 2005). The result would be a more reliable supply of electricity that will help spur local economic development, while at the same time displacing polluting and expensive diesel fuel as well as kerosene and fuel wood use.

The other key project is the Mt. Elgon Hydropower Project. The objective of this project is to build a small hydro facility that will provide power to villages, business and industries that are not currently connected to the grid, supplying electricity on the same rationale as for the Kilembe Project (Kasimbazi, 2005). The Mount Elgon Hydro Power Company Ltd has permits to develop five sites, totalling about 14 MW, near a mountain on the border with Kenya. The project will install small turbines to provide electricity. Low voltage lines will be connected to villages and businesses. The facility itself will include a diversion weir and canal, an intake weir, an outdoor powerhouse and an access road. The technology to be deployed will be small hydro generators and a 110 kV transmission line to connect the site to the grid in order to sell excess power, as well as transformers and LV transmission lines to consumers.

**The Wetlands Sector**

With an estimated coverage of 30,000 square kilometres (13 per cent) of Uganda's land surface (Kasimbazi, 2005), wetland ecosystems constitute an important natural resource in Uganda, from an ecological, social and economic point of view (Bakema and Lyango, 2000). Wetlands affect the levels of atmospheric carbon in two ways. First, many wetlands are carbon reservoirs. Carbon is contained in the standing crops, trees and other vegetation and in litter, peat, organic soils and sediments that have been built up, in some instances, over thousands of years. It has been estimated that wetlands hold 35 per cent of the total terrestrial carbon (Kusler, 1999). The magnitude of storage depends upon wetland type and size, vegetation, the depth of wetland soils, ground water levels, nutrient levels and other factors. Such carbon reservoirs may supply large amounts of carbon to the atmosphere if water levels are lowered or land management practices result in the oxidation of soils. Second, many wetlands also continue to sequester carbon from the atmosphere through photosynthesis by wetland plants; many also act as sediment traps for carbon-rich sediments from watershed sources (ibid.).

The wetlands sector has considerable potential for the CDM. A number of policies, laws and programmes are in place for the protection and sustainable management of wetlands. Those relevant for the implementation of CDM are reviewed below.

## The policy framework for the implementation of CDM for the wetlands sector

The major policy dealing with wetlands management in Uganda is the National Policy for the Conservation and Management of Wetland Resources (1995). The overall aim of this policy is to promote the conservation of Uganda's wetlands in order to sustain their ecological and socio-economic functions for the present and future well-being of the people (Republic of Uganda, 1995, p. 4). One of the goals of the policy is to maintain the functions and values of wetlands throughout Uganda and to promote the recognition and integration of wetlands functions in resource management and economic decision-making with regard to sector policies and programmes in other areas such as forestry, agriculture and environmental management (Republic of Uganda, 1995).

One of the strategies of the policy is to ensure that there is no drainage of wetlands unless justified by the most important environmental management requirements. It is only those uses that have been proved to be non-destructive to wetlands that can be allowed or encouraged and any decisions to use wetlands must consider the requirements of all other users in the community (Republic of Uganda, 1995, p. 6). All wetlands are a public resource, controlled by the government on behalf of the public. Therefore, no leasing of any wetland to any person in Uganda at any time for any reason is allowed (Republic of Uganda, 1995). As noted, in the forestry sector, the trust obligation imposed on the state ensures quick implementation and sustenance of CDM projects in relation to wetlands sector.

The policy makes provision for recovery of previously drained wetlands, otherwise referred to as restoration (Republic of Uganda, 1995, p. 7). Many wetlands have been drained or modified, especially in south-west and eastern Uganda. As a strategy therefore, government may require that some wetlands which have already been drained should be allowed to regenerate (Republic of Uganda, 1995). The CDM could be one mechanism that may be employed to regenerate these wetlands by providing financial support to the regeneration projects.

The National Environment Management Policy in relation to wetlands has the objective of promoting the conservation of wetlands to sustain their ecological and socio-economic functions for the present and future well-being of the people (NEMP, 1994, p. 14). The policy recognises that wetlands are important and productive natural resource systems which should be sustainably managed. It also calls for the involvement of the local authorities/users in wetland resource planning and management. This ensures participation in the

CDM projects at all levels. Public participation is important as it promotes awareness and a sense of responsibility among members of the public regarding environmental conservation and climate change. The policy also lays down strategies for the management of wetland resources. It requires the carrying out of a full inventory of major wetlands to determine their location, status, ecological and socio-economic value, as well as their capacity to perform their various functions on a sustainable basis. Through this inventory, it is possible to identify wetlands that may be appropriate subjects for CDM projects.

The Wetlands Sector Strategic Plan 2001–2010 has the overall goal of ensuring that the contribution of Uganda's wetlands to human welfare and the health of the environment are increased (Republic of Uganda, 2001, p. 19). The strategic objectives of the plan include the development and maintenance of an institutional framework for the management of wetlands (Republic of Uganda, 2001, p. 19). Key actions here include: ensuring allocation from the Government recurrent budget of sufficient monies to cover the ongoing costs of the national lead agency – the Wetland Inspection Division (WID); training and equipping District Environment Officers to carry out wetlands management functions; supporting the formation and operation of District and Local Environment Committees; and establishing and maintaining a National Wetland Inter-Agency Co-ordination Committee (Republic of Uganda, 2001). A strong institutional framework under the plan has a significant part to play in the implementation and success of CDM projects in the wetlands sector.

**Legal framework for the implementation of CDM in the wetlands sector**

The National Environment Act 2000 restricts activities in wetlands. Therefore, no activity is allowed in a wetland unless a person has written permission from NEMA following an EIA (required under s. 19 of the National Environment Act) to determine the effects of that activity on wetlands and the environment in general (s. 36). Under the Act, NEMA is required to establish guidelines for the identification and sustainable management of all wetlands in Uganda. It is also required to identify wetlands of local, national and international importance as ecosystems and habitats of species of fauna and flora and to compile a national register of wetlands. NEMA is also given discretion, in consultation with the lead agency and the District Environment Committee, to declare any wetland to be a protected wetland, thereby excluding or limiting human activities in that wetland (s. 37).

The National Environment (Wetlands, River Banks and Lake Shores Management) Regulations 2000,[24] which were made under NEA, have important provisions for the implementation of the CDM in the wetlands sector. Part II of these regulations applies to all wetlands in Uganda. Central or local government is required to hold in trust for the people and protect wetlands for the common good of the citizens of Uganda.[25] The Regulations further set out principles that form the basis for the management of all wetlands. For instance, wetland resources shall be utilised in a sustainable manner, compatible with the continued presence of wetlands and their hydrological functions and services; environmental impact assessment as required under the statute is mandatory for all activities in wetlands that are likely to have an adverse impact on it; and wise use of wetlands shall be integrated into the national and local approaches to the management of their resources, through awareness campaigns and dissemination of information.[26] These Regulations are important because any CDM project to be implemented under the wetlands sector must comply with the requirements of the 2000 Regulations.

## 4. CHALLENGES TO THE IMPLEMENTATION OF THE KYOTO PROTOCOL IN UGANDA

Uganda faces a number of legal challenges in the implementation of the CDM. One of the critical legal issues arising from the operation of the CDM lies in the property and contract law issues surrounding sequestered carbon. As sequestered carbon is a relatively new 'commodity', introduced by the Kyoto Protocol and enjoying some unique characteristics (Kusler, 1999), complex legal issues arise when defining the property rights it engenders and in drafting carbon sequestration sales contracts. The problem is how to approve, monitor and verify the carbon credits earned under clear and transparent rules, for permanence and sustainability (Brown et al., 2004). Carbon credits are certificates awarded to countries that are successful in reducing the greenhouse gases emissions. Carbon credits can be used to finance carbon reduction schemes between trading partners around the world (World Bank, 2007). Further, contractual concerns arise because participating in CDM projects requires signing international contracts. These contracts require expert negotiation by people exposed to international contracts, commercial law and CDM legal issues (UNIDO, 2007) with which most Ugandans are not familiar. This issue is relevant beyond the law, as there are low levels of awareness of the CDM, particularly due to inadequate circulation of, and the complex language contained in, materials that concern the projects that are implemented under the Kyoto Protocol. One consequence of this is that these projects receive low support from the public and other civil society organisations, limiting their participation in this area (Brown et al., 2004).

A related concern lies in the fact that CDM projects are also more likely to flow to countries that are already successfully attracting direct foreign investment. This is because the substantial levels of private investment in such countries attracts CDM projects much more easily than is the case in countries where direct foreign investment is still low (UNIDO, 2007). Uganda does not as yet attract major investments and this partially explains why the CDM projects in Uganda are still relatively few in number.

An additional area of concern is that, despite considerable state activity in this area, Uganda lacks a strong national institutional framework to implement the Kyoto mechanisms. There are failures at different institutional and policy levels in environmental management for implementing the Kyoto Mechanisms. Policies such as the National Environmental Management Policy for Uganda lack financial facilitation and skilled manpower. Whereas it is now largely accepted that climate is of fundamental importance and worth protecting, and whereas implementation of the Kyoto Protocol is expected to be done through a hierarchy of enforcement from the Ministry of Water and Environment, through NEMA and local government, down to community level, the enforcement capacity available at all these levels does not appear to be commensurate with the widespread nature of the problem. In particular, administration at district and local environment committee levels lack adequate human resources and funds to implement and monitor all the CDM projects (NEMA, 2001/2002, p. 5). As a result, enforcement of the Kyoto implementation mechanisms under the national policy and legal framework is weak (Rose, 2001). The legal and policy measures taken by Uganda, as discussed above, though they appear to be adequate, are not strictly enforced owing to a number of reasons such as inadequate logistics, corruption, and poor institutional linkages.

An additional burden is placed on government resources with respect to the CDM by the fact that the Kyoto Protocol requires parties to submit national communications containing information regarding actions taken to implement the protocol. However, preparing such a national communication is often a complex and expensive exercise that a country like Uganda may struggle to afford.

Further, under Art. 12.8 of the Kyoto Protocol, two percent of the Certified Emission Reductions (carbon credits issued by the Clean Development Mechanism Executive Board for emission reductions achieved by CDM projects, known as CERs) generated by the CDM are earmarked for the Kyoto adaptation fund for developing countries that are particularly vulnerable to the negative effects of climate change. In practice, this means that 2 per cent of the CERs generated from the CDM would be deducted from the project (UNFCCC, 2002). Therefore, in practical terms, the implementation of CDM projects in Uganda is rendered more costly. This may be expensive for a country like Uganda where nearly half of its budget is donor funded.

## 5. CONCLUSION

Uganda has attempted to implement the Kyoto Protocol mechanisms through developing policy and legislative measures to combat climate change and its effects. The successful application of these policies and enforcement of the laws will obviously contribute to climate change mitigation through the reduced emission of greenhouse gases and enhancement of sinks. This is an important step towards environmental sustainability. However, as observed above, these efforts are constrained by a number of factors, though most of these are extraneous to the legal framework itself. There is room to improve in the key areas of state and private law activity alluded to above to ensure that the problem of climate change is more effectively addressed in practice, both in relation to the Kyoto Protocol mechanisms and their successors.

## NOTES

1. See Article 1 of the United Nations Framework Convention on Climate Change (UNFCCC), UN Doc. A/AC.237/18 (Part II) (Add. 1), Misc 6 (1993), 31 ILM 848.
2. Note 1, Art. 2 of the UNFCCC.
3. The Kyoto Protocol to the United Nations Framework Convention on Climate Change, UN Doc FCCC/CP/1997/L.7/add.1, 37 ILM (signed 11 December 1997).
4. Note 3 Art. 3 read together with Annex A.
5. These include the Vienna Convention for the Protection of the Ozone Layer (UNTS 293, 324, 26 ILM 1529) and the Montreal Protocol on Substances that Deplete the Ozone Layer (S. Treaty Doc. No. 9, 99th Cong., 1st Sess. 22, (1987) 26 ILM 1550).
6. Uganda signed the UNFCCC on 13 June 1992 and ratified it on 8 September 1993; it ratified the Kyoto Protocol on 25 March 2002. It acceded to the Vienna Convention for the Protection of the Ozone Layer on 24 June 1988; it signed the Montreal Protocol on 15 September 1988 and ratified it on the same date.
7. The Kyoto Protocol, Background; see http://www.envocare.co.uk/kyoto_protocol.htm.
8. The Kyoto Protocol, Art. 3 read together with Annex A to the Protocol.
9. Note 3, Annex A to the Kyoto Protocol.
10. Copenhagen Accord, Art. 6: 'We recognize the crucial role of reducing emission from deforestation and forest degradation and the need to enhance removals of greenhouse gas emission by forests and agree on the need to provide positive incentives to such actions through the immediate establishment of a mechanism including REDD-plus, to enable the mobilization of financial resources from developed countries.' UNFCCC COP, Decision 2/CP.15, at http://unfccc.int/resource/docs/2009/cop15/eng/11a01.pdf.
11. Section 20 (D) Marrakech Accords 2001.
12. Note 3, Art. 12 (5).
13. Note 3, Art. 12 (5).
14. Note 3, Art. 12 (5).
15. MWLE (1994, p. 3).
16. The Constitution of the Republic of Uganda, 1995, Art. 245.
17. Note 16, Principle XIII.
18. The National Environment Act, Uganda, 2000 ('NE ACT').
19. The National Forestry and Tree Planting Act, 2003, s. 6 ('NFTP Act, 2003').

20. The policy therefore, by promoting the exploration of fossil fuels, is bound to reverse the benefits of carbon reduction derived from the implementation of various CDM projects under the energy sector.
21. The Constitution of Uganda, Republic of Uganda, 1995.
22. Note 21, Principle XXVII (iii).
23. The Electricity Act, Cap 145 of the Laws of Uganda.
24. The National Environment (Wetlands, River Banks and Lake Shores Management) Regulations, 2000,Statutory Instruments No. 3, 2000.
25. Note 24, Regulation 3.
26. Note 24, Regulation 5.

# REFERENCES

Akiiki, Magezi (2002), *Overview of Climate Change and its Impacts on Socio-economic Development in Uganda – Exploring the Past, Present and Future Trends*, Entebbe Uganda: Department of Meteorology.

Bakema, R.J. and L. Lyango (2000), 'Engaging Local Users in the Management of Wetland Resources: The Case of the National Wetlands Programme, Uganda', in E. Maltby (ed.), *The Wetlands Handbook*, Oxford: Blackwell.

Baumert, K.A., R. Bhandari and N. Kete (1999), *What Might a Developing Country Climate Commitment Look Like?*, Washington, DC: World Resources Institute.

Brown, K., E. Boyd, E. Corbera and W.N. Adger (2004), *How Do CDM Projects Contribute to Sustainable Development*, Tyndall Centre for Climate Change Research, Technical Report, Norwich University of East Anglia.

Carbon Emission Reduction Association (CERA) Uganda (2010), *Uganda Sustainable Projects*, at http://www.adrai.net/cera/rubriquec8fe.html?id_rubrique=11.

De Sadeleer, N. (2002), *Environmental Principles. From Political Slogans to Legal Rules*, Oxford: Oxford University Press.

Food and Agriculture Organization (FAO) (2006), *FAONewsroom*, 'Forests and Climate Change': see http://www.fao.org/newsroom/en/focus/2006/1000247/index.html.

Kasimbazi, E. (2005), 'In the Defence of Prosperity: Challenges of Implementing Clean Development Mechanisms in Uganda', in Ole Kristian Fauchald and Jacob Werksman (eds), *Yearbook of International Environmental Law*, Vol. 16, Oxford: Oxford University Press.

Kerr, Michael (2002), 'Tort Based Climate Change Litigation in Australia', A Discussion Paper Prepared for the Climate Change Litigation Forum London, March 2002 hosted by Friends of the Earth International: http://www.acfonline.org.au/uploads/res_climate_change_litigation.pdf.

Kusler, Jon (1999), *Climate Change in Wetland Areas Part II: Carbon Cycle Implications*, Berne, New York: Institute for Wetland Science and Public Policy: see http://www.usgcrp.gov/usgcrp/Library/nationalassessment/newsletter/1999.08/Wet.htm.

Metz, Bert, Stewart Ogunlade and Pan Jiahua (eds) (2001), *Climate Change 2001: Mitigation*, Contribution of Working Group III to the Third Assessment Report of the Intergovernmental Panel on Climate Change, Cambridge: Cambridge University Press.

Ministry of Agriculture, Animal Industry and Fisheries (MAAIF) (2002), *The Second National Report to the Conference of Parties on the Implementation of the United Nations Convention to Combat Desertification* (UNCCD) in Uganda, Entebbe, Uganda.

Ministry of Energy and Mineral Development (MEMD) (2002), *The Energy Policy for Uganda*.

Ministry of Finance Planning and Economic Development (MFPED) (1998), *Uganda Vision 2025: A Strategic Framework for National Development*.

Ministry of Water, Lands and Environment (MWLE) (1995), *The National Environment Action Plan*, Uganda.

Ministry of Water, Lands and Environment (MWLE) (2001), *The Uganda Forestry Policy*, Uganda.

National Environment Management Authority (NEMA) (2000/2001), *State of Environment Report 2000/2001*, Uganda.

National Environment Management Policy (NEMP) (1994), *The National Environment Management Policy for Uganda*, Ministry of Water, Lands and Environment, Uganda.

Orindi, Victor A. and Siri Eriksen (2005), 'Mainstreaming Adaptation to Climate Change in the Development Process in Uganda', *Ecopolicy* Series No. 15, African Centre for Technology Studies.

Republic of Uganda (1995), *National Policy for the Conservation and Management of Wetland Resources*, Uganda.

Republic of Uganda (2001), *The Wetland Sector Strategic Plan 2001–2010*, Uganda.

Republic of Uganda (2005), *The Uganda National Water Development Report*.

Rose, G. (2001), 'A compliance system for the Kyoto Protocol', *UNSW Law Journal*, 24 (2), 588.

United Nations Framework Convention on Climate Change (UNFCCC) (2002), Report of the Conference of the Parties on its Seventh Session, held in Marrakech 29 October–10 November (UNFCCC).

United Nations Framework Convention on Climate Change (UNFCCC/COP–13) (2007), conference held in Bali, December 2007 COP-13.

United Nations Industrial Development Organization (UNIDO) (2007), *Negotiating the Transfer and Acquisition of Project-based Carbon Credits under the Kyoto Protocol*, Vienna, UNIDO.

Waiswa, M.M. (2003), 'Strategic Choices for Enhancing Capacity of Rural Communities to Adapt to Climate Variability: The Case of Uganda', Contribution to the NOAA Office of Global Programs Workshop, *Insights and Tools for Adaptation, Learning from Climate Variability*, Washington, DC, 18–19 November 2003.

World Bank (2007), *State and Trends of the Carbon Market*, Washington, DC, May, 2007.

World Commission on Environment and Development (WCED) (1987), *Our Common Future*, Oxford: Oxford University Press.

PART FIVE

# Nature conservation and sustainability

# 19. Contractual tools for implementing the CBD in South Africa*

## Alexander Paterson

## 1. INTRODUCTION

South Africa, in common with fellow parties to the Convention on Biological Diversity,[1] has been grappling with designing a new legal regime to comply with its core international obligations as set out in the Convention's objectives. Those objectives are to conserve biological diversity, provide for the sustainable use of its components and ensure the fair and equitable sharing of the benefits derived from such use (Art. 1). This process culminated in the National Environmental Management: Biodiversity Act 2004 (hereafter Biodiversity Act). This Act regulates a broad range of issues such as biodiversity planning, threatened and protected ecosystems and species, alien invasive species, bio-prospecting, access and benefit-sharing. In addition, the National Environmental Management: Protected Areas Act 2003 (hereafter Protected Areas Act) prescribes the country's new protected areas regime. Cumulatively, they encompass South Africa's attempt to give domestic effect to the Convention on Biological Diversity.

These laws are a clear acknowledgement that the Government cannot alone halt the rapid demise of the nation's biodiversity. The public, including individuals, community associations, non-profit institutions and legal entities engaged in public benefit activities, are recognised as indispensable allies in this process. Subsumed within the broad principle of public participation are two further principles: the need to move away from the traditional exclusionary approach to conservation to a contemporary human-centred approach that recognises that one cannot divorce people from conservation and protection from sustainable use; and the need to shift from the traditional command-and-control approach to a more cooperative incentive-based approach.

The signing of the Convention on Biological Diversity initiated the shift in thinking about biodiversity regulation, which is now reflected in the Biodiversity Act and the Protected Areas Act. This chapter critiques the manner in which South Africa's new biodiversity regime seeks to implement the human-centred, incentive-based approach to biodiversity regulation through innovative contractual arrangements aimed at enabling active public participation.

## 2.  THE TRADITIONAL APPROACH TO BIODIVERSITY REGULATION

### Overview of the Traditional Approach

South Africa ranks as the world's third most biologically diverse country (Wynberg, 2002, p. 233), but this biodiversity is one of the most threatened on the planet.[2] Although occupying less than 2 per cent of the world's land surface, it is home to nearly 10 per cent of the world's plant species and 7 per cent of the world's reptile, bird and mammal species.[3] This rich biological diversity is, however, one of the most threatened on the planet (ibid.). In an assessment of the nation's biological resources, 34 per cent of terrestrial ecosystems, 82 per cent of significant rivers and 67 per cent of marine bio-zones were classified as threatened (Driver et al., 2005b).[4] In addition, 50 per cent of South Africa's wetlands have been destroyed (Kotze et al., 1995) and many species situated within and outside these ecosystems have been identified as vulnerable, endangered or critically endangered.[5] Recent assessments have indicated that approximately 10 per cent of South Africa's birds and frogs, 20 per cent of its mammals (Friedmann and Daly, 2004; Minter et al., 2004) and 36 per cent of its freshwater fish are threatened (Driver et al., 2005a). Currently being reassessed, some 10 per cent of the country's plant species are threatened with extinction (ibid.).

These statistics are somewhat surprising given the enactment of a complex network of laws to regulate the numerous threats posed to South Africa's biological resources in the past few decades.[6] These laws have generally adopted traditional legal approaches to conserving and managing biodiversity, namely protected area regimes and species regimes.

Approximately 6 per cent of South Africa's terrestrial environment and 19 per cent of the marine environment have been accorded formal protected areas status. Prior to the Protected Areas Act, 20 laws provided for the designation of over 25 different types of protected areas.[7] This specific protected areas legislation is supplemented by an array of national[8] and provincial planning laws and municipal zoning schemes, which have secured additional land for conservation. Each province in South Africa has promulgated its own Planning Ordinance or Act to regulate planning at provincial level. Zoning schemes, developed and implemented by local government, currently provide for a range of land-use categories, including open space. Land zoned as 'open space' is typically reserved for nature reserves and conservation use. Development is subject to strict control and generally requires an environmental authorisation preceded by an environmental impact assessment.

Species regimes, by which various species of fauna or flora are listed and activities are strictly regulated are also prevalent. The lists of species and permitting arrangements are found in national and provincial legislation.[9] A licence is generally required prior to undertaking any activity that may impact on a listed species. Finally, various laws identify activities and permitting arrangements generally, or in respect of certain specific areas, which may negatively impact on South Africa's biodiversity.[10] Listed activities generally require formal authorisation and environmental impact assessment.

## Key challenges facing the traditional approach

Notwithstanding this extensive network of laws which preceded the enactment of the Biodiversity Act and the Protected Areas Act, the decline of South Africa's biological resources continued at an alarming rate, partly due to South Africa's ineffective and outdated regulatory framework (Kumleben et al., 1998); (Hanks and Glavovic, 1992, pp. 712–714). Contributing factors included: a lack of political will; the absence of an adequate planning framework; legislative and institutional fragmentation; capacity and resource constraints; reliance on command-and-control strategies; and the adoption of an exclusionary approach to conservation. The latter three are central when considering the role of the public as vital actors in biodiversity regulation.

## Capacity and resource constraints

Biodiversity conservation is an expensive exercise. Associated expenses include: developing strategic planning frameworks; identifying and monitoring the status of vital biological resources; formulating policy and legislation to manage these resources; funding administration, compliance and enforcement; securing land for inclusion within protected areas; managing the biological resources situated both within and outside these areas; and increasing public awareness. Raising sufficient funds is a significant challenge especially where competing socioeconomic imperatives are prioritised over environmental concerns. This is evident in South Africa's decreasing national budgetary allocation to biodiversity conservation over the past 15 years. In 1996, only 0.28 per cent of the national budget was directly allocated to biodiversity conservation (Kumleben et al., 1998, pp. 32–34) decreasing to 0.08 per cent in 2008.[11] This significantly undermined the ability of key national and provincial institutions to implement and enforce biodiversity legislation. For example, obligations imposed on landowners to clear alien invasive vegetation under the Conservation of Agricultural Resources Act have not resulted in one conviction despite the fact that alien invasive vegetation poses one of the greatest threats to the nation's biodiversity (Preston and Siegfried, 1995, p. 49). It has also significantly impacted on the Government's ability to properly administer South Africa's protected areas. Some management responsibilities have been neglected placing many protected areas in jeopardy (Kumleben et al., 1998, p. 37).[12] Given that funding will not be significantly increased soon and given the fallacy of protected areas becoming economically self sufficient, the Government has recognised the need to identify alternative sources of funding (ibid., p. 31 and pp. 37–39).

The Government has confirmed its commitment to increase the proportion of terrestrial territory situated in protected areas from 6 per cent to 10 per cent.[13] With the decreasing availability of suitable state-owned land, the focus is now on privately owned land, which constitutes 84 per cent of the country's territory. This land is often of high premium, and the Government has thus created alternative mechanisms to enable, and incentives to encourage, the incorporation of privately owned land within protected areas, and to share the management costs with willing conservation organisations, local communities and individuals (Crowe, 1996, p. 218).

## Reliance on the command-and-control approach

A further problem, integrally associated with these resource and capacity constraints, has been the Government's historic reliance on the command-and-control approach to biodiversity regulation. The majority of laws which preceded the introduction of the country's contemporary conservation regime prescribe a range of legislative standards, prohibitions and restrictions.[14] Non-compliance is generally subject to potential prosecution and sanction.

However, as has been identified both internationally (Pearce et al., 1989; Bruce and Ellis, 1993; James 1997; Milne et al., 2003; Wilke, 2005) and domestically (Stauth and Baskind, 1992; Henderson, 1994, p. 50; Paterson, 2005a, p. 182; Paterson, 2005b, p. 97; Paterson, 2006, p. 1), wholesale reliance on this command-and-control approach in any regulatory context is problematic. High costs associated with the administration, compliance and enforcement of direct regulation often plagues effective implementation. Prescribed standards, prohibitions and restrictions are frequently inflexible and unable to cater for geographical, sectoral or individual specificities. In addition, the command-and-control approach does not generally facilitate and encourage voluntary initiatives.

These problems played out very vividly in the context of biodiversity regulation in South Africa. Funding direct regulation was not possible and given the diversity of species, ecosystems, threats and stakeholders, inflexible regulation proved unworkable. As the majority of biological resources are on privately owned land, the failure to facilitate and encourage extensive voluntary public action was unviable. The Government was therefore compelled to reassess its regulatory approach and consider a more cooperative and incentive-based approach aimed at enabling and encouraging the public to become active participants in biodiversity regulation.

**Adoption of an exclusionary approach**

The Government's traditional approach to biodiversity regulation was largely based on the premise that effective conservation required the exclusion of the public. The result saw the alienation of conservation from people, and people from conservation, which was particularly clearly reflected in the previous protected areas legislation. Express provision for public participation in the formation and management of protected areas was almost entirely absent, as too was recognition of the need to ensure equitable access, use and benefit sharing. Protected areas were often established on land formerly owned or occupied by local communities who were frequently displaced and denied access and use rights (Kumleben et al., 1998; Summers, 1999, p. 189). This problem was not confined, however, to within the borders of protected areas. With the majority of South Africa's territory being privately owned by the white minority (a result of *apartheid* land policies), the bulk of the population had no opportunity to access and use the nation's biological resources. Conservation therefore became regarded as an elitist concern, the 'preserve of the privileged members of society' (Kumleben et al., 1998, p. 42), and protected areas, the 'playgrounds for the privileged elite'.[15]

This exclusionary approach was subject to extensive domestic criticism. Commentators argued that it was unsustainable, especially in a developing economy such as South Africa where broad sectors of society were dependent on accessing biological resources to sustain their livelihoods (Summers, 1999, p. 258). Calls were made for the introduction of a more human-centred approach to biodiversity regulation, with a focus on community-based natural resource management (Summers, 1999, p. 191; Mandondo, 2005). It was urged that in order for such an approach to be successfully implemented in South Africa, both within and outside of protected areas, genuine proprietorship, with the right to use resources and determine the mode of usage, distribution of such benefits and rules of access, had to be granted to local communities (Murphree, 1991). In the context of protected areas, critics argued that public participation needed to extend to determining reserve boundaries, preparing management plans and sharing in the economic benefits derived from their establishment (Bothma and Glavovic, 1992, p. 258).

In light of the above domestic concern and growing international acceptance of the view that effective regulation of biodiversity must be socially and economically relevant and requires public support and co-operation, as recognised within many international conventions and policy documents,[16] the Government acknowledged the need to shift away from the traditional exclusionary approach (Summers, 1999, pp. 55–57).

**Towards a More Sustainable Regulatory Approach**

To guide its formulation of a novel biodiversity regime, the Government commissioned various policy papers and reports, the most notable of which are the White Paper on Biodiversity[17] and the Report of the Board of Investigation into the Institutional Arrangements for Nature Conservation in South Africa.[18] These documents reflected many of the above criticisms and advocated a fundamental shift in approach to biodiversity regulation 'from preservation to conservation and sustainable use; from exclusivity to participation and sharing; ... from fences and fines to incentives and individual responsibility'.[19]

This approach is now embodied in the Biodiversity Act and the Protected Areas Act, which in turn give domestic effect to the Government's obligations under the Convention on Biological Diversity by cumulatively providing for: national biodiversity strategies, plans and programmes (Art. 6); identification and monitoring procedures for protecting important components of biological diversity and regulating activities which may negatively impact on them (Art. 7); a range of *in-situ* and *ex-situ* conservation mechanisms (Arts. 8 and 9); the sustainable use of components of biological diversity (Art. 1); impact assessment and minimisation (Art. 14); access to genetic resources (Art. 16); and the handling of biotechnology and distribution of its benefits (Art. 19). A key tool prescribed in the Biodiversity Act and the Protected Areas Act for overcoming the problems inherent in South Africa's old biodiversity regime, and for practically implementing the above components of the Convention on Biological Diversity, is a range of novel contractual arrangements. It is to these that the focus of this chapter now shifts.

## 3.   A NOVEL REGIME UNDER THE BIODIVERSITY ACT

The Biodiversity Act is the Government's first attempt to regulate the nation's biological resources in a holistic manner and fundamentally reforms the traditional approach to biodiversity regulation. The Act appoints the Government as the trustee of South Africa's biodiversity. Underpinning its implementation is a three-tier planning framework to manage biodiversity that comprises a national biodiversity framework, bioregional plans and biodiversity management plans.

Against this framework, the Act regulates a broad range of issues relevant to biodiversity. First, it provides for the declaration of threatened and protected ecosystems and species by regulation. Once declared, activities that may threaten or impact on these ecosystems or species are restricted in various ways. Secondly, it regulates species and organisms that pose potential threats to biodiversity, such as alien species, invasive species and genetically modified organisms. The Act lists a range of restricted activities relating to these species and organisms that cannot be undertaken without permission, and imposes a broad duty of care on persons who are so permitted. Thirdly, it regulates the vexed issue of bio-prospecting, access and benefit sharing. This is principally achieved through permitting schemes that must be preceded by benefit-sharing agreements or material transfer agreements, and the establishment of a Bio-prospecting Trust Fund to hold and distribute all money generated from these agreements. Finally, the Biodiversity Act provides for the establishment and functions of the South African National Biodiversity Institute to assist the Government in future biodiversity planning and regulation.

In acknowledgement of the failings of the previous regime, the Biodiversity Act provides various opportunities for the public to become active participants in its implementation. These take the form of two key contractual schemes: the first relating to the implementation of the biodiversity planning framework; and the second, to bio-prospecting.

## Contractual Tools for Facilitating Biodiversity Management

One of the most significant improvements introduced by the Biodiversity Act is the prescription of a three-tier planning framework at national, regional and local level.

First, the Minister of Environmental Affairs and Tourism is required to prescribe a national biodiversity framework to provide an integrated, co-ordinated and uniform approach to biodiversity management at all levels. This framework, complemented by a National Spatial Biodiversity Assessment (2005) and National Biodiversity Strategy and Action Plan (2005), was promulgated in 2007. Secondly, the Minister or relevant provincial MEC responsible for environmental affairs may determine certain geographical regions as bioregions and publish bioregional plans for the management of the biodiversity in the region. No such plans have been declared to date.

Although these provide a vital planning context, it is the third tier of the planning framework, namely biodiversity management plans, that holds the real potential for facilitating public participation in the management of biological resources. Any person, organisation or organ of state wishing to contribute to biodiversity management may submit to the Minister a biodiversity management plan for an ecosystem, indigenous species or migratory species in need of protection. The biodiversity management plan must be aimed at ensuring the long-term survival in nature of the species or ecosystem to which the plan relates and must be consistent with the national biodiversity framework and any applicable bioregional plan. The Minister must identify a suitable entity to be responsible for implementing the plan, must assign responsibility to it for doing so, and may enter into a biodiversity management agreement with it to regulate its practical implementation.

These biodiversity management agreements provide the practical tool for engaging public support and action. The public can enter into these potentially vast agreements with relevant authorities. Parties can include government authorities, individual landowners, landowner associations, communities and conservation organisations. The core function of these agreements could relate to formally listed threatened and protected species and ecosystems as well as unlisted species and ecosystems deemed worthy of special conservation attention. The form and content is not yet prescribed. Although potentially proving to be an important tool for facilitating public participation in biodiversity management both within and outside the borders of protected areas, no such agreement has been concluded to date.

### Prerequisites for the Success of Biodiversity Management Agreements

### Raising public awareness

Ignorance often undermines implementation. Prescribing a statutory framework for biodiversity management agreements may therefore prove ineffective in the absence of an extensive public awareness campaign. Given the significant proportion of land, and accordingly biological resources, they currently own, this campaign should target private landowners. In the absence of public awareness, these valuable tools may remain 'paper potentials'.

The Government has recognised the need for such an environmental awareness campaign and launched *Indalo Yethu* ('our environment') to promote, encourage and support responsible environmental actions, programmes and projects. Although still a fledgling initiative, it would appear to provide the ideal vehicle for promoting awareness about biodiversity management agreements.

## Prescribing planning frameworks

Biodiversity management agreements are aimed at implementing biodiversity management plans. In the absence of the latter, the former are unviable. Concerted effort therefore needs to be invested to facilitate the development of biodiversity management plans, which can be initiated by the public.

These biodiversity management plans are in turn primarily aimed at managing ecosystems and species which are listed as threatened or in need of protection under the Biodiversity Act. In the absence of these lists, the potential of biodiversity management plans and, accordingly, biodiversity management agreements, may be undermined. Although certain species have been listed recently, no ecosystems have been listed to date. Provision is, however, also made for biodiversity management plans and hence biodiversity management agreements to relate to the management of unlisted species and ecosystems 'warranting special conservation attention'.

## Clarifying contractual formalities

The nature and form of these agreements are currently undefined. Although creating flexibility which should enable the public to tailor any agreement to suit the location, target and nature of their intended action, it may ultimately lead to uncertainty and public inaction. The prescription of additional formalities through regulation or guidelines regarding the nature and form of these agreements would be beneficial.

## Providing incentives

A very small sector of the public generally undertakes voluntary action for purely philanthropic reasons. The creation of an environment which rewards the public for concluding biodiversity management agreements therefore appears to be a further prerequisite for their widespread use. Although incentives in the form of tax deductions are currently available in certain conservation contexts, these do not extend to costs incurred by persons implementing biodiversity management agreements. The Government has recognised this as a distinct possibility for future implementation (Paterson, 2005a, p. 201).[20]

## Contractual Tools for Regulating Bio-prospecting

Prior to the commencement of the Biodiversity Act, bio-prospecting was largely unregulated. Factors which led the Government to recognise the need for extensive regulation of this burgeoning industry include: the proliferation of bio-prospecting initiatives in South Africa; the problematic benefit-sharing arrangements associated with these initiatives; the failure of the country's intellectual property regime to adequately and equitably regulate these initiatives; the need to regulate the flow of South Africa's valuable biological capital out of its borders; and the potential economic value of bio-prospecting initiatives to traditional communities and the country as a whole.

The Biodiversity Act prescribes a comprehensive set of contractual arrangements to regulate bio-prospecting involving 'indigenous biological resources', the export of indigenous biological resources from South Africa, and the fair and equitable sharing of benefits derived from these activities. A permit is required prior to undertaking bio-prospecting involving indigenous biological resources or exporting from South Africa any indigenous biological resources for the purpose of bio-prospecting, making sure that the interests of various stakeholders are adequately protected. Several of the prescribed protective mechanisms are based in contract.

The applicant must have entered into a material transfer agreement that regulates the provision of or access to the indigenous biological resources, and have concluded a benefit-sharing agreement with relevant stakeholders that provides for the sharing of any future benefits derived from the relevant bio-prospecting activity.

No permits may be issued to undertake any form of bio-prospecting prior to the conclusion of the above agreements. The agreements must be preceded by full disclosure of all material information and the prior consent of relevant stakeholders. Provision is made for the Minister to exempt indigenous biological resources or bio-prospecting activities from the above scheme. This process must, however, be preceded by extensive public consultation to ensure that the bio-prospecting regime is not avoided. The Regulations on Bio-prospecting, Access and Benefit-sharing[21] govern the implementation of the above scheme.

### Prerequisites for the Success of Bio-prospecting Agreements

#### Clarifying contractual formalities

Given the often controversial nature of bio-prospecting activities, stringent guidance regarding the form, content and procedures for concluding the above agreements appears essential. Although being fairly explicit on the mandatory content for benefit-sharing and material transfer agreements, the Biodiversity Act provides inadequate guidance on the procedure for concluding these agreements. Additional procedural formalities are contained in the Bio-prospecting Regulations, which include pro-forma material transfer and benefit-sharing agreements.

In addition, provision for regular monitoring and review appears essential. Bio-prospecting activities are often long-term enterprises that are significantly influenced by variations in technology and market conditions. Accordingly, any contractual scheme that seeks to regulate such concerns needs to be able to cater for these changing conditions. The Biodiversity Act provides for the regular review of benefit-sharing agreements but not material transfer agreements. However, the omission of the latter agreements does not appear problematic, as these are different in nature, regulating the initial transfer of indigenous biological material and not the long-term benefits associated with its commercial application.

### Identifying stakeholders

The Biodiversity Act prescribes that bio-prospecting applicants must conclude material transfer agreements and benefit-sharing agreements with all relevant stakeholders. Although these stakeholders are defined in the Act, their identification in practice may prove problematic, given the collective and oral nature of 'indigenous knowledge'. 'Indigenous use or knowledge' is defined in the Bio-prospecting Regulations to include 'knowledge of, discoveries about or the traditional use of indigenous biological resources, if that knowledge, discovery or use has initiated or will contribute to or form part of a proposed bio-prospecting or research project to which an application for a permit relates'. Additional issues associated with the identification of stakeholders include: the potential desire of all, even those with fringe interests, to be party to these potentially lucrative arrangements; the interwoven and migratory nature of many relevant indigenous communities; language and capacity constraints; and differing and overlapping land-tenure systems.

Fortunately, the draft Bio-prospecting Regulations contain additional principles for identifying stakeholders. One factor which may, however, undermine the interests of various stakeholders, particularly relevant indigenous communities, is that 'community' is defined as 'a coherent, social group of persons, or a part of such a group, that is organised in terms of a democratically agreed founding document that protects the rights and interests of each member of the community'. Although aspiring to the ideal of democracy, many relevant communities are not currently organised in terms of 'democratically agreed founding documents' which would therefore disqualify them as potential stakeholders. Care therefore needs to be exercised in redefining the principles. Alternatively, efforts will need to be made to rapidly formalise the governance structures of all relevant indigenous communities in South Africa.

### Ensuring equitability in negotiations

Bio-prospecting ventures are often based on indigenous knowledge held by traditional communities. These communities are potentially at a significant disadvantage when entering into negotiations with large, well-resourced and influential bio-prospecting companies. Minimising the potentially negative impact of inequitable power imbalances therefore becomes a key prerequisite for ensuring the success of the contractual scheme. The Biodiversity Act provides for various safeguards in this regard. Both material transfer and benefit-sharing agreements are subject to Ministerial oversight and approval. Provision is made for full disclosure of all material information relevant to the bio-prospecting activity to relevant stakeholders. In addition, authorities are empowered to engage the relevant parties on the terms of any such agreement, facilitate negotiations and, when requested by the Minister, to ensure that the terms of any relevant agreement are fair and equitable. The latter aspect is reinforced in the Bio-prospecting Regulations which prescribe detailed criteria for both forms of agreements and provide that the Minister must be satisfied that such agreements are fair and equitable to all parties before approving them.

If properly implemented, the above mechanisms should mitigate the impact of any power imbalances between the contracting parties. However, an extensive public awareness campaign is required, especially amongst traditional communities, to raise awareness of the existence of the above bio-prospecting regime and the value of indigenous biological resources and knowledge. This could similarly be implemented through the *Indalo Yethu* initiative mentioned above.

**Public oversight vs confidentiality**

Public oversight provides a further valuable mechanism for ensuring fairness and equitability, as well as ensuring that all relevant stakeholders are party to negotiations. Although the Biodiversity Act does not itself provide for such oversight, the Bio-prospecting Regulations enable the Minister to invite public comment prior to approving a benefit-sharing agreement. This public oversight is unfortunately discretionary in nature and only relates to benefit-sharing agreements. In addition, the ambit of potential public participation is further limited in that the Minister may only invite public comment on the agreement to the extent that no 'confidential information' is disclosed – a term which is so broadly defined that it effectively nullifies the commenting procedure.

**Monitoring compliance**

The financial interests of stakeholders and bio-prospectors will be regulated in the material transfer and benefit-sharing agreements. As traditional communities will frequently be a party to such agreements, some form of Government oversight for the duration of the contract is desirable. Otherwise the entire purpose of such agreements may be undermined, particularly where indigenous communities are a party thereto and do not have the capacity or resources to monitor and enforce compliance.

**Aligning the intellectual property regime**

The Patents Act 1978 regulates applications for patents in South Africa and operates as a double-edged sword in the context of protecting indigenous biological resources and indigenous knowledge. First, the requirement for registering a patent effectively precludes the protection of indigenous biological resources and indigenous knowledge.[22]

Further, the products of bio-prospecting activities based on these biological resources and/or indigenous knowledge are patentable, which may create the undesirable scenario of the developer securing lucrative proprietary rights over the product to the exclusion of those contributing to its development. It is therefore imperative that some link be forged between the environmental regime and the intellectual property regime so as to ensure that any prospective patents based on indigenous biological resources or indigenous knowledge are subject to the benefit-sharing arrangements in the Biodiversity Act.

The Government has recently moved to create checks and balances of this nature. In terms of the Patents Amendment Act 2005, which is yet to come into force, patent applicants must disclose whether or not the invention for which protection is claimed is based on or derived from an indigenous biological resource, genetic resource, traditional knowledge or use. If the invention is derived from such information, the authorities will require proof of the applicant's title or authority to make use of it, which includes: securing the prior informed consent of all relevant stakeholders; concluding a material transfer and/or benefit-sharing agreement; securing the approval of these agreements from the Minister; and obtaining a permit under the Biodiversity Act. In addition, the Patents Amendment Act enables the authorities to revoke any patent if the applicant made a false statement or representation in the above regard. These provisions, once implemented, should complement the bio-prospecting agreements prescribed under the Biodiversity Act and minimise the threat of bio-piracy.

## 4. A NOVEL REGIME UNDER THE PROTECTED AREAS ACT

The second component of the nation's new biodiversity regime is the Protected Areas Act. It introduces a fundamental shift in approach to establishing and managing protected areas in South Africa as is evident from the express objectives of the Act, which include: providing for a representative network of protected areas on state, private and communal land; promoting the sustainable utilisation of protected areas for the benefit of the people; and promoting the participation of local communities in the management of protected areas.

The Government is similarly appointed as the trustee of South Africa's protected areas. The Act preserves the validity of various forms of current protected areas including: provincial protected areas under provincial conservation ordinances and Acts; world heritage sites under the World Heritage Convention Act 1999; marine protected areas under the Marine Living Resources Act 1998; forest nature reserves and forest wilderness areas under the National Forests Act 1998; and mountain catchment areas under the Mountain Catchment Areas Act 1970.

The Act simultaneously provides for the declaration of four additional types of protected areas: special nature reserves;[23] national parks;[24] nature reserves[25] and protected environments.[26] Protected areas can generally be declared in respect of private land if the owner has consented to the declaration by way of written agreement. Provision is made for these agreements to be registered against the title deeds of the private property, which makes them binding on successive owners.

The authorities are required to assign the management of the protected area to a management authority which must prepare and submit a management plan for approval. The contents of the management plan will effectively identify the conservation-related activities to be undertaken by the management authority. Provision is made for monitoring compliance with these plans and restricting various activities in these areas. Finally, the Protected Areas Act sets out the powers and functions of South African National Parks (SANParks), the authority responsible for managing the nation's national parks.

The Protected Areas Act specifically directs that its implementation must take place in partnership with the people. Accordingly, the Act prescribes a range of contractual tools which provide for the incorporation of privately-owned land within protected areas, public management of protected areas, public access and use rights in respect of biological resources situated within protected areas, and the equitable sharing of benefits derived from such use.

### Contractual Tools for Incorporating Private Land within Protected Areas

Prior to the Protected Areas Act, predominantly state-owned land was converted to protected areas. However, as indicated above, owing to the unavailability of state-owned land, and in order to attain its international targets, the Government has sought to acquire private land. Owing to funding constraints, alternative mechanisms have been introduced to incorporate private land within all four types of protected areas.

Either party can instigate agreements between private landowners and the Government, and the agreement is registered against the title deed of the property. This effectively constitutes the Government's first attempt to recognise the notion of conservation servitudes in South Africa.

Very few agreements have been concluded to date, partly due to: their novelty; a lack of clarity regarding their form, content and procedures for conclusion; delays in the development of the biodiversity planning framework essential for identifying land worthy of incorporation; and a failure to effectively 'market' them.

## Prerequisites for the Success of Land Incorporation Agreements

### Clarifying contractual formalities

Although creating a vital tool for incorporating private land within the protected area network, the Act is unfortunately very vague on the content, nature and form of these agreements. It is unclear whether the content of these agreements should vary across different forms of protected areas and, if so, how; and whether they should only record the formal consent to incorporate private land or extend to cover issues such as management responsibilities, land-use restrictions, management costs, income distribution and commercial activities. It is also unclear whether: the agreements constitute a form of servitude and, if so, what type of servitude; the entire agreement, or only certain terms thereof, need be recorded against the title deeds of the property concerned; and what formal procedures need to be followed to effect Deeds Office registration and endorsement.

The Protected Areas Act does enable the Government to clarify these issues by way of regulation but the Regulations for the Proper Administration of Special Nature Reserves, National Parks and World Heritage Sites[27] (Protected Areas Regulations) unfortunately provide no clarity on the issue.

### Identifying priority areas

Given the scarcity of available resources, conservation efforts need to be directed at land of high conservation value. A key prerequisite for implementing the land incorporation agreements is therefore biodiversity planning through which priority areas and species are mapped, enabling the authorities to identify which private land should be targeted.

The Government has made progress with the national biodiversity planning process, including the publication of the National Biodiversity Framework, National Spatial Biodiversity Assessment, National Biodiversity Strategy and Action Plan and the Threatened and Protected Species Regulations. However, key components of the planning scheme yet to be finalised are the identification of bioregions, the formulation of bioregional plans and the listing of threatened ecosystems.

## Marketing the agreements

Failing to properly promote the virtues of any new product may undermine its successful introduction into the market. This principle similarly applies to the land incorporation agreements. Owing to their novelty, effort is required to raise public awareness about the existence of these agreements and potential benefits accruing to landowners who conclude them. The Government's *Indalo Yethu* Programme could once again be used for such an initiative. The Government has recently identified the need to develop and support provincial initiatives encouraging public biodiversity stewardship through various mechanisms such as land-incorporation agreements under the National Biodiversity Framework.

In addition, owing to the fact that private landowners will effectively forego development opportunities on land contracted into protected areas, it may be necessary to reward those landowners entering such agreements. One of the more successful international approaches in this regard is the use of fiscal instruments, such as tax incentives (Paterson, 2005a). South Africa's recently amended property tax regime, the Local Government: Municipal Property Rates Act 2004, offers various incentives to landowners who contract their land into protected areas. These take the form of various property tax rebates, reductions, exemptions and prohibitions. These incentives are, however, limited in their ambit and plagued by anomalies, which require urgent resolution (Paterson, 2005b). There are also numerous additional forms of tax incentives that could be used to facilitate public participation such as donations tax, estate duty and transfer duty. Recent policy documents have recognised the importance of implementing incentives of this nature.

## Contractual Tools for Managing Protected Areas

The second manner in which the Government has sought to enter into partnerships with the public relates to managing protected areas. Once established, the Government must assign the management of the protected area to a management authority, with the concurrence of the prospective management authority. The range of entities to which this function can be assigned includes suitable persons, organisations and organs of state, thereby enabling the Government to devolve the management of protected areas to the public where appropriate.

A management authority must submit a comprehensive management plan to the Government for approval. The protected area must be managed in accordance with the management plan and the Protected Areas Act, read together with its Regulations, prescribes a range of mandatory and discretionary content.

Although the Protected Areas Act does not provide for the conclusion of a formal contract between the Government and the management authority, it in fact constitutes a form of contractual relationship, a 'management agreement', in that: the management authority must agree to its appointment; the management plan sets out the reciprocal obligations of the Government and the management authority; the content of the management plan needs to be approved by both parties; and provision is made for the termination of the management relationship if the appointed management authority fails to comply with the plan's terms.

These management agreements provide an important mechanism for the Government to share the responsibility and cost of managing South Africa's protected areas with the public, a function which historically fell within its exclusive purview. The prescribed content of the management agreements also reflects an express recognition by the Government of the need to move towards a more human centred approach to conservation and to manage protected areas within their broader socioeconomic context.

## Prerequisites for the Success of Management Agreements

### Clarifying contractual formalities

Although a few details regarding the form, content and procedure for concluding these management agreements are prescribed in the Protected Areas Act, read together with the Protected Areas Regulations, these are unfortunately far too vague and will no doubt cause uncertainty. As with the array of contracts discussed above, uncertainty may lead to disuse and therefore the prescription of detailed guidance regarding these issues appears warranted.

### Aligning planning frameworks

Given that protected areas are one of the practical tools for implementing biodiversity planning frameworks, it would have been nonsensical for individual protected areas management plans to be at odds with relevant local, provincial and national plans. The Protected Areas Act provides for the mandatory alignment of management plans with all relevant biodiversity-planning frameworks and compels management authorities to consult all relevant organs of the state, local communities and other affected parties when preparing such plans.

## Flexibility vs coherence

South Africa's protected areas differ significantly biologically, topographically and climatically, and are subject to differing environmental, social and economic challenges. The management agreements should ideally be sufficiently flexible to cater for varying specificities. Although the Protected Areas Act is very flexible regarding the authorities appointed to manage these areas and the content of the management plans, it needs to be counterbalanced against the need for consistency and coherence. Similar types of protected areas should be subject to similar management, and similar management authorities should be subject to similar obligations. The Protected Areas Act includes an array of mechanisms to achieve such consistency. Management plans are subject to government oversight and approval, must comply with prescribed guidelines and relevant planning frameworks, and have prescribed mandatory and discretionary content. These mechanisms should ensure the desired level of consistency. However, owing to the exclusion of a number of other types of protected areas from the ambit of the Act's management regime, their management remains subject to inconsistent regulation under a fragmented array of laws[28] and, in certain circumstances, no regulation at all.[29] In the interests of promoting consistent and coherent governance, perhaps consideration should be given to including all forms of protected area within the ambit of the Protected Areas Act with provision being made for differential management formalities for areas of differential status.

## Periodic review

Given the potential long-term nature of management agreements and the fact that management imperatives change over time, the terms of management plans and the performance of management authorities should be subject to periodic review. A failure to do so could lead to inappropriate management or mismanagement.

The Protected Areas Act empowers the authorities to establish indicators for monitoring the management of protected areas. This provides a valuable tool for frequently reviewing management performance and provision is made for the amendment of management plans by agreement. SANParks has developed a biodiversity management reporting system for national parks although it has not been formally prescribed under the Protected Areas Act. The Government could draw from this valuable SANParks initiative and implement similar national and provincial reporting systems across other national, provincial and local protected areas.

The above review and reporting process, once formally prescribed, may uncover instances of mismanagement which warrant serious sanction. In this regard the Protected Areas Act provides effectively for the termination of management agreements.

## Co-opting public support

As with all the above contractual mechanisms, raising public awareness about their existence is essential. In addition, given resource constraints, serious consideration needs to be given to financial mechanisms to support management authorities, especially where these responsibilities are undertaken by the public. A failure to do so may see the above termination provisions being frequently invoked, as the public is effectively precluded from undertaking effective management owing to financial constraints. The result could see the management of all protected areas reverting to the state, which would undermine the entire tenor of South Africa's new regime aimed at effecting implementation in partnership with the people.

## Providing for co-management

One protected area may frequently incorporate land owned by many different people. Furthermore, many stakeholders may have complementary or competing interests in the resources located within a protected area. The Protected Areas Act recognises this potential and therefore makes provision for management authorities to conclude co-management agreements with organs of state, local communities or individuals to co-manage the protected area. These co-management agreements can provide for the apportionment of income generated; the use of biological resources within the area; access; occupation of the protected area; development of economic activities within and adjacent to the protected area; development of local management capacity; and knowledge exchange.

The Government has taken significant strides in the past several years to practically implement the Protected Areas Act's management provisions. Various co-management agreements have been concluded but these relate primarily to national parks. A concerted effort is required to ensure that similar initiatives are undertaken in respect of the many other forms of protected areas regulated under the Act.

## Contractual Tools for Facilitating Access, Sustainable Use and Benefit Sharing Within Protected Areas

In line with the shift away from an exclusionary approach to conservation, the Protected Areas Act expressly recognises the need to entrench a more human-centred approach to conservation within South Africa's protected areas. This is reflected in the objectives of the Protected Areas Act and the purposes for which protected areas can be declared. Inherent in this approach is the need to enable the public to access, use and share any benefits derived from the use of natural resources situated within protected areas, using an array of contractual tools, the availability and applicability of which is dependent on a person's relationship to the land.

For private landowners, the land incorporation agreements will principally regulate such issues. Where the person has been appointed the area's manager, it will principally be the management agreements that will regulate them. However, individuals and communities may frequently not be the owners or managers of the land, and in these circumstances, their interests could be significantly prejudiced by the incorporation of the land within a protected area. The Protected Areas Act prescribes an array of additional contractual mechanisms that can be used to potentially mitigate this scenario.

It will frequently be land incorporation, management and co-management agreements which regulate access, use and benefit-sharing issues and accordingly all the prerequisites associated with these contractual mechanisms will be relevant. There are, however, various additional issues which may impact on their potential.

## Prerequisites for the Success of Access, Use and Benefit-sharing Agreements

### Promoting uniformity and clarity

Given the broad array of agreements that may be relevant to regulating access, use and benefit-sharing issues within protected areas, perhaps it would be advisable to prescribe detailed substantive and procedural guidelines or regulations to promote certainty, consistency and equity across all relevant contractual schemes. Although the Government has recently published *Guidelines for the Implementation of Community-based Natural Resource Management in South Africa*,[30] they lack the necessary specificity and therefore require comprehensive revision or the promulgation of complementary guidelines or regulations.

### Rethinking discretions and overcoming power imbalances

Individuals and local communities appear to be well placed to protect their interests where they own the land in question or are appointed as the management authority. However, where they are not, their ability to do so is very tenuous, as the use of the majority of these contractual mechanisms falls to the discretion of the management authority, including: the content of the management plans; the conclusion of co-management agreements; and the conclusion of agreements regulating community activities within national parks, nature reserves and world heritage sites.

An associated concern relates to the relative bargaining power of parties seeking to conclude agreements of this nature. Where a management authority does elect to use these contractual tools, existing power imbalances may undermine the ability of individuals and local communities to protect their interests, as public and governmental oversight occurs only in limited circumstances. Additional mechanisms are therefore required to increase Government authority to oversee and in appropriate circumstances intervene to compel the use of these contractual mechanisms and ensure that the terms thereof are fair and equitable. One method of doing so would be to include such procedures in the guidelines or regulations proposed above.

## Extending application

The provisions regulating access, use and benefit sharing generally only apply to protected areas declared under the Protected Areas Act. A failure to extend the scheme to protected areas declared under other laws may undermine the goal of fostering a human-centred approach to conservation throughout South Africa.[31] In addition, the application of various access, use and benefit-sharing provisions are limited to certain forms of areas declared under the Protected Areas Act and consideration should therefore similarly be given to extending their application to all forms of protected areas declared under it.

## Shifting the conservation consciousness

The prescription of the above tools aimed at facilitating public access, use and benefit sharing within protected areas will not alone achieve the ideological shift from exclusion to inclusion and protection to sustainable use. These tools need to be accompanied by extensive public education regarding the nature, availability and virtues of the above contractual schemes.

The environmental authorities have implemented an array of non-statutory initiatives to complement and raise awareness about the link between people and conservation. These include the establishment of a dedicated People and Conservation Division; the introduction of the People and Parks Programme and People and Parks Forum; and the establishment of individual national park forums. These initiatives should go some way toward shifting the conservative conservation ideology that underpinned the formation and management of protected areas in the past.

## 5.   CONCLUSION

The recent legal reforms undertaken in South Africa have recognised the value of the nation's rich biodiversity and the need for urgent action to halt its rapid decline. The Government has acknowledged the inadequacies of the previous biodiversity regime and introduced a novel regime that entrenches a more contemporary human-centred, cooperative and incentive-based approach to biodiversity regulation, through which it seeks to honour its international commitments, particularly under the Convention on Biological Diversity.

Central to the successful implementation of this novel regime is an array of contractual mechanisms. Cumulatively, these mechanisms attempt to enable and encourage the public to become active participants in biodiversity regulation as: biodiversity planners; biodiversity managers; bio-prospecting stakeholders; land donors; protected area managers; and sustainable users.

New legal regimes are frequently imperfect and numerous flaws have been identified here. These do not, however, render the novel approach to biodiversity regulation in South Africa fatally flawed. Laws are living instruments subject to constant change. The identification of flaws provides opportunities for future improvement and a little tinkering with the formulation of the current contractual mechanisms should see them achieving the lofty ideal of co-opting the public as the future stewards of biodiversity regulation in South Africa.

## NOTES

*     This chapter reflects the position as at 1 March 2008.
1.    (1992) 31 ILM 818. South Africa ratified the *Convention on Biological Diversity* on 2 November 1995.
2.    World Conservation Monitoring Centre, Global Biodiversity Status of the Earths Living Resources (1992) Chapman and Hall; *White Paper on the Conservation and Use of South Africa's Biodiversity (White Paper)* (GN 1095, *Government Gazette* 18163, 28 July 1997), 12.
3.    Endangered Wildlife Trust, The Biodiversity of South Africa – Indicators, Trends and Global Impacts (2002) Struik, Cape Town.
4.    See generally 'Chapter 5: Biodiversity and Ecosystem Health', in Department of Environmental Affairs and Tourism; *South African Environmental Outlook: A Report on the State of the Environment* (2006), 108–137.
5.    Department of Environmental Affairs and Tourism, *South Africa's National Biodiversity Strategy and Action Plan* (2005) 14–16.
6.    Key Acts are: National Environmental Management Act 1998; World Heritage Convention Act 1999; National Heritage Resources Act 1999; National Forests Act 1998; National Water Act 1998; Mountain Catchment Areas Act 1970; Marine Living Resources Act 1998; Environment Conservation Act 1989; Forest Act 1984; Genetically Modified Organisms Act 1997; Conservation of Agricultural Resources Act 1983; National Parks Act 1976; Animal Improvement Act 1998; Plant Improvement Act 1976;

Plant Breeders' Rights Act 1976; Lake Areas Development Act 1975; Sea Birds and Seals Protection Act 1973; and various provincial nature conservation and land-use planning Ordinances and Acts.

7.   National laws include the: National Parks Act; Environment Conservation Act; Forests Act; National Forests Act; Marine Living Resources Act; Mountain Catchment Areas Act; World Heritage Convention Act; National Heritage Resources Act; Lake Areas Development Act; and Sea Birds and Seals Protection Act. Provincial laws include: Mpumalanga Nature Conservation Act 1998; Limpopo Environmental Management Act 2003; Kwazulu-Natal Nature Conservation Management Act 1997; Provincial Parks Board Act (Eastern Cape) 2003; and Western Cape Nature Conservation Laws Amendment Act 2000; Nature and Environmental Conservation Ordinance 1974 (Cape); Nature Conservation Ordinance 1983 (Transvaal); and Nature Conservation Ordinance 1969 (Orange Free State).

8.   The main national planning laws are the: Development Facilitation Act 1995; Local Government Transition Act 1993; Physical Planning Act 1991; Black Communities Development Act 1984; and Less Formal Townships Establishment Act 1991.

9.   The main national law is the Threatened and Protected Species Regulations promulgated under the Biodiversity Act (GNR 151–152 *Government Gazette* 29657, 23 February 2007, as amended). The main provincial laws are listed in note 7.

10.   The main law is the Environmental Impact Assessment Regulations (GNR 385–387, Government Gazette 28753, 21 April 2006) promulgated under the National Environmental Management Act.

11.   See National Treasury; *Estimates of National Expenditure* (2008).

12.   C. Mathys, 'Cape Nature Needs R20m to get out of the Woods', *Cape Argus* (21 June 2005); M. Gosling, 'Cape Nature Managers take a 5% Pay Cut amid Crises', *Cape Times* (23 June 2005); and R. Davies, 'Shortages, Infighting Cripple Cape Nature', *Cape Times* (24 July 2007).

13.   Department of Environmental Affairs and Tourism, *10 Year Review (1994–2004)* (2005) at 44. See also the *Durban Accord*, the *Durban Action Plan* and *World Park Congress Recommendations*, <www.iucn.org/themes/wcpa/wpc2003/>.

14.   See laws listed at notes 6 and 7.

15.   *White Paper on Biodiversity*, note 2 at 33.

16.   See: Convention on Biological Diversity, Art. 8(j); Resolution VII.8 on Local Communities and Indigenous People, adopted by the Conference of the Parties (San José, 1999) to the Convention on the Protection of Wetlands of International Importance Especially as Waterfowl Habitats (1983) 22 ILM 698; Borrini-Feyerabend, Kothari and Oviedo, *Indigenous and Local Communities and Protected Areas: Towards Equity and Enhanced Conservation* (2004) *IUCN Best Practice Protected Area Guidelines Series No.11*, at pp. 8–10.

17.   *White Paper on Biodiversity*, note 2.

18.   The *Kumleben Report* was commissioned by the Minister of Environmental Affairs and Tourism to investigate and make recommendations on certain practical aspects relating to South Africa's protected areas regime such as: institutional arrangements; classification of protected areas; declaration and management regimes; financing protected areas; and increasing local community involvement.

19.   10 Year Review (1994–2004), note 13 at 44.

20.   National Treasury (2006, pp. 95–100).

21.   Regulations were promulgated on 8 February 2008. *Government Gazette*, 30739.

22.   The Patents Act requires that to register a patent, the invention must be: novel; an inventive step; and have commercial application (s. 25(1)). The Patents Act further provides that an invention 'shall be deemed to be new if it does not form part of the state of the art immediately before the priority date of any claim to the invention' (s. 25(5)) and 'state of the art' is defined as all material that has been made available to the public 'by written or oral description, by use or any other way' (s. 25(6)). Accordingly, there are various obstacles to using the Patents Act to protect indigenous knowledge. First, the indigenous biological resources themselves are un-patentable as they do not constitute an

invention. Secondly, the nature of indigenous knowledge renders it similarly unpatentable. It is collective in nature and it may be difficult to determine who the inventor is to whom the patent should be issued. In addition, it is frequently oral in nature and passed down from one generation to another which potentially renders it 'state of the art' and therefore unpatentable.

23. Highly sensitive areas, outstanding ecosystems, species, geological or physical features, or to make the area available primarily for scientific research.

24. An area of national or international biodiversity importance; prevent exploitation or occupation inconsistent with the protection of the ecological integrity of the area; provide spiritual, scientific, educational, recreational and tourism opportunities which are environmentally compatible; and, where feasible, to contribute to economic development.

25. To supplement the system of national parks in South Africa; protect areas which have significant natural features or biodiversity, are of scientific, cultural, historical or archaeological interest; protect areas which are in need of long-term protection; and to provide for a sustainable flow of natural products and services to meet the needs of a local community.

26. To regulate the area as a buffer zone for the protection of other forms of protected areas; enable owners to take collective action to conserve biodiversity on their land and to seek legal recognition for this; protect the area if it is sensitive to development; and to protect a specific ecosystem outside a special nature reserve, national park, world heritage site or nature reserve.

27. GNR 1061 in *Government Gazette* 28181, 28 October 2005.

28. These include: marine protected areas declared under the Marine Living Resources Act; world heritage sites declared under the World Heritage Convention Act; specially protected forest areas, forest nature reserves and forest wilderness areas declared under the National Forests Act; and mountain catchment areas declared under the Mountain Catchment Areas Act.

29. These include non-statutory protected areas such as conservancies, biosphere reserves and transfrontier conservation areas.

30. Department of Environmental Affairs and Tourism, *Guidelines for the Implementation of Community-based Natural Resource Management in South Africa* (2003).

31. These areas would include: marine protected areas declared under the Marine Living Resources Act; specially protected forest areas, forest nature reserves and forest wilderness areas declared under the National Forests Act; mountain catchment areas declared under the Mountain Catchment Areas Act; and the various forms of heritage areas declared under the National Heritage Resources Act.

# REFERENCES

Barnes, K. (ed.) (2000), *The Eskom Red Data Book of Birds of South Africa, Lesotho and Swaziland*, Johannesburg: Birdlife South Africa.

Bothma, K. and P. Glavovic (1992), 'Wild Animals', in R. Fuggle and M. Rabie (eds), *Environmental Management in South Africa*, Cape Town: Juta Law.

Bruce, N. and G. Ellis (1993), 'Environmental Taxes and Policies for Developing Countries', *World Bank Policy Research Working Paper*, No. WPS1177, Washington, DC.

Crowe, T. (1996), 'Developing a national strategy for the protection and sustainable use of South Africa's biodiversity', *South African Journal of Science*, **92** (5), 218–219.

Driver, M., T. Smith and K. Maze (2005a), *Specialist Review Paper on Biodiversity for the National Strategy for Sustainable Development*, Report compiled by the

National Biodiversity Institute on behalf of the Department of Environmental Affairs and Tourism, Pretoria.

Driver, M., K. Maze, M. Rouget, A. Lombard, J. Nel, J. Turpie, R. Cowling, P. Desmet, P. Goodman, J. Harris, Z. Jonas, B. Reyers, K. Sink and T. Strauss (2005b), *National Spatial Biodiversity Assessment 2004: Priorities for Biodiversity Conservation in South Africa*, Strelitzia, 17, Pretoria: South African National Biodiversity Institute.

Friedmann, Y. and B. Daly (eds) (2004), *Red Data Book of the Mammals of South Africa: A Conservation Assessment*, CBSG Southern Africa, Conservation Breeding Specialist Group (SSC/IUCN), Pretoria: Endangered Wildlife Trust.

Hanks, J. and P. Glavovic (1992), 'Protected Areas', in R. Fuggle and M. Rabie (eds), *Environmental Management in South Africa*, Cape Town: Juta Law.

Henderson, P. (1994), 'Fiscal incentives for environmental protection – introduction', *South African Journal of Environmental Law and Policy*, **1**, 49–60.

James, D. (1997), *Environmental Incentives: Australian Experience with Economic Instruments for Environmental Management*, Environmental Economics Research Paper No. 5, Canberra: Environment Australia.

Kotze D., C. Breen and N. Quinn (1995), 'Wetland Losses in South Africa', in G. Cowan (ed.), *Wetlands of South Africa*, Pretoria: Department of Environmental Affairs and Tourism.

Kumleben, M., S. Sangweni and J. Ledger (1998), *Board of Investigation into the Institutional Arrangements for Nature Conservation in South Africa: Report*. Minister of Environmental Affairs and Tourism, South Africa.

Mandondo, A. (2005), 'Dialogue of Theory and Empirical Evidence: a Weighted Decision and Tenurial Niche Approach to Reviewing the Operation of Natural Resource Policy in Rural Southern Africa', *Commons Southern Africa: CASS Occasional Paper Series* (No. 10) Centre for Applied Social Studies (University of Zimbabwe) and Programme for Land and Agrarian Studies, Harare/Cape Town: University of the Western Cape.

Milne, J., K. Deketelaere, L. Kreiser and H. Ashiabor (2003), *Critical Issues in Environmental Taxation*, Oxford: Oxford University Press.

Minter, L., M. Burger, J. Harrison, H. Braack, P. Bishop and D. Kloepfer (eds) (2004), *Atlas and Red Data Book of the Frogs of South Africa, Lesotho and Swaziland*, SI/MAB Series No. 9.

Murphree, M. (1991), 'Communities as Institutions for Resource Management', *CASS Occasional Paper Series*, Centre for Applied Social Studies (University of Zimbabwe) and Programme for Land and Agrarian Studies, Harare/Cape Town: University of the Western Cape.

National Treasury (2006), *A Framework for Considering Market-Based Instruments to Support Environmental Fiscal Reform in South Africa – Draft Policy Paper*, Pretoria: Tax Policy Chief Directorate.

Paterson, A. (2005a), 'Tax incentives – valuable tools for biodiversity conservation in South Africa', *South African Law Journal*, **1**, 182–216.

Paterson, A. (2005b), 'Property tax – a friend or foe for landscape protection in South Africa', *South African Journal of Environmental Law and Policy*, **12** (2), 97–111.

Paterson, A. (2006), 'Pruning the money tree to ensure sustainable growth', *Potchefstroom Electronic Law Journal*, **9** (3), 1–27.

Pearce, D., A. Markandya and E. Barbier (1989), *Blueprint for a Green Economy*, London: Earthscan.

Preston, G. and W. Siegfried (1995), 'The protection of biological diversity in South Africa: profiles and perceptions of professional practitioners in nature conservation agencies and natural history museums', *South African Journal of Wildlife Research*, **25** (2), 49–56.

Stauth R. and P. Baskind (1992), 'Resource Economics', in R. Fuggle and M. Rabie (eds), *Environmental Management in South Africa*, Cape Town: Juta Law.

Summers, R. (1999), 'Legal and Institutional Aspects of Community-based Wildlife Conservation in South Africa, Zimbabwe and Namibia', *Acta Juridica*, Cape Town: Juta, pp. 188–210.

Wilke, K. (2005), *What Is In It for Me: Exploring Natural Capital Incentives*, Canada West Foundation: Calgary.

Wynberg, R. (2002), 'A decade of biodiversity conservation and use in South Africa: tracking progress from Rio Earth Summit to the Johannesburg World Summit on Sustainable Development', *South African Journal of Science*, **98**, 233–243.

# 20. Mangrove swamps and sustainability

## Marcelo Nogueira Camargos and Solange Teles da Silva

## 1. THE SITUATION OF MANGROVES IN BRAZIL

This chapter analyses the constitutional and federal norms of the Brazilian legal system related to the protection of mangroves, questioning whether they conform to the principle of ecologically sustainable development. The first section of the chapter deals with the situation of Brazilian mangroves, including their ecological, environmental and social importance, and the variety of human impacts over this ecosystem in Brazil. The second section is a critical review of the concepts of sustainable development. The third explores the associated constitutional and infra-constitutional federal norms.

Mangroves, found only in the coastal zone of the tropical and subtropical regions, are transitional ecosystems between terrestrial, fluvial and marine environments, of great importance not only for the coastal environment but also for the local people. Mangroves are of value for their great biological productivity, as an essential environment for reproduction and habitat of many marine species, sheltering larvae, fish fingerlings and crustaceans, and supporting innumerable food chains. They are thus a natural nursery for many marine organisms. Moreover, their vegetal formation softens and balances the transition between the land and the sea and protects the coast against erosion produced by currents, tides and flooding. Mangroves also act as a biological filter, holding back sediments, nutrients and pollutants in the water. This ecosystem can also be used for ecological tourism, environmental education, and for the exploitation of marine species. Their social importance lies in the dependence of traditional populations[1] on the natural resources provided by this ecosystem. These people, as explained by Vannucci (2002, p. 112), do not live in the mangrove forest, which would be practically impossible, but in higher areas close to them along rivers and streams.

Generally, the use of and exploitation of natural resources derived from mangroves by traditional populations are carried out in an ecologically sustainable way, since they depend on those resources for their survival. Diegues (2004) explains that traditional populations and cultures are comprised of groups of minor producers deriving from the colonial period, frequently involved in monoculture. Because of their relative isolation, they have developed particular ways of life that involve great dependence on and deep knowledge about biological cycles and natural resources, transferred verbally between generations. These cultures and societies are characterised by their dependence on and even symbiosis with nature; their ways of using and managing environmental resources acquired through empiricism; their notion of territory or space deriving from where the social group has been reproducing economically and socially for generations. The areas occupied by these people are generally environmentally well conserved because they manage and exploit natural resources by paying attention to natural cycles and the capacity of species to recover. Diegues (2004) emphasises that the contribution of traditional communities to the conservation of nature is acknowledged in the international sphere by the Convention on Biological Diversity (Art. 8, (j)). Diegues also explains that the current degree of occupation and use of the Brazilian coastal zone constitutes a threat to the physical, material and cultural survival of traditional populations for a variety of reasons. For instance, the advance of real estate speculation in the coastal zone may force people to leave their territories and cause them to take other jobs, such as bricklayers and housekeepers. Mass tourism also contributes to the disruption of traditional communities due to the demand for workers, especially during summer. Another factor that puts these communities at risk is the transformation of their traditionally used lands into protected areas such as natural parks and reserves. This process often brings with it serious limitations to their traditional activities of agriculture, hunting, fishing and wood extraction, and might force their migration to urban areas where they are often forced to live in slum areas (Diegues, 2004).

Mangroves are mainly constituted by a form of vegetation adapted to live in an environment characterised by constant flooding, high salinity and predominantly muddy ground where there is a lack of oxygen. The most notable adaptation is related to mangrove roots, which stay above the surface of the ground in order to fix the trunk to the soft soil and to obtain oxygen, which is lacking in the wet soil. It is a fragile ecosystem, and once having being damaged does not recover easily. For these reasons, it must be managed in a careful and sustainable manner.

Brazil has an estimated area of mangrove swamps that ranges from 10,000 to 25,000 km² along the coast and bordering estuaries and lagoons from the State of Amapá up to Santa Catarina (Santos and Camera, 2002, p. 118). The incidence of this ecosystem on the Brazilian coast varies considerably. De Lacerda (2002, pp. 196–197) reports that the mangroves from the north coast, where 85 per cent of the total area of this ecosystem is located in Brazil, have the most complex structures, with trees that can reach 40 metres in height and trunks up to one metre in diameter. They form forests stretching more than 40 kilometres inland along the rivers and estuaries. On the northeast coast from Ceará to Rio de Janeiro, the mangroves are lower and structurally less complex, with trees that grow up to 20 metres, forming forests that generally develop in narrow fringes throughout estuaries and lagoons. This region holds 10 per cent of the total mangrove area in Brazil. On the southeast coast, from Rio de Janeiro to Santa Catarina, the extension of the coastal plain is limited by a mountain range called 'Serra do Mar'. This region thus possesses only 5 per cent of the total area of mangroves in Brazil, the ecosystem being restricted to the interior of the bays and formed by low trees that rarely exceed 10 metres.

The Brazilian coastal region presents a worrying panorama with regard to environmental degradation, which is worse in metropolitan areas. Due to the nature of the settlement process, the most populated areas were established along the Brazilian coast. As a result, some highly populated and industrialised metropolitan regions are located by the sea, such as Fortaleza, Recife, Salvador, Rio de Janeiro, Vitória, Belém, Baixada Santista, among others. Population growth as well as economic activities (infrastructure, construction and tourism industries, for example) represent the main form of pressure on the coastal environment where the mangroves are located, with major releases of domestic and industrial effluent in the air, water and soil. Half of the Brazilian population lives no further than 200 kilometres from the sea, and coastal economic activities are responsible for about 70 per cent of the national gross domestic product (Santos and Camara, 2002, p. 119). For these reasons, mangrove swamps are impacted by various intense environmental impacts caused by human activities, such as deforestation, contamination and other degradation from industrial, thermoelectric energy, port, urban and tourist projects, and also by unauthorised occupation of land. On the Brazilian northeast coast, an economic activity that has grown substantially and has major impacts on mangrove swamps is shrimp farming, producing tens of thousands of tons per annum.

While the level of production has fluctuated considerably in recent years, serious environmental damage and threats continue to be visited on traditional communities settled in areas focused on by shrimp breeders. Among the social and environmental problems caused by this activity, the following can be highlighted: tide flow modification; reduction and destruction of numerous species' habitats and areas used for fishing and crab capture; water contamination; landscape deterioration; expulsion of fishermen from their working environment; and human deaths caused by contamination from chemicals used for shrimp conservation. On the coast of São Paulo State, some 52 per cent of its total area of mangroves is found in the Metropolitan Region of Baixada Santista, composed of the following municipalities: Santos, Guarujá, Bertioga, Cubatão, São Vicente, Praia Grande, Mongaguá, Itanhaém and Peruíbe. In the region of Santos, 43 per cent its mangrove areas have already been damaged or even destroyed by irregular human occupation.[2] Thus, the great industrial concentration, port activities and human population in the Metropolitan Region of Baixada Santista are determinative factors that form the current picture of environmental degradation of its ecosystems, including mangroves (Gutberlet, 1996).

De Lacerda explains that historically in Brazil, mangrove areas have been exploited mainly by traditional populations, such as the 'caiçaras',[3] using natural resources for their own survival. For this reason, most of these areas remain environmentally balanced, particularly on the north coast; a region of low population density. On the other hand, the situation of the mangroves located in the northeast and southeast coasts is very different, since their intense urbanisation and industrialisation have resulted in the elimination of a significant percentage of their original vegetation (De Lacerda, 2002). Thus, the diverse forms of human activities and their impact over mangrove swamps must be taken into account in terms of legal regulation, ranging from harmful activities in urban and industrial centres to those that are practically insignificant in terms of environmental impact, such as activities of traditional populations, some of which serve to assist in conserving nature.

There is a paradox regarding the situation of mangroves in Brazil: a high percentage of these ecosystems are well conserved because they are located in the low-density north coast region. Yet in the northeast and southeast coasts where the incidence of mangroves is scarcer, their state of degradation is infinitely higher. The legal protection and management of mangroves must necessarily, therefore, promote the three main factors inherent in the concept of sustainable development: environmental protection, social/cultural matters equity and economics.

## 2.   MANGROVES AND SUSTAINABILITY

On the international political plane, the expression sustainable development gained traction with the Brundtland Report, published in 1987 under the title *Our Common Future* (WCED, 1987), which became a preparatory text for the Rio Earth Summit in 1992. Sustainable development was defined as 'development that meets the needs of the present without compromising the ability of future generations to meet their own needs'. This is a model of development based on solidarity with future generations through the rational exploitation of the environment.

Although still an enigma, the expression 'sustainable development', according to Veiga (2006), represents basic values to be adopted, since it consists of the future vision on which the current civilisation must base its hopes. He explains that 'development' is not the spontaneous result of free interaction of market forces, since markets represent only one amongst many other institutions that play an important role in the development process. Reflecting on the studies of Ignacy Sachs, the author argues that 'development' involves qualitative changes in the lives of the people. In other words it means that the development process must make it possible for people to live the type of life they have chosen, and provide the instruments and opportunities for them to make their choices. He understands development as a process that seeks the consolidation of human rights protection and democracy, whereas growth is a simply quantitative change (Veiga, 2006, p. 80 *et seq.*).

For Sachs (2002, p. 60), the notion of development must be understood as an effective appropriation of human, political, social, economic and cultural rights, including the collective right to a healthy environment. He highlights that the development process must necessarily be inclusive, sustainable and enduring. He sees inclusiveness as being in opposition to the current growth standard, which concentrates income and wealth and excludes part of the consumption market, characterised mainly by strongly segmented labour markets and weak participation in politics. Sachs explains that for the development process to be inclusive, it must be intrinsically related to the issue of decent work for all, which involves equal chances of access to public services such as education, health care and housing, amongst others. 'Sustainable', in relation to environmental conservation, requires the development process to take into account current and future generations, as well as 'enduring', in terms of being a continuous process (Sachs, 2004). Therefore, when applied to mangrove protection, the development process will be inclusive, sustainable and enduring if: it guarantees the participation of traditional populations that exploit its natural resources in the process of public policy making; it considers environmental conservation as a fundamental factor of the policies to be applied; and the management adopted in mangrove areas generates income and promotes the survival of those traditional populations.

## 3.   LEGAL PROTECTION OF MANGROVES

The protection of mangroves is both generally and specifically promoted in the Brazilian legal system. Article 225 of the Brazilian Federal Constitution of 1988 includes the right of all to an ecologically balanced environment and the duty of public authorities to defend and preserve the environment for current and future generations. Article 225 also lists the Coastal Zone and the Mata Atlântica (Atlantic Forest) as part of the national heritage, which means that these areas can only be used according to legal norms and under conditions that assure their environmental preservation.[4] The Forest Code, Federal Law of 1965,[5] as a general rule, establishes that existing forests in national territory and other types of vegetation are of common interest to all Brazilians and it defines two types of protected areas or protected spaces: 'legal reserve areas' ('áreas de reserva legal')[6] and 'permanently protected areas' ('áreas de preservação permanente' – APP). The latter have been defined as areas 'protected under the provision of Articles 2 and 3 of this Law, whether or not covered by native vegetation, which has the environmental role of preserving water resources, landscape, geological stability, biodiversity, the gene flow of fauna and flora, protecting the soil and ensuring the well-being of the human population'.

Based on the right to an ecologically balanced environment established by the Brazilian Constitution, the Forest Code highlights the importance of mangrove swamps when constituting the areas where *restingas* exist (a kind of vegetation found on tropical beaches) as permanently protected areas for the fact that they fix dunes and stabilise mangrove vegetation. The National Environmental Council (CONAMA)[7] is the central consultative and deliberative organ of the Environment National System (SISNAMA), charged with defining environmental quality standards and criteria. CONAMA adopted Resolution n. 303/2002, and developed the legal definition of mangroves, constituting permanently protected areas (Art. 3, x).[8] In a 2007 case, the High Court of Brazil affirmed that the 'present Brazilian legislation reflects the scientific, ethical, political and legal transformation that reoriented the position of mangroves from being regarded as a public health risk to the condition of being a critically endangered ecosystem. Aiming to protect their ecological, economic and social functions, the legislator has given them the legal status of Permanent Preservation Areas'.[9]

Individual landowners have the obligation to preserve or restore the native vegetation of these permanently protected areas, but enforcement of this provision is still weak (Drummond and Barros-Platiau, 2006). There is a deficit of permanently protected areas – there are 103 million hectares of permanently protected areas, but only 59 million hectares have natural vegetation cover (Sparokev et al., 2010).

The devegetation of permanently protected areas can be applied in cases of public utility or social interest, under appropriate administrative procedures,[10] when there are no other alternative production methods and site alternatives to the enterprise proposed (Forest Code, Art. 4). The Forest Code defines the concepts of public utility and social interest, and establishes that work, plans, activities or projects can also be defined by CONAMA as public utility or social interest.[11] Under CONAMA Resolution 369/2006, there are only two possibilities regarding the removal of mangrove forests located in permanently protected areas. These are: (a) public utility: namely activities of national security and sanitary protection; the essential infrastructure work destined for public services of transport, sanitation and energy; the establishment of public green space in urban regions; archaeological research; public works to implant necessary installations to collect and transport water and treated effluent; and for the building of necessary installations for private projects of aquaculture; (b) access of people and animals to the permanently protected area, only allowed for the supply of water, as long as it does not result in adverse effects on native vegetation.

A gap exists between reality and the rules related to mangrove protection that cannot be addressed at state or municipal levels. This is because the restrictions mentioned above in relation to the use of mangroves proceed from general norms, which means that they must be observed by all federated entities according to Article 24, (1) and (2) of the Brazilian Federal Constitution of 1988.

In fact, the legal protection of mangrove swamps does not correspond to the reality of what occurs in these ecosystems, since their exploitation by traditional populations has historically always occurred, and we can see here that the legislation does not consider that in this case social diversity and biodiversity are part of the same logic. It is important to stress that the knowledge, practices and culture of traditional populations are constitutionally protected and feature as a part of the national cultural heritage (Art. 216 Brazilian Federal Constitution). This implies a duty by the public authorities to establish rules and public policies that promote the conservation of the environment as well as the cultural heritage.

## 4. CONCLUSION

As indicated above, both an ecologically balanced environment and the cultural heritage are equally protected by the Federal Constitution, which places an affirmative duty on the public authorities to establish rules and public policies that deal holistically with environmental rights and cultural rights. The strong restrictions on the use of mangrove swamps imposed by the legal system to guarantee their conservation are due to their environmental importance. These restrictions are fundamental, considering their current state of degradation. However, because of the exceptions to the restrictions mentioned above, the general norms related to the protection of mangrove swamps are misdirected. On the one hand, the removal of mangroves for the building or expansion of infrastructure for the purposes of transport, such as ports, generally causes major environmental impacts, while being recognised as important to national development. On the other hand, the environmentally sustainable exploitation of this ecosystem carried out by traditional populations, which can actually assist in conserving mangroves,[12] is forbidden. In light of this prohibition, it can be concluded that the social factors inherent to the concept of sustainable development are not taken into consideration by the Brazilian general infra-constitutional norms – federal norms – insofar as they apply related to mangrove protection.

Another problem that must be faced is the fact that those general federal norms, when regulating the use and exploitation of mangrove areas, should consider these ecosystems holistically. The variations, in terms of structure, use and state of conservation of mangrove areas along the Brazilian coast are not taken into account by those norms. In the light of these variations, land use planning and environmental zoning are instruments of fundamental importance in protecting and conserving mangrove swamps in Brazil. However, in order for these provisions to be effective the participation of all stakeholders, including traditional populations, must be guaranteed in terms of decision making, which means that the general norms related to mangrove protection must be changed to address these issues.

## NOTES

1.  'Traditional population' is defined by law as the population living in close relationship with the natural environment, depending on their natural resources for their socio-cultural reproduction, through activities with low environmental impact (Federal Law, n. 11.428/2006, entitled Law of Atlantic Forest Protection).
2.  The slum called México 70, located in Baixada Santista, is considered the largest one in Brazil and was built entirely in mangrove areas. Two federal programmes – the Program for Accelerated Growth and 'My House, My Life' (Federal Law, n. 11.977/2009) – are directed at solving the problem of 1,417 households that occupy this slum through processes of housing access and land tenure regularisation.
3.  The term 'caiçara', which refers to the stakes placed around the huts and villages, and corrals made of tree branches stuck in the water to surround the fish, became the name given to all individuals and communities of the coastal states of Paraná, São Paulo and Rio de Janeiro (Adams, 2000).
4.  For an overview of environmental protection law and policy in Brazil, see Drummond and Barros Platiau (2006) and Patriota (2008/2009). For biodiversity protection in Brazil see Crawford and Pignataro (2007); see also Federal Law n. 11.428/2006, Law of Atlantic Forest Protection and Federal Law n. 7.661/1988 setting forth the National Plan for Coastal Management.
5.  The first 'Forest Code' ('Código Florestal'), Decree 23.793, of 23 January 1934, stated that forests were of 'common interest' for all Brazilians and had established several preservationist provisions. It distinguishes four types of forests: 'protective', 'remnant', 'model' and 'productive'; see Drummond and Barros Platiau (2006); Silva et al. (2010).

6. Areas located inside a rural property or landholding, except those for permanently protected areas, which are necessary for the sustainable use of natural resources, conservation and recovery of ecological processes, conservation of biodiversity and shelter and protection for native fauna and flora, under Provisional Measure n. 2.1666-67/2001.

7. The National Environmental Council (CONAMA) is composed of members representing many federal departments and agencies, all state governments, local governments, businesses, workers, scientists and environmental NGOs (Drummond and Barros-Platiau, 2006).

8. CONAMA Resolution 303/2002 provides the parameters, definitions and boundaries of permanently protected areas. See also CONAMA Resolution 302/2002 which defined the parameters, definitions and limitations of permanently protected areas of artificial reservoirs and the land-use regime of surrounding areas.

9. Justice Antonio Herman Benjamin. REsp 650728/SC Recurso Especial. Editors' note: *Areas de Preservação Permanente – APP* (in Portuguese), or Permanent Preservation Areas (in literal translation), are defined in the 1965 Brazilian Forest Code as those that, because of their topography and vulnerability, cannot be cleared or even have their vegetation sustainably exploited. They include, among others, fringing or riparian vegetation, steep areas with an incline of over 45 degrees, and mangroves.

10. The authorisation must be given by the State Environmental Agency, with previous consent from the Environmental Federal or Municipal Agencies when the destruction of vegetation is required. In cases where the removal of the vegetation of permanently protected areas occurs in an urban area, the administrative procedure must be submitted to the municipality, if there is a branch or Office of the Environment with jurisdiction to deliberate, with the previous consent of the State Agency for the Environment. The decision must be based on a technical environmental assessment. The Environment Agency which has jurisdiction must, before issuing the authorisation, point out the impacts and also the mitigating and compensatory measures that should be adopted by the entrepreneur.

11. See CONAMA Resolution 369/2006 that provides for the exceptional cases of public utility, social interest or low environmental impact which justify interventions and the suppression of vegetation in permanently protected areas; see also CONAMA Resolution 425/2010, which provides additional criteria that allows the intervention or suppression of vegetation in permanently protected areas, defining as social interest those activities of sustainable agriculture performed by family farmers, rural entrepreneurs, and traditional people and communities.

12. The mangrove forest and artisan fishing in the Acupe District (Santo Amaro, Bahia State, Brazil): an ethno-ecological approach – DOI: 10.4025/actascibiolsci.v30i3.5014 Acta Sci. Biol. Sci. Maringá, v. 30, n. 3, pp. 275–282, 2008.

# REFERENCES

Adams, Cristina (2000), 'As populações caiçaras e o mito do bom selvagem: a necessidade de uma nova abordagem interdisciplinar' ('The Caiçaras population and the myth of the noble savage: the need for a new interdisciplinary approach'), *Rev. Antropol*, **43** (1), 145–182; see http://www.scielo.br/scielo.php?script=sci_arttext&pid=S0034-77012000000100005&lng=en&nrm=iso.

Crawford, Colin and Guilherme Pignataro (2007), 'The insistent (and unrelenting) challenges of protecting biodiversity in Brazil: finding "the law that sticks"', *University of Miami Inter-American Law Review*, **39** (1), 301–365.

De Lacerda, Luiz D. (2002), 'Os manguezais do Brasil' ('Mangrove swamps in Brazil') in *Os Manguezais e Nós: Uma Síntese de Percepções*, São Paulo: Edusp.

Diegues, Antônio C.S. (2004), *O Mito Moderno da Natureza Intocada* (*The Modern Myth of Untouched Nature*), 5th edn, São Paulo: Hucitec.

Drummond, José and Ana Flávia Barros-Platiau (2006), 'Brazilian environmental law and policies, 1934–2002: a critical overview', *Law & Policy*, **28** (1), 83–108.

Gutberlet, Jutta (1996), *Cubatão: Desenvolvimento, Exclusão Social e Degradação ambiental* (*Cubatão: Development, Social Exclusion and Environmental Degradation*), São Paulo: USP, Fapesp.

Patriota, Antonio de Aguiar (2008/2009), 'An introduction to Brazilian environmental law', *The George Washington International Law Review*, **40** (3), 611–617.

Sachs, Ignacy (2002), 'Pensando Sobre o Desenvolvimento na Era do Meio Ambiente: Do Aproveitamento Racional da Natureza para a Boa Sociedade' (Thinking About Development in the Era of the Environment: The Rational Exploitation of Nature for the Good Society') in Paula Y. Stroh (ed.), *Caminhos Para o Desenvolvimento Sustentável* (*Paths towards Sustainable Development*), Rio de Janeiro: Garamond.

Sachs, Ignacy (2004), *Desenvolvimento: Includente, Sustentável, Sustentado* (*Development: Inclusive, Sustainable and Sustained*), Rio de Janeiro: Garamond.

Santos, T.C.C. and J.B.D Camara (eds) (2002), *GEO Brasil 2002: Perspectivas do meio Ambiente no Brasil* (*GEO Brazil 2002: Brazilian Environmental Outlook*), Brasilia: IBAMA.

Silva, Solange Teles da, Sandra Cureau and Márcia Diegues Leuzinger (eds) (2010), *Código Florestal: Desafios e Perspectivas* (*Forest Code: Challenges and Perspectives*), São Paulo: Fiuza.

Sparokev, Gerd, Alberto Barretto, Israel Klug and Göran Berndes (eds) (2010), *Considerações sobre o Código Florestal Brasileiro* (*Reflections on the Brazilian Forest Code*), see http://www.ekosbrasil. org/media/file/OpCF_gs_010610_v4.pdf.

Vannucci, Marta (2002), *Os Manguezais e Nós: Uma síntese de Percepções* (*Mangrove Swamps and Us: A Synthesis of Perceptions*), São Paulo: Edusp.

Veiga, José E. (2006), *Desenvolvimento Sustentável: o Desafio do Século XXI* (*Sustainable Development: The Challenge of XXI Century*), Rio de Janeiro: Garamond.

World Commission on Environment and Development (WCED) (1987), *Our Common Future*, Oxford: Oxford University Press.

# 21. The Amazonian Treaty and harmonisation of environmental legislation

## José Augusto Fontoura Costa, Solange Teles da Silva and Fernanda Sola

## 1. INTRODUCTION

Generally, environmental problems can be separated into two distinct classes: local and global. There is no clear line that separates these, but it is important to understand the dynamics of each. Global issues, such as global warming, depletion of highly migratory fish stocks and the ozone layer, need an all-embracing international system which binds each and every country. Local issues can be limited to the territory of a single country, or can include several countries of a region. Regional international regimes can be created to deal with local issues. It is important to stress that even regional regimes that deal with similar issue areas – drainage basins, for instance – can show several differences within them regarding both normative and institutional aspects.

Rather than being ends in themselves, harmonisation and unification of law are traditional tools for the formulation and achievement of common goals in international relations. In the environmental arena the legal and political tools are especially significant in achieving the goals set by political actors. Thus the theoretical study of construction and implementation of international environmental regimes is useful only if it is able to inform the political actors on their potentialities and limits.

This chapter aims to identify the possible instruments relevant to a broader and more international treatment of environmental problems related to the Amazon Region, including the state parties of the 1978 Amazonian Cooperation Treaty (ACT). It begins with a description of international regime theory, focusing on the divide between institutionalists and cognitivists. The main features of the Amazon Cooperation Treaty (ACT) and a general description of Amazonian environmental problems are provided in order to give an understanding of their range as well as the roles of some actors in the making of an international environmental regime. Finally, a synthesis on the perspectives of the making of an Amazonian international environmental regime is presented.

## 2.　BUILDING INTERNATIONAL REGIMES: NEOLIBERAL AND COGNITIVIST PERSPECTIVES

The theory of international regimes has been significantly boosted since the 1980s. Though originally concerned with Cold War bilateral tensions, its focus has changed to deal with the institutionalisation and legalisation of the treatment of international issues and problems in a multilateral framework.

One of the central aims of regime theory is to understand cooperation under conditions of anarchy or, at least, considering the absence of a central authority; as Axelrod (1984, p. 3) asks: 'under what conditions will cooperation emerge in a world of egoists without central authority?'

Cooperation is described both as inter-subjective action which is not underpinned by force or need, but rather is legitimately institutionalised, as well as cooperation under a decentralised international order. The explanation of the second can be based on altruistic feelings and/or on self-interest. Rationalists such as Meyers state that value calculation is enough to describe accurately and realistically the results and institutionalisation of cooperation (Meyers, 2000).

Analysts have classified regime theory in a number of ways. Krasner (1982) finds three perspectives: 'conventional structural', 'modified conventional' and 'grotian' (named for the Dutch legal theorist Hugo Grotius). This classification refers to the question of whether a regime really matters. The first perspective denies the influence of regimes in actual international relations; the second regards regimes as a variable quantity and the third looks at regimes as an inherent feature of relations among states. In this study, the first two perspectives have been discarded, and the influence of international regimes is focused on.

Stein (1990) deals with the main divide between theorists of world politics as embracing realists, which takes a conventional view of international relations, and liberals. It is important to stress here that the second, roughly similar to 'modified conventional' in Krasner's classification and 'rationalists' in that of Meyers, borrows its name from economic classical liberalism, extended to relations among states or nations (regarded as the primary actors). Cooperation is considered a result of a calculation of costs and benefits, which shows that conflict normally is disadvantageous and promotes commercial relations based on comparative advantages, leading to an international division of labour. Liberals in particular believe that full information and institutions will facilitate global politics.

Baldwin (1993) identifies six dimensions which are debated between neorealists and neoliberals:

- the nature and consequences of anarchy, considered more serious by realists;
- cooperation, regarded as harder to achieve by realists;
- relative (neoliberals) and absolute gains (neorealists);
- priority of security (neorealists) and economic (neoliberals) goals of the state;
- intentions and perception of actors (neoliberals) and objective capabilities (neorealists); and
- institutions and regimes, considered as relevant by neoliberals.

To sum up, liberals and neoliberals, under a stronger influence of institutionalism, consider the regimes as an intervening variable of state behaviour, which changes as a function of the absolute gains of the long-term positive effects of cooperation.

In considering the methodological approach, Haggard and Simmons (1987) identify four kinds of theories: structural, game-theoretic, functional and cognitive. Hasenclever et al. (1997) consider interest-based (neoliberalism), power-based (realism) and knowledge-based theories (cognitivism). This classification takes into account the principle that explains the birth and growth of international regimes.

Departing from a similar analysis, though more focused on the function of rules, Trubek et al. (2005) divide the theories into rationalist and constructivist. The first, linked to economic analysis, regards rules as a device to stabilise expectancies and the second – theoretically a tributary of sociology – regards rules as instruments which promote the diffusion of norms. The authors submit that *both* theoretical views bring contributions to the effective legalisation of international issues and that a hybrid approach would be worthwhile.

It is also necessary to remember here that regime theories are in part about the construction and maintenance of cooperation in an otherwise anarchic world, or at least a world of complex and fuzzy hierarchies. The mainstream theories are mainly engrossed with the need to understand the relations among states (primary actors of international relations), although the recognition of greater power and influence of non-state actors, especially under the influence of globalisation, leads to a possible new paradigm (Mittelman, 2000) or, at least, a new dichotomy and debate on international relations (Puchala, 2003). The previously presented hybridism can also be regarded as an effect of globalisation.

The neoliberal perspective, which constitutes the mainstream of regime theories, is intent on understanding how states (primary actors) cooperate without a single international order, considering the calculation of interests. Since the interests of distinct states are commonly counter-posed, regimes and institutions seem to be the result of compromise. In this context, full information is a prerequisite to the making of rational choices by the various actors, throwing light onto the establishment of interests and preferences, thus leading states to the most reasonable decisions. Globalisation produces effects over these theories, since new actors – such as transnational companies, non-governmental organisations, epistemic communities and internal structures of state power – must be considered.

The cognitivist perspective concentrates its thrust on the generation of consensus. Epistemic communities, international organs and sets of professional administrators seem to support this view. As Haas (1992) explains, epistemic communities are networks of experts in scientific or technological fields as well as politically informed groups whose members share beliefs and validity criteria based on internal evaluation and normative commitments. The knowledge of a specific epistemic community affects the decision-making of other groups or even states, as it offers scientific legitimation by defining the relationship between cause and effect, explaining the complexity of issues, and helping to define self interest in clearer terms. Considering that these communities diminish the costs of information, their proposed patterns of knowledge and legitimacy are spread among political actors and help to build consensus.

The cognitivist perspective regards the growth and diffusion of knowledge as an instrument of consensus building as well as an influence on determining the self interest of political and legal decision-makers. It is therefore important to explain international regimes in the field of environmental issues, since most of the chemical and biological effects of entropy action are crucial to an understanding of needs and possible actions in this field. Moreover, neoliberal perspectives, which consider states to be well-informed and rational actors, find that choices are limited, since the knowledge held by state negotiators and decision-makers depends on the projects of epistemic communities.

Nevertheless, since this chapter deals with the perspectives of the use of a legal instrument, the Amazonian Cooperation Treaty (ACT), it should be stated that international regimes and international *legal* regimes are not synonymous expressions, since the first one refers to 'principles, norms, rules and decision-making procedures' (Krasner, 1982), which are not necessarily legal, but can also be political and economic. Legal regimes, on the other hand, are special discourses which have a normative aspect and are subject to control by a special community where 'discussion of issues purely in terms of interests or power is no longer legitimate' (Abbott et al., 2000).

So, if a primary task of regime theories is to explain cooperation in an anarchic or complex world, the role of legalisation theories is to explain why and how political decisions sometimes transfer a set of decisions from the economic or political decision-making jurisdiction to the specifically legal one.

This brief analysis of international regimes and legalisation theories implies that the research on legal regime-building related to the ACT should take into account both the actual Amazonian problems, as described by epistemic communities, as well as the advantages and disadvantages of legalisation.

## 3.  ORIGINS AND LIMITS OF THE AMAZONIAN COOPERATION TREATY

The legal regimes of international drainage basins are quite traditional in international law. Originally, the treaties and commissions on drainage basins were mainly concerned with international navigation and access of land-locked countries to the sea.  For example, the Congress of Vienna in 1815 dealt with river basin questions and established a Central Commission for the Navigation of the Rhine. In South America, quarrels over control of river estuaries and navigation permissions marked the tensions between Spain and Portugal and, thereafter, among the new states (Góes Filho, 2001). After World War Two, the focus switched to waterpower plants and the negotiation of the 1969 River Plate Basin Treaty, among other legal instruments, which were, in spite of some ancillary environmental references, guided by diplomatic disputes on hydroelectric energy production (Caubet, 1989).

It is important to note that international legal treatment of both navigational and energy issues are better explained by neoliberal theories, since the self-interest of states is clearly defined and there are opposing objectives. Knowledge diffusion and consensus building are not as decisive in these disputes as they would be with reference to environmental issues.

In this context, the interest in the waterpower potential of the Amazon River Basin was not as central as in the River Plate Basin. In the 1970s, the population of consumers in the northern region of the subcontinent was relatively small, which made the construction of dams far more difficult and expensive.

The initiative to negotiate and the first drafts of ACT came from Brasilia. In fact, the development and security goals of the military regime provided the main impulse for the treaty, which was also driven by the fear of internationalisation manoeuvres against state sovereignty attracted by the 'population gap' and the wealth of natural resources (Ricupero, 1984).

The ACT came into force in 1978 when adopted by eight states: Bolivia, Brazil, Colombia, Ecuador, Guyana, Peru, Surinam and Venezuela, six years after the Stockholm Declaration on the Human Environment (United Nations, 1972)[1] and four years after the special session of United Nations General Assembly (UNGA) on the New International Economic Order.[2] This treaty is not open to new adherences, even by French Guyana, which is in the territory of the basin. In fact, its status as a French overseas territory – regarded as a colony – was a reason for the denial of its participation, though France tried at an early stage to join the negotiations (Soares, 1993).

The context of the creation of the Treaty was less clear with regard to the interests and objectives of each state. On the one hand, the protection of the principle of permanent sovereignty over natural resources[3] was still at the centre of interests and discussions of developing states. On the other hand, environmental international regulation was regarded suspiciously by these countries, since the Stockholm Conference was considered a diversionist manoeuvre and the international environmental principles were seen as limitations on the sovereign use of natural resources (Nascimento and Silva, 1995; Schrijver, 1997; Costa, 2001; Silva, 2009).

It is significant that the Brazilian Foreign Office in 1976 conceived the idea of the Treaty and presented the plan to the other Amazonian countries. The Treaty originally focused on the needs of economic and industrial integration. In order to reach these goals, some instruments for freedom of trade were put forward. Nevertheless, also due to the overlapping jurisdiction of the scope and subject matter of the Andean Pact[4] and the Latin American Integration Association (ALADI) (Ricupero, 1984), this original plan was transformed into a proposal for a wide but loose cooperative scheme based on research into and exploitation of their resources, as well as the interactions in the region through transportation and communication networks. The question of access to information was central to this process, including plans to establish 'an information centre to process local data, as well as to exchange complementary information with other Latin American cooperation systems for the purpose of aiding specific national projects, giving priority to the joint efforts of the less-developed members of the Pact' (Mendes, 1993, p. 201).

In this context, it is important to note Article IV of the ACT:

> The Contracting Parties agree to undertake joint actions and efforts to promote the harmonious development of their respective Amazonian territories in such a way that these joint actions produce equitable and mutually beneficial results and also achieve the preservation of the environment, and the conservation and rational utilization of the natural resources of those territories. To this end, they shall exchange information and prepare operational agreements and understandings, as well as the pertinent legal instruments to permit the aims of the present Treaty to be attained.

In the light of doubts and uncertainties about the further development of international law, this international legal text became a broad framework that focused on permanent sovereignty over natural resources and proposed cooperation in the use of shared resources. It is also interesting to note that the lack of strong legal language of the ACT allows it to be classified as soft law (Freire et al., 2007). As the legal framework is quite loose, the limits imposed over state action are virtually absent: it does not create clear obligations for states. This may be due to the unwillingness of the major power in the region, Brazil, to deal with the use of shared resources and environmental protection through a detailed legal instrument that creates such obligations, as the exercise of power and regional leadership may bring more benefits through a softer regulatory approach.

Thus this Treaty can be seen as an 'umbrella agreement' that requires for 'its full implementation, the subscription of specific agreements and understandings, eliminating the possibility that its execution affects the existing boundary disputes among signatories' (Mendes, 1993, p. 201).

The original treaty also did not provide for the creation of an international organisation in its original draft. In fact, its institutional structure (Arts 20 to 23) adopts provisions for exceptional meetings of Foreign Affairs Ministers and yearly meetings of a Council of Amazonian Cooperation, composed of governmental diplomatic representatives. Since there was no specific country designated as the seat of the organisation, these organs rotate through the members in alphabetical order and the country where the next meeting is scheduled is responsible for the executive secretarial tasks, performed by a national permanent commission, a *pro tempore* secretariat. So, due to budgetary constraints at the time (Ricupero, 1984), no permanent secretariat was established, nor a management organ like the International Consultancy Commission of Treaty of the River Plate Basin.

Nevertheless, in 1995 the eight members decided to give birth to the Amazon Cooperation Treaty Organization (ACTO). A formal treaty amendment was approved in 1998 and the General Secretary was installed in 2002. The ACTO has a relatively weak mandate, since the decisions are not binding and the two main political bodies – Ministerial Meetings and the Council of Representatives – make decisions by unanimous vote.

Effectively, the most important change that resulted from the creation of the ACTO is the transformation of the *pro tempore* secretariat into a permanent secretariat, the seat of which is Brasilia. The General Secretary coordinates the particular issues of environment, health, science and education, transport and tourism, and indigenous and traditional peoples. Considering its institutional structure and its legal framework, it is possible to assert that the ACTO conducts its activities through technical cooperation and fostering of scientific studies on the region, since it cannot make legally binding decisions.

In fact, there have been no substantive changes in the legal structure of the treaty institutions since the ACTO was created. Domestic law is still the main legal instrument of environmental protection as well as international negotiation and political bargaining, which leads to *ad hoc* solutions, and remains the most effective means of international coordination and cooperation in the region.

Therefore, although there is no coordination of legal issues, the harmonisation of domestic law is a possible means of generating similar instruments of environmental protection and sustainable use of natural resources. In this sense, epistemic communities – both of lawyers and law scholars as well as of social and natural scientists – play a key role in the diffusion of harmonic patterns and standards of environmental state regulation.

It is not likely that the international legal framework in the region will become stronger in the short term, since states are not keen to accept the imposition of international decision-making, or the delegation of dispute resolution to international bodies. In regime-theory language, it would be possible to assert that insufficient information and some potentially emerging conflicts make the calculation of costs and benefits of cooperation impossible and, as a consequence, prevent the creation of a legally narrow cooperation system.

However, the structure of the General Secretariat promotes cooperation based on consensus and on the knowledge developed by epistemic communities fostered and, in some extent, selected by Contracting Parties of the ACTO.


## 4.   AMAZONIAN ISSUES

As Becker (2004) states, the Amazonian environment is perceived in global, regional and local terms. The need for preservation of the Amazon can be seen as global, since it affects all of humanity. As a frontier of exploitation of natural resources and economic development, the national features are also easy to recognise as a means of addressing local societal needs.

Whatever perception of the Amazonian environment is accepted, an accurate analysis of any environmental problem must take all three perspectives into account. Considering that each state holds the sovereign right to exploit its own natural resources, it is also obliged to make sure that the acts performed inside its jurisdiction will not affect the environment of the other states, consistent with Principle 21 of the Stockholm Declaration on Human Environment of 1972, and Principle 2 of the Rio Declaration on Environment and Development.

Under international law it is possible to scrutinise the environmental problematic from regional or international perspectives. The Amazonian environment thus leads first, to an analysis concerning its limits and boundaries, and thereafter, to a study of transboundary and global environmental problems that impact on the region. It is also fundamental to take into account the sustainable development of this region, considering the quality of life of the population, including indigenous and traditional communities.

## The Amazonian Region

The Amazonian Region can be defined as a huge and complex river system that encompasses an area of '6.5 million km², the equivalent of two-fifths of South America. It covers 52 per cent of Brazil, 50 per cent of Peru, 30 per cent of Colombia, large expanses of Bolivia, Venezuela and Ecuador and the entire territories of Suriname, Republic of Guyana and French Guyana' (Nogueira, 1993, p. 2). Although it includes the territory of nine states, the territorial scope of the Amazon Cooperation Treaty (ACT), as stated in Article II, covers the Amazon River Basin as well as land, because its geographical, ecological or economic features are related to this watercourse in the territories of the Contracting Parties of Bolivia, Brazil, Colombia, Ecuador, Republic of Guyana, Peru, Suriname and Venezuela. Thus it is necessary to examine the territorial extent of this treaty.

A proposed definition of the territorial extent of the treaty was presented in a seminar organised by the European Commission and ACTO (Eva and Huber, 2005) based on the following criteria: (a) hydrological criteria, covering the regions of Amazon and Tocantins Rivers; (b) ecological criteria, departing from the division of the Amazon River Basin in several sub-regions, which belong to distinct eco-regions; (c) biogeographical criteria, which include both the rainforest areas as well as the deforested areas that were historically covered by the biome. The proposal also included French Guyana. Although France itself is not a member of the ACTO because of its status as a colonial power, French Guyana presents common ecological and bio-geographical features. Thus the region was divided into five sub-regions (Eva and Huber, 2005):

(a)   Central – *stricto sensu* Amazon – defined by the limits of the Amazon River Basin in the north, an area comprehended by a contour 700 km westwards, and the biome limits (before deforestation) in the south and southeast;

(b)   Andean, from the contour of 700 km to the source of the Amazon River;

(c)   High plains, between the limits of Amazonian Plains and the limits
      of rivers Tocantins and Amazon rising in Bolivia and Brazil;
(d)   Guyana, limits go north to the Atlantic baseline and the rivers
      Orinoco and Vichada. Its southern limit is marked by the waters of
      Amazon River Basin; and
(e)   Gurupí, which covers the Northeast of the Brazilian State of Pará
      and the western half of the Brazilian State of Maranhão.

It must be made clear, however, that limits and boundaries projected on the
territorial basis are not exclusively the result of geographical, economic or
ecological criteria, comprising also their historical and cultural situation (see
Bourdieu, 2005, p. 114). In other words, the delimitation of Amazonian
territory does not depend exclusively on geographical or biological criteria.
The Amazonian Region is not a territory without people and history that can
be subjected to proposals for major infrastructure projects (roads,
hydropower plants, mineral plants and others) that do not consider the
interests and needs of the local population (Ab'Sáber, 2004). The historical
and cultural dimensions must be added and the visions of traditional
populations and Indigenous peoples should also be considered.

It is important to highlight the relationship between socio-diversity and
biodiversity. Neves underlines that there are two hypotheses that seem
important in the Amazonian Region: (a) the relationship between socio-
diversity and biodiversity, and (b) the maintenance of human socio-diversity.
The first one deals with the fact that this relationship goes far beyond the mere
relationship expressed in the statement that by 'protecting the first one, we
protect the second'. The second one expresses the idea that 'the maintenance of
human socio-diversity, in addition to its concern for the ethics related to self-
determination of peoples, is also concerned with the ethics of survival of the
species itself' (Neves, 1995, p. 92).

**Environmental Problems**

It is common to hear that the Amazon encompasses the most extensive area
of rainforest and the largest drainage basin of the world, as well as hosting
one of the most vulnerable and complex ecosystems of the planet. Through
the process of human occupation, it is apparent that the modes of
appropriation of natural resources were led by an economic misconception of
the inexhaustibility of those resources. Thus, it is the case that continuing
high deforestation rates promote the widening of the agrarian frontier as well
as providing coal for the steel-making industry. In addition water pollution
from the use of mercury for the processing of gold (Worthington and Brown,
1993) and the depletion of fish stocks and biopiracy add to the environmental

issues of the region. Moreover, some social-environmental questions are observed as well. In the words of Ferreira and Salati (2005, p. 32): 'expansion of gold mining, drug trafficking and the poverty belt of cities, ... provide evidence of the environmental disorder in the contemporary Amazon'. Limiting these considerations to Brazilian Amazonia, or at least to Brazilian 'Legal Amazonia' that covers 5,217,423 square kilometres, almost 60 per cent of Brazilian territory, five categories of environmental impacts on the region are described by Nogueira: (a) the opening of roads and financial incentives for the large cattle industry that have resulted in the deforestation of large areas to create pastures with adverse consequences for the health of the population; the increase of tropical diseases such as malaria and leishmaniasis; (b) mining and ore processing, noting that wealth generated by mineral riches has little positive impact on the quality of life of the local population, while mining by *garimpeiros* (small-scale independent miners) has also caused severe environmental degradation in Amazonia; (c) hydropower plants have caused some ecological and social problems in the region, such as deforestation, decomposition of organic materials that generate obnoxious gases, interference with indigenous communities, displacement of riparian communities; and (d) the growth of urban environments without adequate sanitation and other urban impacts (Nogueira, 1993, pp. 9–12).

Of course, the three perspectives of environmental problems – local, regional and global – must be considered to ensure environmental order and security in the region (Silva and Mele, 2006). In other words, the development of a regional legal framework must take into account the local specificities as well as the international environmental issues.

If these problems are analysed through a global lens, they cannot be confined to the Amazon. Since they constitute global menaces to environmental equilibrium and human security, they demand responses from the international community. On the one hand, the effects of deforestation on climate change and biodiversity make clear that the problems related to forests must be treated in an integrated manner and also as global considerations (Rosendal, 2001). On the other hand, the United Nations concept of human security (UNDP, 1994) includes environmental security at the same time as economic, food, health, personal, community and political security. As Slaughter (2005) makes clear, human security underpins the solidarity of states under a collective security umbrella.

Particularly important to global issues is the question of global warming, since it affects the whole world, although it affects the developing and poor regions more profoundly (Watkins, 2007). In this regard, all countries of the region are parties to the 1992 United Nations Convention on Climate Change[5] and the 1997 Kyoto Protocol.[6] Similarly, the 1992 United Nations Convention on Biological Diversity[7] as well as the Cartagena Protocol on Biosafety have been ratified by all ACT countries.

Moreover, air and water pollution also can be transboundary problems, since economic activities that take place in the territory of a state of the ACT can produce effects in the territory of another member. Transboundary pollution is defined as the direct or indirect human introduction of substances or energy into the environment in the form of pollution originating from one country resulting in effects on other jurisdictions, such as endangerment of human health, damage to biological resources and ecological systems, ecological damage, or preventing other legitimate uses of the environment (Silva, 2007). Transboundary impacts correspond to damage caused by an activity under the jurisdiction of a given state, the physical origin of which is wholly or partially under the jurisdiction of another state.

The sources of pollution must be identified and preventive action and integrated management of natural resources taken in border regions. It is therefore necessary for environmental impact studies to take the transboundary aspects into account and assess the potential damage that could be caused in foreign territory. For example, Brazil has conducted environmental impact assessment for the construction of two hydroelectric plants in the Madeira River – the 'Madeira River Complex', beginning with the Santo Antônio and Jirau hydroelectric dams (Rubinson, 2006). However, this study aroused controversy (see for example Manifesto on the Madeira River Complex, 2009) and was the subject of a motion approved in May 2007 by the National Environment Council – the Brazilian consultative and deliberative organ on the national environmental policy. This motion pointed out, among other things, various irregularities in the procedure, concealment of the real interests of the Madeira River Complex, and adverse impacts that will arise, profoundly affecting local people, fauna, flora and biodiversity of the Amazon ecosystem. It also referred to the fact that the territorial unity of the Madeira River Basin, which encompasses Bolivia, Brazil and Peru, covering 4,225 kilometres of river upstream from Porto Velho, including the rivers Guaporé (Brazil), Marmoré (Bolivia and Brazil), Bene (Bolivia) and Madre de Dios (Peru), as well as its tributaries, have not been taken into account in this environmental impact assessment. The Bolivian government has also indicated that possible impacts could be produced in Bolivian territory. As a result, Brazil and Bolivia began a dialogue, with a recognition of the obligation to make sure that the acts performed inside their jurisdictions will not affect the environment of the other states, and the obligation to inform being inherent in the principle of prevention, as found in customary international law, as confirmed in the International Court of Justice case concerning the pulp mills on the River Uruguay (*Argentina v Uruguay*, April 2010).[8]

Environmental issues require common management of natural resources and participation opportunities, which also include traditional populations and indigenous peoples, and the need to take their rights into account. Consequently, environmental regulation occurs within a very complex set of conditions, which reach far beyond the international relations among Amazonian countries themselves and include broad issues of human security and human rights.

## 5. CONCLUSIONS

The theoretical models of international regimes and institutional modelling shed some light on the formulation of an Amazonian legal framework. At first sight, it is possible to assert that the construction of international regimes concerning traditional issues such as navigation, hydroelectricity generation and even fisheries can be well explained by the neoliberal model, which takes as its starting point the fact of states being primary actors which carry out decisions well informed and guided by rational choice. However, the highly complex Amazonian cultural context and the scientific and technical aspects of environmental questions points to the necessity of the cognitivist model basis for understanding the creation, as well as some limits, of environmental regimes. Since the information produced by epistemic communities and political groups is also incorporated by states, the cognitivist explanation of regimes also includes some neoliberal perspectives, though states are now not necessarily always regarded as the primary actors.

The ACT and the ACTO are, of course, created by the states in the region. The original functions of the ACT, which reasserted permanent sovereignty over natural resources, has been supplemented by a scheme devoted to the production and broad transmission of information, as well as the establishment of an international political forum.

As an instrument of legal harmonisation, the Treaty and the ACTO established a set of conventional principles which cannot by themselves generate international obligations and were, in some aspects, overridden by subsequent environmental principles of international declarations and conventions. Moreover, as ACTO's structures do not include any dispute resolution or delegation rules, the domestic legal regulations are still the main driver of environmental regulation in the Amazon region. Considering the structure of ACT and ACTO, as well as the features of environmental problems and the complexity of Amazonian issues, the efforts toward legal harmonisation, as a result of the building of an international regime, are still concentrated on the production and diffusion of information on domestic legal issues, as well as on scientific, technical and cultural ones. In this sense, the diffusion function of normative and informative ACTO instruments, and its function as a political forum, are its most important attributes, in light of the fact that the hardening of international regional law is not yet in prospect.

## NOTES

1.  See United Nations Conference on the Human Environment 1972, A/CONF.48/14/Rev.1, at http://www.unep.org/Documents.Multilingual/Default.asp?documentid=97&articleid =1503.
2.  United Nations General Assembly Resolution 1974 Declaration on the Establishment of a New International Economic Order, A/RES/S-6/3201.
3.  United Nations General Assembly Resolution Permanent Sovereignty over Natural Resources, UN Doc. A/5217 (1962).
4.  The Andean Pact was established through the 1969 Cartagena Agreement and was the name of the Andean Community of Nations until 1996.
5.  (1992) 31 ILM 849.
6.  (1998) 37 ILM 22.
7.  (1992) 31 ILM 818.
8.  *Pulp Mills on the River Uruguay (Argentina v. Uruguay)*, 20 April 2101; majority judgment available at http://www.icj-cij.org/docket/files/135/15877.pdf.

## REFERENCES

Abbott, Kenneth W., Robert O. Keohane, Andrew Moravcsik, Anne Marie Slaughter and Duncan Snidal (2000), 'The concept of legalization', *International Organization*, **54** (3), Cambridge, MA: IO Foundation and MIT.

Ab'Sáber, Aziz Nacib (2004), *Amazonia: o Discurso à Praxis (Amazon: Discourse to Praxis)* (2nd edn), São Paulo: Edusp.

Amazon Cooperation Treaty Organization, Amazon Cooperation Treaty 1978, at http://sedac.ciesin.columbia.edu/entri/texts/amazonian.cooperation.1978.html.

Axelrod, Robert (1984), *The Evolution of Cooperation*, New York: Basic Books.

Baldwin, David A. (1993), 'Neoliberalism, Neorealism, and World Politics', in David A. Baldwin (ed.), *Neorealism and Neoliberalism – The Contemporary Debate*, New York: Columbia University Press.

Becker, Bertha K. (2004), *Amazônia: Geopolítica na Virada do III Milênio (Amazon: Geopolitics at the Turn of the Third Millennium)*, Rio de Janeiro: Garamond.

Bourdieu, Pierre (2005), *O Poder Simbólico (Symbolic Power)* (8th edn), Rio de Janeiro: Bertrand Brasil.

Caubet, Christian G. (1989), *As Grandes Manobras de Itaipú – Energia, Diplomacia e Direito na Bacia do Prata (The Great Maneuvers of Itaipú – Energy, Diplomacy and Law in La Plata Basin)*, Florianópolis: Acadêmica.

Costa, José A.F. (2001), 'Aspectos Fundantes da Conferência de Estocolmo de 1972' (Foundational aspects of the Stockholm Conference in 1972), in C. Derani and J.A.F. Costa (eds), *Direito Ambiental Internacional (International Environmental Law)*, Santos: Leopoldianum.

Eva, H.D. and O. Huber (eds) (2005), Proposta para definição dos limites geográficos da Amazônia – Síntese dos resultados de um seminário de consulta a peritos organizado pela Comissão Européia em colaboração com a Organização do Tratado de Cooperação Amazônica – JRC Ispra, 7–8 de junho de 2005. European Commission, OTCA, at http://ies.jrc.cec.eu.int/fileadmin/Documentation/Reports/ (A proposal for defining the geographical boundaries of Amazonia. Synthesis of the results from an Expert Consultation Workshop organised by the European Commission in collaboration with the Amazon Cooperation Treaty Organization – JRC Ispra, 7–8 June 2005), at http://ecosynapsis.net/RANPAold/Contenido/ MainPages/preAmac /articulosPDF/ Amazonia%20Limites.pdf. Global_Vegetation_ Monitoring/EUR _2005/eur21808_bz.pdf.

Ferreira, Antonia M.M. and Enéas Salati (2005), 'Forças de transformação do ecossistema amazônico' (Forces of transformation of the Amazon ecosystem), *Estudos Avançados*, **19** (54), 32.

Freire, Cristiniana C., Carla C.A. Torquato and José A.F. Costa (2007), 'Juridificação Internacional – Análise do Tratado de Cooperação Amazônica em Face dos Desafios Ambientais Internacionais' (Juridification International – Analysis of the Amazon Cooperation Treaty in the Face of International Environmental Challenges), *Anais do XV Congresso Nacional do CONPEDI*, Manaus, at http://www.conpedi.org/manaus/arquivos/anais/manaus/direito_ ambiental_ cristiniana_cavalcanti_freire_e_outros.pdf.

Góes Filho, Synésio S. (2001), *Navegantes, Bandeirantes, Diplomatas (Mariners, Pioneers, Diplomats)*, São Paulo: Martins Fontes.

Haas, Peter M. (1992), 'Introduction – Epistemic Communities and International Policy Coordination', in Peter M. Haas (ed.), *Knowledge, Power, and International Policy Coordination*, Columbia: University of South Carolina Press.

Haggard, Stephan and Beth A. Simmons (1987), 'Theories of international regimes', *International Organization*, **41**, 491–517.

Hasenclever, Andreas, Peter Mayer and Volker Rittberger (1997), *Theories of International Regimes*, Cambridge: Cambridge University Press.

Krasner, Stephen D. (1982), 'Structural causes and regime consequences: regimes as intervening variables', *International Organization*, **36** (2), Cambridge, MIT.

Manifesto on the Madeira River Complex (2009), at http://www.banktrack.org /download/world_social_forum_manifesto_on_rio_madeira/090129_fsm_rio_madaira_ manifesto.pdf.

Mendes, Luis Barrera (1993), 'The Amazon Pact', in Michael Bothe (ed.), *Amazonia and Siberia: Legal Aspects of the Preservation of the Environment and Development in the Last Open Spaces*, London: Graham & Trotman, pp. 199–207.

Meyers, Reinhard (2000), 'Theorien Internationaler Kooperation und Verflechtung', in Wichard Woyke (ed.), *Handwörterbuch Internationale Politik* (6th edn), Opladen: Leske and Budrich.

Mittelman, James H. (2000), 'Globalization: an ascendant paradigm?' *International Studies Perspectives*, **3** (1).

Neves, Walter (1995), 'Sociodiversity and Biodiversity, Two Sides of the Same Equation', in M. Clusener-Godt and I. Sachs (eds), *Brazilian Perspectives on Sustainable Development of the Amazon Region*, Paris: UNESCO, pp. 91–124.

Nogueira, Vicente de P.Q. (1993), 'Ecological Aspects of Development in Amazonia', in Michael Bothe, T. Kurzidem and C. Schmidt (eds), *Amazonia and Siberia: Legal Aspects of the Preservation of the Environment and Development in the Last Open Spaces*, London: Graham & Trotman, pp. 1–34.

Puchala, Donald (2003), *Theory and History in International Relations*, New York: Routledge.

Ricupero, Rubens (1984), 'O Tratado de Cooperação Amazônica' (The Amazon Cooperation Treaty), *Revista Informação Legislativa*, n. 81 January/March.

Rosendal, G. Kristin (2001), 'Overlapping international regimes – the case of the Intergovernmental Forum on Forests (IFF) between climate change and biodiversity', *International Environmental Agreements: Politics, Law and Economics*, **1** (4), Dordrecht: Kluwer.

Rubinson, Abby (2006), 'Regional projects require regional planning: human rights impacts arising from infrastructure projects', *Michigan Journal of International Law*, **28**, 175–205.

Schrijver, Nico (1997), *Sovereignty over Natural Resources – Balancing Rights and Duties*, Cambridge: Cambridge University Press.

Silva, Geraldo (1995), *Direito Ambiental Internacional: Meio Ambiente, Desenvolvimento Sustentável e os Desafios da Nova Ordem Mundial (International Environmental Law: Environment, Sustainable Development and the Challenges of the New World Order)*, Rio de Janeiro: Thex Editora.

Silva, Solange Teles da (2007), 'Le droit international et la protection de l'eau et de l'air' (International law and water and air protection), *Anuário Brasileiro de Direito Internacional*, **II** (1), 224–247.

Silva, Solange Teles da (2009), *O Direito Ambiental Internacional (International Environmental Law)*, Belo Horizonte: Del Rey.

Silva, S.T. and João Leonardo Mele (2006), 'Segurança ambiental na Região Amazônica' (Environmental security in the Amazon Region), *Anais do XV Congresso Nacional do CONPEDI*, Manaus, at http://www.conpedi. org/manaus/arquivos/anais/manaus/violencia_criminalidade_solange_da_silva_ e_ joao_mele.pdf.

Slaughter, Anne-Marie (2005), 'Security, solidarity, and sovereignty: the grand themes of UN reform', *American Journal of International Law*, American Society of International Law, **99**, 619.

Soares, Guido F. da S (1993), 'The Impact of International Law on the Protection of the Amazon Region and the Further Development of Environmental Law in Brazil', in Michael Bothe et al. (eds), *Amazonia and Siberia: Legal Aspects of the Preservation of the Environment and Development in the Last Open Spaces*, London: Graham & Trotman.

Stein, Arthur A. (1990), *Why Nations Cooperate – Circumstance and Choice in International Relations*, Ithaca: Cornell University Press.

Trubeck, David M., Patrick Cottrell and Mark Nance (2005), '"Soft Law"', "Hard Law", and European Integration: Toward a Theory of Hybridity' (Working paper), Wisconsin: University of Wisconsin.

UNDP (1994), *Human Development Report – New Dimensions of Human Security*, New York: UN Press.

Watkins, Kevin (2007), 'Climate Justice Demands Action for the Poor', at UNDP (Working paper), at http://hdr.undp.org/hdr2007/Climate_justice_KW_26Feb07.pdf.

Worthington, Simon and Nigel Brown (1993), 'Mercury Pollution in the Amazon: The History of Gold Production in the Amazon Basin', in Michael Bothe et al. (eds), *Amazonia and Siberia: Legal Aspects of the Preservation of the Environment and Development in the Last Open Spaces*, London: Graham & Trotman, pp. 35–55.

# Index